MARKET TO MARKET

Presented by
The Service League
of
Hickory, North Carolina, Incorporated

Featuring

Tested Recipes
International Cuisine
Microwave Delights
Menus

1

The purpose of the Service League of Hickory, is to assist those in the community who are in need and to foster interest among the members in the charitable, civic and cultural conditions of the community.

Proceeds from the sale of **Market to Market** will be used for community projects approved or sponsored by the Service League of Hickory, North Carolina, Incorporated.

Additional copies may be obtained by addressing
Market to Market
Post Office Box 1563
Hickory, North Carolina 28603

First Printing, 10,000 — September, 1983
Second Printing, 10,000 — July, 1984

ISBN 0-9611356-0-3

Printed in the United States of America
Wimmer Brothers Books
4210 B.F. Goodrich Blvd.
Memphis, Tennessee 38118

"Cookbooks of Distinction"™

INTRODUCTION

The flavor of "Hickory" is a special one to experience—for Hickory, North Carolina, is a unique kind of town. Nestled in the Piedmont region of the Blue Ridge Mountains, it is known not only for its beauty, but also for the environment that its variety of citizens have created.

Hickory is said to be more cosmopolitan than most cities of its size due to the varied backgrounds of its natives and those citizens who have moved to it from across the breadth of our country, attracted by its industries and location.

The major industries in this area include furniture manufacturing, textile manufacturing and a large hosiery manufacturing contingency. Each industry has gathered its own artisans, craftsmen and executives from across the nation and from abroad. Creativity is in the atmosphere,and this makes for an exciting and forward moving community which is dedicated to the arts, sciences, music, education and the sharing of gracious life styles.

People come to our area by the thousands during "Market" time for our industries—thus the name of this book, MARKET TO MARKET, came into being. It is our desire to share with the reader of this cookbook the special "Hickory flavor" that comes from the essence of our community.

3

ACKNOWLEDGEMENTS

The Cookbook Committee is deeply appreciative to all our League members for their imaginative contributions and unselfish sharing of treasured recipes with our Committee. They have tasted, tested, typed and proofread. Our one regret is that each recipe could not be included due to similarity or lack of space.

We thank our husbands and children who gave up their favorite menu to try something "different" and their patience for our time away from them.

We would like to especially thank two league husbands—Edward Gerrard for sharing his expertise in selecting our wines and Robert Mitchell for artfully designing our menus. Their contributions highlight our *Hickory Entertains* section.

COOKBOOK COMMITTEE

EDITOR
Anne F. Mitchell

CO-EDITORS
Shirley L. Ballew   Joanne M. Martin

COPY EDITOR
Camille M. Gardner

ARTIST
Sally T. Blackwelder

Phyllis D. Cauble	Lynn L. Lyerly
Carole J. Cumming	Judy B. Pierce
Lindy M. Dillow	Polly H. Shook
Carolyn W. Glass	Pat Y. Tolbert
Beverly A. Guarino	Carol H. Tuttle
Susanne M. Gunter	Kay J. Webber
Susan L. Ingle	Judy C. West
Carolyn W. Lyerly	Barbara F. Williams

TABLE OF CONTENTS

MARKET TO MARKET has been
assembled with great
enthusiasm and devotion
presented with
delight
and is dedicated to
all cooks everywhere
who
will read its pages
and share it

APPETIZERS
&
BEVERAGES

APPETIZERS AND BEVERAGES

( ) Denotes: **(HE)** Hickory Entertains   **(I)** International   **(M)** Microwave Recipes

APPETIZERS

CHAFING DISH CHEESE DIP WITH APPLES

Yield: 4 cups

1 (8-ounce) package cream
  cheese, cut in pieces
1/2 pound sharp Cheddar cheese,
  shredded
6 tablespoons light cream
1 teaspoon Worcestershire
  sauce

1/4 teaspoon dry mustard
3 drops hot pepper sauce
apples, unpared and cut in
  wedges
lemon juice
fruit pectin

In heavy saucepan, combine cream cheese, Cheddar cheese, cream, Worcestershire sauce, mustard, and hot pepper sauce. Heat over low heat, stirring until cheese melts and mixture is hot. If mixture becomes too thick, add more cream. Serve in a chafing dish, surrounded with apple wedges that have been dipped in lemon juice and fruit pectin.

Marianna M. Raugh

CRABMEAT AND BLEU CHEESE IN A CHAFING DISH

Yield: 10 servings

2 tablespoons butter, melted
2/3 cup onion, finely chopped
1/2 cup green pepper, finely
  chopped
1 cup celery, chopped
1 cup milk (or light cream)
6 ounces bleu cheese, crumbled
1 cup ripe olives, pitted and
  sliced

4 (6-ounce) cans crabmeat,
  frozen, thawed, and drained
  (or fresh)
2 teaspoons paprika
2 tablespoons parsley, chopped
  (or 1 tablespoon dried)

In a large skillet, sauté onion, pepper, and celery until soft in butter. Remove from heat. In the top of a double boiler, combine milk and cheese over hot water until cheese is melted and smooth; stir occasionally. To the skillet with the vegetables, add the cheese mixture, olives, and crabmeat. Stir until well combined and heat slowly for about 20 minutes. Serve on toast points, in pastry cups, crêpes, or seafood shells. Sprinkle with paprika and parsley. Serve in a chafing dish as an appetizer.

Judy B. Smith

CHIP BEEF TOMATO CHEESE DIP

May prepare ahead   *Yield: 20 to 30 servings*

4 tablespoons butter
16 ounces pasteurized process
  cheese spread
2 (2½-ounce) packages (or 1
  [5-ounce] jar) chip beef,
  frizzled
1 (16-ounce) can tomatoes,
  chopped

1 medium onion, grated
1 tablespoon Worcestershire
  sauce
10 drops of hot pepper sauce
  (or to taste)

Melt butter and cheese in double boiler; stir until thoroughly melted and blended. Add remainder of ingredients and stir. Put into a chafing dish and serve with corn chips, celery, or other vegetables.

Nancy F. Matheson

CRABMEAT MORNAY

Yield: 100 to 125 servings

24 tablespoons butter, melted
3 small bunches green onions,
  chopped
2 cups fresh parsley, finely
  chopped
7 tablespoons all-purpose flour
2 pints light cream
1½ pounds imported Swiss
  cheese, shredded

1 (8-ounce) package deluxe
  Swiss cheese, shredded
red pepper to taste
salt to taste
3 pounds fresh lump crabmeat
2 tablespoons dry sherry

In a heavy saucepan at low temperature, sauté onions and parsley in butter. Blend in flour and cream and cook a few minutes until well blended. Add cheese and blend until cheese melts. Add the seasonings, except sherry, and gently fold in crabmeat. It is important to continually stir to keep from scorching. Just before serving, blend in sherry. Serve in chafing dish with small pastry shells or toast points.

Phyllis D. Cauble

OYSTERS IN A CHAFING DISH

Yield: 20 to 25 servings

1 pound butter	1 gallon oysters, drained well
1 (5-ounce) jar creamed horseradish	1/4 teaspoon Worcestershire sauce
1 (10¾-ounce) can mushroom soup	salt to taste

Place butter, horseradish, and soup in a saucepan; heat until butter melts. Remove from heat and add oysters, Worcestershire sauce, and salt. Place in a chafing dish over low heat and serve with crackers.

Note: Serve with a bowl of chilled, bottled seafood sauce which has been mixed with juice of one lemon.

Camille M. Gardner

SAUSAGE STROGANOFF

May prepare ahead   *Yield: 20 to 25 servings*

2 pounds hot sausage	1 pint sour cream
1/2 cup onion, chopped	1 teaspoon garlic salt
1 (10¾-ounce) can mushroom soup	1 tablespoon all-purpose flour
2 (4-ounce) cans mushrooms (or 8-ounces fresh mushrooms, sliced)	pepper to taste
	2 tablespoons parsley, chopped

Fry sausage and onion; drain, then return to pan, and add mushroom soup, mushrooms, sour cream, garlic salt, flour, and pepper. Stir well. Serve in a chafing dish and garnish with parsley.

Variation: May serve over rice or grits as entrée.

June P. Wilfong

ITALIAN CAPONATA

May be frozen   *Yield: 3 quarts*

2 medium eggplants, cut into cubes
½ cup olive oil
2 large onions, chopped
1½ cups celery, sliced
2 bell peppers, red (or green), cut into chunks
2 cloves garlic, chopped
2½ pounds tomatoes, seeded and diced (or 1 [28-ounce] can Italian plum tomatoes, undrained, cut-up)

⅓ cup red wine vinegar
2 tablespoons salt (or to taste)
2 tablespoons sugar
¼ cup fresh basil, chopped (or 2 tablespoons dried basil)
3 tablespoons tomato paste
½ cup parsley, chopped
1 teaspoon pepper
¾ cup stuffed green olives, sliced

Optional:
4 tablespoons capers, drained
2 carrots, thinly sliced
2 to 3 zucchini, sliced

½ cup pine nuts, lightly browned in olive oil

Heat olive oil in a 5-or 6-quart casserole or Dutch oven. Add eggplant and onions and sauté for 5 minutes or until lightly golden. Add celery, peppers, garlic, tomatoes, red wine vinegar, salt, sugar, basil, tomato paste, parsley, pepper, olives, and optional vegetables; stir gently but thoroughly. Simmer, covered, for 30 minutes, stirring occasionally. Remove lid, simmer for about 10 minutes or until thickened. Serve at room temperature in a bowl surrounded by sliced French or Italian bread, or serve as a salad on Romaine lettuce. Will keep refrigerated for three weeks.

Note: This is pretty served in a copper pan, or it can be placed in a chafing dish.

Helen M. Brooks

SHRIMP FLAMBÉ

Partially prepare ahead   *Yield: 12 servings*

2 pounds shrimp, shelled and raw

½ pound bacon, sliced
½ cup rum, warmed

Preheat oven to 450°. Wrap each shrimp in bacon and fasten with a toothpick. Spread on a cookie sheet and bake, turning frequently until bacon is crisp. Drain on paper towels. Place in a chafing dish and pour warmed rum over shrimp and ignite. Serve immediately.

June P. Wilfong

BARBECUE MUSHROOMS

Yield: 15 to 20 servings

8 tablespoons butter, melted
1 cup catsup
¼ cup vinegar
¼ cup lemon juice
2 tablespoons Worcestershire
   sauce
1 tablespoon brown sugar

1 tablespoon prepared mustard
1 onion, grated
dash of hot pepper sauce
1 pint large, fresh, whole
   mushrooms
2 tablespoons butter, melted
   (approximately)

Add catsup, vinegar, lemon juice, Worcestershire sauce, brown sugar, mustard, onion, and hot pepper sauce to butter in a large skillet; simmer 10 minutes. Barely sauté mushrooms in small amount of butter. Mushrooms should still be raw on the inside. Add to sauce and serve in chafing dish with toothpicks.

Variation: Add small meatballs to sauce and mushrooms.

Phyllis D. Cauble

ROSEMARY'S MARINATED MUSHROOMS

Must prepare ahead   *Yield: 1 quart*

3 pounds fresh mushrooms,
   (caps or whole)
⅓ cup red wine vinegar
⅓ cup salad oil
1 small onion, sliced in rings
1 teaspoon salt
1 teaspoon dried parsley
1 teaspoon prepared mustard

1 teaspoon brown sugar
1⅓ cups red wine vinegar
1⅓ cups salad oil
3 small onions, sliced in rings
3 teaspoons salt
3 teaspoons dried parsley
3 teaspoons prepared mustard
3 teaspoons brown sugar

Place mushrooms, vinegar, oil, onion, seasonings, and sugar in large pot. Boil for 3 minutes; drain in collander. Combine red wine vinegar, salad oil, onions, salt, parsley, mustard, and brown sugar, and pour over mushrooms in a large bowl. Marinate at room temperature until cool. Place, covered, in refrigerator for at least 24 hours. Will keep as long as mushrooms last.

Note: May use fewer mushrooms to marinade proportions and pour off excess marinade after cooking.

Joanne M. Martin

DELICIOUS MUSHROOM DIP WITH TOAST

May prepare ahead   *Yield: 15 to 20 servings*

16 ounces mushrooms, chopped   ¼ cup dry sherry
   and drained   bread
4 tablespoons butter   8 tablespoons butter
2 onions, finely minced   garlic salt
2 (10¾-ounce) cans mushroom
   soup

Preheat oven to 225°. Fry onions in butter; add mushrooms and sauté, then add soup and sherry. Let simmer until hot. Cut crust off small loaf of bread; cut into triangles. Melt butter and spread over bread. Sprinkle with garlic salt. Bake for 2 hours. Store in a tight container. To serve, dip bread into warm mushroom sauce.

Linda P. Frye

HOT ARTICHOKE DIP

May prepare ahead   *Yield: 6 to 8 servings*

1 (14-ounce) can artichoke   dash of garlic powder
   hearts, cut in quarters   dash of hot pepper sauce
   (or chopped)   paprika
1 cup mayonnaise
1 cup Parmesan cheese, freshly
   grated

Preheat oven to 350°. Mix artichoke hearts, mayonnaise, Parmesan cheese, garlic powder, and hot pepper sauce. Place in a 9-inch baking dish and sprinkle paprika on top. Bake for 20 to 30 minutes and serve hot with bland crackers.

Note: Can also be put on party rye and broiled for several minutes. Tastes like crab.

Ann B. Whitener, Lynne G. Leffler & Sherry S. Abernethy

KATTY'S HERB DIP

Must prepare ahead   *Yield: 1 ½ cups*

1 (8-ounce) carton sour cream
2 tablespoons mayonnaise
1 tablespoon dried onion,
   minced
1 tablespoon dried chives
¼ teaspoon lemon juice

1 teaspoon dried dill
½ teaspoon dried garlic, minced
1 teaspoon parsley patch mix
   (or ½ lemon and ½ bell
   pepper)
½ teaspoon salt

Mix all ingredients and let stand overnight. Serve with a vegetable tray, artichokes, or put in a baked potato.

Note: It is superb for beef or shrimp fondue.

Katty D. Lefler

VEGETABLE DIP

May prepare ahead   *Yield: 2 ½ cups*

1 (8-ounce) carton sour cream
¼ cup green onion, chopped
¼ cup cucumber, chopped and
   drained
¼ cup green pepper, chopped
¼ cup radishes, chopped

½ cup mayonnaise
1 tablespoon sugar
1 teaspoon salt
dash pepper
dash garlic powder

Blend all ingredients and serve with assorted raw vegetables.

Margaret Ann W. Powell

APPETIZERS

ARTICHOKE NIBBLES

May be frozen   *Yield: 6 dozen*

2 (6-ounce) jars marinated
  artichokes
1 clove garlic, minced
1 small onion, chopped
4 eggs
8-ounces Cheddar cheese,
  shredded

2 tablespoons parsley, chopped
1/4 cup dry bread crumbs
1/4 teaspoon salt
1/8 teaspoon pepper
1/8 teaspoon oregano, ground
hot pepper sauce to taste

Preheat oven to 325°. Drain juice from *one* jar of artichokes and place in a sauté pan. Sauté garlic and onions in the juice. Chop both jars of artichokes and set aside. In a bowl, beat eggs and add artichokes, and all other ingredients. Pour into a greased 8x12-inch pan and bake for 30 minutes. Cut into small squares to serve.

Note: Reheat for 10 minutes if frozen.

Carole J. Cumming

BETTY'S CATAWBA COUNTY MEAT BALLS

Must prepare ahead   *Yield: 8 to 10 servings*

1/2 pound bacon, fried and
  crumbled
1 medium onion, sliced
8 tablespoons of butter
vegetable oil, as needed
1/2 cup bread crumbs
1/2 cup milk or (cream), warm
1 pound lean chuck, ground
2 egg yolks, slightly beaten

1/4 teaspoon salt
pepper to taste
1/2 teaspoon Worcestershire
  sauce
garlic salt to taste
1/2 pound saltine crackers,
  crumbled
hot oil, for frying
1 cup sour cream

Set crumbled bacon aside. Sauté onion in bacon drippings, butter, and extra oil if needed; set aside. Soak bread crumbs in milk and add to meat; then add egg yolks, salt, pepper, Worcestershire sauce, and garlic salt. Put in refrigerator to chill. Crush crackers fine. Roll meat into small balls and roll in cracker crumbs. Fry balls in oil until brown and put into a chafing dish. Place sour cream on top of balls and sprinkle bacon and onions on top.

Betty P. Cooke

COCKTAIL QUICHES

May be frozen   *Yield: 40 to 50 shells*

Pastry:

1 cup butter, softened   2 cups all-purpose flour
6-ounces cream cheese,
    softened

Beat butter and cream cheese until smooth; add flour and form into ball. Wrap in wax paper and chill for 30 minutes or longer. Make miniature pie shells by shaping the dough into 1-inch balls and pressing it into the bottom and sides of 1½-inch muffin cups.

Filling:

8-ounces ham (or shrimp,   ½ cup milk
    bacon, crabmeat), cooked   ½ cup light cream
1 cup Swiss cheese, shredded   ¼ teaspoon nutmeg
4 eggs, lightly beaten   pepper to taste

Preheat oven to 400°. In each miniature shell place ½ teaspoon chopped meat and ½ teaspoon of cheese. Combine the eggs with milk, nutmeg, and pepper; fill cups ¾ full. Bake for 10 minutes. *Reduce heat to 325°* and continue baking for 15 minutes or until lightly browned.

Phyllis D. Cauble

Variation: For Feta cheese filling omit Swiss cheese, cooked meat, and nutmeg. Add milk, 1 pound shredded Feta cheese, eggs, 1 teaspoon corn starch, ½ teaspoon dried thyme, 1 clove crushed garlic, and pepper. Blend ingredients in food processor. Fill shells and garnish with sliced ripe olives.

Camille M. Gardner

CHEESE KRISPIES

May prepare ahead   *Yield: 4 to 5 dozen*

1 cup margarine   2 cups all-purpose flour
8 ounces sharp Cheddar cheese, ½ teaspoon red pepper
    finely shredded   2 cups oven-toasted rice cereal

Cream margarine and cheese; add flour and red pepper, a little at a time. Add rice cereal. Using a teaspoon, drop the size wafers desired on a cookie sheet. Bake at 350° for 15 to 20 minutes.

Frances R. Hilton

CHEESE OLIVE BALLS

May be frozen   *Yield: 6 dozen*

½ pound sharp Cheddar cheese,   cayenne pepper to taste
   shredded   2 cups all-purpose flour
½ pound butter or margarine   stuffed olives, well drained
1 teaspoon salt

Preheat oven to 350⁰. Cream cheese and butter; add salt and pepper. Gradually add flour, working in well with each addition. To make balls, pinch off dough and mold around olives, covering well. Bake about 10 minutes, being careful that balls do not touch. Turn several times so they do not brown too much on bottom. To freeze, place uncooked balls so they do not touch on cookie sheet in freezer. When hard, store in plastic bags in freezer.

Note: Cocktail sausages, nuts, or dates may be used instead of olives.

Joanne M. Martin

DILL WAFERS

May prepare ahead   *Yield: 30 servings*

1 cup all-purpose flour   2 teaspoons dried dill
¾ teaspoon salt   ½ cup creamed cottage cheese
½ teaspoon baking powder   paprika
6 tablespoons unsalted butter,
   cold and cut into pieces

Preheat oven to 425⁰. Into a bowl, sift flour, salt, and baking powder; add butter and dill and blend the mixture until it resembles cornmeal. Add cottage cheese and form the dough into a ball. Knead the dough lightly and form it into a 6-inch log on a double sheet of waxed paper. Using waxed paper as a guide, roll the log tightly into a smooth 6-inch roll and chill it, wrapped in waxed paper, for at least 2 hours. Cut the roll in ⅛-inch slices and arrange the slices ½-inch apart on a buttered baking sheet. Sprinkle the slices with paprika and bake at 425⁰ for 12 to 15 minutes or until browned.

Note: Will store in a tin and keep a long time.

Janet E. Schoonderwoerd

CHRISTMAS WREATH

May prepare ahead   *Yield: approximately 94*

Deviled Ham Balls

1 (3-ounce) package cream
 cheese, softened
1 (4½-ounce) can deviled ham

1 teaspoon paprika
1 cup walnuts, finely chopped,
 divided

Mix cheese, ham, and paprika with ½ cup of the walnuts; chill. Form into 24 balls and roll in remaining walnuts; chill.

Liverwurst Balls

1 (3-ounce) package cream
 cheese, softened
1 (4¾-ounce) can liverwurst
 spread

½ teaspoon instant onion
hot pepper sauce to taste
Worcestershire sauce to taste
½ cup fresh parsley, minced

Mix cheese, liverwurst, onion, hot pepper sauce, and Worcestershire sauce; chill. Form into 25 balls and roll in parsley; chill.

Corned Beef Balls

1 (3-ounce) package cream
 cheese, softened
1 (4½-ounce) can corned beef
 spread

3 tablespoons crushed
 pineapple, drained
½ cup fresh parsley, minced
½ cup walnuts, finely chopped

Mix cheese, corned beef, and pineapple; chill. Form into 12 to 15 balls and roll in a mixture of the parsley and walnuts; chill.

Chicken Balls

1 (3-ounce) package cream
 cheese, softened
1 (4¾-ounce) can chicken
 spread
⅓ cup slivered almonds, finely
 chopped

1 tablespoon mayonnaise
2 teaspoons chutney, finely
 chopped
1 to 1½ teaspoons curry
 powder
1 cup coconut, flaked

Mix cheese, chicken spread, almonds, mayonnaise, chutney, and curry powder; chill. Form into 18 to 20 balls and roll in coconut; chill.

To assemble:

cherry tomatoes   pimento-stuffed olives

Using balls from each group, arrange in wreath fashion on a round tray and intersperse with cherry tomatoes and pimento-stuffed olives. Place a big red bow on it to complete the wreath.

Dorothy Y. Menzies

19

HOT ASPARAGUS ROLL

Must prepare ahead   *Yield: 75 canapés*

25 thin slices white bread
1 egg, beaten
3 ounces bleu cheese, softened
1 (8-ounce) package cream
    cheese, softened

25 small asparagus spears
½ pound butter, melted

Trim crusts and flatten bread slices with a rolling pin. Blend egg, bleu cheese, and cream cheese until smooth. Spread evenly and lightly on each slice of bread. Roll one asparagus spear in each slice. Fasten with a toothpick and dip in melted butter. Place rolls on a cookie sheet and freeze. When frozen, slice each roll into three equal parts. (They may be put back in freezer, then baked before serving.) Remove toothpicks and bake in a 400° oven for 15 minutes or until lightly browned.

Brenda K. Cline

ORANGE MARMALADE TURNOVERS

May be frozen   *Yield: 50 turnovers*

1 (8-ounce) jar spreadable sharp
    Cheddar cheese
¼ pound butter, partially
    softened
1 cup all-purpose flour, sifted

2 tablespoons cold water
dash of Worcestershire sauce
1 (10-ounce) jar orange
    marmalade

Preheat oven to 375°. Cut cheese and butter into flour then mix with cold water and dash of Worcestershire sauce. Shape into a ball and refrigerate overnight. Roll out dough very thin and cut into 2-inch circles. Put small amount of marmalade in center of circle, fold over edge and mash edge together with a fork and prick top with fork. Bake for 10 minutes.

Note: Freeze after baking, then reheat before serving.

Phyllis D. Cauble

HOT CRAB SPREAD

May prepare ahead   *Yield: 6 to 8 servings*

1 (8-ounce) package cream
  cheese, softened
1 (6-ounce) can crabmeat
2 tablespoons milk
¼ teaspoon salt

½ teaspoon horseradish
dash of pepper
2 tablespoons green onion,
  chopped
⅓ cup almonds, slivered

Preheat oven to 375⁰. Mix all ingredients, except almonds. Place in a 6-inch flan pan; top with almonds. Bake for 30 minutes and serve with a variety of crackers or breads.

Beverly R. Hyatt & Carol H. Tuttle

OYSTER ROLL

Must prepare ahead   *Yield: 25 servings*

2 (8-ounce) packages cream
  cheese, softened
3 tablespoons mayonnaise
2 teaspoons Worcestershire
  sauce
2 to 3 drops hot pepper sauce

1 tablespoon plus 1 teaspoon
  onion, finely chopped
½ teaspoon salt
2 (3¾-ounce) cans smoked
  oysters, drained
toast points

Mash cream cheese by hand; then add mayonnaise and seasonings. Mix well and spread mixture about ¼-inch thick on aluminum foil which has been placed on a cookie sheet. The cream cheese should be rectangular in shape but will not be as large as cookie sheet. Mash oysters and spread on top of cheese mixture. Let chill in refrigerator. Take out and roll as for jelly roll and refrigerate 24 hours. Serve on **toast points**.

Toast Points:
Preheat oven to 150⁰. One large sandwich loaf (24-ounce) of white bread will make about 100 toast points. With electric knife or very, very sharp carving knife, cut crusts off bread slices and then slice each piece of bread into 4 triangles. Bake on cookie sheet for 3 to 4 hours.

Phyllis D. Cauble

21

PEAPOD HORS D'OEUVRES

Partially prepare ahead   *Yield: 30 servings*

½ pound Chinese snowpeas
1 cup cottage cheese with
   chives
1 (3-ounce) package cream
   cheese, softened

2 tablespoons cocktail sauce
1 teaspoon dry mustard
few dashes hot pepper sauce
1 (4½-ounce) can tiny shrimp,
   drained

Shell the peas, separating peas and pods but leaving the pods attached on one side. In blender or processor combine cottage cheese, cream cheese, peas, cocktail sauce, mustard, and hot pepper sauce. Process until well blended and smooth. Chill. At serving time, stuff peapods with cheese-pea mixture. Garnish with shrimp.

Note: If you don't have time to stuff peapods, leave them unshelled. Prepare the filling and use as a dip for 1 pound of unshelled peas.

Anne F. Mitchell

STUFFED MUSHROOMS

Yield: 6

2 tablespoons butter
18 mushroom caps
2 tablespoons butter
3 shallots, chopped
9 chicken livers, cut in half

¼ cup Madeira
1 truffle, chopped
parsley, or a truffle sliced, to
   garnish

Preheat oven to 350°. In a sauté pan melt butter and sauté the mushrooms lightly. Reserve. In the same pan, melt 2 more tablespoons butter and sauté the shallots. Add the chicken livers and brown. Do not overcook. The chicken livers should be pink in the center. Add the Madeira and the truffle. Reduce the mixture until the liquid is an essence. Put ½ a liver into each mushroom cap. Top with the truffle and shallots in the Madeira essence. Heat the stuffed mushrooms for 5 minutes or until thoroughly hot. Garnish and serve.

Anne Byrd
"Instructor of Creative Cookery"

RIPE OLIVE CANAPÉS

Yield: 15 to 20 servings

1 (6-ounce) can ripe olives,
    pitted and chopped
¾ cup sharp Cheddar cheese,
    shredded
3 tablespoons mayonnaise

¼ teaspoon curry powder
1 tablespoon onion, chopped
dash Worcestershire sauce
1 (16-ounce) loaf of bread

Preheat oven to 350°. Combine olives, Cheddar cheese, mayonnaise, curry powder, onion, and Worcestershire sauce. Cut out little rounds of bread and toast on one side. Spread with olive mixture and bake for 5 minutes.

Dorothy Y. Menzies

SMOKED OYSTER PUFFETS

Yield: 20 servings

1 (8-ounce) package cream
    cheese, softened
6 tablespoons light cream
4 tablespoons onion, finely
    minced
1 teaspoon Worcestershire
    sauce

1 clove garlic, finely minced
1 egg yolk, beaten
1 (3½-ounce) tin smoked
    oysters
20 slices bread, whole wheat

Preheat oven to 425°. Blend together cheese, cream, onion, Worcestershire sauce, garlic, and egg yolk until thoroughly mixed. Fold in oysters. Cut bread in rounds and toast on one side. Spread with mixture. Place in hot oven for about 8 minutes, or until mixture is puffed and lightly browned. Serve hot.

Dorothy Y. Menzies

POLYNESIAN SHRIMP

May prepare ahead   *Yield: 10 to 12 servings*

1 pound medium shrimp,   ³/₄ cup sour cream
  cooked   ¹/₄ cup mayonnaise
1 large pineapple, halved   1 tablespoon horseradish,
  lengthwise   grated

Scoop out pineapple and cut into bite-size pieces. Spear each shrimp on a toothpick with a piece of pineapple and heap into one half of the pineapple shell. In the other half of the shell place a dip made of sour cream, mayonnaise and horseradish.

Camille M. Gardner

SPINACH OR MUSHROOM EMPAÑADAS

Yield: 4 to 5 dozen

Spinach Filling:
4 slices bacon, fried and   1 cup cottage cheese
  crumbled   salt and pepper to taste
2 garlic cloves, finely minced ⅛ teaspoon nutmeg, grated
2 small onions, finely minced
1 (10-ounce) package frozen
  spinach, thawed and
  chopped

Sauté garlic and onion in bacon drippings until tender. Add spinach and cook until tender. Stir in cheese, seasonings, and bacon. Cool before using.

Mushroom Filling:
2 tablespoons butter, melted   1 cup sharp Cheddar cheese,
1 (16-ounce) box fresh   shredded
  mushrooms, sliced   2 tablespoons all-purpose flour
1¹/₂ cups sour cream
1 (1.38-ounce) envelope dry
  onion soup mix

Sauté mushrooms in butter until browned. Turn off heat. Combine sour cream, soup mixture, and cheese. Sprinkle flour over mushrooms and blend. Add sour cream mixture to mushrooms and blend. Cool.

24

Pastry:

1 (12-ounce) package cream cheese, softened
12 tablespoons butter, softened
1½ teaspoons salt

2½ cups (scant) all-purpose flour, sifted
1 egg, beaten

Preheat oven to 325°. Beat cream cheese and butter until smooth and creamy. Gradually add salt and flour and knead only until it just clings together. Wrap dough and refrigerate 3 to 4 hours or overnight. (If overnight, let stand 30 minutes before rolling.) Roll out pastry ¼ at a time on lightly floured pastry cloth until ⅛-inch thick. Cut into 3-inch rounds; place 1 teaspoon filling in the middle of each and fold to make half moons. Seal with a little water. Place on ungreased cookie sheet and chill or freeze before baking. Brush the surface with beaten egg and make a pinpoint hole for steam. Bake at 325° for about 30 minutes or until lightly browned.

Variation: Can use mushroom filling as a spread by decreasing quantity of mushrooms by half. Place ingredients in a 9-inch plate and top with Cheddar cheese. Bake at 350° until hot and bubbly.

Anne F. Mitchell and Carol H. Tuttle

SPICY NIBBLES

May prepare ahead   *Yield: 3½ quarts*

3 (5-ounce) cans chow mein noodles
2½ cups pecans, chopped
1 (3½-ounce) package sunflower kernels (optional)
10 tablespoons butter (or margarine), melted

5 tablespoons soy sauce
4 tablespoons sesame seeds
2½ tablespoons chili powder
¼ teaspoon garlic salt
¼ teaspoon dry mustard

Preheat oven to 325°. Place noodles, nuts, and kernels into large, deep bowl. In another bowl, mix remaining ingredients. Add seasoned liquid to noodle mixture, stirring and tossing to cover well. Place in two 9x13-inch baking pans. Bake for 20 minutes. Stir often to prevent over cooking. Cool; place in airtight containers. Serves a large crowd.

Joanne M. Martin

PARTY NUT MIXTURE

May prepare ahead   *Yield: 1½ pounds of mix*

2 (2½-ounce) packages   1 (12-ounce) can peanuts
  almonds, sliced   1 (12-ounce) can cashews
2 tablespoons butter,   1 (12-ounce) can mixed nuts
  approximately   ½ (15-ounce) box raisins
dash of salt   (or more)
1 (3¾-ounce) package sunflower 1 (6-ounce) package dried
  seeds   apricots

Preheat oven to 200° or 250°. Put almonds on cookie sheet, dot with butter, and toast in low oven until lightly brown. Salt and drain on paper towels; mix with sunflower seeds, peanuts, cashews, mixed nuts, raisins, and apricots.

Phyllis D. Cauble

STUFFED MUSHROOMS

Partially prepare ahead   *Yield: 8 to 10 servings*

12 to 15 large mushrooms,   ⅓ cup soft bread crumbs
  separated into caps and   4 anchovy fillets, drained and
  stems   chopped
6 tablespoons butter, melted   1 pimento, chopped
  and divided   salt and pepper to taste
⅛ teaspoon ground ginger   2 tablespoons parsley, chopped
1 tablespoon shallots, finely ¼ cup Parmesan cheese, grated
  chopped

Preheat oven to 375°. Combine 1 tablespoon butter with ginger and brush the caps. Put into a shallow baking dish. Chop mushroom stems and sauté with the shallots in 3 tablespoons of remaining butter. Add bread crumbs, anchovies, pimento, salt, pepper, and parsley. Fill caps with filling and sprinkle with cheese. Drizzle the remaining butter over all and bake for 15 minutes. Serve at once.

Anne M. Boyer

TERIYAKI FLANK STEAK

Must prepare ahead   *Yield: 4 to 6 servings*

2 pounds flank steak
1/2 cup soy sauce
2 tablespoons vinegar
2 tablespoons honey

1 1/2 teaspoons ginger, ground
1 teaspoon garlic powder
1 scallion with top, finely
   chopped

Score flank steak diagonally on both sides. Combine soy sauce, vinegar, honey, ginger, garlic powder, and scallion. Pour over steak; marinate 24 hours. Broil 4 to 7 minutes per side over hot coals (4 minutes for rare). To serve, carve across grain into thin slices.

Note: This can be rolled pinwheel fashion, secured with a toothpick, and served as an hors d'oeuvre. Also, the sauce can be used to marinate other meats. This can be cut into strips and placed on bamboo skewers and served as an appetizer.

Ruth L. Hord, Carol S. Teague & Nikki I. Gillespie

CHEESE BALLS WITH BRANDY

May be frozen   *Yield: 4 large-size balls*

1 pound sharp Cheddar cheese,
   shredded
1/2 pound bleu cheese, shredded
1 pound cream cheese, softened
1 onion, grated
6 tablespoons Worcestershire
   sauce

1/4 cup brandy
2 teaspoons hot pepper sauce
1/2 teaspoon celery salt
1/2 teaspoon garlic salt
2 dashes garlic powder
1 cup nuts, chopped
1 cup parsley, chopped

Put cheeses, onion, Worcestershire sauce, brandy, hot pepper sauce, celery salt, garlic salt, and garlic powder in large mixer bowl; cream thoroughly. Chill several hours, then shape into balls, wrap, and refrigerate. Mix nuts and parsley together and roll balls in mixture before serving.

Note: Recipe may be halved. Make another batch instead of doubling, as there will be too much to beat smoothly.

Katty D. Lefler

CAVIAR MOUSSE

Must prepare ahead   *Yield: 4 cups*

1 tablespoon unflavored gelatin	1 tablespoon lemon juice
¼ cup cold water	½ teaspoon salt
1 (4-ounce) jar caviar	1 cup sour cream
2 tablespoons onion, grated	1 cup heavy cream, whipped

Soften gelatin in cold water for 5 minutes; then dissolve over low heat. Cool slightly. Combine caviar, onion, lemon juice, salt, and sour cream and blend. Stir in gelatin and fold in whipped cream. Put mixture in oiled 4-cup mold and chill until firm. Serve on party rye or melba toast.

Helen S. Moretz

BEEF CHEESE BALL

May be frozen   *Yield: 25 servings*

3 (2½-ounce) packages dried beef, chopped and finely cut with scissors, divided	1 small onion, chopped
	2 tablespoons Worcestershire sauce
3 (8-ounce) packages cream cheese, softened	2 tablespoons flavor enhancer for meat

Reserve one package of beef to roll ball in. Mix cheese, onion, Worcestershire sauce, flavor enhancer, and beef. Shape into a ball and roll in reserved beef.

Note: May make into three balls. This will keep several weeks in the refrigerator.

Nancy F. Matheson

Variation for Beef Dip for Vegetables: Add only 1 (3-ounce) package of beef and 1 (8-ounce) package cream cheese. Add 4 teaspoons vinegar and ½ cup mayonnaise. Blend and chill. Serve with raw vegetables.

Variation for Beef Dip for Vegetables: Add 1 (3-ounce) package of beef and 1 (8-ounce) package cream cheese. Add 4 teaspoons vinegar, ½ cup mayonnaise, Worcestershire sauce, and ½ teaspoon onion powder. Blend and chill. Serve with raw vegetables.

Frances R. Hilton

CAVIAR LAYER SUPREME PIE

Must prepare ahead   *Yield: 35 servings*

Egg Layer:

1 tablespoon unflavored gelatin	¼ cup parsley, minced
¼ cup cold water	1 onion, minced
4 hard-cooked eggs, finely chopped	¾ teaspoon salt
	¼ teaspoon pepper
½ cup mayonnaise	

Lightly oil an 8-inch cake pan. Soften gelatin in cold water in a measuring cup. Dissolve gelatin by setting cup in hot water or in microwave oven for 20 seconds. This gelatin will be divided between the three layers. Combine all ingredients with 1 tablespoon of softened gelatin. Spread mixture into prepared cake pan. Cover and refrigerate overnight.

Avocado Layer:

2 avocados, finely chopped	2 tablespoons mayonnaise
1 onion, minced	½ teaspoon salt
2 tablespoons lemon juice	¼ teaspoon pepper

Lightly oil an 8-inch cake pan. Combine all ingredients with 1 tablespoon of softened gelatin. Spread mixture into pan; cover and refrigerate overnight.

Sour Cream Layer:

1 cup sour cream	1 (4-ounce) jar caviar, black or red
¼ cup onion, minced	

Lightly oil an 8-inch cake pan. Combine above ingredients, except caviar, with remaining 2 tablespoons of softened gelatin. Spread mixture in pan, cover and refrigerate overnight.

To Assemble:

Thirty minutes before serving, gently remove egg layer by turning upside down on platter or cake plate. Place avocado layer on top of egg layer, then sour cream layer. Place caviar in fine sieve and rinse gently under cold water; drain. Spread caviar over top of sour cream layer. Decorate around the bottom of cake with parsley and thinly sliced lemon. Serve with party pumpernickel bread or wheat crackers.

Pat Y. Tolbert

29

LIPTAUER CHEESE

May prepare ahead   *Yield: 10 to 12 servings*

6 ounces cream cheese,
  softened
3 ounces bleu cheese, softened
5 tablespoons butter, softened

1½ tablespoons Dijon mustard
1 tablespoon onion, chopped
sweet Hungarian paprika

Cream the cheeses and butter with mustard and onion until soft. Add enough paprika to give a pink color; then form into a ball. Place ball in center of a large tray.

Garnishes:

7 lettuce cups

2 (2-ounce) cans anchovy fillets,
  drained and chopped
⅔ cup green onion, finely
  chopped
⅔ cup cucumber, finely chopped
⅔ cup radishes, diced

½ cup capers, drained
1 (3½-ounce) jar caviar, black
  or red
1 (2-ounce) jar caraway seeds
thinly sliced pumpernickel bread

Place garnishes in individual lettuce cups around the cheese ball. Serve with sliced pumpernickel.

Note: Each guest spreads the pumpernickel with some of the cheese ball, then adds any condiment he chooses.

Robin T. Mills

HOT JEZEBEL

May prepare ahead   *Yield: 2½ cups*

1 cup apricot preserves
1 cup pineapple preserves
¼ cup horseradish, drained
3 teaspoons dry mustard

1 teaspoon pepper
1 (8-ounce) package cream
  cheese

Mix preserves, horseradish, mustard, and pepper; store in a covered jar in the refrigerator. To serve, place ⅓ cup of hot Jezebel on cream cheese.

Sarah S. Raney

PÂTÉ EN CROÛTE

May be frozen   *Yield: 7 to 8 slices per roll*

Pâté:

1 cup butter, divided	½ teaspoon dried thyme
1 cup onion, finely chopped	1 tablespoon lemon juice
½ pound fresh mushrooms,	¼ teaspoon pepper
chopped	pinch of nutmeg (optional)
½ pound chicken livers, cut in	3 eggs, hard-boiled
half, membranes removed	cognac to taste (optional)
2 teaspoons salt	

In 8 tablespoons hot butter in medium skillet, sauté onion until very soft and golden. Add mushrooms and chicken livers; cook, stirring occasionally, until livers and mushrooms are well done and soft. Remove from heat. Add rest of butter, salt, thyme, lemon juice, pepper, and nutmeg; stir until butter melts and divide mixture into 4 parts. Cut eggs into quarters. In electric mixer or food processor purée the chicken liver-mushroom mixture, one part at a time, adding three of the egg quarters to each part. Add cognac to taste; then turn into bowl and refrigerate.

Croûte:
12 to 14 sour dough rolls

Slice ends off rolls. Remove inside of bread, leaving a crust about ¼-inch thick. With a spoon, push pâté mixture into hollow and fill completely. Refrigerate, wrapped in foil, several hours, or until cool enough to slice. (May be frozen at this point.) To serve: cut into slices about ¼-inch thick.

Phyllis D. Cauble

CARROT MOLD

Must prepare ahead   *Yield: 1 pint*

1 tablespoon unflavored gelatin
¼ cup water
1 (8-ounce) package cream
   cheese, softened
1 cup carrots, grated

1 tablespoon onion, grated
1 tablespoon mayonnaise
red pepper to taste
salt to taste
⅛ teaspoon lemon juice

Soften gelatin in water, then heat to dissolve. Mix with cream cheese, carrots, onion, mayonnaise, red pepper, salt, and lemon juice. Shape into a ball or carrot shape and chill until firm. Serve with crackers. Stores several weeks in refrigerator.

Carolyn W. Lyerly

CHEESE MOLD WITH APRICOT TOPPING

Must prepare ahead   *Yield: 25 to 30 servings*

1½ pounds sharp Cheddar
   cheese, shredded
1 cup walnuts, finely chopped
1 cup mayonnaise

1½ medium onions, finely
   chopped
½ teaspoon hot pepper sauce
apricot topping

Grate cheese; *but do not put in food processor,* then combine with other ingredients and mix well. Grease a 1½-quart ring mold and pack cheese mixture into mold. Chill 24 hours before unmolding. *Do not put in hot water to unmold.* Spread apricot topping on top and serve with crackers.

Apricot Topping:
1 (6-ounce) package dried
   apricots
½ cup water
¼ cup sugar

2 tablespoons butter
2 tablespoons sherry (or more
   to taste)

Put apricots and water in a saucepan and simmer until apricots are thick like jam. Mash as it cooks and add more water to prevent burning. Add sugar and butter; taste to adjust sweetness. Take off heat and add sherry. Cool and put in a glass jar. Can be stored in refrigerator about 1 week.

Phyllis D. Cauble

SHERRIED-CURRIED CHEESE

Must prepare ahead   *Yield: 4 to 6 servings or 3 cups as mold*

2 (3-ounce) packages cream   dash of salt
    cheese   ¹/₂ teaspoon curry powder
1 cup sharp Cheddar cheese,   1 (9-ounce) jar chutney, chopped
    shredded   2 scallions with tops, chopped
4 tablespoons dry sherry

Place cream cheese, Cheddar cheese, sherry, salt, and curry powder in a food processor; mix until well blended. Spread in a 9-inch pie plate. Spread chutney on top and top with scallions.

Josephine L. Hambrick

Variation: Clam and Chutney Mold: omit Cheddar cheese, sherry, and curry powder. Add 16-ounces cream cheese, scallions, dash of Worcester-shire sauce, 8-ounces clams, ¹/₂ pound of bacon, crumbled, and 1 cup chives. Mix ingredients; mold. At serving, unmold, and sprinkle bacon and chives on top.

Anne F. Mitchell

CRAB DIP OR SPREAD

May prepare ahead   *Yield: 2¹/₂ cups as dip*
                                       6 to 8 servings as spread

1 (8-ounce) package cream   1¹/₂ tablespoons dried onion,
    cheese   minced
¹/₃ cup mayonnaise   1 (6-ounce) can crabmeat
1 teaspoon prepared mustard   1 tablespoon parsley, chopped
    with horseradish   dash garlic powder

Blend cream cheese, mayonnaise, mustard, and onion. Mix in crabmeat, parsley, and garlic powder until well blended. Serve with wheat thins.

Pat R. Speagle

Variation: Crab Spread—omit mayonnaise and dried onion; add 1 table-spoon milk and 1 small onion, minced. Mix and spread in a 9-inch dish. Pour 1 (12-ounce) jar of cocktail sauce over top. Serve with bland crackers.

Linda P. Frye

SHRIMP MOUSSE MOLD

Must prepare ahead   *Yield: 25 to 30 servings*

1 (8-ounce) package cream
  cheese, softened
1 cup mayonnaise
1 cup celery, chopped
1/2 cup onion, chopped
1/4 cup green pepper, chopped

2 (41/2-ounce) cans shrimp,
  drained
salt and pepper to taste
11/2 teaspoons unflavored gelatin
1/4 cup cold water
1 (103/4-ounce) can tomato soup

Combine cream cheese and mayonnaise and beat well until blended. Add celery, onion, green pepper, shrimp, salt, and pepper to taste. Dissolve gelatin in water, then add to warm soup; stir until well blended. Add to cheese mixture. Oil a large fish mold or a 2-quart mold, fill with mixture, and chill. Garnish with an olive for the eye, strips of green pepper for fins and tail.

Marion G. Cline

SALMON MOUSSE WITH SOUR-CREAM DILL SAUCE

Must prepare ahead   *Yield: 20 to 25 servings as an appetizer
or 8 as a salad*

1 tablespoon unflavored gelatin
1/4 cup cold water
1/2 cup boiling water
1/2 cup mayonnaise
1 tablespoon lemon juice
1 tablespoon onion, finely
  minced
1/2 teaspoon hot pepper sauce

1/4 teaspoon paprika
1 teaspoon salt
16-ounces canned salmon,
  drained and finely chopped
1 tablespoon capers, chopped
1/2 cup heavy cream
3 cups cottage cheese

Soften gelatin in cold water; add boiling water and stir until gelatin has dissolved; cool. Add mayonnaise, lemon juice, onion, hot pepper sauce, paprika, and salt; mix well. Chill to the consistency of unbeaten egg whites. Add the salmon and capers and beat well. Whip the cream, fold into the salmon mixture, and turn into a 2-quart oiled fish mold. Add the cheese to fill the mold. Chill until set. Unmold on a serving platter and garnish with watercress, lemon slices, and salmon roe. Serve with sour-cream dill sauce.

Sour-Cream Dill Sauce:

1 egg	4 teaspoons lemon juice
1 teaspoon salt	1 teaspoon onion, grated
pinch of pepper, freshly ground	2 tablespoons dill, finely cut
pinch of sugar	1½ cups sour cream

Beat the egg until fluffy and lemon-colored. Add the remaining ingredients, blending in the sour cream last. Stir until blended and chill.

Note: For a cocktail party, double this recipe.

Anne F. Mitchell & Helen M. Brooks

CRAB RING OR MOLD

Must prepare ahead   *Yield: 36 servings*

2 tablespoons unflavored gelatin	16-ounces crabmeat
½ cup water	1 cup mayonnaise
1 (10¾-ounce) can mushroom soup	¼ cup onion, finely minced
½ cup celery, minced	sauce

Soften gelatin in water; set aside. Heat soup, add gelatin, and heat until dissolved; mix well. Add other ingredients and mix well. Pour into an 11-cup ring mold or a 2-quart mold and chill until firm.

Sauce:

1 cup mayonnaise	½ teaspoon Worcestershire
1 teaspoon lemon juice	sauce
½ teaspoon onion, finely minced	½ teaspoon red pepper
1 teaspoon curry powder	¼ cup chili sauce

Mix well and refrigerate.

Note: Can be served with bland crackers as an appetizer, a first course, or a salad. Place bowl of sauce in center of ring when serving.

Dorothy Y. Menzies

Variation: Omit ½ cup cold water. Add ¼ cup cold water, mushroom soup, 6-ounces cream cheese, gelatin, celery, onion, 1 (5-ounce) can of crabmeat, and ¼ teaspoon curry powder. Heat soup and dissolve cheese in it; add other ingredients.

Mary Ayers P. Campbell

35

LOBSTER MOLD

Must prepare ahead   *Yield: 20 to 30 servings*

2 tablespoons unflavored gelatin
¼ cup hot water
1 (10¾-ounce) can mushroom
    soup
1 (8-ounce) cream cheese,
    softened
1 (16-ounce) package of frozen
    lobster or crabmeat, cut
    into small pieces

1 (4½-ounce) can baby shrimp,
    drained
½ cup celery, chopped
1 small onion, chopped
3 teaspoons dried chives
¾ cup mayonnaise

Dissolve gelatin in ¼ cup *hot* water. Heat soup and cream cheese over low heat. Add lobster, shrimp, celery, and onion; stir together. Add gelatin and chives; stir together. Remove from heat, cool; then add mayonnaise and mix. Turn into a greased 3-quart mold and chill completely. Serve with crackers.

Note: Can refrigerate 2 to 3 weeks.

Jeanette S. Johnson

BEVERAGES

BLOODY MARYS

Must prepare ahead   *Yield: ten 10-ounce servings*

1 (32-ounce) bottle clam-tomato
    juice
1 (16-ounce) can cocktail
    vegetable juice
1 fifth Bloody Mary Mix

juice of 3 lemons
4 dashes Worcestershire sauce
4 dashes hot pepper sauce
2 cups vodka

Mix all ingredients, except the vodka. Place in an airtight container and refrigerate for up to five days. Add the vodka just before serving over ice.

Carole J. Cumming

CHARLESTON EGGNOG

Must prepare ahead   *Yield: 25 to 30 servings*

10 eggs, separated   2 cups heavy cream
½ cup sugar   1 cup whiskey or bourbon
2 quarts commercial eggnog   2 cups light rum
2 cups light cream

Beat yolks in a mixer with sugar until light and fluffy; add eggnog and creams. Stir together, but *do not beat.* Add whiskey and rum very slowly, stirring constantly. Store overnight in refrigerator tightly covered. Beat 6 reserved egg whites until stiff and gently fold into mixture. Stir before serving. Place in mugs or punch bowl; top with a dash of nutmeg.

Sally T. Blackwelder

DEEP FREEZE DAIQUIRI

Must prepare ahead   *Yield: 2 quarts*

2 (6-ounce) cans frozen   1 fifth rum
   lemonade concentrate   6 lemonade cans water
1 (6-ounce) can frozen limeade
   concentrate

Place 1 can lemonade, ½ can limeade, ½ bottle rum, and 3 cans of water in blender or food processor; blend thoroughly. Pour into a large container. Repeat blending with remaining ingredients; pour into container and stir. Cover and freeze mixture for at least 12 hours. Approximately 30 minutes before serving, remove mixture from freezer and stir. Pour into small (4-ounce) glasses. Refreeze any unused portion.

Note: This mixture will not freeze solid.

Roddy S. Dixon

FRENCH 75

Yield: 1 (4-ounce) drink

dash of lemon juice   ½-ounce Cointreau
1-ounce gin   champagne

Place ingredients in a glass and fill with champagne.

Beverly A. Guarino

DEEP FREEZE PIÑA COLADA

May prepare ahead   *Yield: 6 servings*

1 (4-ounce) can coconut drink   20 ice cubes
   mix   6 pineapple chunks
1 (8-ounce) can pineapple juice   6 maraschino cherries
6-ounces light rum

Combine coconut drink mix, pineapple juice, light rum, and ice cubes;
place in blender. Blend and store in freezer. Serve in champagne glasses
and garnish with pineapple chunk and a cherry.

Note: Will not freeze hard.

Roddy S. Dixon

IRISH COFFEE

Yield: 1 serving

1 teaspoon French-style instant   1½-ounces Irish whiskey
   coffee   whipped cream (or all-natural
1 teaspoon brown sugar   vanilla ice cream) for
¾ mug boiling water   garnish

Into an Irish coffee mug, put coffee and sugar; pour in boiling water to
¾ full. Stir well to dissolve coffee and sugar. Add whiskey. Garnish to
brim with cream or ice cream.

Joanne M. Martin

WHISKER

Yield: 4 to 6 servings

5-ounces crème de cacao   4 to 5 scoops coffee ice cream
5-ounces Cointreau   2 tablespoons cracked ice

Mix all ingredients in blender and serve.

Catherine H. Yeager

TEQUILA SOUR

May prepare ahead   *Yield: 5 to 6 servings*

1 tray ice cubes   12-ounces tequila
1 (12-ounce) can frozen limeade   12-ounces water
   concentrate

Crush ice; add with other ingredients to blender container. Blend until combined and thickened. Serve in large (8-ounce) cocktail glasses or champagne glasses.

Note: If made ahead, omit ice cubes; blend with cubes just before serving.

Catherine H. Yeager

VODKA SLUSH

Must prepare ahead   *Yield: sixteen 8-ounce servings*

1 (6-ounce) can frozen orange   1 cup sugar
   juice concentrate, thawed   3½ cups water
   and undiluted   2 cups vodka
2 (6-ounce) cans frozen   2 (28-ounce) bottles lemon-lime
   lemonade concentrate,   carbonated beverage, chilled
   thawed and undiluted
2 (6-ounce) cans frozen limeade
   concentrate, thawed and
   undiluted

Combine orange juice, lemonade, limeade, sugar, water, and vodka; mix well. Freeze 48 hours, stirring occasionally. For each serving, spoon ¾ cup frozen mixture into a tall glass; fill with carbonated beverage. Serve at once.

Kay J. Webber

Variation: For Gin Slush, omit limeade and vodka; add 2 cups gin to other ingredients.

Patti C. Owens

B
E
V
E
R
A
G
E
S

LONDON FOG

Yield: six 4-ounce servings

1 cup strong black coffee   1 cup vanilla ice cream
1 cup bourbon

Place ingredients in a blender and mix well; serve in punch cups.

Note: The coffee removes cloying sweetness, the ice cream gives it body, and it goes down so smoothly you enter into a fog sooner than expected.

Betty N. Hudson

STRAWBERRY DAIQUIRIS

Yield: 6 to 8 servings

1 (6-ounce) can frozen limeade   6-ounces rum
   concentrate   3-ounces vodka
1 (10-ounce) package frozen   8 to 10 ice cubes
   strawberries, partially   sugar (or heavy cream) to taste
   thawed

Place limeade, strawberries, rum, vodka, and ice cubes into blender; mix and serve. Add a little sugar if strawberries seem tart, or a little heavy cream may be added.

Chris R. Bates

PEPPERMINT LIQUEUR

Must prepare ahead   *Yield: 3 pints*

4 cups sugar   3 teaspoons peppermint extract
2 cups water   (use 2 teaspoons for lighter
3 cups vodka   taste)

Boil sugar and water together to make a syrup. Cool. Mix with vodka and peppermint extract. Pour into glass container. Cover tightly and let stand 2 weeks before serving. Delicious in coffee. Add a couple of drops of green food coloring, if desired.

Joyce S. Trado

COFFEE LIQUEUR

Must prepare ahead   *Yield: ½ gallon*

4 cups sugar   1 fifth rum (for Jamaican
2 cups water   variety)
⅔ cup instant coffee   1 vanilla bean
1 fifth vodka (for Mexican
   variety) or

Combine sugar, water, and coffee in saucepan. Bring to rolling boil. Skim off froth on top and allow to cool. Pour in a half-gallon wine jug or jar. Add vodka or rum and vanilla bean. Store in dark place for at least two weeks, preferably longer. Remove vanilla bean and store in sealed glass containers until ready to serve.

Joyce S. Trado

APRICOT BRANDY

Must prepare ahead   *Yield: 1 fifth of brandy*

1 pound dried apricots   1 pound rock candy
1 fifth vodka

Combine apricots, vodka, and rock candy in a jar with a tightly fitting lid. When the rock candy dissolves, the brandy is ready. Store, unopened, for eight weeks. Remove apricots before serving brandy.

Note: 2 cups sugar can be substituted for the rock candy. If sugar is used, turn the jar upside down every few days until the sugar dissolves. Any dried fruit may be substituted for apricots.

Joyce S. Trado

41

EASY PARTY PUNCH

May prepare ahead   *Yield: forty 4-ounce servings*

1 fifth gin (optional)
2 (28-ounce) bottles Tom Collins
   Mix, chilled
1 (24-ounce) can pineapple
   juice, chilled

2 (6-ounce) cans frozen orange
   juice concentrate, thawed
   but chilled
1 (28-ounce) bottle ginger ale,
   chilled

Mix all ingredients, except ginger ale if made ahead; add ginger ale at serving time.

Martha F. Powell

STRAWBERRY PUNCH

Partly prepare ahead   *Yield: approximately 20 servings*

1 quart strawberries, lightly
   sugared
1 fifth Rhine wine

1 fifth champagne
1 pint club soda
ice (or ice ring)

Place strawberries in a container or jar. Pour ½ bottle of wine over berries; cover and let stand for 1 to 3 hours. Add remaining wine, champagne, and club soda. Chill; serve over ice or ice ring in a punch bowl.

Carolyn W. Lyerly

EASY CHRISTMAS WASSAIL

Yield: 5 servings

1 (32-ounce) bottle cranberry
   juice
2 cups apple juice
6 inches stick cinnamon, broken

24 whole cloves
1 lemon, sliced
2 fifths red wine
sugar to taste

In a 4-quart saucepan, combine cranberry and apple juices. Tie spices in a cheesecloth bag; add to pan along with sliced lemon. Cook on high heat for 10 minutes, or until almost boiling. Add wine. Continue cooking on high heat for 15 minutes, or until heated through. Remove spice bag; add sugar to taste and serve hot.

Joanne M. Martin

GLÜHWEIN

Yield: 8 to 10 servings

2 quarts Burgundy, (inexpensive
   brand)
1 cup sugar
4 orange slices

4 lemon slices
2 (3-inch) cinnamon sticks,
   broken into eight pieces
10 whole cloves

Heat Burgundy in a stainless steel pan until very hot but *do not boil.* Add sugar and fruit slices from which white centers have been removed. Stir in cinnamon and cloves. Cover and allow to steep over low heat for 15 minutes. Pour into warmed mugs and enjoy!

Note: This is a traditional German warm-up.

Sally T. Blackwelder

CHATHAM COUNTY ARTILLERY PUNCH

Must prepare ahead

*Yield: 12 gallons or
two hundred 4-ounce servings*

1 pound green tea
2 gallons cold water
3 dozen oranges
3 dozen lemons
5 pounds brown sugar
2 quarts maraschino cherries
3 gallons Catawba (or Rhine)
   wine

1 gallon light (or St. Croix) rum
1 gallon brandy
1 gallon rye whiskey
1 gallon gin
2 or 3 large stone or glass
   crocks

Put tea in 2 gallons water; let stand overnight. Strain and add juice of the oranges and lemons. Add brown sugar, cherries, and all of alcoholic beverages. Cover lightly; allow to ferment in crocks, at room temperature, for 2 to 6 weeks. Strain off cherries and pour mixture into gallon or quart bottles. At party time, mix 1 gallon of this base with 1 quart of champagne or club soda. Pour over ice in a punch bowl and serve with a *warning about the potency!*

Camille M. Gardner

43

MIMOSA PUNCH

Partially prepare ahead   *Yield: 20 servings*

1 (6-ounce) can frozen orange
   juice concentrate
2 quarts fresh orange juice
½ cup confectioners sugar
1 navel orange, thinly sliced
½ cup Grand Marnier (or Triple
   Sec)

1 cup to 1 fifth vodka,
   depending on strength
   desired
2 fifths champagne, chilled

Stir juices and sugar until sugar dissolves. Marinate orange slices in Grand Marnier. Just before serving, combine juice mix, orange slices in liqueur, and vodka. At serving time, add chilled champagne; serve over ice in large (8-ounce) wine glasses or brandy snifters.

Note: Wonderful with brunch!

Camille M. Gardner

BANANA PUNCH

Partially prepare ahead   *Yield: thirty-five to forty*
                                             (4-ounce) cups

4 cups sugar
5 cups water
1 (12-ounce) can frozen orange
   juice concentrate
1 (24-ounce) can pineapple
   juice

2 lemons, juiced
5 bananas, mashed
5 or 6 (28-ounce) bottles
   ginger ale

Boil sugar and water together until sugar dissolves; then cool. Mix all ingredients into sugar and water except ginger ale. Add ginger ale with equal amounts of mix to punch bowl at serving time.

Note: Freeze mixture without ginger ale; this will keep for months!

Carolyn S. Moretz

CRANBERRY PUNCH

Partially prepare ahead   *Yield: approximately fifty*
(4-ounce) cups

1 (64-ounce) bottle cranberry   1 (67½-ounce) bottle ginger ale
  juice   1 tablespoon almond extract
1 (46-ounce) can pineapple juice   ½ gallon pineapple sherbet

Chill cranberry juice, pineapple juice, and ginger ale; pour into a punch bowl. Add almond extract and sherbet.

Patti C. Owens

PERCOLATOR PUNCH

May prepare ahead   *Yield: twenty to twenty-five*
(4-ounce) cups

9 cups pineapple juice   4½ teaspoons whole cloves
9 cups cranberry juice   4 cinnamon sticks
4¼ cups water   ¼ teaspoon salt
1 cup brown sugar, packed

In a large coffee maker, combine juices, water, and brown sugar. In the basket, place cloves, cinnamon sticks, and salt. Plug in coffee maker.

Note: This makes the house smell wonderful!

Brenda K. Cline

SPECIAL HOT CHOCOLATE

Yield: 1½ cups

2 cups milk   2 tablespoons molasses
½ cup little round candy-coated ¼ teaspoon ginger, ground
  chocolates   whipped cream

Heat milk to 212°. Combine candy, molasses, and ginger in a blender; add milk. Blend on high speed 1 minute or until smooth. Top with whipped cream.

Linda P. Frye

ORANGE SLUSH

May prepare ahead   *Yield: 4 cups*

2 cups orange juice,   ¼ teaspoon vanilla extract
   unsweetened   8 ice cubes
½ cup instant nonfat dry milk

Add all ingredients in blender container and process on high until mixture is combined and thickened. Serve immediately.

Shirley P. Thomason

SUMMERTIME ICED TEA

May prepare ahead   *Yield: 1 gallon*

9 tea bags, regular-size   1 (6-ounce) can frozen
4 cups boiling water   lemonade, thawed and
1½ cups sugar   undiluted
10 cups cold water   6 ounces fresh orange juice

Place tea bags in boiling water; remove from heat and steep for 5 minutes. Discard bags. Add sugar; stir to blend. Into a gallon container, pour cold water; add lemonade and orange juice, then tea. Serve over ice.

Stevi S. Dozier

RUSSIAN TEA

Must Prepare ahead   *Yield: 1 gallon*

2 tea bags, family-size   1 (6-ounce) can frozen lemonade
10 cups boiling water   concentrate
1 (24-ounce) can pineapple   30 whole cloves
   juice, unsweetened   4 small sticks cinnamon
1 (12-ounce) can frozen orange
   juice concentrate

In a Dutch oven, add tea bags to boiling water; remove from heat and steep for 30 minutes. Remove tea bags and add remaining ingredients. Bring to a boil; watch carefully for it will boil over. Turn off heat, cover, and let stand at least 1 hour. Strain. Store in refrigerator or freezer until ready to reheat and serve.

Roddy S. Dixon

SOUPS &
SANDWICHES

SOUPS AND SANDWICHES

( ) Denotes: (HE) Hickory Entertains   (I) International   (M) Microwave Recipes

SOUPS

APPLE VICHYSSOISE

Yield: 6-8

3 leeks, sliced
1 onion, sliced
2 tablespoons butter
3 potatoes, peeled and sliced
3 cups chicken stock
1 cup milk
1 cup heavy cream
salt to taste

2 bunches watercress
juice of ½ lemon
2 apples, peeled and grated
6-8 sprigs watercress, to
    garnish
12-16 apple slices, sprinkled
    with lemon juice to garnish

In a saucepan, sauté the leeks and onion in the butter until they are golden. Add the potatoes and chicken stock. Simmer for 35 minutes or until the potatoes are very soft. Purée the mixture in a blender. Stir in the milk, cream, and salt.

Cook the watercress in boiling water for a few minutes. Drain well and purée in the blender. Stir the watercress purée into the soup. Add the juice of ½ a lemon. Chill the soup well. Just before serving stir in the apples. Garnish each portion with a sprig of watercress and apple slices sprinkled with lemon juice.

Anne Byrd
Instructor of Creative Cookery

CARROT VICHYSSOISE
(PROCESSOR)

Yield: 6 servings

2 cups potatoes, pared, diced
2¼ cups carrots, sliced
1 leek, sliced
3 cups chicken stock
salt

pepper
1 cup heavy cream
dried dill (garnish)
raw shredded carrots (garnish)

Simmer vegetables in chicken stock for 25 minutes, or until vegetables are tender. Place half of mixture in food processor or blender and purée. Repeat with second half. Combine all puréed vegetables with salt and pepper to taste. Add cream. To serve, sprinkle with dried dill and raw shredded carrots. Serve hot or cold.

Roddy S. Dixon

49

OLD-FASHIONED POTATO SOUP

Yield: 8 to 10 servings

6 to 8 white potatoes, peeled
    and sliced
3 medium onions, sliced
1½ teaspoons salt
4 cups water

6 cups milk, scalded
black pepper
salt
2 tablespoons parsley, chopped

Put the potatoes and onions in a 4-quart kettle with salt and cover with cold water. Bring to the boiling point. Cover and cook gently for 20 minutes. Transfer to a blender and purée the vegetables or simply mash them to a pulp in the water. Add the milk and season to taste with salt and pepper. Garnish liberally with chopped parsley.

Frances R. Hilton

WESTERN CHRYSANTHEMUM BOWL

Yield: 6 servings

6 cups chicken broth or
    consommé
1 (8-ounce) can water chestnuts,
    thinly sliced
2 large scallions, chopped fine
peel of 1 lemon, sliced
    matchstick thin

6 large spinach leaves, shredded
2 slices cold boiled ham, cut
    in strips
1 tablespoon sherry
1 tablespoon soy sauce
1 large chrysanthemum

Heat broth to boiling and add all remaining ingredients except chrysanthemum. Bring to boil again and transfer to serving tureen. At table, just before serving, pull petals from chrysanthemum and scatter over the hot soup.

Helen M. Brooks

CRABMEAT SOUP

Yield: 6 servings

2 tablespoons butter
4 tablespoons all-purpose flour
1 quart hot milk
2 hard boiled eggs, pressed
  through strainer
1/2 pound crabmeat or 1
  (6 1/2-ounce) can crabmeat

grated rind of 1 lemon
salt and pepper to taste
1 cup heavy cream, whipped
2 tablespoons sherry

Melt butter and blend in flour. Add hot milk and stir until thick. Add eggs, crabmeat, and lemon rind. Season with salt and pepper. Stir over heat until boiling. Just before serving add whipped cream and sherry. Reheat, but do not boil.

Louise H. Jones

COLD CUCUMBER SOUP

Yield: 4 to 6 servings

1 large cucumber, peeled and
  sliced
1 (10 1/2-ounce) can cream of
  chicken soup

1 cup sour cream
1 or 2 teaspoons celery salt
1/2 cup milk
chives (optional)

Put cucumber in blender or food processor and blend. Add other ingredients. Chill thoroughly.

Caroline B. Bumbarger

INDIAN MOCK TURTLE SOUP

Yield: 4 servings

1 tablespoon butter
1 small onion, chopped
1 to 2 teaspoons curry powder
1/4 teaspoon sweet basil

1 (10 1/2-ounce) can green pea
  soup
1 (10 1/2-ounce) can tomato soup
2 cups water

Sauté onion in butter until slightly browned. Add curry powder and basil. Add remaining ingredients and heat thoroughly.

Dorothy Y. Menzies

51

CREAMY BROCCOLI SOUP

Yield: 6 to 8 servings

1 small onion, minced	1 to 2 cups chicken broth
4 tablespoons butter or	2 (10-ounce) packages frozen
margarine	chopped broccoli, slightly
5 tablespoons all-purpose flour	thawed
1 teaspoon salt	1/2 teaspoon nutmeg
3 cups light cream	

Sauté onion in butter until tender; stir in flour and salt. Gradually add cream, stirring constantly. Add broth according to desired thickness of soup. Add broccoli and nutmeg. Cook over low heat 25 minutes. Stir occasionally.

Variation: 1/8 teaspoon mace may be substituted for nutmeg. Cauliflower can be used in lieu of broccoli.

Linda P. Frye

LENTIL SOUP

Yield: 12 to 15 servings

2 cups lentils, soaked overnight	1 (16-ounce) can tomatoes
1/2 pound sweet sausage	2 1/2 teaspoons salt
1/2 pound hot sausage	1/2 teaspoon oregano
8 cups water	1/4 teaspoon sage
2 cups chicken broth	1/4 teaspoon red cayenne pepper
8-ounces pepperoni, thinly	2 medium carrots, sliced
sliced	2 stalks celery, sliced
1 cup onion, chopped	

Cut sausage in small pieces, fry, and drain. Place lentils and sausage in a 6-quart heavy pot with water, chicken broth, pepperoni, onions, tomatoes, salt, oregano, sage, and cayenne. Bring to a boil. Reduce heat, cover, and simmer for 30 minutes, stirring occasionally. Add carrots and celery, cover, and simmer for another 40 minutes.

Note: All ingredients can be put into a crockpot and cooked on low, 8 to 10 hours.

Carol H. Tuttle

COLD TOMATO SOUP

Yield: 6 to 8 servings

3 cups tomato juice (or cocktail vegetable juice)
2 tablespoons tomato paste
4 green onions, minced
salt to taste
¼ teaspoon thyme

½ teaspoon curry powder
grated rind of ½ lemon
½ teaspoon sugar
1 cup sour cream
1 tablespoon parsley

Mix all ingredients except sour cream and parsley and chill. Before serving, add sour cream and parsley. Stir with wire whip. The sour cream does not dissolve, but remains in small dollops throughout. Serve in mugs or bowls.

Sarah S. Raney

FRENCH ONION SOUP

Yield: 6 servings

½ cup butter
1 pound yellow onions, sliced or chopped
2 tablespoons all-purpose flour
6 cups water
5 beef bouillon cubes

1 (1.37-ounce) package dried onion soup (optional)
6 thin slices French bread
2-ounces mozzarella cheese, shredded

Melt butter in a heavy 3-quart saucepan. Add onions and flour; cook 15 minutes until brown, but not crisp. Add water and bouillon cubes. Heat to boiling, stirring to dissolve bouillon. Cover tightly; reduce heat and simmer 15 minutes or longer. Toast bread to golden brown; place a piece in the bottom of each of 6 soup bowls. Ladle in soup and sprinkle with cheese.

Variation: After making broth, place in individual oven-proof bowls. Top with French bread and 2 cups grated Gruyère or ½ cup Swiss and ½ cup Gruyère cheese. Bake 30 minutes in 350° oven until hot and bubbly.

Linda P. Frye

53

NEW ENGLAND CLAM CHOWDER

Yield: 6 to 8 servings

2 cups new potatoes, diced
1 cup water
6 tablespoons butter, divided
2 tablespoons all-purpose flour
2 cups milk
1 (10½-ounce) can cream of
　shrimp soup
¼ cup sautéed and diced salt
　pork

3 (6½-ounce) cans minced
　clams and juice
1 tablespoon Worcestershire
　sauce
juice of 1 lemon
salt and pepper to taste

Cook potatoes in a heavy 2-quart saucepan, uncovered, in 1 cup water. Do not drain. In a small, heavy saucepan make a thick, smooth white sauce using 2 tablespoons butter, flour, and 1 cup milk. Add cream of shrimp soup and stir until smooth. Add to potatoes and water. Add ¼ cup diced salt pork, 4 tablespoons butter, 1 cup milk, clams, Worcestershire sauce, lemon juice, salt, and pepper. Simmer slowly over low heat about 30 minutes being careful that soup does not stick. If soup becomes too thick, add a little more milk.

Sally T. Blackwelder

WINTER SQUASH SOUP

Yield: 8 to 10 servings

3 large onions, chopped
1 cup celery, chopped
1 clove garlic
4 tablespoons butter
3 cups chicken stock
2 cups cooked yellow squash,
　mashed, or 2 (10-ounce)
　packages frozen yellow
　squash, cooked and mashed

1 teaspoon fresh rosemary or
　½ teaspoon dried caraway
½ teaspoon winter savory or
　½ teaspoon summer savory
2 tablespoons parsley, chopped
2 cups heavy cream
salt and pepper to taste
dash of nutmeg

Sauté onions, celery, and garlic in 2 tablespoons butter until golden. Add to chicken stock with cooked squash, rosemary, savory, and parsley. Bring to a boil, simmer for 10 minutes. Add 2 tablespoons butter. Remove from heat and add cream. Season with salt and pepper. Dust with nutmeg and serve in warmed tureen.

Lou Ellen J. Goodwin

BACON AND POTATO SOUP

Yield: 8 to 10 servings

3 tablespoons butter
2 medium yellow onions, sliced
2 pounds potatoes, peeled
    and sliced
3 cups milk

3 cups chicken stock
1 cup light cream
parsley, chopped
8 slices bacon, crumbled

Melt butter in heavy saucepan, add sliced onions and cook gently. Do not let them brown. Add potatoes, season to taste, then pour the milk and stock over potatoes. Cover and cook gently for about one hour. Put potatoes into food processor or blender and purée. Return puréed potatoes to saucepan and add cream. Gently reheat, but do not boil. Garnish with parsley and bacon.

Judy C. West

MOTHER'S GRAND CHICKEN STOCK OR BROTH
(Fond de Volaille)

Yield: 1 gallon

2½ to 3 pound chicken or
    pieces
3½ to 4 quarts water
3 carrots, sliced
3 stalks celery with tops

2 leeks (white part only) or
3 onions, sliced
½ teaspoon salt
½ teaspoon whole peppercorns
Bouquet Garni (See page 315)

Place chicken in a stockpot with cleaned vegetables cut into 1-inch pieces, add water and seasonings. Bring to a boil and skim as necessary. Cook for one hour or until chicken is tender. Remove whole chicken or pieces and strain stock into a clean bowl or stockpot. Remove chicken meat from bones, discard skin, and save for salad or casserole. Freeze in 1 or 2 cup portions any stock not used within a week. Always bring stored stock to a boil before using in a recipe.

Camille M. Gardner

SQUASH SOUP

Freezes well   *Yield: 4 to 6 servings*

4 medium-sized yellow squash,   1½ cups chicken broth
  sliced   salt and pepper to taste
1 zucchini squash, sliced   Swiss cheese (garnish)
1 medium onion, sliced

Steam squash and onion slowly in chicken broth in heavy saucepan until tender. Cool. Purée in food processor or blender. Heat and serve, topped with shredded Swiss cheese.

Note: This is low calorie.

Jennie S. Case

FRESH MUSHROOM SOUP

Yield: 4 servings

2 tablespoons butter   1 clove garlic, crushed
3 medium onions, coarsely   ¼ teaspoon freshly ground
  chopped   pepper
1 pound fresh mushrooms,   ½ cup dry white wine
  sliced   4 to 6 slices cocktail rye
2 tablespoons chicken bouillon   bread, toasted and halved
  granules   1 cup Jarlsberg cheese,
3 cups hot water   shredded
⅓ cup minced fresh parsley   1 cup Parmesan cheese, grated
3 tablespoons tomato paste   1 cup Cheddar cheese, shredded

Melt butter in Dutch oven over medium-high heat. Add onions and sauté until almost tender. Add mushrooms and sauté briefly. Dissolve bouillon in hot water. Stir into vegetables and add parsley, tomato paste, garlic, and pepper. Increase heat and quickly bring soup to a boil. Reduce heat and add wine. Cover and simmer 5 minutes. Meanwhile, combine cheese. Divide toast and cheese among 4 (16-ounce) mugs. Ladle hot soup over top of cheese and toast. Serve immediately.

Susanne M. Gunter

56

MUSHROOM CLAM SOUP

Yield: 6 to 8 servings

½ cup butter
½ cup all-purpose flour
1 quart clam broth or 1 quart
   shrimp broth
1½ cups water
1½ pounds fresh mushrooms,
   chopped

2 cups heavy cream
salt and pepper to taste
dash of hot sauce (optional)
dash of lemon-pepper
   (optional)

Melt butter in a heavy Dutch oven and add the flour, stirring until it is absorbed by the butter. Cook slowly until the mixture turns medium brown. Add clam broth, water, and mushrooms. Simmer 5 minutes, add cream and season to taste with salt and pepper and optional seasonings.

Joyce S. Trado & Barbara F. Williams

COLD TOMATO COBB

Must prepare ahead   *Yield: 6 servings*

6 large tomatoes
1 small white onion, finely
   minced
1½ teaspoons salt

¼ teaspoon pepper, freshly
   ground
sauce

Scald and skin the tomatoes and put through grinder or processor. Mix the tomatoes, onions, and seasonings and place in the freezing tray of refrigerator until thoroughly chilled but not frosty.

Sauce:
5 tablespoons mayonnaise
1 heaping tablespoon parsley,
   minced

1 teaspoon imported curry
   powder

Mix the mayonnaise, parsley, and curry and keep in the refrigerator until the tomatoes are served. Garnish with sauce. Serve in crystal bowls with warmed crackers.

Note: This recipe, from a great cook the late Josephine Murphy Grimes, is the most delicious thing you could possibly eat on a hot summer day.

Dorothy Y. Menzies

57

ROMAINE LETTUCE SOUP

Yield: 8 to 10 servings

2 tablespoons butter
1 small onion, minced
1 quart chicken broth
2 quarts chopped romaine
    lettuce

salt and freshly ground pepper
4 egg yolks
1 cup heavy cream

Melt butter in a large saucepan, add the onion and cook until tender. Add the chicken broth and bring to a boil. Add the romaine, salt, and pepper and cook over low heat 10 minutes or until the romaine is wilted. Beat together the egg yolks and heavy cream. Stir into the soup mixture and cook over low heat, stirring until the soup begins to thicken but before the boiling point is reached. Correct the seasonings.

Helen M. Brooks

PUMPKIN SOUP

Yield: 8 servings

¼ cup butter
1 large onion, sliced
½ teaspoon curry powder

2 cups canned pumpkin
2 cups heavy cream
2½ cups chicken stock

Melt butter in a skillet. Add the onion and sauté until limp. Sprinkle with curry powder and sauté an additional minute or two. Purée onions and pumpkin in food processor or blender. Pour heavy cream into processor beaker or blender container while processing or blending. Transfer purée to a large saucepan and heat slowly with chicken stock. Garnish with a dash of nutmeg, and serve steaming hot.

Note: This soup is best when refrigerated overnight, as the flavors blend well together. We have served this as an appetizer for Thanksgiving and Christmas dinners. We have found that a steaming mug of pumpkin soup, some interesting cheeses and crackers, and cold vegetables and a creamy dip served a few hours before the "big dinner" are satisfying and not too filling.

Josephine L. Hambrick

ALMOND SOUP

May prepare ahead   *Yield: 4 to 6 servings*

1 tablespoon butter
1 tablespoon cornstarch
3 cups chicken stock

1 cup cream
⅓ cup almonds, chopped
chopped celery leaves, garnish

Place all ingredients in blender or food processor. Blend to combine. Heat until hot. To serve sprinkle each serving with celery leaves.

Anne F. Mitchell

HAMBURGER SOUP

Yield: 8 servings

1 medium onion, sliced
3 tablespoons butter or
   margarine
2 pounds ground beef
1 (28-ounce) can tomatoes
3 (10½-ounce) cans beef
   consommé
2 (10½-ounce) cans water

1 tablespoon salt
½ teaspoon pepper
1 tablespoon celery seed
2 tablespoons parsley flakes
1 bay leaf
5 medium-size potatoes, diced
4 carrots, diced

Sauté onion in butter in a heavy 4-quart saucepan. Add ground beef and brown. Add tomatoes, consomme, water, salt, pepper, celery seed, parsley flakes, bay leaf, potatoes, and carrots. Simmer about 1 hour.

Kay J. Webber

59

GAZPACHO FOR TWO

Must prepare ahead   *Yield: 2 servings*

3 cups cocktail vegetable juice
1 cup cucumber, seeded and
   chopped
1 cup tomatoes, chopped
½ cup green pepper, chopped
¼ cup onion, chopped

2 cups celery, chopped
1 tablespoon lemon juice
¼ teaspoon salt
¼ teaspoon pepper
¼ teaspoon hot sauce
2 tablespoons olive oil

Combine all ingredients in a large bowl. Chill at least 6 hours. Mix well before serving. Garnish with shredded Cheddar cheese and garlic croutons.

Carolyn H. Walker

ANTIQUES FAIR VEGETABLE SOUP

Must prepare ahead   *Yield: 1 gallon*

1 pound lean stew beef
water
1 pound potatoes, peeled and
   cubed
½ pound onions, peeled and
   chopped

2 stalks celery, chopped
1 (20-ounce) package frozen
   vegetables
1 cup canned tomatoes
1 (6-ounce) can tomato paste
seasonings to taste

Brown meat; then cover meat with water and simmer until meat is very tender. Add potatoes, onions, celery, vegetables, tomatoes, and tomato paste; season with salt and pepper. Simmer for several hours.

Note: Soup may be thinned with vegetable juice and/or beef bouillon to desired consistency.

The Service League of Hickory

CORN CHOWDER

Yield: 6 to 8 servings

4 slices bacon
2 medium onions, sliced
3 to 4 potatoes, diced
2 cups water
1 teaspoon salt

⅛ teaspoon pepper
1 (1-pound) can cream-style
  corn
2 cups milk

Fry bacon, drain and set aside. In the bacon drippings sauté the onion slices until transparent. Add potatoes, water, salt, and pepper. Cover and simmer until potatoes are tender. Add canned corn and milk and bring to serving temperature. Crumble bacon and sprinkle over top of each serving.

Frances R. Hilton

 SANDWICHES

HOT BROWN SANDWICH

Yield: 4 servings

2 tablespoons butter
1½ to 2 tablespoons flour
1 cup milk
salt to taste
pinch of cayenne pepper
¼ cup American cheese,
  shredded

4 slices of toast
4 slices baked chicken or turkey
fresh mushrooms
8 strips bacon, fried
4 tablespoons Parmesan cheese,
  grated

Melt butter over low heat. Blend in flour and slowly stir in milk, salt, and cayenne. Simmer and stir until thickened. Blend American cheese with cream sauce until the cheese melts. To assemble sandwiches, place a piece of chicken on each slice of toast. Cover with ¼ cup of sauce. Place two strips of cooked bacon on each sandwich. Sprinkle with one tablespoon of grated Parmesan cheese. Place sandwich in pan under broiler until cheese melts and is golden brown. Serve at once.

Carol H. Tuttle

PICNIC SANDWICH

Yield: 12 servings

1 cup cooked ham, ground
mayonnaise
1 teaspoon horseradish
1 cup cooked chicken, chopped
½ cup celery, chopped and
   divided

4 eggs, hard boiled
sweet pickle relish
Dijon mustard
1 loaf bread, unsliced
1 (8-ounce) package cream
   cheese, whipped

Make ham salad with ground ham, mayonnaise, and horseradish. Make chicken salad with chopped chicken, celery, and mayonnaise. Make egg salad with chopped eggs, celery, pickles, mustard, and mayonnaise. Slice bread 4 times lengthwise. Butter layers. Put one salad mixture on each layer. Use pimento cheese as filling for last layer. Ice loaf with whipped cream cheese; garnish with vegetable flowers.

Note: Make this lovely sandwich with a round loaf of bread for the look of a cake.

Nancy F. Matheson

BAKED CHICKEN SANDWICH

Must prepare ahead   *Yield: 8 sandwiches*

2 cups chicken, cooked
1 (10½-ounce) can cream of
   mushroom soup
1 (10½-ounce) can prepared
   chicken gravy
2 tablespoons pimento, chopped

2 tablespoons onions, minced
1 cup water chestnuts, sliced
16 slices sandwich bread
4 eggs, beaten
2 tablespoons milk
4 cups crushed potato chips

Slice chicken into small pieces and mix with soup, gravy, pimento, onions, and water chestnuts. Trim crusts from bread. Spread chicken mixture on bread and top with another slice making a sandwich. Wrap each sandwich in aluminum foil and freeze. When ready to use, dip frozen sandwich into egg and milk batter. Roll sandwich in potato chips until well coated. Place sandwiches on a buttered baking sheet. Bake at 300° for 1 hour.

Chris I. Shuford

SUNDAY NIGHT MUSHROOM SANDWICH

thinly sliced mushrooms	salt and pepper
butter	white wine
minced garlic	English muffins
minced onion	mayonnaise
Parmesan cheese	cooked bacon strips
oregano	Provolone or Muenster cheese

Sauté mushrooms in butter. Add garlic, onion, Parmesan, oregano, salt, pepper, and white wine. Cook until mushrooms are light brown in color. Toast an English muffin; spread with butter and mayonnaise. Add mushrooms, bacon strips, and thick slices of cheese. Broil until cheese melts.

Camille M. Gardner

HOT CHEESE TOAST

Yield: forty ½x5-inch strips

8 slices bacon, fried until crisp	⅛ teaspoon dry mustard
⅓ cup mayonnaise	½ teaspoon Worcestershire
1 cup sharp Cheddar cheese, shredded	sauce
1 small onion, grated	several dashes Tabasco
1 egg, lightly beaten	8 slices firm white, day old
freshly ground black pepper, to taste	bread

Fry bacon until crisp. Drain and set aside. Combine all remaining ingredients except bread. Crumble bacon and add to mixture. Cut crust from bread and toast both sides. Spread each slice generously with cheese mixture. Cut each bread slice into squares or strips. Sprinkle with paprika. Bake in a 350⁰ oven for 20 minutes. Serve hot. If made ahead, cover with waxed paper and refrigerate. Remove from refrigerator 30 minutes before baking.

Note: Serve with soup or salad.

Linda P. Frye

63

VEGETABLE POCKETS

Yield: 8 to 10 servings

4 cups cabbage, shredded
2 green onions including top,
 thinly sliced
1 stalk celery, thinly sliced
1 large carrot, thinly sliced
1/2 cup green pepper, chopped,
 (or 5 or 6 radishes, sliced)
1 cup (4-ounces) sharp Cheddar
 cheese (or Swiss cheese),
 shredded

salt and pepper to taste
4 or 5 pita breads (or taco
 shells), halved
1 to 1 1/2 cups salad dressing
 (creamy Ranch or Thousand
 Island)
1 (2.8-ounce) can french-fried
 onion rings

Store vegetables, separately, in refrigerator. Just before serving, toss vegetables with dressing; then stuff into bread pockets. Garnish with onion rings.

Note: This sandwich is a great accompaniment to soup or chili.

Judy B. Pierce

BROILED MUSHROOM SANDWICH ROMANO

Yield: 3 servings

6 thick slices of bread or rolls
soft butter or margarine
Romano or Parmesan cheese,
 grated
6 thin slices tomato
8 to 10 fresh mushrooms,
 sliced

salt
seasoned pepper
1 cup mayonnaise
2 tablespoons lemon juice
2 tablespoons chopped chives
3/4 cup Romano cheese, grated

Spread bread with butter on each side. Toast one side lightly. Turn and sprinkle with a little cheese; toast lightly. Top with tomato, cover with sliced mushrooms. Sprinkle with salt and seasoned pepper. Mix mayonnaise, lemon juice, chives, and Romano cheese. Spread over mushrooms, covering bread completely. Broil slowly about 6-inches from heat, until bubbly hot and flecked with brown; 3 to 5 minutes. Serve hot.

Note: This is delicious for a Sunday night supper or a luncheon dish.

Anne F. Mitchell

SPRING SANDWICH PUFF

Yield: 6 servings

6 slices bread
6 sandwich-sized slices
  Cheddar cheese

6 thin slices ham
18 asparagus spears, cooked

Toast 6 slices of bread on one side. Place cheese on other side of each slice and melt under broiler. Top bread and cheese slices with ham and 3 asparagus spears. Add some topping to each sandwich and bake at 350° for 12 to 15 minutes.

Sandwich Topping:
3 eggs, separated
¼ cup mayonnaise

¼ teaspoon salt
dash pepper

Beat egg whites until stiff and set aside. Beat egg yolks until lemon colored and combine with mayonnaise, salt, and pepper. Fold in stiffly beaten egg whites.

Lindy M. Dillow

"OLD NO. 8"

Yield: 1 serving

1½ slices rye bread
shredded lettuce
2 to 3 slices tomato
2 to 3 slices roast beef
1 slice Swiss cheese, cut into
  strips

2 slices bacon, fried and
  drained
dressing (your choice,
  Roquefort recommended)

Place three ½-slices of rye bread on plate. Add the following in order; shredded lettuce, tomato, meat, cheese, and bacon. Top with 1 to 1½ tablespoons dressing.

Note: This was a favorite at Rich's Tearoom in Atlanta many years ago. It was dropped from the menu, but you could still order "Old No. 8" and be served this delicious sandwich.

Helen L. Bowman

65

BROILED OPEN FACED CRAB SANDWICH

Yield: 3 to 4 sandwiches

1 (6½-ounce) can crabmeat,
    drained
⅓ cup celery, finely chopped

½ teaspoon onion, minced
½ cup mayonnaise
½ cup sharp cheese, shredded

Combine crabmeat, celery, and onion. Add mayonnaise and spread on a buttered and toasted bun. Top with cheese. Broil until bubbly.

Helen L. Bowman

PIMENTO CHEESE

Freezes well   *Yield: 2½ to 3 quarts*

1 pound sharp Cheddar cheese,
    shredded
2 (10-ounce) packages longhorn
    cheese, shredded
1 cup mayonnaise

1 tablespoon sugar
6 (4-ounce) jars diced pimento
    with juice
salt, Worcestershire sauce,
    and onion salt to taste

Mix all ingredients and store in refrigerator or freezer.

Roddy S. Dixon

VEGETABLE SANDWICH SPREAD

May prepare ahead   *Yield: 3 to 4 dozen*

1 tomato, finely chopped
1 large carrot, grated
1 small onion, grated
1 cucumber, peeled and grated
1 green pepper, grated
1 tablespoon unflavored gelatin

2 tablespoons vegetable juice,
    reserved
1 cup mayonnaise
salt to taste
pepper to taste

Grate or mix vegetables in food processor, then place in cheese cloth and squeeze, reserving 2 tablespoons juice. Mix juice with gelatin and melt in double boiler, then combine gelatin mixture with vegetables, mayonnaise, salt, and pepper. Chill overnight. When ready to spread, add mayonnaise if needed. Spread on trimmed bread.

Pat Y. Tolbert

BREADS

BREADS

( ) Denotes: (HE) Hickory Entertains   (I) International   (M) Microwave Recipes

ANGEL BISCUITS

Freezes well   *Yield: approximately 3 dozen*

2 (¼-ounce) packages yeast
½ cup warm water (105° to
   110°)
2 teaspoons sugar
5 cups all-purpose flour

1 teaspoon baking soda
1 teaspoon baking powder
1 cup shortening
1¾ cups buttermilk

Dissolve yeast in warm water. Add sugar; set aside. Sift dry ingredients together in large bowl. Cut in shortening with pastry blender or fork. Add buttermilk and yeast mixture. Stir until moistened. Turn dough onto floured board and knead several times. Store dough in covered bowl in refrigerator. To bake: roll dough to ½-inch thickness and cut with biscuit cutter, or drop into greased muffin tins. Bake at 400° 12 to 15 minutes or until lightly browned.

Note: Dough can be stored in refrigerator one week.

Nellie W. Barnes & Janice S. Thornton

MELT IN YOUR MOUTH BISCUITS

Yield: 18 to 24 biscuits
(depending on thickness)

1 cup heavy cream   1¾ cups biscuit mix

Preheat oven to 450°. Lightly stir cream into mix. Gently turn out on lightly floured board. Knead quickly several times. Pat out to one inch thickness. Cut and place on greased baking sheet. Bake 10 to 20 minutes.

Alice B. Davidson

BUTTERMILK BISCUITS

Yield: 18 to 20 biscuits

2 cups self-rising flour
5 tablespoons shortening

1 cup buttermilk

Preheat oven to 450º. Cut shortening into flour with pastry blender or fork. Stir in buttermilk until all flour is moistened. Do not over mix. Turn out dough onto floured waxed paper. Pat dough down with hand and cut with doughnut size cutter. Place on greased cookie sheet and bake 10 to 12 minutes.

Peggy R. Yancey

MEXICAN CORN BREAD

*Yield: one 8-inch square or
9-inch square pan*

1½ cups self-rising cornmeal
⅓ cup vegetable *or* corn oil
3 eggs, beaten
1 jalapeño pepper, finely diced
1 small-sized green pepper,
   chopped

1 (8½-ounce) can cream style
   corn
1 large onion, chopped
1 cup longhorn cheese,
   shredded

Preheat oven to 425º. Grease an 8-inch or 9-inch square pan. Combine all ingredients and bake for 20 to 25 minutes.

Della Marie V. McKinnon

LOUISIANA POPADUMS

May prepare ahead

Yield: 2 to 3 dozen

16-ounces French bread (or
   rye bread)

melted butter
sesame seed or grated cheese

With a sharp knife, slice French bread or rye as thin as possible. Dip in melted butter, spread on a cookie sheet, and bake at 250º until crisp; or bake at 375º for about 12 minutes. These may be sprinkled with sesame seed or grated cheese. They keep well in a tin box or they may be frozen.

Beverly A. Guarino

APPLE DATE BREAD

Freezes well

*Yield: 10-inch bundt pan or
two 9x5x3-inch loaves*

2 cups sugar
1½ cups vegetable oil
3 eggs
juice of ½ lemon
2 teaspoons vanilla
½ teaspoon salt

3 cups cake flour
1¼ teaspoons baking soda
2 cups apples, chopped
1 cup dates, chopped
1½ cups chopped pecans

Preheat oven to 325°. Grease and flour either two 9x5x3-inch loaf pans or a 10-cup fluted tube pan. Combine sugar, oil, eggs, lemon juice, vanilla, and salt. Mix well. Stir in flour and soda. Fold in apples, dates, and pecans. Batter will be thick. Pour into pan(s). Bake 1½ hours for tube pan or 45 minutes to 1 hour for loaf pans.

Pat R. Speagle

BANANA NUT BREAD

Freezes well

*Yield: two 7x5x2-inch loaves or
one 9x5x3-inch loaf*

½ cup margarine, softened
1½ cups sugar
2 eggs, unbeaten
1¾ cups all-purpose flour
1 teaspoon baking soda

4 tablespoons buttermilk
4 bananas, *very* ripe, mashed
1 cup chopped pecans
2 teaspoons vanilla

Preheat oven to 350°. Grease pans and dust with flour. Cream margarine and sugar until light and fluffy. Add eggs, one at a time, beating well after each addition. Mix flour and soda together and add alternately with buttermilk. Blend in bananas, pecans, and vanilla. Bake in two 7x5x2-inch loaf pans for 30 minutes, or one 9x5x3-inch loaf pan for 45 minutes.

Mickey R. Maynard

71

APRICOT BREAD

Yield: one 9x5-inch loaf

1 cup dried apricots ½ cup water

Soak apricots in water for 1 hour. Drain and reserve ¼ cup apricot water.

2 cups all-purpose flour
1 tablespoon baking powder
¼ teaspoon baking soda
1 teaspoon salt
1 egg, beaten
1 cup sugar
¼ cup butter, melted
½ cup orange juice
1 cup chopped nuts

Preheat oven to 325°. Sift flour, baking powder, baking soda, and salt together. Set aside. Combine egg, sugar, and butter. Combine juice and apricot water. Alternately add egg mixture and juices to dry ingredients, mixing well. Stir in chopped nuts. Bake in greased 9x5-inch loaf pan for 1 hour. Serve with cream cheese.

Roddy S. Dixon

SESAME CHEESE ROUND

Freezes well *Yield: 6 to 8 servings*

3 tablespoons sesame seed
1 egg, well beaten
1½ cups milk
3¾ cups biscuit mix
1½ cups sharp cheese, shredded
1 tablespoon parsley flakes

Preheat oven to 350°. Grease a 2-quart casserole. Sprinkle sesame seeds on bottom and sides of dish. In large bowl combine egg, milk, biscuit mix, cheese, and parsley. Mix well. Pour into casserole and bake for 40 to 45 minutes or until oven tester comes out clean. Invert on plate and remove casserole. Serve warm with butter.

Variation: Use poppy seed.

Joanne M. Martin

SPOON BREAD

Yield: 6 servings

2 cups milk
1 cup corn meal
1 teaspoon salt
2 tablespoons butter

1 teaspoon sugar
3 teaspoons baking powder
3 eggs, separated

Mix milk and corn meal. Cook on medium heat until thick, stirring constantly. Remove from heat and add salt, butter, sugar, baking powder, and slightly beaten egg yolks. Beat egg whites until stiff and fold into mixture. Turn into a well buttered 1½-quart baking dish. Bake at 400° for 20 to 25 minutes. Serve immediately.

Connie H. Abernethy

SPICED ZUCCHINI BREAD

Freezes well   *Yield: two 9x5-inch loaves*

3 cups all-purpose flour
2 teaspoons baking soda
1 teaspoon salt
½ teaspoon baking powder
1½ teaspoons ground cinnamon
¾ cup chopped walnuts
3 eggs

2 cups sugar
1 cup vegetable oil
2 teaspoons vanilla extract
2 cups zucchini, coarsely
   shredded
1 (8-ounce) can crushed
   pineapple, drained

Preheat oven to 350°. Combine flour, baking soda, salt, baking powder, cinnamon, and nuts; set aside. Beat eggs lightly in a large mixing bowl. Add sugar, oil, and vanilla; beat until creamy. Stir in zucchini and pineapple. Add dry ingredients, stirring only until dry ingredients are moistened. Spoon batter into 2 well greased and floured 9x5-inch loaf pans. Bake for 1 hour or until done. Cool 10 minutes before removing from pans. Turn out on rack and cool completely.

Note: The crushed pineapple is the real secret; it keeps the bread moist once cut and adds greatly to the flavor.

Variation: Use 2¼ cups sugar and 3 teaspoons cinnamon. Add ½ teaspoon ground cloves, 1 teaspoon nutmeg and 1 cup raisins.

Mickey C. Shuford

73

CINNAMON RAISIN BREAD

Yield: two 9x5x3-inch loaves

2 cups milk, scalded
¼ cup butter
2 cups all-purpose flour
½ cup sugar
½ teaspoon salt
1 (¼-ounce) package yeast
3¼ to 3¾ cups all-purpose
   flour

1½ cups raisins
2 tablespoons plus 2
   teaspoons sugar
2 teaspoons ground cinnamon
¼ cup butter, melted, divided

Combine milk and ¼ cup butter, stirring until butter melts. Cool mixture to 105° to 115°. Combine 2 cups flour, ½ cup plus 1 tablespoon sugar, salt, and yeast. Gradually add milk mixture to dry ingredients, mixing at low speed. Beat 2 minutes on medium speed, scraping bowl occasionally. Add ¾ cup flour; beat at medium-high speed 2 minutes. Stir in enough remaining flour to make a soft dough (2½ to 3 cups). Stir in raisins. Turn dough out onto a lightly floured surface. Knead until smooth and elastic. Place dough in a greased bowl, turning to grease top. Cover and let rise in a warm place, free from drafts, 1 hour and 20 minutes, or until doubled in bulk. Punch dough down; turn out on a lightly floured surface. Cover and let dough rest 15 minutes. Combine 2 tablespoons plus 2 teaspoons sugar and cinnamon. Divide in half and set aside. Divide dough in half, and place on a lightly floured surface. Roll each half into an 18x8-inch rectangle; brush each rectangle with 2 tablespoons melted butter. Sprinkle each with half of sugar mixture. Roll up rectangles in jellyroll fashion, beginning at narrow edge. Pinch seams and ends together to seal. Place rolls, seam side down, in 2 well-greased 9x5x3-inch loaf pans. Cover and let rise 55 minutes or until doubled in bulk. Bake at 350° for 25 to 30 minutes or until loaves sound hollow when tapped. Brush with melted butter, if desired. Remove from pan. Cool on wire racks.

Frances R. Hilton

ENGLISH MUFFIN BREAD

Yield: two 9x5x3-inch loaves

1 cup milk
2 tablespoons sugar
1 teaspoon salt
3 tablespoons margarine
1 cup warm water (105° to 115°)

1 (¼-ounce) package yeast
5½ cups all-purpose flour
corn meal

Scald milk; stir in sugar, salt, and margarine. Cool to lukewarm. Measure warm water into large warm bowl. Sprinkle in yeast; stir until dissolved. Stir in lukewarm milk mixture. Add 3 cups flour; beat until smooth. Add enough flour to make soft dough. Turn onto floured board; knead for about 2 minutes, or until dough is manageable and can be formed into a ball. Place in greased bowl; grease top. Cover; let rise until doubled, about 1 hour. Punch down; divide in half. Shape into loaves. Roll each loaf in corn meal. Place in greased loaf pans. Cover; let rise until doubled, about 1 hour. Preheat oven to 400°. Bake for 25 minutes or until done. Remove from pans and cool on wire racks.

Frances R. Hilton

DILLY CASSEROLE BREAD

Yield: 8 to 10 servings

1 (¼-ounce) package yeast
¼ cup warm water (105°)
1 cup creamed cottage cheese, heated to lukewarm
2 tablespoons sugar
1 tablespoon minced onion
1 tablespoon butter, melted

2 teaspoons dill seed
1 teaspoon salt
¼ teaspoon baking soda
1 egg
2¼ to 2½ cups all-purpose flour

Dissolve yeast in warm water. In mixing bowl, combine cottage cheese, sugar, onion, butter, dill seed, salt, baking soda, egg, and yeast. Gradually add flour to form a stiff dough, beating well after each addition. Cover; let rise in warm place 50 to 60 minutes or until doubled in bulk. Stir down dough with a spoon. Place in well greased casserole dish. Let rise until doubled (30 to 40 minutes). Preheat oven to 350° and bake 40 to 50 minutes, until golden brown. Brush top of warm bread with soft butter and sprinkle with coarse salt.

Margaret F. Tallant & Juanita T. Isenhower

GREEK CHEESE-FILLED BREAD

Freezes well   *Yield: one 9-inch bread round*

Dough:

½ cup warm water (105° to 115°)

1 (¼-ounce) package yeast

1 tablespoon sugar

6 tablespoons butter

1 cup warm milk (110° to 115°)

1 tablespoon sugar

1 teaspoon salt

3¾ to 4 cups all-purpose flour

1 egg yolk, beaten

Combine first three ingredients. Set aside until foamy (10 minutes). Melt butter in small saucepan. Remove from heat and blend in warm milk, sugar, and salt. Place 3½ cups flour in large bowl. Make a well in flour and add yeast mixture and milk mixture. Stir and add remaining flour until dough forms. Knead in bowl for 5 minutes. Turn out on lightly floured board and roll into 22 to 24 inch circle. Place dough into buttered cake pan, letting excess hang evenly around edges. Combine all ingredients for filling and spoon onto dough. Fold and pleat excess dough around pan, bringing dough over filling and meeting in center. Twist to form knob. Bake at 375° for 45 minutes. Remove from oven, brush top with yolk and return to oven for 15 minutes or until golden. Remove from pan immediately. Cool several minutes before slicing.

Filling:

¾ pound Muenster cheese, shredded

½ pound Swiss cheese, shredded

¼ pound Mozzarella cheese, shredded

2 eggs, lightly beaten

½ cup fresh mint leaves, chopped (or 1 tablespoon dried mint) (optional)

white pepper, freshly ground, to taste

Note: Good with salad or soup. Dough may be divided for two small round loaves.

Anne F. Mitchell

REFRIGERATOR BRAN MUFFINS

Stores well   *Yield: 36 muffins*

1 cup boiling water
3 cups bran, divided
1 cup sugar
1/2 cup shortening
2 eggs
2 1/2 cups all-purpose flour

2 1/2 teaspoons baking soda
1/2 teaspoon salt
2 cups buttermilk
3/4 cup raisins
3/4 cup chopped pecans

Pour boiling water over 1 cup of bran and set aside to cool. Cream together shortening and sugar until fluffy. Add eggs and continue beating. Combine flour, soda, and salt. Add flour mixture to creamed mixture, alternating with buttermilk. Add wet cereal mixture. Add remaining bran, raisins, and nuts. Refrigerate batter until ready to bake. To bake: Preheat oven to 400°. Spoon batter into greased muffin pans. Bake for 20 minutes. Cool 10 minutes before turning out on rack.

Note: Batter keeps in refrigerator, tightly covered, for 4 weeks. Recipe may be varied by using half dates and half raisins or substituting black walnuts for pecans.

Sally T. Blackwelder

BLINTZ BUBBLE RING

Yield: 12 servings

20 refrigerator biscuits
1/2 cup butter
1 cup sugar
3 to 4 tablespoons cinnamon
    (depending on taste)

1 (8-ounce) package cream cheese

Preheat oven to 375°. Melt butter and set aside. Mix sugar and cinnamon; cut cream cheese into 20 pieces. Flatten biscuits and put 1 teaspoon cinnamon sugar on each biscuit. Put a piece of cream cheese on each biscuit and pinch the edges closed. Dip each biscuit in butter and roll in cinnamon sugar. Place biscuits in a tube pan with the seam side up. Layer biscuits to fit all in the pan. Bake for 30 minutes.

Lynn G. Young

77

CREAM CHEESE BRAIDS

Must prepare ahead   *Yield: four 12-inch loaves*

1 cup sour cream   2 (¼-ounce) packages yeast
½ cup sugar   ½ cup warm water (105° to
1 teaspoon salt   115°)
½ cup butter or margarine,   2 eggs, beaten
   melted   4 cups all-purpose flour

Heat sour cream over low heat; stir in sugar, salt, and butter. Cool to lukewarm. Sprinkle yeast over warm water in a large mixing bowl, stirring until yeast dissolves. Add sour cream mixture, eggs, and flour. Mix well. Cover tightly and refrigerate overnight. The next day, divide dough into four equal parts. Roll out each part on a well floured board into a 12x8-inch rectangle. Spread one fourth of cream cheese filling on each rectangle. Roll up jelly roll fashion, beginning at long sides. Pinch edges together and fold ends under slightly. Place the rolls, seam side down, on greased baking sheets. Slit each roll at 2-inch intervals about two thirds of way through dough to resemble a braid. Cover and let rise in a warm place, free from drafts, until doubled in bulk. (About 1 hour.) Bake at 375° for 12 to 15 minutes. Spread with glaze while warm.

Cream Cheese Filling:
2 (8-ounce) packages cream   1 egg, beaten
   cheese, softened   ⅛ teaspoon salt
¾ cup sugar   2 teaspoons vanilla extract

Combine cream cheese and sugar in a small mixing bowl. Add egg, salt, and vanilla. Mix well. Yield: 2 cups.

Glaze:
2 cups powdered sugar   2 teaspoons vanilla extract
4 tablespoons milk

Combine all ingredients in a small bowl. Mix well. Yield: about 1 cup.

Anita G. Anderson

PANE ALL'OLIO

Must prepare ahead   *Yield: 2 loaves*

1 package active dry yeast   2 teaspoons salt
1 cup lukewarm water, divided   1 tablespoon olive oil
3 cups unbleached flour, divided

Dissolve the yeast in ½ cup lukewarm water. Measure 1½ cups flour onto a working surface, making a well in the center. Add the yeast into the
well, incorporate the flour into the yeast gradually, then knead for 10
minutes. Grease a bowl and place the dough in it. Cover and allow to
rise in a warm spot for 3 hours or until doubled in bulk. Place the remaining flour on the work surface. Place the ball of dough on the flour,
punching it down, flattening it, and making a well in it. Add the remaining ½ cup water, salt, and olive oil. Knead for 10 minutes. Shape into a
ball. Return to greased bowl, cover, and let rise again until doubled in
bulk (approximately 3 hours). After the second rising, knead the dough
for a few seconds. Divide the dough in half and shape into 2 loaves
about 8-inches long. Place on a greased baking sheet that has been
sprinkled with corn meal. Allow the dough to rest for a few minutes,
then slash with a sharp knife lengthwise (about 1-inch deep). Brush with
water until lightly moistened. Bake at 375⁰ for 12 minutes, reduce heat
to 350⁰ and bake for 45 minutes more. Remove and allow to cool for at
least 2 hours before eating.

Note: All kneading may be done in your food processor.

Mary Ann K. Forehand
(The Apron String—A kitchen specialty shop)

ITALIAN EGG BREAD

Yield: three 9x5x3-inch loaves

1 (¼-ounce) package yeast
½ cup warm water
½ cup butter, softened
½ cup sugar
6 eggs, room temperature
2¼ tablespoons lemon extract

1 cup cream (or ¾ cup
  evaporated milk)
dash of salt
¼ cup water
8 cups all-purpose flour

Dissolve yeast in ½ cup warm water. Cream butter and sugar. Add eggs, lemon extract, cream, salt, and ¼ cup water. Gradually add flour until the dough is workable. Knead for 15 minutes. Place in greased bowl and let rise until double in bulk. Knead again and divide dough into 3 equal parts. Shape into 3 loaves and place in greased loaf pans. Let rise one hour. Bake at 350⁰ for 30 to 35 minutes.

Kay B. Melton

WHOLE WHEAT BREAD

Yield: two 9x5x3-inch loaves

3 cups whole wheat flour
½ cup powdered milk
1 tablespoon salt
2 (¼-ounce) packages yeast
3 cups warm water

½ cup honey
2 tablespoons oil
1 cup whole wheat flour
4 to 4½ cups all-purpose flour

Mix together 3 cups whole wheat flour, powdered milk, salt, and yeast. Add water, honey, and oil; mix. Add 1 cup wheat flour and all-purpose flour. Knead until dough is smooth and elastic. Cover dough with warm damp cloth and let rise until doubled. Punch down; divide dough into greased pans. Cover; let rise until doubled again. Preheat oven to 375⁰. Bake for 40 to 45 minutes.

Frances R. Hilton

STRAWBERRY COFFEE CAKE

*Yield: one 10-inch tube cake
or two 9x5x3-inch loaves.*

3 cups all-purpose flour
1 teaspoon baking soda
1 teaspoon salt
3 teaspoons ground cinnamon
2 cups sugar

2 cups fresh strawberries,
   halved
4 eggs, well beaten
1¼ cups vegetable oil
1¼ cups chopped pecans

Sift flour, soda, salt, cinnamon, and sugar into a large bowl. Make a well in center and add strawberries, eggs, oil, and nuts. Mix just to moisten all ingredients. Pour into a well greased bundt pan or 2 loaf pans. Bake at 350⁰ for 45 to 60 minutes.

Note: 2 (10-ounce) packages frozen strawberries, thawed, may be substituted for fresh berries. If desired, drizzle a powdered sugar and milk glaze over warm cake.

Judith C. West & Lynn L. Lyerly

DANISH COFFEE CAKE

Yield: 6 servings

2 cups all-purpose flour, divided
1 cup butter, divided
2 tablespoons water
1 cup water
1 teaspoon almond flavoring

3 eggs
¾ cup powdered sugar
½ teaspoon vanilla or almond
   flavoring
3 to 4 teaspoons water

Combine 1 cup flour, ½ cup butter, and 2 tablespoons water. Flatten on a large cookie sheet. Combine remaining butter and water in a saucepan. Bring to boil; remove from heat and add almond flavoring. Stir in remaining flour and add eggs one at a time, beating well after each addition. Spread over flattened dough and bake at 350⁰ for 55 to 60 minutes. While coffee cake bakes, combine powdered sugar, vanilla flavoring, and water for glaze. Frost cake while warm.

Note: A delicately flavored coffee cake. Perfect for morning parties.

Anita G. Anderson & Nell B. Walton

ICED BUTTERHORNS

Yield: 32 rolls

1 cup light cream, divided	½ teaspoon salt
2 (¼-ounce) packages yeast	4½ to 5 cups all-purpose flour,
1 cup butter, sliced	divided
½ cup sugar	¼ cup butter, melted
2 eggs, beaten	

Dissolve yeast in ½ cup warm cream. In a large bowl combine butter, sugar, eggs, salt, yeast mixture, and remaining cream. Add 2½ cups flour and beat until well blended. Add remaining flour plus extra if needed to make dough stiff enough to handle. Knead 10 minutes on floured board. Place dough in greased bowl and grease top of dough. Cover and let rise until doubled in bulk. To prepare, divide dough into 4 equal portions. Roll each portion into a 12-inch circle. Brush with melted butter. Cut each circle into 8 equal wedges. Roll each from the large to small end to form crescent rolls. Brush with melted butter; cover and let rise until doubled. Bake at 350⁰ for 10 to 12 minutes or until lightly browned.

Icing:

3 tablespoons butter	1 teaspoon almond extract
2 cups powdered sugar	½ teaspoon vanilla extract
⅛ teaspoon salt	chopped pecans
3 tablespoons light cream, warmed	

Cream butter. Add sugar and salt; mix thoroughly. Add cream, almond and vanilla extracts. Beat until fluffy. Frost crescents while warm; top with finely chopped nuts.

Note: Butterhorns freeze beautifully, icing and all. Thaw and reheat slowly. Delicious!

Carole J. Cumming

HOT CROSS BUNS

Yield: 30 buns

2 cups hot milk
1 cup butter
1 cup sugar
2 (1/4-ounce) packages yeast
1/3 cup warm water
2 eggs
1/2 teaspoon salt
8 cups all-purpose flour

1/2 teaspoon cinnamon or
  nutmeg
2 cups currants or raisins
1/2 cup candied fruit peels
2 cups powdered sugar
3 to 4 tablespoons milk
1/2 teaspoon vanilla extract

Pour milk over butter and sugar. Stir to dissolve; cool to lukewarm. Dissolve yeast in water and combine with milk mixture. Add eggs; blend well. Gradually beat in salt, flour, and cinnamon. Dust fruit with flour and stir into dough. Place in a buttered bowl, cover, and let rise until doubled in bulk. Punch down dough and turn it out on a floured surface. Shape dough into 30 buns. Place buns on buttered cookie sheets. Cover and let rise for 30 minutes. Press cross shapes into dough with the back of a table knife. Bake at 375° for 10 minutes; then reduce heat to 350° and continue baking for 10 to 15 minutes, or until buns are done and slightly browned. Combine powdered sugar, milk, and vanilla. Frost cross-shaped indentions.

Note: Perfect for Good Friday or Easter.

Nancy F. Matheson

A LUNCHEON MUFFIN

Freezes well   *Yield: 18 to twenty-four 1 1/2-inch muffins*

2 cups self-rising flour   1 cup butter, melted
1 cup sour cream

Preheat oven to 400°. Grease muffin tins. Fold sour cream into flour. Add butter and stir. Batter will be thick. Bake for 15 minutes.

Note: May be frozen and reheated on baking sheet at 325°.

Carolyn W. Glass

83

MARGUERITES

Freezes well   *Yield: twelve 2½-inch or*
                                       twenty-four 1½-inch muffins

2 eggs   ½ teaspoon salt
1 cup brown sugar   1 cup chopped pecans
½ cup all-purpose flour   ¼ teaspoon baking powder

Preheat oven to 350°. Slightly beat 2 eggs. Add sugar, flour, salt, pecans, and baking powder. Pour into greased muffin tins. Place half a pecan on each. Bake until mixture begins to leave sides of pan, usually 8 to 12 minutes. Serve hot or cold. Store in a tin box.

Note: Especially nice served at coffees or teas.

Judy B. Smith

KARIN'S SWEET CRANBERRY MUFFINS

Yield: Twelve 2½-inch muffins

2 cups all-purpose flour   ¼ cup shortening, melted
½ cup sugar   1 egg
3 teaspoons baking powder   1 cup milk
½ teaspoon salt   1 cup cooked cranberries

Preheat oven to 350°. Grease muffin tins. Mix flour, sugar, baking powder, and salt. Add shortening, egg, and milk. Stir to blend ingredients. Fold in cranberries. Spoon into tins and bake for 20 to 25 minutes. Remove and glaze with the following:

Glaze
½ cup butter, melted   1 teaspoon cinnamon
1 tablespoon sugar

Brush each muffin with butter. Sprinkle with sugar and cinnamon. Serve warm.

Camille M. Gardner

SALLY LUNN MUFFINS

*Yield: twenty-four 1½-inch
or twelve 2½-inch muffins*

¼ cup shortening
⅓ cup sugar
2 eggs, beaten
2 cups all-purpose flour

4 teaspoons baking powder
1 teaspoon salt
⅔ cup milk

Preheat oven to 400°. Cream shortening and sugar; add eggs and mix well. Sift together flour, baking powder, and salt; add this alternately with milk to first mixture of shortening and sugar. Pour into greased muffin tins and bake for 30 minutes.

Note: Indent each muffin with thumb. Fill with favorite preserves.

Nancy S. Johnson

SWEET POTATO MUFFINS

Freezes well   *Yield: 2 dozen muffins*

½ cup butter
1¼ cups sugar
1¼ cups sweet potatoes,
    mashed
2 eggs
1½ cups all-purpose flour
2 teaspoons baking powder
¼ teaspoon salt

1 teaspoon cinnamon
¼ teaspoon nutmeg
1 cup milk
¼ cup pecans or walnuts,
    chopped
½ cup raisins, chopped
cinnamon-sugar

Preheat oven to 400°. Have all ingredients at room temperature. Cream butter, sugar, and sweet potatoes until smooth. Add eggs and blend well. Sift flour, baking powder, salt, and spices, and add alternately with milk to the egg batter. Do not over mix; fold in nuts and raisins. Sprinkle a little cinnamon-sugar on top before baking. Bake in greased muffin tins for approximately 25 minutes or until done.

Kay J. Webber

REFRIGERATOR ROLLS

Freezes well   *Yield: approximately 3 dozen rolls*

1 cup shortening   1 cup lukewarm water
¾ cup sugar   7½ to 8 cups all-purpose flour
1 cup boiling water   2 teaspoons salt
3 eggs, beaten   2 tablespoons vegetable oil
2 (¼-ounce) packages yeast

Cream shortening and sugar. Stir in boiling water. Cool to lukewarm.
Add eggs. Dissolve yeast in lukewarm water. Allow yeast to proof (5
minutes), then add to shortening mixture. Sift salt and flour. Add four
cups flour to shortening mixture. Blend until smooth. Gradually add remaining flour. Knead dough until smooth and elastic. Place dough in a
greased bowl. Brush top of dough with oil. Cover tightly and refrigerate.
Use *before* dough is three days old. To make rolls: Form dough into
rolls. Let rise in warm area for 1½ to 2 hours. Bake at 450⁰ for 12 to 15
minutes, or until golden brown.

Note: Freezes well when baked until barely golden.

Mary King L. Spainhour

CRESCENT YEAST ROLLS

Freezes well   *Yield: 60 rolls*

⅔ cup shortening   2 teaspoons salt
1 cup sugar   6 eggs, beaten
2 cups milk, scalded   9 to 11 cups all-purpose flour
2 (¼-ounce) packages dry yeast   butter or margarine, melted

Cream shortening and sugar. Scald milk. Add yeast and salt to cooled
milk. Beat eggs. Add milk and eggs to shortening mixture. Add 1 cup
flour and beat 2 minutes. Add enough flour to make a workable dough.
Knead until dough is smooth and satiny. Put dough in a greased bowl,
cover and let rise until doubled. Divide dough into 6 parts. Roll each
part into a circle and cut into pie-shaped pieces. Roll each from the large
to small end to form crescent rolls. Grease top with additional melted
butter or margarine. Allow to rise in a draft-free place until doubled in
bulk. Preheat oven to 375⁰ and bake for about 15 minutes, or until lightly browned.

*Note: To freeze, bake rolls until set but not brown. When ready to serve,
brown in a 375° oven.*

Frances R. Hilton

CINNAMON ROLLS

Yield: 2½ to 3 dozen rolls

¾ cup milk
¼ cup sugar
3 tablespoons butter
1 teaspoon salt
1 (¼-ounce) package yeast
¼ cup warm water (105° to
    115°)

1 egg, beaten
4 cups all-purpose flour, divided
½ cup butter, melted
1 cup brown sugar
1 teaspoon cinnamon
¾ cup brown sugar
3 tablespoons butter, melted

Scald milk and add sugar, butter, and salt. Cool to lukewarm. Dissolve yeast in water; set aside for 5 minutes. Add yeast and egg to milk mixture. Add 2 cups flour and beat well. Add remaining flour and mix thoroughly. Cover and let rise until doubled (1 to 1½ hours). Roll dough on floured board into a rectangle approximately ½-inch thick. Brush dough surface with butter. Combine sugar and cinnamon; sprinkle evenly over dough. Roll dough into jelly roll, pinching seam to seal. Cut into 1-inch slices. Combine remaining brown sugar and butter. Spread mixture on the bottom of a 9x13x2-inch pan. Place rolls in pan and let rise 30 minutes. Bake in 400° oven for 30 to 35 minutes. Remove from pan while warm; serve warm.

Peggy E. Hill

PUFFS OF PASTRY

Yield: 16 to 18 puffs

½ cup butter or shortening
1 cup water, boiling
1 cup all-purpose flour

½ teaspoon salt
4 eggs

Melt butter in boiling water. Sift flour and salt together and add to water. Cook over medium heat, stirring constantly, until mixture leaves sides of pan and is smooth and compact. (About 2 minutes.) Remove from heat and cool for 1 minute. Blend in eggs, one at a time, beating vigorously after each addition, until mixture is smooth and glossy. Drop dough by rounded tablespoonfuls onto greased baking sheets. Bake 20 to 25 minutes until golden brown. Turn oven off. Prick each puff with a sharp knife to let steam escape. Leave puffs in oven for 10 minutes. Cool, split and fill with chicken salad, creamed chicken, pudding, ice cream, etc.

Peggy L. Lyerly

WAFFLES

Yield: 4 to 5 servings

1 cup all-purpose flour
½ teaspoon salt
2 teaspoons baking powder

2 eggs, separated
1 cup milk
2 tablespoons melted butter

Sift together flour, salt, and baking powder. Add egg yolks and milk. Beat until batter is smooth. Stir in melted butter. Beat egg whites until stiff and add to batter. Cook and serve immediately.

Jane F. Hunsucker

PAM'S PANCAKES

Yield: 12 to 15 pancakes

1⅛ cup milk
1 cup oatmeal
½ cup whole wheat flour
2 tablespoons vegetable oil

2 eggs, beaten
1 tablespoon brown sugar
1 teaspoon baking powder
salt to taste

Soak oatmeal in milk until softened. Add remaining ingredients, stirring until blended. Fry on heated griddle, turning once. Serve with honey or maple syrup.

Jan J. Smithson

SILVER-DOLLAR PANCAKES

Yield: 12 pancakes

1¼ cups all-purpose flour
2 teaspoons baking powder
¾ teaspoon salt

1 egg, lightly beaten
1½ cups skim milk

Mix and sift flour, baking powder, and salt. Place dry mixture in a mixing bowl. Combine egg and milk, add to dry mixture, and blend well. Spoon onto a greased griddle or skillet and cook on both sides.

Variations: 1. Use ½ cup whole wheat flour with ¾ cup all-purpose flour for whole wheat pancakes. 2. Add blueberries and chopped pecans to mixture before cooking for a delicious treat.

Kay I. Showfety

FRENCH TOAST FONDUE

Yield: 4 to 6 servings

1 loaf French bread
2 eggs, well beaten
½ cup milk

¼ teaspoon salt
cooking oil for fondue pot

Cut bread into approximately fifty 1-inch cubes. Combine eggs, milk, and salt. Dip cubes into egg mixture, being certain to soak a bit of mixture into each cube. Heat cooking oil in fondue pot. Spear cubes and fry. Dip each into maple butter and enjoy.

Maple Butter:
½ cup butter, softened
1½ cups powdered sugar

1 egg, separated
½ cup maple syrup

Cream butter and sugar. Add syrup and egg yolk; stir to blend. Beat egg white until stiff and fold into mixture.

Note: This is great fun for breakfast or Sunday supper. Serve with small link sausages and fresh fruit.

Sally T. Blackwelder

DADDY'S TURKEY DRESSING

Yield: stuffing for a 20 pound turkey

16 cups coarse dry bread
   crumbs
3 cups celery, chopped
4 cups pecans, chopped
¾ cup onion, chopped
1 (6-ounce) can sliced
   mushrooms, drained

1 tablespoon salt
2 teaspoons dried basil
⅛ teaspoon pepper
2 cups butter, melted
1 cup milk
½ cup dry white wine

In large bowl, combine bread crumbs, celery, pecans, onion, mushrooms, salt, basil, and pepper. Gradually add butter, milk, and wine, tossing with fork until combined. To make dressing balls, use ½ cup dressing for each ball. Place in a greased baking dish, brush with butter and cover. Bake with turkey for 30 minutes, remove cover, and bake 15 minutes more.

Nancy F. Matheson

HUSH PUPPIES FOR A CROWD

Yield: 50 to 75 servings

5 pounds corn meal
4 eggs, beaten
4 tablespoons salt
1 tablespoon sugar

1 teaspoon baking soda
1 quart buttermilk
water

Thoroughly mix ingredients in a very large bowl. Add just enough water to make a thick batter. Drop by a teaspoon into deep fat (375⁰) and fry until golden brown.

Note: Double recipe for a larger gathering.

Stevi S. Dozier

BASIC CRÊPES

May prepare ahead, freezes well   *Yield: Approximately 12*

1 cup all-purpose flour, sift
    before measuring
pinch of salt, sifted into flour
1 cup milk

2 eggs, at room temperature
1 tablespoon butter, melted
butter for cooking

Place flour and salt mixture into a bowl and add milk. Beat eggs and add to flour mixture, stirring until smooth. Stir in butter and let batter rest in refrigerator for 2 hours. Brush the bottom of a 6 or 7-inch crêpe pan or skillet with a small amount of butter. Heat over *medium* heat until hot. Pour a scant ¼ cup of batter into pan. Quickly tilt pan in all directions to run batter over the bottom of the pan in a thin film. (Return excess batter to bowl.) Cook for 1 minute; then turn and cook the other side about ½ minute. (This is the side where filling is placed.) Throw the first crêpe away. Repeat process with remaining batter and either use immediately, between layers of waxed paper and store in refrigerator, or wrap layered crêpes in foil and freeze.

Dessert Crêpes:
Add 1 tablespoon of sugar to Basic Crêpe recipe. If desired, 2 table-spoons of Grand Marnier, rum, brandy or other flavoring may be added.

Carolyn W. Lyerly

CHEESE & EGGS

I N D E X

CHEESE AND EGGS

CHEESE
Artichoke-Mushroom Pie 95
Blender Cheese Soufflé 93
Fabulous Ham and Cheese
  Soufflé. 101
Swiss Alpine Pie 95
Swiss Cheese Croquettes with
  Tomato Sauce 94
Wine Strata 93

EGGS
Bacon Casserole (HE) 100
Cheese, Artichoke Casserole 96
Company 96
Fluffy Golden Omelet (M) 377
Overnight Scrambled Casserole . . . 97
Salmon Soufflé 100
Sausage Strata 98
Stuffed Mornay 99
Tomato and Eggs in Ramekins 98
Quiche
Artichoke-Mushroom Pie 95
Cocktail (HE). 17
Crab Pie 101
Incredible 102
Spinach. 102
Swiss Alpine Pie 95

( ) Denotes: (HE) Hickory Entertains   (I) International   (M) Microwave Recipes

 # CHEESE AND EGGS

BLENDER CHEESE SOUFFLÉ

Yield: 6 servings

8-ounces sharp Cheddar cheese
5 slices white bread, trim crusts
3 eggs
2 cups whole milk

1 teaspoon dry mustard
salt and pepper to taste (½ teaspoon salt is enough)

Put all ingredients into blender or food processor. Blend for 1 to 2 minutes. Bake at 325° for 1 hour, or until firm.

Sherry S. Abernethy

CHEESE WINE STRATA

Must prepare ahead   *Yield: 8 servings*

⅔ cup butter, softened and divided
1 clove garlic, crushed
1 tablespoon dry mustard
1 loaf French bread, sliced
4 cups Swiss cheese, shredded and divided

3 tablespoons onion, grated
1 teaspoon salt
1 teaspoon paprika
¼ cup all-purpose flour
1 cup white wine
3 cups milk
3 eggs, beaten

Cream ⅓ cup butter with garlic and mustard; spread on bread slices. Line the bottom of a 13x9x2-inch casserole with bread, buttered side down. Combine 3 cups of cheese, onion, and seasonings; toss until blended. Melt remaining butter; remove from heat. Add flour, wine, and milk; cook until thickened. Add a little sauce to eggs and pour all back into the saucepan. Stir until well blended. Arrange alternating layers of cheese, bread, and sauce in the casserole, ending with bread, buttered side up. Sprinkle with remaining cheese on top. Refrigerate overnight. Preheat oven to 350°. Bake for 35 to 40 minutes.

Note: An unusual version of mock cheese soufflé.

Carole J. Cumming

93

SWISS CHEESE CROQUETTES WITH TOMATO SAUCE

Yield: 6 servings

4 tablespoons butter
⅓ cup all-purpose flour, sifted
½ cup milk
dash of white pepper

dash of ground nutmeg
3 egg yolks, beaten
4 cups Swiss cheese, shredded

In a skillet, melt butter; blend in flour and milk all at once. Cook and stir until it thickens. Add pepper and nutmeg. Stir a moderate amount of the hot mixture into egg yolks. Return to pan and cook 10 minutes, stirring constantly. Add cheese, and stir until mixture is smooth. Oil an 11x7x1½-inch baking pan. Spread mixture; chill until firm. Cut into 12 portions.

Batter:
2 eggs, beaten
½ cup milk

½ cup all-purpose flour
1 cup fine dry bread crumbs

Combine eggs and milk. Roll chilled croquettes into flour, dip into egg mixture, and roll gently in bread crumbs to coat. Heat cooking oil to 375°. Fry in deep fat until golden brown and heated thoroughly (about 3 minutes).

Tomato Sauce:
1 tablespoon butter or
   margarine
1 slice raw bacon, diced
⅓ cup onion, minced
½ cup tomato purée

¼ cup catsup
1 (10½-ounce) can beef broth
2 tablespoons carrot, diced
1½ slices bread

In a saucepan, melt butter and cook bacon and onion until tender. Stir in remaining ingredients. Cover and cook over low heat for 30 minutes. Press through a sieve; reheat to serve. Makes 1¼ cups sauce.

Note: This is an unusual first course at a dinner party, or delightful for a brunch or luncheon. Well worth the preparation time.

Anne F. Mitchell

ARTICHOKE-MUSHROOM PIE

Yield: 6 servings

2 (9-inch) deep dish pie shells
2 cloves garlic, minced
1 tablespoon cooking oil
1 (14-ounce) can artichoke
  hearts, drained
1 (4-ounce) can mushroom
  stems and pieces, drained
4 eggs beaten

1 cup mozzarella cheese,
  shredded
1 cup Cheddar cheese,
  shredded
1 cup Gruyere cheese, shredded
¼ cup chopped pitted ripe olives
⅛ teaspoon pepper

Preheat oven to 350°. Turn 1 pie shell out onto waxed paper; let it thaw for 10 minutes. Press gently to flatten. Halve artichoke hearts. In a small skillet, cook garlic in hot oil; stir in artichokes and mushrooms. Spoon mixture into the bottom of remaining pie shell. In a bowl, combine eggs, cheeses, olives, and pepper; pour over vegetables. Place flattened shell on top; turn under and crimp edges of both shells together. Cut slits in top. Place on a baking sheet and bake for 40 to 50 minutes. Let pie cool before cutting in wedges.

Note: To use as an appetizer, cut into 12 smaller wedges.

Grace W. Menzies

SWISS ALPINE PIE

Yield: 4 servings

1 (10-inch) pie shell
1 (10-ounce) package frozen
  broccoli, cooked
2 cups cooked ham, cut into
  ½ inch cubes
2 cups Swiss cheese, shredded

3 tablespoons chopped onion
1½ cups hot milk
3 eggs, slightly beaten
⅛ teaspoon salt
⅛ teaspoon pepper

Preheat oven to 450°. Drain and chop broccoli. Layer ½ broccoli, ½ ham, and ½ cheese in pie shell. Repeat with remaining broccoli, ham, and cheese. Sprinkle onions on top and set aside. Gradually stir milk into eggs; add salt and pepper. Pour into pie shell. Bake for 10 minutes; reduce heat to 325° and continue baking for 30 to 35 minutes. Remove from oven and let stand a few minutes before serving.

Shirley L. Ballew

COMPANY EGGS (FOR A CROWD)

Must prepare ahead   *Yield: 18 servings*

½ cup butter or margarine
3 dozen eggs, well beaten
½ cup milk
2 (10¾-ounce) cans mushroom
   soup

½ pound sharp Cheddar cheese,
   shredded
½ cup dry sherry
1 pound mushrooms, sliced

Melt butter over low heat in a large frying pan. Combine eggs and milk and soft scramble in the butter; remove from heat. Combine soup, cheese, and sherry in a saucepan. Heat, stirring constantly, until cheese melts. In a 2½ to 3-quart casserole, pour ½ of the egg mixture; then ½ of the sauce, repeating with remaining egg mixture and ending with sauce. Cover and refrigerate 24 hours. Preheat oven to 250°. Top casserole with mushrooms. Cover and bake for 50 minutes.

Note: Easy and delicious for brunch.

Joanne M. Martin

EGG, CHEESE, ARTICHOKE CASSEROLE

Freezes well   *Yield: 4 servings*

1 bunch green onions
2 (6½-ounce) jars marinated
   artichoke hearts
1 clove garlic, finely minced

4 eggs, beaten
1 cup medium Cheddar cheese,
   shredded
6 crackers, crumbled

Preheat oven to 350°. Finely mince onions, including only ½ of the tops. Cut artichoke hearts into thirds and reserve oil. Sauté onions and garlic in artichoke oil. Combine remaining ingredients with onions and garlic. Grease a 9x9-inch glass dish, pour in mixture, and bake for 40 minutes.

Note: Tripled, this recipe serves 30 for brunch if it's cut into 2-inch squares. Can be served at room temperature or hot. May be prepared a day ahead and refrigerated. Reheat 15 to 20 minutes to warm. If frozen, thaw, and reheat as if refrigerated.

Anne F. Mitchell

OVERNIGHT SCRAMBLED EGG CASSEROLE

Must prepare ahead   *Yield: 12 to 15 servings*

1 cup cooked ham, cubed
¼ cup green onion tops,
    chopped
3 tablespoons butter or
    margarine

12 eggs, beaten
1 (4-ounce) can sliced
    mushrooms, drained

Sauté ham and onions in margarine until onions are tender. Add eggs; cook over medium-high heat, stirring to form large curds. When set, stir in mushrooms and cheese sauce. Place in a greased 13x9x2-inch baking dish.

Cheese Sauce:
2 tablespoons butter or
    margarine
2½ tablespoons all-purpose
    flour
2 cups milk

½ teaspoon salt
⅛ teaspoon pepper
dash of hot pepper sauce
1 cup Cheddar or processed
    American cheese, shredded

Melt margarine, blend in flour, and cook 1 minute. Gradually add milk; cook on medium heat until thickened. Add salt, pepper, hot sauce, and cheese. Stir until cheese melts and mixture is smooth.

Topping:
¼ cup butter or margarine,
    melted

2¼ cups soft bread crumbs
paprika to taste

Combine and spread over egg mixture. Sprinkle with paprika. Cover and place in refrigerator overnight. The next day, preheat oven to 350⁰, uncover, and bake for 30 minutes or until eggs are heated thoroughly.

Joyce S. Trado

EGG-SAUSAGE STRATA

Yield: 6 to 8 servings

6 to 8 slices bread
1½ pounds pork sausage
1 teaspoon prepared mustard
1 cup (or ¼ pound) Swiss
    cheese, shredded
4 eggs, slightly beaten
1½ cups milk

¾ cup light cream
½ teaspoon salt
dash of pepper
dash of nutmeg
1 teaspoon Worcestershire
    sauce

Trim bread crusts. Grease a 10x6-inch or an 11x7-inch casserole. Place bread in bottom of dish. Brown sausage; drain fat. Stir mustard into sausage and pour over bread. Sprinkle on cheese. Combine eggs, milk, cream, salt, pepper, nutmeg, and Worcestershire sauce. Pour over cheese. Bake at 350° for 25 to 35 minutes.

Note: Great combination for brunch.

Lou Ellen J. Goodwin

TOMATO AND EGGS IN RAMEKINS

Yield: 2 servings

2-ounces butter or margarine
4 slices tomato
pinch of salt

pinch of pepper
2 eggs

Preheat oven to 200°. For each serving, put 1-ounce butter in each of 2 ramekins (or custard cups). Place ramekins in oven until butter melts. Remove; place 2 slices of tomato in each ramekin and add salt and pepper. Increase oven temperature to 400°. Bake for 4 minutes. Remove and break 1 egg in each ramekin; salt and pepper to taste. Continue baking for 9 to 10 minutes.

Note: A dollop of hollandaise sauce may be placed on top after baking. Carefully broil to heat. Or, top tomatoes with piece of ham before adding eggs.

Frances D. Norman

STUFFED EGGS MORNAY

May prepare ahead   *Yield: 12 servings*

12 hard-cooked eggs
½ pound fresh mushrooms,
   minced
4 tablespoons butter
2 tablespoons parsley, chopped

½ teaspoon leaf tarragon,
   crumbled
cheese sauce
bread crumb topping

Slice eggs lengthwise, remove egg yolks to small bowl. Reserve egg whites. Sauté mushrooms in butter for 5 minutes or until mixture is almost dry. Add parsley and tarragon. Mash egg yolks with ½ cup cheese sauce. Add mushroom mixture. Stuff egg whites with mixture. Spread a thin layer of cheese sauce in a buttered 12x8x2-inch glass baking pan. Place stuffed eggs in pan and spoon remaining sauce over eggs. Casserole may be cooled, covered and refrigerated up to 24 hours at this point. When ready to serve, top with bread crumb topping and bake uncovered in preheated 350⁰ oven for 30 minutes.

Cheese Sauce:
4 tablespoons butter or
   margarine
1 teaspoon salt
½ cup all-purpose flour
dash cayenne pepper
¼ teaspoon black pepper

3 cups hot milk
2-ounces Swiss cheese,
   shredded
4 tablespoons grated Parmesan
   cheese

Combine butter, salt, flour, peppers, and 2 cups of milk in blender or food processor. Process 30 seconds. Pour into heavy 2-quart sauce pan; add remaining hot milk and cook over medium heat, stirring constantly until thickened. Add cheeses and stir until cheeses melt. Cover and set aside.

Topping:
1 cup fresh bread crumbs
2 tablespoons Parmesan cheese,
   grated

2 tablespoons butter, melted

Toss bread crumbs and Parmesan cheese with melted butter. Sprinkle over eggs.

Lindy M. Dillow

EGG AND BACON CASSEROLE

Yield: 6 servings

4 tablespoons all-purpose flour
1 teaspoon salt
1 teaspoon dry mustard
6 tablespoons butter or
   margarine, melted
2 cups milk

½ pound sharp cheese,
   shredded
10 hard-cooked eggs, quartered
½ pound bacon, cooked and
   crumbled

Combine flour, salt, dry mustard, butter, milk, and cheese in a saucepan. Cook over low heat, stirring often, until cheese melts and sauce thickens. Layer 2-quart casserole or souffle dish with eggs, bacon, then sauce. Bake at 350° for 30 minutes.

Mary Kathryn F. Hemphill

SALMON SOUFFLÉ

Yield: 3 to 4 servings

3 tablespoons butter
3 tablespoons all-purpose flour
1 cup milk
1 cup cooked salmon, flaked
   (fresh or canned)
1 tablespoon minced green
   pepper
1 tablespoon minced chives

1 tablespoon sherry
1 tablespoon lemon juice
½ teaspoon dry mustard
sea salt and pepper to taste
4 egg yolks
5 egg whites
hollandaise sauce (optional)

Preheat oven to 350°. Melt butter in a saucepan; add flour and stir until smooth. Slowly add milk, whisking constantly. Cook over low heat until sauce is thick (about 5 minutes). Remove from heat and stir in salmon, green pepper, chives, sherry, lemon juice, dry mustard, sea salt, and pepper. Beat in egg yolks; set aside for 15 minutes. Beat egg whites until stiff but not dry. Stir ¼ egg whites into salmon mixture. Gently fold in remaining egg whites. Pour mixture into a 1 to 1¼ quart souffle dish. Bake for 35 minutes. Serve at once. If desired, pass hollandaise sauce on the side.

Shirley L. Ballew

FABULOUS HAM AND CHEESE SOUFFLÉ

Must prepare ahead   *Yield: 8 to 10 servings*

16 slices white sandwich bread
1 pound ham, cubed
1 pound sharp Cheddar cheese,
    shredded
1½ cups Swiss cheese, cut in
    small pieces
6 eggs, beaten

3 cups milk
½ teaspoon onion salt
½ teaspoon dry mustard
3 cups cornflakes, crushed
6 drops hot pepper sauce
½ cup butter or margarine,
    melted

Grease a 9x13x2-inch baking dish. Cut off bread crusts and cube bread. Spread ½ bread cubes evenly in dish. Add ham and both cheeses; cover with remaining bread cubes. Combine eggs, milk, onion salt, and mustard. Pour evenly over casserole. Refrigerate overnight. Preheat oven to 375°. Combine cornflakes, hot pepper sauce, and butter. Cover top of casserole with mixture and bake for 40 minutes.

Shirley L. Ballew

CRAB PIE

Yield: 6 servings

1 (9-inch) pastry shell, unbaked
1 cup Swiss cheese, shredded
1 (7½-ounce) can crabmeat,
    drained and flaked
2 green onions with tops, sliced
3 eggs, beaten

1 cup light cream
½ teaspoon salt
½ teaspoon lemon peel, grated
¼ teaspoon dry mustard
dash of mace
¼ cup sliced almonds

Sprinkle cheese evenly over bottom of pastry shell. Top with crabmeat and sprinkle with onion. Combine eggs, cream, salt, lemon peel, mustard, and mace. Pour over crabmeat. Top with sliced almonds and bake at 325° for 45 minutes. Remove from oven; let stand 10 minutes before slicing.

Carol H. Tuttle

INCREDIBLE QUICHE

Yield: 6 servings

3 eggs
½ cup biscuit mix
½ cup butter or margarine,
  melted
1½ cups milk

¼ teaspoon dry mustard
¼ teaspoon salt
1 cup Swiss cheese, shredded
½ cup ham, bacon or
  vegetables, chopped

Place eggs, biscuit mix, butter, milk, dry mustard, and salt into blender or food processor. Process a few seconds to blend well. Pour mixture into well greased 9½-inch pie pan. Sprinkle cheese, meat, or vegetables over top of mixture. Push gently below surface. Bake at 350⁰ for 45 minutes or until done. Let quiche set 10 minutes before cutting. Crust forms while baking.

Joanne M. Martin

SPINACH QUICHE

Freezes well   *Yield: 8 to 10 servings*

1 (9-inch) unbaked deep-dish
  pie shell
1 (10-inch) package frozen
  chopped spinach
8-ounces Swiss cheese, diced
2 tablespoons all-purpose flour

1 cup milk
3 eggs, beaten
½ teaspoon salt
⅛ teaspoon pepper
dash ground nutmeg

Prick bottom and sides of pie shell with a fork. Bake at 425⁰ for 6 to 8 minutes. Set aside. Cook spinach, drain well, and let cool. Combine cheese and flour; set aside. Combine milk, eggs, salt, pepper, and nutmeg. Mix well. Stir in spinach and cheese. Pour mixture into partially baked pie shell. Bake at 350⁰ for 50 to 60 minutes. Cool slightly before serving.

Note: To freeze, bake only 40 minutes, wrap tightly in foil and freeze. To serve, thaw and bake 15 to 20 minutes.

Frances R. Hilton

SALADS &
DRESSINGS

SALADS AND SALAD DRESSINGS

( ) Denotes: (HE) Hickory Entertains   (I) International   (M) Microwave Recipes

❧ SALADS ❧

CRANBERRY SALAD MOLD

Must prepare ahead   *Yield: 8 to 10 servings*

4 cups fresh cranberries,
  washed and chopped
1 cup sugar
1 envelope unflavored gelatin
½ cup orange juice

1 cup celery, chopped
1 cup apple, chopped
1 cup pecans (or walnuts),
  chopped

Put cranberries through a food chopper or food processor. Add sugar and let stand 15 minutes, stirring occasionally. Sprinkle gelatin over orange juice in a small saucepan to soften. Place over low heat and stir until dissolved. Add gelatin mixture, celery, apple, and nuts to cranberries and mix well. Turn into a 1-quart mold and refrigerate until firm. Serve with mayonnaise.

Nell B. Walton

CAPER SALAD

Must prepare ahead   *Yield: 12 to 15 servings*

1 (20-ounce) can pineapple,
  cut into cubes
1 (¾-ounce) jar capers
2 (3-ounce) packages lemon
  gelatin

2 cups cold water, divided
1 (4-ounce) jar pimentos,
  chopped
1½ cups pecans, chopped

Drain pineapple and capers; reserve liquid. Heat liquid with enough water to measure 2 cups. Dissolve gelatin in ½ cup cold water and add to hot liquid. Add 1½ cups cold water. Cool and fold in pineapple, capers, pimento, and pecans. Mold in an 11-cup ring mold or a 2-quart mold. Serve with mayonnaise on a bed of lettuce.

Alice G. Shuford

105

ASHEVILLE SALAD

Must prepare ahead   *Yield: 8 to 10 servings*

1 (10½-ounce) can tomato
   soup
3 (3-ounce) packages cream
   cheese
2 tablespoons unflavored gelatin
½ cup cold water

1½ cups celery, chopped
1 tablespoon onion, chopped
1 green pepper, chopped
1 cucumber, chopped or
   2 (2-ounce) jars pimento
1 cup mayonnaise

Heat soup on low heat; stir in cream cheese and stir until dissolved. Dissolve gelatin in cold water, then heat until dissolved in soup mixture. When partially cool, fold in vegetables and mayonnaise. Pour into greased 1½-quart mold or 8-inch square pan.

Carol D. Triplett & Janet E. Schoonderwoerd

LEMON FRUIT SALAD

Must prepare ahead   *Yield: 15 to 18 servings*

2 (3-ounce) packages lemon
   gelatin
2 cups boiling water
2 cups carbonated lemon-lime
   drink

1 (2-ounce) can crushed
   pineapple, drained, reserve
   juice
2 large bananas, sliced
2 cups miniature marshmallows

Combine gelatin and boiling water; stir until dissolved. Add lemon-lime drink, pineapple, bananas, and marshmallows; mix well. Pour into a 13x8¾x¾-inch casserole and chill until firm.

Topping:
1 cup sugar
¼ cup all-purpose flour
¼ cup margarine
2 eggs, lightly beaten

2 (3-ounce) packages cream
   cheese, softened
1 (8-ounce) container of
   whipped topping

Add enough water to reserved pineapple juice to make 1 cup. Combine pineapple liquid, sugar, flour, margarine, and eggs in a saucepan; cook over medium heat, stirring constantly, until thickened. Add cream cheese and stir until melted; cool. Spoon over gelatin layer, then spread whipped topping over cooked layer. Chill, cut into squares.

Dot L. Bishop

BROCCOLI BAVARIAN SALAD

Must prepare ahead   *Yield: 8 servings*

1 tablespoon plain gelatin   juice of 1/2 lemon
1/4 cup cold water   2 cups broccoli, chopped and
1 cup hot consomme   cooked
   (or bouillon)   2 hard cooked eggs, chopped
3/4 cup mayonnaise   2 hard cooked eggs, sliced
1/4 teaspoon salt   1/8 teaspoon pepper

Soften gelatin in water for five minutes. Dissolve in consomme, then chill until slightly thickened. Fold in mayonnaise and seasonings, mixing well until blended. Mix broccoli and chopped eggs and fold into mixture. Pour mixture into a greased one-quart mold and chill until firm. Unmold on a large platter and garnish with lettuce greens and egg slices.

Isabel F. Whaley

MOTHER-IN-LAW FRUIT SALAD

Must prepare ahead   *Yield: 4 to 6 servings*

3 apples, peeled and chopped   1 1/2 cups miniature
2 bananas, sliced   marshmallows
1 (8 1/2-ounce) can crushed
   pineapple, drained,
   reserve liquid

Cut fruits into bite-sized pieces. Combine with pineapple and marshmallows and serve on lettuce with dressing, or in a compote as a dessert.

Dressing:
2 tablespoons all-purpose flour   2 tablespoons vinegar
1/2 cup sugar   1 egg, beaten
juice from drained pineapple

In a small saucepan, combine flour, sugar, juice, vinegar, and egg. Cook until thickened, stirring constantly. Refrigerate until chilled.

Martha F. Powell

SALADS

107

ELEGANT LAYERED CHAMPAGNE SALAD

Must prepare ahead   *Yield: 12 servings*

1st layer:
2 envelopes unflavored gelatin   1 (6-ounce) can frozen
2 cups cold water, divided   lemonade, unthawed
¼ cup sugar   ½ cup champagne

In a pan over low heat, dissolve gelatin in 1 cup water, stirring constantly for several minutes. Remove from heat. Add sugar and stir until dissolved. Add lemonade and stir until melted. Add remaining water and champagne. Pour mixture into a 12-cup mold and chill until almost firm. While chilling, prepare second layer.

2nd layer:
3 envelopes unflavored gelatin   1 cup champagne
1¾ cups cold water   2 cups heavy cream, whipped
½ cup sugar   strawberries or blueberries
2 (6-ounce) cans frozen   (for garnish)
    lemonade, unthawed

In a 2½-quart pan over low heat, dissolve gelatin in water, stirring constantly for 3 to 4 minutes. Remove from heat. Add sugar, stirring to dissolve. Add lemonade and stir until melted. Add champagne. Chill until mixture thickens to an unbeaten egg white consistency. Fold whipped cream into gelatin mixture. Gently turn into mold over 1st layer. Chill until firm. Before serving, lightly oil serving platter to help center salad. Garnish with fruit.

Note: A beautiful and delicious salad. Perfect for a wedding or any special occasion. Must be made ahead.

Helen M. Brooks

RHUBARB SALAD

Must prepare ahead   *Yield: 12 servings*

2 cups rhubarb, cooked   2 cups apples, chopped
2 cups pineapple juice   1 cup pecans, chopped
2 (3-ounce) packages strawberry
   gelatin

Add pineapple juice to rhubarb and bring to a boil. Remove from heat, add gelatin, stir to dissolve and cool. Add apples and nuts. Pour into 2-quart mold and chill.

Dressing:
1 (3-ounce) package cream   ¼ cup pineapple juice
   cheese

Thin cream cheese with pineapple juice and serve with Rhubarb Salad.

Joanne F. Underdown

CONGEALED COMBINATION SALAD

Must prepare ahead   *Yield: 16 servings*

1 (3-ounce) package lime jello   ⅔ cup celery, chopped
1 (3-ounce) package lemon jello   ⅔ cup cucumber, diced
2 cups boiling water   1 (8-ounce) can crushed
2 cups ginger ale   pineapple, drained
⅔ cup white grapes
⅔ cup apple, chopped (do not
   peel)

Dissolve lime and lemon jello in water. When cool, add remaining ingredients. Congeal until firm.

Note: A tasty blend of vegetables and fruits. Very good for a luncheon.

Mary Lou E. Dixon

MOLDED GRAPEFRUIT SALAD

Must prepare ahead   *Yield: 6 servings*

1½ envelopes unflavored gelatin   1 cup apples, unpeeled and
¼ cup cold water   chopped
½ cup boiling water   2½ cups fresh grapefruit with
½ cup sugar   juice
dash of salt   ½ cup black walnuts, chopped

Soften gelatin in cold water, dissolve in hot water; add sugar and salt, then cool. Add apples, grapefruit, and juice, then chill until partially set. Add nuts and chill in a 1½-quart mold.

Note: Men love this.

Ann B. Whitener

SURPRISE CONGEALED SALAD

Must prepare ahead   *Yield: 8 to 10 servings*

1 (16-ounce) can cling peaches,   2 cups buttermilk
   sliced (fresh or frozen)   1 (8-ounce) carton whipped
1 (6-ounce) package apricot   topping, room temperature
   gelatin

Chop peaches, heat on medium heat, add gelatin and stir until dissolved. Remove from heat, stir a few minutes until slightly cooled; add buttermilk and fold in whipped topping. Stir until mixture has a milky texture. Pour into a 9x13-inch casserole and chill at least four hours. Cut into squares.

Variation: Frozen strawberries and strawberry gelatin may be substituted. Also dietetic fruit and gelatin may be used.

Juanita T. Isenhower

EASY CRANBERRY FROZEN SALAD

Must prepare ahead   *Yield: 12 servings*

1 (16-ounce) can whole   ½ cup pecans, chopped
   cranberry sauce   2 tablespoons fresh orange
1 (8¼-ounce) can crushed   juice (optional)
   pineapple, undrained   dash of salt
1 cup sour cream   dash of cayenne pepper

Line a 2½-inch muffin tin with cupcake papers. Combine all ingredients and spoon into muffin tins. Freeze, then remove from tins and store in freezer bags. Serve on a bed of lettuce.

Lib M. Houston

CUCUMBER JELLY SALAD

Must prepare ahead   *Yield: 12 servings*

6-ounces lemon gelatin   2-ounces pimento, chopped
2 cups boiling water   1 medium cucumber, diced
1 cup mayonnaise   1 teaspoon salt
2 cups celery, finely chopped   2 cups cottage cheese, cream
2 tablespoons onion, grated   style

Dissolve gelatin in water and chill until partly set. Fold in mayonnaise, celery, onion, pimento, cucumber, salt, and cottage cheese; turn into 2½-quart mold. Chill until firm.

Pat Y. Tolbert & June V. Brehm

SUMMER FRUIT SALAD

Must prepare ahead   *Yield: 8 servings*

1 cup strawberries, halved   1 canteloupe, cut in ¾-inch
2 bananas, sliced in ¼-inch   cubes
   sections   1 apple, unpeeled and cubed
2 fresh peaches, cut in wedges   1 (6-ounce) can frozen orange
1 (20-ounce) can pineapple   juice concentrate, thawed
   chunks, undrained

Put all fruits in bowl and gently mix. Spoon orange juice on top. Cover and chill six hours.

Anne C. Brock

NO-NAME SALAD

Do not prepare ahead   *Yield: 4 to 6 servings*

1 small head lettuce
1 banana
1 small avocado
1 (16-ounce) can pear halves,
   drained

½ cup mayonnaise
2 tablespoons vinegar
1 teaspoon sugar
¾ cup bleu cheese, crumbled

Tear lettuce into bite-size chunks; slice banana, dice avocado, and pears. Combine remaining ingredients and stir into salad.

Note: You may use fresh pears. This is a different and delicious salad.

Mickey C. Shuford

RED CABBAGE SALAD

Yield: 4 to 6 servings

½ head red cabbage, sliced thin
1½ cups seedless grapes (white
   or seeded red)

1 avocado, sliced
Poppy seed dressing

Combine vegetables and fruit.

Dressing:
1½ cups sugar
2 teaspoons dry mustard
2 teaspoons salt
⅔ cup vinegar

3 tablespoons onion, chopped
2 cups salad oil
3 tablespoons poppy seed

Combine sugar, dry mustard, salt, vinegar, and onion. Add oil slowly until mixture thickens. Add poppy seed. Pour over cabbage mixture and toss.

Note: This dressing is good to serve over fruit salad.

Dorothy Y. Menzies

PICKLED FRESH PEACH SALAD

Must prepare ahead   *Yield: 4 to 6 servings*

½ cup light corn syrup   ½ teaspoon salt
½ cup white vinegar   2 envelopes unflavored gelatin
2 tablespoons sugar   2 cups ginger ale
½ teaspoon whole cloves   4 medium peaches
1½ cups water, divided

Combine corn syrup, vinegar, sugar, cloves, 1 cup water, and salt in a saucepan and heat to boiling. Lower heat and simmer 20 minutes. Sprinkle gelatin over ½ cup water. Discard cloves; stir in dissolved gelatin. Slowly pour in ginger ale. Refrigerate 1½ hours. Peel and cut peaches into bite-sized pieces. Stir into salad; place into a 2-quart mold and chill until firm.

Dorothy Y. Menzies

TOMATO ASPIC

Must prepare ahead   *Yield: 12 to 15 servings*

2 stalks celery, with leaves   4 tablespoons unflavored gelatin
1 small onion, chopped   ½ cup water
8 cups cocktail vegetable juice   1 (6-ounce) package cream
2 tablespoons celery seed   cheese, softened
3 tablespoons vinegar   2 teaspoons onion, grated
½ teaspoon sugar   1 cup celery, chopped
¼ teaspoon pepper   1 avocado, sliced
several dashes hot pepper sauce

Cut celery stalks in several pieces; combine with onion, vegetable juice, celery seed, vinegar, sugar, pepper, and hot pepper sauce. Simmer for 30 minutes; strain. Dissolve gelatin in water and add to hot vegetable juice mixture; cool. Pour into an 11-inch ring mold or a 2-quart mold. Cool until syrupy. Mix cream cheese with onion and roll into 1-inch balls. Add chopped celery, avocado, and cream cheese balls to tomato mixture. Chill until firm.

Dorothy Y. Menzies

S
A
L
A
D
S

GOLDEN RICOTTA CREAM

May prepare ahead   *Yield: 4 to 6 servings*

¾ cup puréed apricots,   skim milk to thin
  papaya or mango   fruits: honeydew, canteloupe,
1 cup ricotta cheese   grapefruit, orange,
1 cup cottage cheese   pineapple, strawberry
4 tablespoons honey

Set puréed fruit aside. Put ricotta cheese in a blender or food processor
and blend. Add cottage cheese and blend; then add purée and honey.
Add skim milk to thin, if necessary. Make a pyramid with rings of fruit;
ice between rings with ricotta cream. The bottom ring should be
honeydew, then canteloupe, then grapefruit, then orange, then pineapple, and top with a strawberry. Serve on a bed of Boston lettuce.

Peggy B. Shuford

HONEYDEW-LIME CONGEALED SALAD

Must prepare ahead   *Yield: 12 to 15 servings*

2 (3-ounce) packages lime jello   1 (12-ounce) carton cottage
1½ cups hot water   cheese
2 (16-ounce) cans applesauce   honeydew slices
1 tablespoon lemon juice

Combine water and jello, stirring to dissolve. Stir in applesauce and
lemon juice. Pour into a 1½-quart ring mold. When set, unmold and surround with honeydew slices. Place cottage cheese in a bowl which fits
into center of ring mold. Serve with Poppy Seed Dressing, page 112.

*Note: An interesting blend of flavors. The combination of pale green and
white is cool and refreshing.*

Dorothy Y. Menzies

KATTY'S SPINACH SALAD SUPREME

SALADS

Partially prepare ahead   *Yield: 6 servings*

1 clove garlic, cut
½ cup salad oil
½ teaspoon Worcestershire
  sauce
¼ teaspoon dry mustard
¼ teaspoon paprika
1 teaspoon sugar
2 teaspoons salt
dash of pepper
1½ cups crisp croutons

1 quart crisp spinach or other
  salad greens
1 (11-ounce) can mandarin
  orange sections
1 (6-ounce) can artichoke
  hearts
1 avocado, peeled and diced
  (optional)
juice of ½ lemon

Combine garlic, salad oil, Worcestershire sauce, dry mustard, paprika, sugar, salt, and pepper. Let stand several hours to overnight. Ten minutes before serving, discard garlic and pour oil over croutons. When ready to serve, break salad greens in a large salad bowl. Pour oil-crouton mixture over greens. Arrange oranges, artichoke hearts, and avocado on top of greens; squeeze lemon juice over salad. Toss gently.

Katty D. Lefler

GREEN SALAD WITH VINAIGRETTE DRESSING

May prepare ahead   *Yield: Varies according to number served*

Romaine lettuce, torn
watercress, torn
Boston lettuce, torn

curly endive, torn
Vinaigrette dressing

Wash and dry salad greens, then store in refrigerator until serving time.

Dressing:
½ teaspoon dry mustard
salt and pepper to taste

4 tablespoons red wine vinegar
½ cup olive oil

Mix mustard, salt, and pepper, then add vinegar. Add oil slowly and whisk until blended. At serving time, mix with greens.

Camille M. Gardner

ARTICHOKE SALAD

Must prepare ahead   *Yield: 8 to 10 servings*

1 (8-ounce) package chicken-
   flavored rice
2 (6-ounce) jars marinated
   artichokes, drained and
   cut in pieces
1 tablespoon onion, finely
   chopped

3 rings green pepper, finely
   chopped
15 stuffed green olives, sliced
3/4 teaspoon curry powder
1/3 cup mayonnaise

Cook rice according to package directions, leaving out butter. Cool completely. Drain artichokes and save liquid. Add onion, pepper, and olives to cooled rice. Mix one half of artichoke liquid with curry powder and mayonnaise. Add artichokes to rice mixture; pour marinade mixture over all and refrigerate overnight.

Note: This is attractive served in a glass bowl or platter on a bed of lettuce.

Josephine L. Hambrick

CHINESE SALAD

Yield: 6 to 8 servings

3 tablespoons butter, melted
1 teaspoon garlic salt
1 teaspoon curry powder
2 teaspoons Worcestershire
   sauce
dash of hot pepper sauce

1 (16-ounce) can Chinese
   noodles
2-quarts salad greens (Bibb,
   Boston)
2 tablespoons ripe olives, sliced
French dressing

Combine butter, garlic salt, curry powder, Worcestershire sauce, and hot pepper sauce. Pour over noodles and heat in a 200° oven for 15 minutes. Combine greens and olives. Add noodles and enough French dressing to coat salad.

Note: Men love it!

Dorothy Y. Menzies

BROCCOLI-CAULIFLOWER DELIGHT

Must prepare ahead   *Yield: 12 to 16 servings*

1 head broccoli, cut in pieces   1 cup mayonnaise
1 head cauliflower, cut in pieces   2 tablespoons vinegar
1 small onion, minced   ¹/₂ teaspoon sugar
1 cup sharp Cheddar cheese,   ¹/₂ teaspoon salt
  shredded   pepper to taste

Place broccoli and cauliflower in a large bowl. Add onion and cheese. Mix mayonnaise, vinegar, sugar, salt, and pepper in a separate bowl and stir until smooth. Pour the dressing over the broccoli-cauliflower mixture and *refrigerate overnight.*

Note: The amount of vinegar, salt, sugar, and pepper can be varied according to taste.

Carolyn S. Moretz & Coco W. Teeter

WILTED LETTUCE

Partially prepare ahead   *Yield: 4 to 6 servings*

several small heads leaf lettuce   ³/₄ cup water
3 green onions, sliced   ³/₄ cup vinegar
2 to 3 hard-cooked eggs, sliced   salt and pepper to taste
3 to 4 strips bacon   pinch of sugar

Fry bacon and crumble; reserve drippings. Tear lettuce into bite-size pieces and place in bowl. Add onion, eggs, and bacon. Combine water and vinegar with bacon drippings. Add salt, pepper, and sugar; simmer a few minutes. Pour hot sauce over lettuce, toss and serve immediately.

Note: Curly edges on large tender leaves make the best salad. Spinach may be used also.

Mary Stuart M. Tarrant & Mary Ayers P. Campbell

117

RICE SALAD

Must prepare ahead   *Yield: 8 to 10 servings*

1 cup rice, cooked, rinsed,
    and cooled
soy sauce to taste
1 (16-ounce) can small green
    peas

½ cup celery, chopped
1 bunch green onions, chopped
½ to ⅔ cup mayonnaise
1 (5-ounce) can chow mein
    noodles

Sprinkle rice well with soy sauce. Add peas, celery, and onions, including the tops. Mix well with mayonnaise. Serve salad surrounded by chow mein noodles.

Carol H. Tuttle

SEA SHELL SALAD

Must prepare ahead   *Yield: 12 to 14 servings*

4 hard cooked eggs, diced
1 cup cooked shrimp, diced
1 (6½-ounce) can tuna, drained
    and flaked
¼ cup chopped sweet pickles
1 (8-ounce) box shell noodles,
    cooked and drained
1 cup celery, chopped
1 cup green pepper, chopped

1 (4-ounce) can pimentos, cut in
    strips
1 cup mayonnaise
1 tablespoon celery seeds
1 teaspoon dry mustard
dash of Worcestershire sauce
dash of hot pepper sauce
salt and pepper to taste
Garnish, whole shrimp

In a large mixing bowl combine all ingredients. Mix well. Chill several hours or overnight. Serve on a nest of lettuce leaves and garnish with whole shrimp and sprinkle with paprika.

Dorothy Y. Menzies

LOUISIANA CHEF'S SALAD

Partially prepare ahead   *Yield: 6 servings*

1 head of lettuce, washed, dried,
    and chilled
1 cup Romano or Parmesan
    cheese, freshly grated

½ cup imported olive oil
2 cloves garlic, finely chopped
1 teaspoon salt
juice of ½ lemon

Mix olive oil, garlic, salt, and lemon juice. Chill in refrigerator or freezer, if in a hurry. Break lettuce into bite-sized pieces and sprinkle cheese over it. Pour salad dressing over all and mix well.

Beverly A. Guarino

BILL'S COLE SLAW

Must prepare ahead   *Yield: 12 to 15 servings*

1 large head of cabbage, grated   1 green pepper, chopped
1 medium onion, chopped

Mix cabbage, onion, and pepper well with dressing.

Dressing:
1/2 teaspoon celery seed   3/4 cup oil
1/2 teaspoon salt   3/4 cup vinegar
1/4 cup sugar

Combine celery seed, salt, sugar, oil, and vinegar; bring to boil. Cool and pour over cabbage mixture. Stir well and marinate for 2 hours in refrigerator before serving.

Phyllis D. Cauble

TAHITI SALAD

Must prepare ahead   *Yield: 6 to 8 servings*

3 cups potatoes, cooked and   2 tablespoons pimento, chopped
    chopped   2 tablespoons onion, minced
1 1/2 cups cottage cheese   2 tablespoons fresh parsley
3 hard-boiled eggs, chopped   1/3 cup green pepper, chopped
2 tablespoons French dressing   1 teaspoon salt
1/4 cup mayonnaise

Mix all ingredients and chill several hours. Seasonings may be increased for additional flavor.

Note: This is the best, most flavorful, and different potato salad I've ever had!

Judy C. West

119

MARINATED VEGETABLE SALAD

Must prepare ahead   *Yield: 6 to 8 servings*

1 (16-ounce) can French green
  beans
1 (12-ounce) can shoe peg corn
1 (17-ounce) can petite peas
1 (14-ounce) can artichoke
  hearts

1 (2-ounce) jar pimento
1 (4½-ounce) can button
  mushrooms
1 small onion, finely chopped
1 green pepper, chopped
marinade

Marinade:
1 cup sugar
1 cup vinegar

½ cup oil

Melt sugar in vinegar and oil, let cool and pour over vegetables. Chill
and serve.

Brenda K. Cline

INSALATA MISTA

May partially prepare ahead

Romaine and Boston lettuce,
  torn into bite-size pieces
carrots, sliced

celery, sliced
tomatoes, cut in pieces
dressing

Mix together the lettuces, then add carrots, celery, and tomatoes. Toss
with a dressing made of the finest olive oil, a good red wine vinegar, and
a little salt. No other seasoning is necessary.

Note: A true Italian salad does not have cheese or croutons.

Emily N. Garrett
(The Apron String—A kitchen specialty shop)

BEST HAM SALAD

Yield: 8 to 10 servings

2½ pound pre-cooked buffet
ham
3 eggs, hard cooked
½ cup sweet pickle relish
2 tablespoons Worcestershire
sauce

2 tablespoons prepared mustard
½ cup mayonnaise
salt and pepper to taste

Grind ham (or have butcher grind it for you). Do not chop! Grind eggs and add to ham. Combine remaining ingredients and add extra mayonnaise to moisten. A dash of olive juice adds flavor and will also help moisten the ham.

Note: The better the ham, the better the taste.

Sally T. Blackwelder

TACO SALAD

Yield: 4 to 6 servings

1 pound ground beef
½ envelope (¼ cup) dry onion
soup mix
¾ cup water
1 medium head lettuce, torn
into bite size pieces
1 large tomato, cut in wedges
1 small onion, thinly sliced
and separated into rings

¼ cup green pepper, chopped
½ cup ripe olives, sliced
(optional)
4-ounces sharp natural Cheddar
cheese, shredded
1 (6-ounce) package corn chips

In a skillet brown beef; drain off fat. Pour soup mix over meat; stir in water and cook uncovered for 10 minutes. In salad bowl, combine lettuce, tomato, onion, green pepper, olives, and cheese; toss well. Place lettuce mixture on individual salad plates and spoon on meat. Top with corn chips.

Anita G. Anderson

121

SHRIMP SALAD

May prepare ahead   *Yield: 4 servings*

1 pound shrimp, cooked and
    deveined
½ cup onion, chopped
½ cup celery, chopped
3 hard-boiled eggs, chopped

1 tablespoon mayonnaise
1 tablespoon vinegar
1 teaspoon prepared mustard
1 teaspoon salt

Mix all ingredients; serve on lettuce.

Variation: Add ½ cup chopped green pepper and/or 1 large boiled potato, and/or sweet pickle relish to taste.

Peggy R. Yancey

CHICKEN OR TURKEY SALAD INDIENNE

Freezes well   *Yield: Varies*

1 cup cooked poultry per person
celery stalk
small onion, quartered
¼ cup mayonnaise per cup meat
¼ cup coleslaw dressing per
    cup meat
1 teaspoon curry powder per
    cup meat
3 mandarin orange sections,
    chopped, per cup meat

¼ cup white raisins per cup
    meat
1 tablespoon chutney per cup
    meat
2 to 3 strips bacon, per cup
    meat
toasted almonds

Combine celery, onion, and water in a sauce pan. Poach chicken. Remove meat from bones. Combine mayonnaise, coleslaw dressing, and curry powder; mix with the meat. Add orange sections, raisins, chutney, and bacon. Just before serving, sprinkle the top generously with toasted almonds. Salad may be served hot or cold.

Note: Try this in puff pastry shells served hot—delicious!

Martha T. Kurad

CONFETTI CRAB SALAD

May prepare ahead   *Yield: 6 servings*

1 pound crabmeat
8 hard-boiled eggs, chopped
1 (4-ounce) jar chopped
   pimentos
1 cup celery, diced
1 green pepper, diced

4-ounces commercial tangy
   mustard mayonnaise
   dressing
3 tablespoons mayonnaise
2 tablespoons lemon juice

Mix all ingredients. May be served hot or cold. To serve hot, put in greas-ed 9x13-inch casserole and bake 15 minutes at 425°.

Anne F. Mitchell

SERVICE LEAGUE TURKEY SALAD

May prepare ahead   *Yield: 12 to 16 servings*

10 cups cooked turkey, cut up
   (reserve ⅓ cup stock)
4 cups celery, finely chopped
8 hard-cooked eggs, grated

¼ cup lemon juice
1 tablespoon salt
1 teaspoon pepper
1 quart mayonnaise

Start with a quart of mayonnaise for each recipe. (If turkey is moist, all of this will not be needed.) To turkey, add celery, eggs, lemon juice, salt, pepper, and reserved stock. Mix in mayonnaise until it is a good spreading consistency.

The Service League of Hickory

SALAD DRESSINGS

CREAMY FRENCH DRESSING

Yield: 2½ cups

2 egg yolks
½ cup sugar
dash of red pepper
1 scant teaspoon salt
1 tablespoon sweet Hungarian
  paprika

½ cup vinegar (⅔ white, ⅓
  tarragon)
16-ounces vegetable oil
1 garlic clove, crushed

Beat yolks until creamy and add dry ingredients. Beat in ½ of the vinegar, then add small amounts of oil until about 1 cup is used. Oil may be added more quickly as dressing begins to thicken. Add remaining vinegar and continue beating until completely blended. Add the crushed garlic.

Note: This is a very thick dressing.

Mary King M. Spainhour

FRUIT SALAD DRESSING

May prepare ahead   *Yield: 1½ cups*

½ cup sugar
2 tablespoons onion, grated
2 tablespoons vinegar
1 tablespoon dry mustard

1 teaspoon salt
1 teaspoon celery salt
1 cup salad oil

Into a mixer, blender, or food processor, put sugar, onion, vinegar, mustard, salt, and celery salt; blend to mix. Add oil, slowly, and mix until well blended.

Margaret Y. Smith

COOKED DRESSING

Yield: 1 cup

2 tablespoons all-purpose flour
2 tablespoons sugar
1 teaspoon dry mustard
1/4 teaspoon cayenne pepper
1 teaspoon salt

3/4 cup milk
2 egg yolks
1/4 cup vinegar
1 tablespoon butter

Place flour, sugar, mustard, pepper, and salt in top of a double boiler. Mix and add milk slowly, blending until all milk is used. Beat in 2 egg yolks and add vinegar. Cook over medium heat, beating constantly, until mixture has thickened. Remove from heat; add butter, stirring until melted and blended.

Note: This dressing is used on chicken salad, potato salad and as a sandwich spread.

Duart J. Johnston

BLEU CHEESE DRESSING

May prepare ahead   *Yield: 3 1/2 cups*

2 (3-ounce) packages of bleu
    cheese, crumbled
1 cup sour cream
1 cup mayonnaise

1 cup buttermilk
garlic salt to taste
seasoning salt to taste

Combine ingredients in a blender or a food processor and blend until well mixed.

Note: If a less rich dressing is desired, use only 1 package of bleu cheese. Good over green or fruit salad.

Alice M. Lee

125

COUNTRY CLUB FRENCH DRESSING

May prepare ahead　　　　　　　　　*Yield: 4 to 5 cups*

2 cloves of garlic, minced
1 onion, minced
1 cup wine vinegar
1½ cups sugar

1 tablespoon dry mustard
1 teaspoon salt
3 cups salad oil

Mix garlic, onion, and wine vinegar and let stand for awhile. Mix sugar, mustard, and salt; add vinegar mixture and blend in a blender or food processor. Slowly add 3 cups of salad oil and blend.

Margie S. Petree

THOUSAND ISLAND DRESSING

May prepare ahead　　　　　　　　　*Yield: 1 ½ cups*

1 cup mayonnaise
¼ cup chili sauce
2 hard cooked eggs, finely
　chopped
2 tablespoons celery, finely
　chopped

2 tablespoons green pepper,
　finely chopped
1 tablespoon onion, grated
½ teaspoon salt

Combine ingredients and stir to blend. Refrigerate until ready to serve over vegetable salad. Stores well.

Nancy C. Shuford

TANGY DRESSING

May prepare ahead　　　　　　　　　*Yield: 1 pint*

½ teaspoon dry mustard
1 tablespoon water
¼ cup sugar
2 teaspoons salt
½ teaspoon paprika
½ cup catsup

⅓ cup vinegar
½ teaspoon Worcestershire
　sauce
1 teaspoon onion, grated
1 cup salad oil

Put all ingredients, except oil, into blender or food processor and blend. Add oil slowly until well mixed.

Helen S. Moretz

ENTRÉES

ENTRÉES

( ) Denotes: (HE) Hickory Entertains   (I) International   (M) Microwave Recipes

128

( ) Denotes: (HE) Hickory Entertains   (I) International   (M) Microwave Recipes

❧ BEEF ❧

NANCY'S BARBECUE BEEF

May prepare ahead   *Yield: 8 to 10 servings*

3 pounds beef roast (sirloin   ¹/₂ cup vinegar
   tip, round, or shoulder)   2 tablespoons prepared mustard
2 cups tomato juice   2 teaspoons horseradish
1 cup catsup   2 tablespoons sugar
¹/₄ teaspoon garlic powder

Cover beef and cook in a 325° oven until it falls apart. Cool; remove fat
and shred. Combine the remaining ingredients in a deep saucepan. Heat
and add beef. Simmer over low heat for at least 2 hours or until sauce
has cooked down and meat has absorbed liquid.

*Note: Enough for 15 sandwiches. The sauce is also delicious on chicken or
pork chops. Freezes very well. If more liquid is needed when reheated, add
tomato juice.*

Joanne M. Martin

BEEF CURRY

Must prepare ahead   *Yield: 6 servings*

2¹/₂ pounds chuck steak, cut   ¹/₂ teaspoon ginger
   into cubes   2 tablespoons curry powder
¹/₃ cup all-purpose flour   ¹/₄ cup onion, chopped
1 teaspoon salt   ¹/₂ cup chutney
¹/₄ teaspoon pepper   ¹/₄ cup raisins
3 tablespoons vegetable oil   2 tomatoes, peeled and
2¹/₂ cups beef broth   quartered
¹/₂ teaspoon garlic salt

Roll steak in flour, salt, and pepper mixture. Brown beef in oil in a Dutch
oven. Add beef broth, garlic salt, ginger, curry powder, onion, chutney,
and raisins; simmer for 2 to 2¹/₂ hours. Add tomatoes the last 20
minutes of cooking time. Serve over rice with following condiments:

hard boiled eggs   chutney
bacon   coconut
almonds, toasted   ginger, crystalized
pineapple, crushed

Peggy B. Shuford

PAMPERED BEEF FILLETS

May prepare ahead   *Yield: 8 servings*

8 beef fillets, 1½-inches thick   2 tablespoons all-purpose flour
2 to 3 tablespoons butter   1 cup hot bouillon
2 tablespoons butter   2 tablespoons lemon juice
1 cup mushrooms, sliced (fresh   dash of salt
  or canned)

Melt butter in a heavy iron skillet. Very quickly brown fillets in butter.
Cover and set aside. Melt remaining butter and sauté fresh mushrooms
until golden brown and tender. Lift out and add enough butter to make 2
tablespoons of drippings. (if using canned mushrooms, add to melted
butter and heat.) Add flour to make a paste. Slowly add bouillon until
sauce thickens. Add mushrooms, lemon juice, and salt. Place each fillet
on a 10-inch square of heavy foil. Spoon 2 to 3 tablespoons sauce over
each fillet. Be generous. Fold foil up around fillet, leaving a steam open-
ing in the top. Place in broiler pan. Just before serving, place in a 500°
oven 10 minutes (for rare), or 12 minutes (for medium-rare). Unwrap and
spoon juices over them at serving time.

*Note: These are great and can be prepared ahead, then cooked before ser-
ving. The mushroom sauce is wonderful and versatile. Try it with roast
beef or broiled steaks.*

Sally T. Blackwelder

RUMP ROAST WITH PRUNES

Yield: 8 to 10 servings

5 pound rump roast   ½ cup cider vinegar
2 teaspoons salt   ½ cup water
pepper to taste   1 cup light brown sugar
1 cup dried prunes   ¼ teaspoon ground cloves
2 cups boiling water   1 teaspoon cinnamon

In a Dutch oven, heat a small amount of oil and brown meat on all sides.
Add salt, pepper, prunes, and water. Simmer for 3 hours. Remove meat
to hot platter. Stir in vinegar, water, sugar, cloves, and cinnamon. Cook
rapidly to make a thick sauce. Pour ½ over meat and pass remainder of
sauce when serving.

Catherine H. Yeager

FLANK STEAK WITH RICE STUFFING

Yield: 6 servings

Rice Stuffing:

¼ cup margarine	½ cup Parmesan cheese, grated
½ cup onion, chopped	½ teaspoon salt
½ cup long grain rice, cooked	¼ teaspoon pepper
½ cup parsley, chopped	

Preheat oven to 350°. Sauté the onion in the margarine. Combine with other ingredients.

Flank Steak:

1¾ to 2 pounds flank steak	½ cup beef broth, condensed
2 tablespoons soy sauce	½ cup water
½ teaspoon pepper	1 teaspoon ground ginger
2 tablespoons margarine	

Preheat oven to 350°. Wipe steak with damp paper towels. Score both sides of steak into diamonds and brush each side with soy sauce and pepper. Spread ½ of the margarine on steak and cover with stuffing, keeping it about 1 inch from edges. Roll up from end to end. Tie with twine. Spread remaining margarine over surface of steak. Place in a roasting pan. Mix water and beef broth and pour over steak. Sprinkle with ginger and bake at 350° for 45 to 60 minutes, basting several times. Remove twine, slice, and serve.

Jane S. Monroe

BEEF WELLINGTON

Yield: 2 servings

2 (7-ounce) beef fillets
salt and pepper to taste
garlic powder to taste
1 tablespoon vegetable oil
3 tablespoons chicken liver
 paté

3 sheets filo dough
4 tablespoons butter, melted
Bearnaise Sauce

Season fillets with salt, pepper, and garlic powder. Brush with oil and coat with a thin layer of pate. Refrigerate until pate is firm. Cut each filo sheet into 6 strips. Brush each strip with butter. Wrap each fillet in filo, overlapping strips so meat is completely covered. Bake at 400° for 12 minutes for medium rare. Serve on bed of rice and cover with Bearnaise Sauce.

Susan L. Ingle

BEARNAISE SAUCE

¼ cup dry white wine
3 tablespoons tarragon vinegar
2 tablespoons shallots, finely
 chopped
½ teaspoon tarragon leaves

¼ teaspoon peppercorns,
 crushed
2 egg yolks
9 tablespoons butter, melted
salt and pepper to taste

In a heavy skillet, combine wine, vinegar, shallots, tarragon, and peppercorns; bring to a boil and cook until mixture is reduced by about two-thirds. Let cool. Place wine mixture and egg yolks in top of a double boiler over simmering water and whisk until well blended and heated through. Pour mixture into blender set on low speed and blend. Gradually add melted butter to blending sauce. Blend until smooth and creamy. Add salt to taste.

Susan L. Ingle

FOOLPROOF RARE ROAST BEEF

To cook a standing rib roast so that it will be crusty and brown on the outside and evenly rare and juicy on the inside, follow these 4 rules. Rule #1: The roast must be at room temperature. Leave it out of refrigerator 1 hour for each pound or leave out overnight. Rule #2: Season roast and place it rib side down in a shallow pan. Put it uncovered in a preheated 425° oven. Rule #3: Cook roast according to chart listed below. Rule #4: At the end of the required cooking time, turn oven off and do not open door for at least 3 hours. Meat cooks on retained heat. Resist the urge to peek! The roast will have finished cooking but still be warm after 4-5 hours, depending on size.

Cooking Chart:
 5 pounds—35 minutes
 6 pounds—40 minutes
 7 pounds—45 minutes
 8 pounds—50 minutes
 9 pounds—55 minutes
10 pounds—1 hour

Betty Lou M. Bumbarger

MARY'S YORKSHIRE PUDDING

Yield: 6 servings

2 eggs
½ teaspoon salt
1 cup all-purpose flour

1 cup milk
2 tablespoons beef drippings

All ingredients must be room temperature. Beat eggs and salt with a whisk or rotary beater until frothy. Slowly add flour, beating constantly. Pour in milk in a thin stream and beat until mixture is smooth and creamy. Refrigerate for at least 1 hour. Preheat oven to 400°. Heat beef drippings in 10x15x2-inch pan. Pour cooled egg mixture into pan and bake for 15 minutes. Reduce heat to 375° and bake another 15 minutes. Serve immediately with roast beef.

Camille M. Gardner

FILLET STRASBOURG

Yield: 10 servings

4-5 pounds tenderloin of beef
1 carrot
salt and pepper to taste
2 green onions

2 sprigs parsley
1 cup Madeira wine
1 cup white wine
1 tablespoon all-purpose flour

Preheat oven to 450°. Trim fat from tenderloin. Lightly oil the bottom of a roasting pan. Slice vegetables and lay over bottom of pan. Salt and pepper beef and lay on vegetables. Roast at 450° for 30 minutes. Add Madeira and white wine and cook 15 minutes longer. (Can use a meat thermometer to prevent overcooking.) Transfer meat to a slicing board and cover with foil to keep warm. Strain juices and skim off fat. Reduce sauce and add 1 tablespoon of flour to thicken.

Nancy C. Shuford

SWEDISH POT ROAST

Yield: 6 servings

4 pounds beef roast, chuck or
    round
2 teaspoons salt
1 teaspoon allspice
1/2 teaspoon pepper
3 tablespoons butter
1/4 cup brandy (or bourbon)
1/3 cup hot bouillon
2 onions, sliced

3 anchovy filets, minced (or
    1 1/2 teaspoons anchovy
    paste)
2 bay leaves
2 tablespoons white vinegar
2 tablespoons molasses (or
    dark syrup)
1 or 2 tablespoons heavy cream

Rub meat all over with salt, allspice, and pepper. Brown in butter on all sides in a Dutch oven. Pour brandy over hot meat and flame with a lighted match. Add bouillon, onions, anchovies, bay leaves, vinegar, and molasses. Simmer, covered, over low heat 2 hours or until tender. Remove meat to hot platter; add cream to juices in pan. Pour a little gravy over meat; serve rest separately.

Note: Surround meat platter with buttered peas, carrots, cauliflower buds, and tiny browned potatoes. Decorate with tomato and cucumber slices and parsley sprigs.

Ruth F. Deaton

STUFFED EYE OF THE ROUND ROAST

May prepare ahead   *Yield: 8 to 10 servings*

3-4 pounds eye of round roast
1 sausage, chopped
1 slice ham, chopped
1 clove garlic, minced
1 medium sized Spanish onion,
  chopped
½ green pepper, chopped
salt

pepper
paprika
3 tablespoons bacon drippings
¾ cup hot consommé
piece of suet
1 bay leaf
4 whole cloves

Preheat oven to 325°. Cut lengthwise pocket in center of beef, leaving opposite end closed. Mix sausage, ham, garlic, onion, and pepper, and stuff roast. Secure open end with skewers. Rub salt, pepper, and paprika all over roast and brown well in bacon drippings over medium heat. Add consommé. Lay suet on top of meat; add bay leaf and cloves to liquid. Cover and place in oven; baste occasionally. Cook three hours or until tender. During last 30 minutes potato balls may be added. Serve beef cut in round slices and pass gravy.

Isabele F. Whaley

BUFFET STEW

Must prepare ahead   *Yield: 4 to 6 servings*

2½ tablespoons butter
¼ cup celery, chopped
¼ cup green pepper, chopped
1 clove garlic, minced
½ cup onion, sliced
2 pounds round steak, cut in
  1-inch cubes
2½ tablespoons all-purpose
  flour

1½ teaspoons salt
¼ teaspoon pepper
1 tomato, peeled and diced
1 (4-ounce) can mushrooms
2 cups broth (or water)
½ cup dry red wine
½ teaspoon sugar

Sauté celery, green pepper, garlic, and onion in butter until softened and slightly browned. Dust beef with flour, salt, and pepper. Sauté until brown and stir in tomato, mushrooms, broth, wine, and sugar. Transfer to buttered 3-quart casserole, cover, and let stand several hours. Bake for 2 hours at 350°.

Cathi H. Dillon

MEATBALLS IN CONSOMMÉ

Yield: 16 meatballs

1 (10¾-ounce) can consommé, heated
2 (10¾-ounce) cans water
1 small hard roll
½ pound lean ground beef
½ pound ground veal
2 tablespoons grated onion
½ teaspoon grated lemon peel

3 eggs, beaten
1 tablespoon lemon juice
1 teaspoon salt or salt substitute
½ teaspoon Worcestershire sauce
parsley to taste (optional)

Moisten roll with water and ring out excess. Tear roll apart. Combine remaining ingredients except consommé and mix thoroughly with the roll. Shape into balls and drop into hot consommé. Cover, simmer for 15 minutes. Serve in shallow casserole or tureen. May be garnished with additional chopped parsley or chives.

Lindy M. Dillow

PERFECT STROGANOFF

Freezes well

Yield: 6 servings

2 pounds round, sirloin, or fillet of beef
6 tablespoons butter
1 cup chopped onion
1 clove garlic, minced
½ pound mushrooms, sliced
3 tablespoons all-purpose flour
2 teaspoons steak sauce

1 tablespoon catsup
½ teaspoon salt
⅛ teaspoon pepper
1 can beef bouillon
½ cup dry white wine
½ teaspoon dried dillweed
1½ cups sour cream
noodles or potato sticks

Cut beef into ½-inch squares. Slowly heat skillet and melt 2 tablespoons of butter. Brown beef, remove from pan. Add remaining 4 tablespoons of butter to pan and sauté onion, garlic, and mushrooms for 5 minutes. Add flour, steak sauce, catsup, salt, and pepper and stir until smooth. Gradually add bouillon, bring to a boil and simmer for 5 minutes. Over low heat, add wine, dillweed, and sour cream. Return beef to pan, heat but do not boil. Serve over noodles or potato sticks.

Note: This may be frozen before adding the sour cream. The recipe can be doubled to make 12 to 14 servings.

Carole J. Cumming

137

STUFFED MEAT LOAF

Yield: 8 to 10 servings

2 pounds ground beef
½ cup instant potato flakes
½ cup onion, minced
1 teaspoon Worcestershire
  sauce
¼ cup herb seasoned tomato
  sauce

2 eggs
2 teaspoons salt
¼ teaspoon pepper
1 tablespoon bottled steak
  sauce
1 medium carrot, grated

Combine all ingredients and blend well. Shape meat loaf firmly into a ball. Place on waxed paper; with hands, flatten out and shape into a 16x8½x½-inch rectangle.

Filling:

1 (16-ounce) carton ricotta
  cheese
1 (10-ounce) package frozen
  chopped spinach, thawed
  and drained
1 egg

½ cup Parmesan cheese, grated
1 tablespoon instant potato
  flakes
¼ teaspoon salt
⅛ teaspoon pepper

Combine all ingredients. Spread mixture evenly over meat mixture to within ½-inch of edges. Starting at 8½-inch end, roll up meat, jelly-roll fashion, pulling off waxed paper as you roll. Place seam side down in a deep baking dish.

Glaze:

2 tablespoons brown sugar
1 cup herb seasoned tomato
  sauce

1½ teaspoons dry mustard
2 tablespoons Parmesan cheese,
  grated

Combine all ingredients. Add more seasonings if desired. Spread several spoonsful over top of meat loaf. Reserve remaining sauce; heat and serve with meat loaf. Bake meat loaf at 350° for 1 hour. Remove pan from oven, pour off excess fat. Sprinkle top with Parmesan cheese and bake another 15 minutes.

Note: Takes time to prepare, but this elegant variation of an old stand-by will be well worth the effort. Can be prepared in advance, refrigerated, and baked before serving.

Frances R. Hilton

FAMILY NIGHT CASSEROLE

Freezes well   *Yield: 8 servings*

1 (8-ounce) package elbow
  macaroni, cooked and
  drained
¼ cup butter or margarine
1 cup onion, coarsely chopped
1 clove garlic, crushed
1½ pounds ground chuck
1 teaspoon salt

¼ teaspoon pepper
1 (11-ounce) can tomato soup,
  undiluted
1½ cups dry cottage cheese
1 cup sour cream
½ cup chopped green pepper
¼ cup chopped green onion
1 teaspoon seasoned salt

In a large skillet, melt butter and sauté onion and garlic about 5 minutes, or until golden. Add meat, salt, and pepper and sauté about 5 minutes, or until meat is browned. Add soup and mix well. Remove from heat. Preheat oven to 350°. In a bowl, combine cottage cheese, sour cream, green pepper, green onion, and seasoned salt. Place ½ macaroni in a buttered 3-quart casserole. Spread with cottage cheese mixture. Add remaining macaroni and pour meat sauce over all, spreading evenly. Bake casserole, covered, for 40 minutes, or until bubbling hot.

Garnish: (optional)
rings of green pepper,   sliced onions, sautéed
  sauteed
Arrange around edge of casserole before baking.

Polly D. Walker

CHILI CON CARNE

Yield: 4 servings

2 tablespoons salad oil
½ cup onions, thinly sliced
2 tablespoons green pepper,
  diced
½ pound extra lean ground beef
½ cup boiling water
1 cup canned tomatoes

1½ tablespoons chili powder
2 tablespoons cold water
½ teaspoon salt
1 teaspoon sugar
1½ cloves garlic, minced
2 cups kidney beans, undrained

Cook onions and green pepper in salad oil until tender; add meat and cook until brown. Add boiling water, tomatoes, chili powder mixed with cold water until smooth, salt, sugar, and garlic. Simmer, covered, 1 hour. Uncover, simmer ½ hour. Add a little hot water if mixture thickens too much. Add beans. Heat.

Shirley L. Ballew

CHEESEBURGER PIE

Yield: 6 to 8 servings

1 (9-inch) unbaked pie shell
1 pound lean ground beef
½ teaspoon oregano
4 ounces tomato sauce
¼ cup chopped onion

1 teaspoon salt
¼ cup chopped green pepper
¼ teaspoon pepper
½ cup fine bread crumbs

Preheat oven to 375°. Brown beef and add remaining ingredients. Spread mixture into pie shell.

Cheese Topping:
8 ounces medium-sharp cheese,
   shredded
1 egg, beaten
¼ cup milk

½ teaspoon salt
½ teaspoon dry mustard
½ teaspoon Worcestershire
   sauce

Combine ingredients. Spread over meat and bake until thoroughly heated, about 40 minutes.

Note: To prevent a soggy bottom crust, weight empty pastry shell with grains of uncooked rice and run in preheated oven just long enough to "set", about 5 minutes.

Ann W. Peden

MEAT LOAF

Freezes well   *Yield: 4 to 6 servings*

1½ pounds ground beef
1 cup fresh bread crumbs
1 (8-ounce) can tomato sauce,
   divided
1 egg, beaten,
1½ teaspoons salt
¼ teaspoon pepper

1 green pepper, chopped
1 onion, chopped
2 tablespoons vinegar
2 tablespoons mustard
2 tablespoons brown sugar
2 strips bacon

Preheat oven to 350°. Combine beef, crumbs, ½ cup tomato sauce, egg, salt, pepper, green pepper, and onion. Place in a 9½x5½-inch loaf pan. Combine remaining tomato sauce, vinegar, mustard, and brown sugar. Pour sauce over meat loaf and top with bacon. Cover with foil and bake for 1 hour. Remove foil and continue baking for 30 minutes.

Peggy R. Yancey

 # HAM

VILLA MONTANA BAKED HAM

Yield: 15 servings

pre-cooked, boned ham
whole cloves
1½ cups brown sugar
2 cups pineapple juice

1 tablespoon prepared mustard
2 cups canned or fresh
   pineapple
ginger ale

Preheat oven to 350°. Stud the ham with cloves. Mix in processor or blender sugar, juice, mustard, and pineapple. Place ham on low rack in 12x9-inch pan. Pour pineapple mixture over ham and bake 1 hour at 350°. Reduce heat to 300° and cook for 2 hours. Baste ham every 15 minutes, adding ginger ale as needed. Remove ham from rack and place directly in sauce the last 30 minutes.

Catherine H. Yeager

 # LAMB

DELICIOUS SHISH KEBAB

Must prepare ahead   *Yield: 6 to 8 servings*

2 pounds boneless leg of lamb
salt and pepper to taste
1 cup yogurt
2 garlic cloves, minced
2 tablespoons lemon juice
fresh or dried thyme to taste

2 lemons, quartered
12 small onions, raw or
   parboiled
12 strips green pepper
12 cherry tomatoes, or wedges
   of large tomato

Cut lamb into large cubes and sprinkle with salt and pepper. Combine yogurt, garlic, lemon juice, and thyme. Add lamb and marinate overnight. On each of 4 skewers, thread lemon quarter. Add lamb and alternate with onions, green peppers, and tomatoes. End with lemon quarter. Broil over charcoal for 20 minutes, or until lamb is tender.

Note: Proportions are for 9-inch skewers. Yogurt makes basting unnecessary.

Roddy S. Dixon

CHEESE CAPPED LAMB CHOPS

Yield: 6 servings

6 lamb chops, ¾ to 1-inch thick
salt and pepper
¼ cup bleu cheese

2 tablespoons butter, softened
⅓ cup unpeeled cucumber,
chopped

Broil chops 3-inches from heat for 6 to 8 minutes or until browned on 1 side. Season with salt and pepper. Turn and brown the other side for 3 minutes; season. Combine remaining ingredients and spread on top of chops. Continue to broil for 2 minutes or until mixture is bubbly.

Note: This is tasty served with corn on the cob, coleslaw in tomato cups, crescent rolls and a fruit pie for dessert.

Lindy M. Dillow

HAL'S BUTTERFLY LAMB

May prepare ahead   *Yield: 8 to 10 servings*

1 leg of lamb, approximately
    8 pounds, boned and laid
    out in butterfly shape
1 cup dry red wine
½ cup olive oil
2 tablespoons lemon juice
1 tablespoon chopped fresh
    ginger (or 1 teaspoon
    powdered)
1 teaspoon Worcestershire
    sauce

2 tablespoons fresh parsley,
    snipped
2 tablespoons chives, chopped
¼ teaspoon ground black
    pepper
½ teaspoon rosemary
⅛ teaspoon marjoram
⅛ teaspoon thyme
⅛ teaspoon garlic powder

Combine all ingredients except lamb to make a marinade. Pour over lamb and marinate overnight in refrigerator. Remove 2 hours before cooking. Cook over charcoal or under broiler for 20 minutes per side (very rare) or 30 minutes per side (medium). Lamb should be slightly pink for best flavor. Serve on large platter garnished with small red potatoes tossed with butter and parsley; baby carrots with butter and dill; artichoke hearts (canned, not marinated); peas with chopped mushrooms and broiled cherry tomatoes. To prepare tomatoes, cut each tomato in half, dip into butter, then into seasoned breadcrumbs and broil until crumbs are golden.

Josephine L. Hambrick

WEST INDIAN LEG OF LAMB

Yield: 8 to 10 servings

leg of lamb
1 tablespoon salt
2 cloves garlic, sliced
½ cup strong coffee
½ cup curaçao, divided
1 tablespoon brown sugar

1 tablespoon molasses
½ teaspoon cinnamon
½ teaspoon allspice
½ teaspoon mace
1 tablespoon cornstarch
½ cup water

Rub salt into lamb. Make slits and insert garlic slices. For coffee sauce, combine coffee, ¼ cup·curaçao, brown sugar, molasses, and spices. Brush mixture on lamb. Roast in a 325⁰ oven for 25 to 30 minutes per pound. Baste often with coffee mixture. When lamb is done, combine cornstarch and water. Blend in drippings, adding water to correct consistency. Cook over low heat until thick and clear. Warm remaining curaçao and pour over lamb. Ignite and serve immediately with coffee sauce. Serve with chutney.

Bess S. Cline

BRAISED LEG OF LAMB

Yield: 8 servings

3 tablespoons oil
6 to 7 pound leg of lamb
2 onions, diced
2 carrots, diced
Bouquet Garni (page 315)
1 teaspoon rosemary

1 clove garlic, crushed
salt and pepper to taste
2 cups white wine
1 cup beef stock
1 bunch watercress (for garnish)

Heat oil in a large, deep casserole and brown lamb on all sides. Remove meat, add onions and carrots; lower heat and cook gently for 8 to 10 minutes, or until vegetables are lightly browned. Add lamb, Bouquet Garni, rosemary, garlic, salt, pepper, wine, and stock. Braise in a 325⁰ oven for 2½ hours, or until tender.

Carolyn H. Walker

 PORK

ROAST PIG

Must prepare ahead   *Yield: 50 to 75 servings*

1 pig, 75 to 80 pounds, when   basting sauce
  dressed

Sauce: (make ahead)
2-quarts cider vinegar   4 bay leaves, crumbled
2 tablespoons red pepper   salt
6 cloves garlic, crushed

Mix together the vinegar, red pepper, garlic, and bay leaves. During cooking, apply the sauce to the pig with a new long-handled mop or a new 3-inch paint brush that has been nailed to a broom handle.

To prepare:
Arise at 3:00 or 4:00 A.M. to start the fire! Dig a pit large enough for a bed of coals at least 12-inches deep. The pit should be about 6-inches longer than the pig at both ends, and wide enough to shovel fresh hot coals easily under the pig as it is roasting. Place several iron rods across the pit to hold the pig up a distance of 12 to 15-inches above the coals. Split open the carcass and prop it open with a piece of hardwood. Run an iron rod through the pig for support and easier handling. To build the fire, start with a bed of hardwood (hickory or oak) and top with a layer of pine kindling. Burn the hardwood until an even, glowing bed of coals is established. In order to maintain this even bed of coals, you will need to build a separate fire that is large enough to be a source of fresh coals for several hours.

To cook:
Place the carcass, skin side up, on the iron rods. Leave the pig in this position until it has almost finished cooking. Add more coals carefully so as not to burn the pig. Baste occasionally with the sauce. The pig should cook slowly, from 6 to 8 hours, over the glowing coals. After 6 hours, check on the cooking progress by sticking a long-tined fork into the hams. The pig is done when the juices run clear with no pink tinge. When the pig finishes cooking, rub lard on the skin and turn the pig so that the skin side is down. Let skin brown until crisp. Add plenty of salt to the basting sauce and apply to the up-turned side of the pig. Clear away the coals and allow the pig to cool until you can work with it without getting burned. Remove the iron rod and cut the meat into serving size pieces. Add additional basting sauce to meat when serving.

Stevi S. Dozier

BARBECUED SPARERIBS WITH SAUCE BEAUTIFUL

May prepare ahead   *Yield: 2 to 3 servings*

Sauce Beautiful:
8 tablespoons peach preserves	1 tablespoon salad oil
½ cup water	1 tablespoon vinegar
juice of one lemon	½ teaspoon paprika
3 tablespoons brown sugar	salt, pepper, and Worcestershire
1 tablespoon butter	sauce to taste

Combine all the ingredients in a small saucepan and blend. Cook over medium heat until thickened, stirring occasionally. Makes about 1 cup.

2 pounds pork spareribs

Preheat oven 450°. Place spareribs in a 9x13-inch pan and roast at 450° for 30 minutes. Pour off fat and reduce heat to 350°. Pour 1 cup of Sauce Beautiful over ribs. Bake, uncovered, until ribs are tender (about 1 hour), basting occasionally.

Stevi S. Dozier

GARDEN PORK CHOPS

May prepare ahead   *Yield: 4 servings*

4 pork chops	½ teaspoon salt
1 cup water	½ teaspoon thyme
1 beef bouillon cube	½ teaspoon sage
2 tablespoons onion, minced	

Brown pork chops in skillet, remove. In skillet, stir water, bouillon cube, onion, salt, thyme, and sage until well combined. Add pork chops, simmer for one hour covered. Then add:

1 package green beans, frozen	1 cup potatoes, thinly sliced
1 cup carrots, thinly sliced	

Cover and cook until vegetables are tender (½ to 1 hour).

Elaine A. Myers

CROWN ROAST OF PORK

Yields: 8

4 tablespoons butter
1 green pepper, chopped
1 onion, chopped
1 cup bread crumbs
1 tomato, peeled, seeded,
   chopped
½ teaspoon basil, dried
½ teaspoon thyme, dried
salt and pepper to taste

1 crown roast pork, 16 ribs
1 garlic clove, crushed and
   minced
pepper
½ cup dry white wine
¼ cup onion, chopped
1½ tablespoons flour
1 cup beef or pork stock
¾ cup dry white wine

Preheat oven to 350°. Melt butter, add green pepper, and sauté for about 1 minute. Add the onion and cook for 1 minute more. Remove from the fire. Add bread crumbs, tomato, basil, thyme, salt and pepper. Mix thoroughly adding more melted butter if necessary to make the mixture hold together.

Season by sprinkling the crown roast inside and out with the chopped garlic and pepper. Place the bread crumb mixture in the center. Cover each rib with aluminum foil to prevent the bones from charring. Place in roasting pan. Pour ½ cup of the white wine over the pork. Roast for 30 to 35 minutes a pound. Baste occasionally with the pan juices.

When the roast is done the internal temperature will register 190° on a meat thermometer. Remove pork from oven and place on a hot serving dish. Place a paper frill on each rib. Allow the roast to stand for about 15 minutes.

Meanwhile, skim all fat except 1 tablespoon off the pan juices, leaving all the good brown juices. Add the ¼ cup onion and cook for about 2 minutes. Off the fire blend in the 1½ tablespoons flour and cook for about 1 minute. Return to the fire, add stock and ¾ cup wine and stir over the fire until the sauce comes to a boil. Boil for 3 to 5 minutes. Serve the sauce in a gravy bowl.

Anne Byrd
"Keeping Pace With Anne Byrd"
Published and Copyrighted by Pace Publications
(Used with permission by the Author.)

PORK CHOP CASSEROLE

May prepare ahead   *Yield: 6 servings*

6 pork chops   3 tomatoes, sliced
1½ cups brown rice, uncooked   1 green pepper, sliced
2 onions, sliced   2 cans beef broth

Preheat oven to 375°. Place rice in bottom of 9x13x2-inch casserole. Brown chops in skillet, then arrange on top of rice. Place onions, tomatoes, and pepper rings on top of pork chops. Pour beef broth over chops, cover, and bake at 375° for 1 to 1½ hours. Add water if necessary.

Barbara A. Garlitz

OVEN SPARERIBS

Yield: 6 servings

4 pounds spareribs   1 teaspoon salt
salt and pepper   1 teaspoon paprika
2 onions, sliced   ½ teaspoon black pepper
2 teaspoons vinegar   1 teaspoon chili powder
2 teaspoons Worcestershire   ¾ cup catsup
  sauce   ¾ cup water

Cut spareribs into serving size. Sprinkle with salt and pepper. Place ribs in a roaster and cover with onions. Combine remaining ingredients and pour over meat. Cover and bake at 350° for 1½ hours. Baste occasionally, turning ribs once during cooking time. Remove cover during last 15 minutes to brown.

Pat Y. Tolbert

ORIENTAL PORK CHOPS

May prepare ahead   *Yield: 6 to 8 servings*

4 pounds pork chops   1 clove garlic, minced
½ cup soy sauce   ¼ teaspoon ginger, ground
2 teaspoons sugar   ½ teaspoon MSG

Trim bone and fat from pork chops and render fat in skillet until there are about 2 tablespoons of drippings. Discard pieces of fat, brown pork on both sides. Mix soy sauce, sugar, garlic, ginger, and MSG and pour over pork. Cover and simmer 30 to 45 minutes, turning occasionally.

Kay J. Webber

ROAST LOIN OF PORK À L'ORANGE

Yield: 8 to 10 servings

4 to 5 pound pork loin roast
1½ teaspoons salt
½ teaspoon ginger

orange sauce
fruit spears, mint, or watercress

Place roast, ribs down, on rack in a shallow pan. Combine salt and ginger; rub into meat. Bake in a 325° oven for 2½ to 3 hours, or until thoroughly done. (If using a meat thermometer, a temperature of 170°.) While roast cooks, make orange sauce.

Sauce:

1 cup orange marmalade
1 cup orange juice
2 tablespoons orange rind, grated
2 tablespoons cornstarch

½ teaspoon salt
½ teaspoon ginger
1 cup seedless grapes, halved (optional)
½ cup orange liqueur (optional)

Combine marmalade, orange juice, rind, cornstarch, salt, and ginger in a saucepan. Add grapes and liqueur, if desired. Heat, stirring constantly, until thick and clear. 30 minutes before end of roasting time, brush ½ cup orange sauce over meat. Arrange roast on serving platter, garnish with fruit spears, mint, or watercress, and serve with sauce.

Catherine H. Yeager

FAVORITE PORK LOIN

Yield: 6 servings

4 pound pork loin
2 cloves garlic
2 teaspoons salt
1 teaspoon sage
½ teaspoon pepper
½ teaspoon nutmeg

2 onions, sliced
2 carrots, sliced
1 cup water
¼ cup currant jelly
1 teaspoon dry mustard
whole cloves

Mash garlic with seasonings. Rub into meat, using fingers instead of spoon. Place onions and carrots into the bottom of a shallow roasting pan. Set meat on top of vegetables, fat side up; splash with water. Roast in 325° oven for 1½ hours. Remove from oven. Slash fat into criss-cross pattern. Combine jelly with mustard; spread over meat. Stud with whole cloves and roast 1 hour longer.

Camille M. Gardner

⌒⌒ VEAL ⌒⌒

ROWENA'S SPECIAL VEAL

Sauce freezes well   *Yield: 12 servings*

Sauce:

2 cups carrots

1½ cups celery

1 cup onion

½ teaspoon oregano

½ teaspoon rosemary

½ teaspoon Beau Monde

½ teaspoon parsley flakes

¼ cup margarine

1 cup water (or chicken stock)

¼ cup soy sauce

½ cup sauterne wine

2 tablespoons cornstarch

2 tablespoons all-purpose flour

1 cup water

Cut vegetables in julienne strips 2 to 3 inches long. Place vegetables, spices, margarine, water, and soy sauce in a saucepan. Cook until vegetables are tender. Add wine. Blend cornstarch and flour. Add water slowly. Add thickening to sauce, stirring gently to avoid breaking vegetables. Cook until thick and set aside to cool. Sauce may be stored in refrigerator 2 days ahead of serving or may be frozen.

Veal Cutlets:

12 (4 to 5 ounce) veal cutlets

1 cup milk

1 egg, beaten

flour (to coat veal)

salt to taste

1 cup medium-sharp Cheddar cheese, shredded

½ cup Parmesan cheese, grated

paprika to taste

Combine milk and egg. Dip each cutlet into mixture, then into flour. Brown slowly on both sides in a small amount of oil. Salt lightly. Place cutlets into a shallow baking dish. Do not crowd. Cover each cutlet with 2 tablespoons sauce, 1 tablespoon Cheddar cheese, a sprinkle of Parmesan cheese, and paprika. Bake in a 350° oven for 25 minutes, or until bubbly and slightly browned.

Note: A very good party dish you can assemble ahead and pop into the oven 30 minutes before serving.

Barbara F. Williams

149

VEAL ELLIE

Yield: 4 servings

1½ pounds thin slices of veal
    (scallops)
2 to 3 tablespoons butter,
    melted
½ pound mushrooms, sliced

½ pint sour cream
1 teaspoon chicken bouillon
    granules
imported soy sauce to taste
juice of 1 lemon

Sauté veal in butter until nicely browned. Remove veal, and brown mushrooms in same pan. Remove mushrooms and pour in sour cream, granules, and soy sauce. Add veal, mushrooms, and lemon juice. Simmer until thoroughly heated and veal is done. Serve over rice or noodles.

Lindy M. Dillow

MINCED VEAL BISCAENNE

Yield: 6 to 8 servings

Parisienne potatoes (2 cups):
4 to 6 potatoes
¼ cup butter or margarine,
    melted

Cut balls from raw potatoes using a French ball cutter. Soak in cold water for 1 hour, drain, and dry thoroughly with a paper towel. Brown in butter until tender. Set aside and keep warm.

Veal:
2 pounds ground veal
1 onion, chopped
½ green pepper, chopped
3 tablespoons olive oil
2 tablespoons all-purpose flour

2 cups canned consommé
2 cloves garlic, pressed
2 tomatoes, peeled, seeded,
    and diced
minced parsley to taste

Brown veal, onion, and green pepper in olive oil. When meat has browned, add flour, consommé, garlic, and tomatoes. Simmer for 15 minutes. Add potatoes, and serve sprinkled with parsley.

Lindy M. Dillow

VEAL PARMESAN

May prepare ahead   *Yield: 4 servings*

4 (3 to 4x¹/₂-inch) pieces of veal   ¹/₂ cup Parmesan cheese, grated
all-purpose flour   2 tablespoons chopped parsley
salt and pepper to taste   2 tablespoons salad oil
oregano to taste   1 cup tomato sauce
1 egg   ⅛ teaspoon garlic powder
¹/₄ cup light cream   ¹/₄ cup dry white wine
¹/₂ cup dry bread crumbs   4 slices mozzarella cheese

Combine flour, salt, pepper, and oregano. Beat egg, then beat in cream.
Combine bread crumbs, Parmesan cheese, and parsley. Dust veal with
flour, dip into egg wash, and then coat with crumb mixture. Heat oil and
slowly brown veal on both sides. When browned, combine tomato
sauce, garlic powder, and wine. Pour *around* veal. Place a slice of mozzarella cheese on top of each veal piece. Bake at 325° 30 to 40 minutes,
or until veal is tender and cheese lightly browned.

Nancy S. Spivey

CHICKEN

ALMOND CHICKEN BAKE

Yield: 6 to 8 generous servings

5 to 6 chicken breasts, cooked   2 (11¹/₄-ounce) cans cream of
   and chopped   chicken soup
1 (6-ounce) box long grain   1 small onion, chopped
   and wild rice, cooked   2 stalks celery, chopped
1 (2³/₄-ounce) package almonds,   1 cup Cheddar cheese,
   sliced and toasted   shredded
¹/₄ cup butter or margarine,   ¹/₂ cup bread crumbs, toasted
   melted

Preheat oven to 350°. Combine butter and chicken soup. Add onion,
celery, chicken, rice, and almonds to soup mixture, blending
thoroughly. Pour into a greased 9x13x2-inch casserole. Top with cheese,
and then bread crumbs. Bake for 40 minutes.

Lynn L. Lyerly

151

CHICKEN AND ARTICHOKES

Yield: Allow 1 piece chicken per serving

6 pounds chicken breasts and
   thighs
2 teaspoons salt
1 teaspoon paprika
1/2 teaspoon pepper
1 cup margarine or butter

1 pound fresh mushrooms
4 tablespoons all-purpose flour
1 cup chicken broth
1 1/2 cups sherry
2 (14-ounce) cans artichoke
   hearts, drained

Preheat oven to 325°. Season chicken with salt, paprika, and pepper. Brown seasoned chicken in margarine in a heavy skillet; remove chicken pieces to a casserole dish. Sauté mushrooms in margarine remaining in skillet. (The mushrooms will absorb all of the margarine.) Remove skillet from the heat and stir in flour. Combine chicken broth and sherry and pour over mushrooms; then pour mushroom mixture over chicken in casserole dish. Cover and bake for 1 hour at 325°. Add artichoke hearts and bake for an additional 15 minutes.

Sara C. Shores

COUNTRY CAPTAIN

May prepare ahead

Yield: 6 servings

1 fryer, cut up
1/2 cup all-purpose flour
salt and pepper
1/2 cup vegetable oil
1 medium onion, thinly sliced
1 medium green pepper,
   chopped

1 clove garlic, minced
2 (8-ounce) cans tomato sauce
1 cup water
1/2 teaspoon thyme
2 teaspoons curry powder
1 teaspoon salt
1 package frozen peas, thawed

Coat chicken with flour lightly seasoned with salt and pepper. In a skillet, brown chicken in oil; remove chicken. Cook onion, green pepper, and garlic in drippings; drain off fat. Return chicken to skillet and add tomato sauce, water, thyme, curry powder, salt, and peas. Cover and simmer 45 minutes, or until chicken is tender. Can be served cool.

Note: An easy to prepare dish. Delicious with rice mixed with 1/4 cup raisins and garnished with parsley and almonds.

Anne F. Mitchell

CHICKEN CORDON BLEU

Yield: 2 servings

1 whole chicken breast, split, boned, and skinned	¼ cup Parmesan cheese, grated
	1 tablespoon parsley, minced
1 (1-ounce) slice Swiss cheese, cut into thin strips	⅛ teaspoon salt
	black pepper, freshly ground
1 (1-ounce) slice cooked ham, cut into thin strips	3 tablespoons all-purpose flour
	¼ cup butter or margarine
1 egg, beaten	4 ounces fresh mushrooms, sliced
¼ cup milk	
½ cup bread crumbs	¼ cup Chablis or other dry white wine
¼ cup all-purpose flour	

Place each chicken breast half on a sheet of waxed paper; flatten pieces to ¼-inch thickness, using a meat mallet or rolling pin. Place half the cheese strips and half the ham strips in the center of each chicken piece. Fold ends over ham and cheese; roll up, beginning with a long side. Secure with wooden picks, if desired. Combine egg and milk, mixing well; set aside. Combine bread crumbs, ¼ cup flour, Parmesan cheese, parsley, salt, and pepper; mix well. Dredge chicken rolls in remaining 3 tablespoons flour; dip into egg mixture, and coat well with breadcrumb mixture. Cover chicken rolls and chill at least 30 minutes. Melt butter in a heavy skillet; brown chicken on all sides. Reduce heat; cover and simmer 10 minutes. Remove chicken from pan, reserving drippings. Sauté mushrooms in drippings until tender; add wine. Cook over medium heat, stirring constantly until mixture is reduced by half. Add chicken and simmer 1 to 2 minutes.

Note: For 4 to 6 servings double or triple recipe.

Judy B. Smith

CHICKEN BREASTS CORDON BLEU

Yield: 16 servings

16 chicken breast halves, boned and skinned
16 slices very thin processed ham
16 Swiss cheese slices
1 can cream of mushroom soup
1 (10-ounce) bottle commercial tangy mustard-mayonnaise dressing

Wrap each chicken breast with a slice of ham and then a slice of Swiss cheese. Secure with a toothpick and place side by side in a long casserole dish. Mix soup and sauce together; pour over the chicken and bake at 250° for 2½ hours. Do not salt. Bake covered.

Judy F. Flowers

BETTY'S BRUNSWICK STEW

Freezes well *Yield: 20 servings*

1 (6-pound) fat hen, cut up for stewing
salt and pepper
1 quart chicken broth
3 (28-ounce) cans tomatoes
9 large onions, chopped
9 medium-sized potatoes
butter or margarine
2 (10-ounce) packages frozen baby lima beans
2 (12-ounce) cans cream style corn
2½ fluid ounces Worcestershire sauce

Place cut up chicken in 8-quart soup pot with 3 quarts of water. Season to taste with salt and pepper. Simmer gently for 2 hours or until chicken is fork tender. When cool enough to handle remove meat from bones. (Can refrigerate overnight.) Place chicken and broth in 8-quart pot, add tomatoes and onions. Stew for 1½ hours. While this is cooking, peel potatoes and cook as for mashing, cream with butter or margarine, use *no milk*. Cook frozen lima beans until done, season with butter or margarine. When chicken has stewed down, add cooked lima beans and mashed potatoes; adding corn last. Stir often after adding potatoes to keep from sticking. Add sauce, and salt and pepper to taste. Cook about 20 minutes after adding the corn. Makes 6 quarts.

June P. Wilfong

CHICKEN WITH ARTICHOKES

May not be frozen   *Yield: 4 servings*

4 whole chicken breasts, cooked   1 (4-ounce) can button
    and skinned   mushrooms
¼ cup butter   ½ teaspoon thyme
1 medium onion, thinly sliced   ½ teaspoon sweet basil
1 (10-ounce) package frozen   salt and pepper to taste
    artichoke hearts, thawed   1 chicken bouillon cube
    and halved

Cut chicken into bite-size pieces and brown slowly in butter. Drain liquid
and reserve. Add onion, artichokes, mushrooms (reserving liquid),
thyme, basil, salt, and pepper to chicken. Dissolve bouillon cube in
mushroom and chicken liquid, about ¼ to ⅓ cup, and pour over other
ingredients in pan. Cook, stirring for 5 minutes. Serve with parsley sour
cream sauce.

Parsley Sour Cream Sauce:
1 cup sour cream   ½ teaspoon salt
2 tablespoons parsley, chopped   1 tablespoon lemon juice

Blend all ingredients and serve at room temperature.

*Note: If serving over rice, and gravy is desired, add 2 cups of chicken
bouillon; simmer awhile and add 1 to 2 tablespoons of cornstarch to
thicken.*

Sue Nell C. Fuller

LIZZIE'S CHICKEN

Yield: Allow 1 or 2 pieces chicken per serving.

2 (2½ to 3 pounds) fryers,   1 (8-ounce) bottle of either
    cut up   Italian or Russian salad
1 (1.25-ounce) envelope dry   dressing
    onion soup mix   1 (10-ounce) jar of apricot jam

Preheat oven to 350°. Clean the chicken and arrange in a 2-quart pan.
Mix dry soup mix, salad dressing, and jam together; pour over chicken.
Bake chicken 1 hour. Baste often.

Elaine S. Zerden

BILL'S PECAN-BREADED CHICKEN BREASTS

Yield: 4 servings

4 whole chicken breasts,
    boned and cut in half
salt and freshly ground black
    pepper
10 tablespoons butter, divided

3 tablespoons Dijon mustard,
    divided
5 or 6 ounces pecans, crushed
2 tablespoons safflower oil
2/3 cup sour cream

Preheat oven to 200°. Season chicken breasts with salt and pepper. Flatten between 2 sheets of waxed paper. Melt 6 tablespoons butter in saute pan and whisk in 2 tablespoons of mustard. Dip chicken breasts into this mixture and cover with crushed pecans. Press if necessary. Melt 4 tablespoons butter in a skillet; add safflower oil and saute chicken breasts 4 to 5 minutes per side. Remove to a baking dish and keep warm in oven. Discard oil and butter from skillet. Deglaze pan with sour cream, scraping up all the brown bits. Whisk in 1 tablespoon mustard; adjust seasonings with salt and pepper. Serve breasts topped with sauce.

Phyllis D. Cauble

ORANGE CHICKEN BURGUNDY

Yield: 4 to 6 servings

2½ to 3 pounds frying chicken,
    cut-up
2 tablespoons butter or
    margarine, melted
½ teaspoon seasoned salt blend
    or salt
⅛ teaspoon pepper
3 tablespoons brown sugar
1 tablespoon cornstarch

⅛ teaspoon ground ginger,
    if desired
¼ teaspoon salt
⅓ cup orange marmalade
⅓ cup orange juice
1 teaspoon lemon juice
⅓ cup Burgundy
1 orange, thinly sliced

In large frying pan or electric skillet, brown chicken in butter. Season with salt and pepper. Add remaining ingredients, except Burgundy and orange slices. Reduce heat; cover. Simmer, stirring and basting occasionally until tender. Add Burgundy and orange slices. Continue simmering for 10 minutes. Serve hot.

Note: ⅓ cup additional orange juice can be used for the Burgundy and increase lemon juice to 1 tablespoon. Prepare as directed.

Jerrie J. Yount

CHICKEN-MUSHROOM STROGANOFF

Yield: 8 servings

3 whole chicken breasts
2 cups water
1 (10-ounce) package frozen
   peas and pearl onions
5 tablespoons unsalted butter,
   divided
1 pound small fresh mushrooms
3 tablespoons all-purpose flour
1 tablespoon onion, finely
   chopped

1 teaspoon salt
½ teaspoon celery salt
½ teaspoon paprika
½ teaspoon oregano
½ teaspoon Worcestershire
   sauce
dash black pepper
½ cup sauterne
1 cup light cream
rice

Simmer chicken in 2 cups salted water for 30 minutes; reserve 1 cup broth. Let chicken cool; bone and skin chicken. Cut meat into 1½-inch cubes. Cook peas according to package directions; set aside. Melt 2 tablespoons butter in skillet; sauté mushrooms 3 to 5 minutes. Melt 3 tablespoons butter over low heat in Dutch oven; stir in next 8 ingredients. Cook, stirring constantly, until bubbly. Stir in reserved cup of broth and sauterne; cook over low heat, stirring constantly, until the sauce is smooth and thickened. Slowly add cream to wine sauce, stirring constantly. Stir in chicken, peas with onions, and mushrooms; heat thoroughly. Transfer to chafing dish set over low heat; serve over rice.

Note: Good buffet dish.

Judith C. West

ELECTRIC SKILLET SOUTHERN FRIED CHICKEN

Yield: 9 servings

9 pieces chicken (3 breasts,
   3 thighs, 3 drumsticks)
1½ cups all-purpose flour
1½ teaspoons salt

1 teaspoon white pepper
1 tablespoon paprika
vegetable shortening

Heat 1½-inches of shortening in electric skillet at 360°. Wash chicken and coat each piece in flour and seasoning mixture. Place all 9 pieces in skillet and cook uncovered on one side for 10 minutes. Turn chicken over and cover with skillet lid letting no steam escape. Cook 15 additional minutes. Uncover and let cook 1½ minutes, then remove and drain on paper towels.

Katharyn A. Portwood

CRAB-STUFFED CHICKEN

Yield: 8 servings

8 large chicken breasts, boned
   and skinned
4 tablespoons butter or
   margarine, divided
¼ cup all-purpose flour
¾ cup milk
¾ cup chicken broth
⅓ cup dry white wine
¼ cup chopped onion
1 (7½-ounce) can crabmeat,
   drained and flaked

1 (3-ounce) can chopped
   mushrooms, drained
½ cup coarsely crumbled
   saltine crackers (10
   crackers)
2 tablespoons snipped parsley
½ teaspoon salt
dash pepper
1 cup (4-ounces) Swiss cheese,
   shredded
½ teaspoon paprika

Pound chicken lightly to make cutlet about ⅛-inch thick; set aside. In a saucepan, melt 3 tablespoons butter; blend in flour. Add milk, chicken broth, and wine all at once; cook and stir until mixture thickens and bubbles. Set aside. In skillet, cook onion in remaining butter until tender. Stir in crab, mushrooms, cracker crumbs, parsley, salt, and pepper. Stir in 2 tablespoons of the sauce. Top each chicken piece with about ¼ cup crab mixture. Fold sides in; roll up. Place seam side down in 12x7½x2-inch baking dish. Pour remaining sauce over all. Bake, covered, in 350⁰ oven for 1 hour or until tender. Uncover, sprinkle with cheese and paprika. Bake 2 minutes or until cheese melts.

Judy B. Pierce

EASY CHICKEN PIE

Freezes well

Yield: 4 servings

4 chicken breasts, stewed
   and boned
¼ cup butter or margarine,
   melted
1 cup all-purpose flour
1 cup milk

1 tablespoon baking powder
1 (10¾-ounce) can chicken
   broth
1 (11-ounce) can celery soup,
   undiluted

Preheat oven to 350⁰. Grease an 8x8-inch casserole, put in chicken, and pour butter over chicken. Combine flour, milk, and baking powder and spread over chicken. Combine broth and celery soup and pour over top. Bake for 1 hour.

Linda P. Frye

HOT CHICKEN ON CORN BREAD

May prepare ahead   *Yield: 2 servings*

2 cups cooked chicken or
    turkey, chopped
¹/₂ cup mayonnaise
1 cup sour cream

¹/₂ teaspoon salt
¹/₄ cup toasted slivered almonds
¹/₄ cup sweet pickle relish
¹/₂ cup celery, chopped

Combine all ingredients; stir well. Put over low heat until warmed through. Serve over toasted corn bread, rice, or noodles.

Anne L. Moss

WINE AND CHIVED CHICKEN

Yield: 4 servings

2 whole chicken breasts, halved,
    boned, and skinned
¹/₂ lemon
1 teaspoon sugar
¹/₄ teaspoon black pepper,
    coarsely ground
3 tablespoons butter, divided
1 cup fresh mushrooms, sliced
1 clove garlic, minced

2 tablespoons all-purpose flour
1 cup chicken broth
¹/₃ cup Moselle wine
1 tablespoon dried chives
¹/₃ cup heavy cream
¹/₄ teaspoon paprika
¹/₄ teaspoon salt
4 large slices buttered, oven-
    toasted French bread

Place chicken on large sheet of waxed paper. Squeeze lemon on both sides of chicken. Mix sugar and pepper and sprinkle over both sides of chicken. Fold half of waxed paper over chicken and press with hands to flatten slightly and to help sugar-pepper mixture to adhere to chicken. Melt 1 tablespoon of butter over medium-hot heat in skillet. Add chicken and brown for about 3 minutes. Remove chicken and set aside. In same pan, put remaining 2 tablespoons of butter and melt over medium-low heat. Add mushrooms and garlic; sauté for 2 minutes. Add flour and stir until smooth. Add chicken, broth, wine, and chives; cook, stirring frequently, about 3 minutes or until sauce thickens. Return chicken to sauce in skillet and simmer, uncovered, over low heat. Cook, turning chicken occasionally, about 18 minutes or until chicken is done. Stir in cream, paprika, and salt and heat 2 minutes. To serve, place halved chicken breasts on slices of French bread and generously spoon sauce over top.

Judy M. Bost

159

C
H
I
C
K
E
N

CHICKEN CRÈME PARISIENNE

Yield: 8 servings

8 chicken breasts
2 chicken bouillon cubes
3 carrots, cooked and cut into
   narrow strips
1 (10-ounce) package frozen
   tiny green peas
8 small pearl onions (in a
   glass jar)
12 mushrooms

1 tablespoon all-purpose flour
seasoned salt
pepper
4 tablespoons butter, melted
½ cup white wine
1 cup chicken broth
1 cup sour cream
½ cup mayonnaise
paprika

Simmer chicken breasts and bouillon cubes in water, covered, for ½ hour. Skin and bone the breasts and reserve the cooking broth. Place breasts in a flat, shallow casserole and arrange around them the cooked carrots, frozen peas, onions, and sautéed mushrooms. Make the sauce in a small saucepan by adding flour, seasoned salt, and pepper to melted butter. Stirring constantly, slowly add wine and 1 cup reserved chicken broth. When thickened, add sour cream and mayonnaise. Adjust the consistency by adding more broth if necessary to make a smooth, velvety, rich gravy. Pour over chicken and vegetables; dust with paprika. Cover with foil and bake at 300° for 30 to 45 minutes or until bubbly.

Toni Y. Coleman and Sue Nell C. Fuller

CHICKEN SCALLOP

Yield: 6 servings

1¾ cups herb seasoned stuffing
   mix
2 cups cooked chicken, diced
4 tablespoons butter or
   margarine

¼ cup all-purpose flour
⅛ teaspoon salt
dash pepper
2 cups chicken broth
3 eggs, slightly beaten

Prepare stuffing mix according to package directions. Spread in 10x6x1½-inch baking dish; top with chicken. In a saucepan melt butter, blend in flour, salt, and pepper. Add broth and cook until thickened. Stir small amount of hot mixture into eggs; return to hot mixture. Pour over chicken. Bake at 325° for 40 minutes or until knife inserted in middle comes out clean. Let stand 5 minutes; cut into squares. Garnish with sliced, stuffed green olives if desired and serve with mushroom sauce.

Mushroom Sauce:
1 can cream of mushroom soup   milk to thin if desired
1/2 cup sour cream

Mix all ingredients together. Heat and serve with chicken.

Lynne G. Leffler

CHICKEN BREAST PERIGOURDINE

Yield: 8 servings

8 whole chicken breasts, boned
salt and freshly ground pepper
    to taste
1/2 teaspoon thyme
3/4 cup butter, divided
1/2 pound chicken livers,
    chopped
1/2 pound mushrooms, sliced
    thin

1 bunch spring onions,
    sliced thin
1 small clove garlic, minced
1 teaspoon salt
1 cup Swiss cheese, shredded
1 egg, beaten
1 1/2 cups dry bread crumbs

Flatten each breast and sprinkle with salt, pepper, and thyme. Prepare stuffing as follows: melt 1/4 cup butter in a skillet. Brown livers, mushrooms, onions, and garlic. Sprinkle with salt. Cook for 7 minutes or until livers are done. Remove skillet from heat. Add cheese and stir until blended. Put a portion of stuffing on each breast. Roll breast and secure with picks or skewers. Roll breast in egg, then crumbs. Place in casserole dish and refrigerate, uncovered, for 2 hours. Heat remaining butter in skillet. Brown chicken. Return to dish; bake in 350° oven for 45 minutes or until tender. Spoon a little sauce over each breast. Serve remaining sauce on the side.

Cream Sauce:
1/4 cup butter
1/4 cup all-purpose flour
2 cups chicken stock

1 tablespoon lemon juice
1/2 cup light cream

In saucepan, melt butter. Blend in flour, then stock. Cook and stir until mixture begins to boil. Turn down heat and cook 4 minutes. Stir in lemon juice and cream. Heat for 1 minute.

Note: Dish takes time to prepare but is well worth every minute! Can be prepared ahead and cooked before serving.

Carolyn W. Lyerly

161

CHICKEN AND WILD RICE

Freezes well   *Yield: 10 servings*

3 pounds chicken pieces
5 cups water, divided
1/2 cup dry sherry
1 medium onion, sliced
1/2 teaspoon curry powder
2 teaspoons salt
1 stalk celery with top
1 pound fresh mushrooms,
    sliced

1/4 cup butter, melted
2 (6-ounce) boxes long grain
    and wild rice
1 (10¾-ounce) can cream of
    mushroom soup, undiluted
1 cup sour cream

Combine chicken, 2 cups water, sherry, onion, curry powder, salt, and celery. Simmer 1 hour; cool and remove chicken. Strain and reserve broth. Remove skin and bones. Cut into bite-size pieces; set aside. Sauté mushrooms in butter; drain and set aside. Cook rice in reserved broth and 3 cups water until tender; do not drain. Combine soup, sour cream, chicken, rice, and mushrooms. Pour into a 4-quart casserole dish. Casserole will be soupy, but thickens while baking. Bake at 350⁰ for 1 hour.

Note: Easy, economical dish for a crowd. Can be prepared ahead and cooked before serving.

Nancy F. Matheson

GOURMET CHICKEN

Yield: 8 to 10 servings

12 large chicken breasts,
    skinned
2 tablespoons butter
salt and pepper

sauce
1 (11-ounce) can mandarin
    oranges, for garnish
2 ripe bananas, for garnish

Arrange chicken in casserole. Dot with butter, salt, and pepper. Bake at 425⁰ for 15 minutes.

Sauce:
1½ cups orange juice
1/2 cup raisins
1/2 cup chutney
1/2 cup almonds, slivered

1/2 teaspoon cinnamon
1/2 teaspoon curry powder
dash thyme

Combine all sauce ingredients and simmer for 10 minutes. Pour sauce over chicken. Reduce oven heat to 300⁰ and bake for 1 hour. Garnish platter with oranges and bananas. Extra sauce may be put in sauce boat. Serve with rice.

Sue Nell C. Fuller

C
H
I
C
K
E
N

OYSTER-STUFFED CHICKEN

Yield: 6 servings

1 pint oysters	1 teaspoon freshly ground black
3 tablespoons green pepper,	pepper
chopped	¹/₄ teaspoon cayenne pepper
2 tablespoons celery, chopped	4 tablespoons butter
3 tablespoons parsley, chopped	3 broilers, split in half
2 tablespoons onion, chopped	butter
1 clove garlic, crushed	bread crumbs
1 teaspoon salt	

Drain and chop oysters and save liquor. Sauté oysters and vegetables with seasonings and 4 tablespoons butter for 10 minutes. Meanwhile, place chickens in a shallow baking pan, skin side up and dot with butter. Add ½ cup water to pan. Bake in moderate oven at 375⁰ for 30 minutes or until brown. Remove chicken from oven. Turn skin side down and fill each cavity with oyster stuffing. Sprinkle with bread crumbs moistened with melted butter and a little oyster liquor. Bake 20 minutes, until golden brown. Serve with cranberry preserves.

Sue Nell C. Fuller

CHICKEN SPAGHETTI

Freezes well   *Yield: A lot!*

5 to 6 pound hen or 2 small
    fryers
4 to 5 onions, chopped
4 to 5 green peppers, chopped
4 to 5 celery stalks, chopped
3 to 4 cloves garlic, minced
3 quarts tomatoes, canned or
    fresh
1 to 1½ quarts chicken broth
2 teaspoons basil
1 teaspoon tarragon

1 teaspoon oregano
½ teaspoon red pepper
½ teaspoon black pepper
½ teaspoon chili powder
5 to 6 stars of anise
8 ounces fresh or canned
    mushrooms, sliced
3 or more tablespoons sugar
salt
1 cup Parmesan or Romano
    cheese, grated

Boil or pressure cook hens, bone, and reserve stock. Soften onions, peppers, celery, and garlic in microwave on high about 5 minutes or sauté in small amount of oil. Add chopped vegetables to tomatoes and chicken broth along with herbs, including star anise. Allow to cook slowly at least 3 hours. About ½ hour before serving add chicken, mushrooms, sugar, salt, and Parmesan cheese. Serve over spaghetti with additional cheese.

Joyce S. Trado

 **TURKEY**

ORIENTAL-BROILED TURKEY STEAKS

Must prepare ahead   *Yield: 4 to 6 servings*

1 turkey breast
1 tablespoon ground ginger
1 teaspoon dry mustard
1 teaspoon monosodium
    glutamate (optional)

1 tablespoon honey
½ cup soy sauce
¼ cup salad oil
½ teaspoon garlic, minced

Ask butcher to cut turkey breast crosswise into 1-inch steaks. Combine all remaining ingredients in glass bowl, allow to stand overnight at room temperature. Pour over turkey steaks, cover and refrigerate for several hours or overnight. Drain steaks and cook over hot coals, allowing about 8 minutes on each side. Brush with marinade if desired.

Beth G. Warmuth

164

CAUBLE'S SPINACH AND TURKEY DIVAN

Yield: 4 to 6 servings

2 bags fresh spinach (10 to
12 ounce bags)
1/4 cup onion, chopped
1/4 cup butter
1/4 cup all-purpose flour
1 teaspoon salt
1/4 teaspoon paprika
1/8 teaspoon nutmeg

14 ounces good chicken stock
1/2 cup heavy cream
2 tablespoons dry vermouth
1/4 cup fresh Parmesan cheese,
grated
3/4 pound cooked turkey or
chicken, sliced

Preheat oven to 400°. Wash spinach well; cover in a saucepan and cook in water until leaves are limp (about 5 minutes). Stir a couple of times. Drain spinach well. Place spinach evenly in bottom of casserole. Cook onion in butter until transparent but not brown. Stir in flour, salt, paprika, and nutmeg. Add chicken broth and stir constantly until well-blended and thickened. Add cream, vermouth, and 1/2 of the cheese. Spoon 1/2 of the sauce over the spinach. Put the sliced turkey or chicken over the spinach. Spoon remaining sauce over chicken or turkey. Sprinkle remaining cheese and paprika over top. Bake in hot oven (400°) until sauce is bubbling (about 15 minutes).

Phyllis D. Cauble

 **GAME**

QUAIL CASSEROLE

Yield: 4 servings

8 quail
8 tablespoons butter
1/2 cup onions, chopped
2 carrots, diced
1/2 cup celery, diced

1 (8-ounce) can water chestnuts
1 cup water
1/2 cup Sauterne
2 (5-ounce) cans mushroom
steak sauce

Flour quail and brown slowly in butter. Transfer to casserole dish. Add onions, carrots, celery, and water chestnuts to hot butter. Stir for 3 minutes. Add water and stir. Pour over birds. Add Sauterne. Tightly cover and bake at 350° for 1 hour. Add steak sauce and continue baking for 30 minutes.

Note: Do not let birds get dry; add extra wine and water, if necessary.

Rebecca H. Hart

165

CHRISTMAS GOOSE WITH FRUIT DRESSING AND POTATOES

Yield: 10 to 12 servings

8 to 10 pound goose

Dressing:

½ cup water
⅓ cup chopped dried apricots
½ teaspoon salt
½ teaspoon dried rosemary
    leaves
½ teaspoon sage
½ teaspoon pepper
½ pound pork sausage

2 cups saltine cracker crumbs
2 large apples, unpared and
    chopped (1½ cups)
½ cup celery, minced
¼ cup fresh chives, snipped
2 tablespoons light cream or
    milk

Preheat oven to 350°. Heat water, apricots, salt, rosemary, sage, and pepper in 3-quart saucepan to boiling; reduce heat. Simmer for 5 minutes; remove from heat. Sauté sausage until brown; drain fat. Stir sausage, cracker crumbs, apple, celery, chives, and cream into apricot mixture. Fill goose cavity loosely with dressing. Tie drumsticks together with heavy string. Place goose, breast side up, on rack in open, shallow baking pan. Insert meat thermometer so tip is in thickest part of inside thigh muscle. Roast uncovered until thermometer registers 185° (3 to 4 hours). After 2 hours, drain all fat from pan. When ⅔ done, cut string holding legs, and prepare potatoes, adding them during last baking hour.

Potatoes:

6 large baking potatoes, cut
    lengthwise in half
salt and pepper to taste
paprika to taste
2 tablespoons all-purpose flour

1 teaspoon salt
½ teaspoon pepper
1 cup water
1 orange, divided into segments
parsley

Season potatoes with salt, pepper, and paprika. Bake potatoes in roasting pan. When goose is done, remove from pan and let stand 30 minutes before carving. Remove potatoes; keep warm. Drain all but 2 tablespoons fat from pan. Stir in flour. Cook over low heat, stirring constantly, until mixture is smooth and bubbly. Remove from heat. Stir in salt, pepper, and water. Heat, stirring constantly, to boiling. Boil and stir 1 minute. Place goose and potatoes on platter. Garnish with orange segments and parsley.

Carolyn H. Walker

WILD DUCK WITH CUMBERLAND SAUCE

Yield: allow 1 serving per pound

wild duck
cooking oil
dash of Worcestershire sauce
black pepper

red pepper
1 onion, peeled
salt

For each duck you are preparing, pour a little oil inside cavity. Add Worcestershire sauce to cavity. Mix together enough black and red pepper to rub inside duck. Place 1 onion into duck and add salt. In a roasting pan, add water to half cover duck and bake at 275° for 6 hours. Turn duck every 40 minutes.

Sauce (per duck):

1 orange, unpeeled
1 lemon, unpeeled
1/2 cup currant jelly
1/4 cup port wine

2 teaspoons dry mustard
1 teaspoon cayenne pepper
1/2 teaspoon ground ginger
1 teaspoon cornstarch

Cut orange and lemon into 1-inch pieces; remove seeds. Combine with jelly, wine, dry mustard, cayenne pepper, ginger, and cornstarch in blender container. Blend until rind is slivered. Transfer to saucepan and simmer until sauce thickens. Pour over duck at end of cooking time.

Note: So delicious you will forget the lengthy preparation time!

Rebecca H. Hart

ROASTED QUAIL

Yield: 6 servings

6 quail
1 teaspoon salt
3 teaspoons butter
1/2 cup all-purpose flour

1/2 cup water
1/2 cup dry sherry
1/4 teaspoon tarragon

Clean quail thoroughly. Sprinkle salt lightly over birds. Place 1/2 teaspoon butter inside each bird. Rub each quail with flour. Place in 11x9x2-inch baking dish with water and sherry. Sprinkle tarragon over top of birds. Basting frequently, bake at 350° for 45 minutes.

Carolyn W. Glass & Pat Y. Tolbert

G
A
M
E

CORNISH HENS BURGUNDY

Yield: 2 to 4 servings

2 Cornish hens
salt and pepper to taste

1 (6-ounce) box seasoned wild
and long-grain rice, cooked

Preheat oven to 400°. Salt and pepper hens and stuff with rice. Cover with foil and bake for 1 to 1½ hours. Baste often with burgundy glaze.

Glaze:

½ cup red Burgundy wine
(good quality)
½ cup currant jelly
2 tablespoons butter
1 tablespoon lemon juice

2 teaspoons cornstarch
2 teaspoons Worcestershire
sauce
½ teaspoon ground allspice
dash salt and pepper

Combine all ingredients in a saucepan. Cook until mixture thickens and bubbles. After cooking, slice hens down the back into 2 sections. Serve with remaining glaze.

Note: 2 (6-ounce) boxes of rice mix will stuff 7 hens.

Mickey C. Shuford

BAKED QUAIL WITH DRESSING

Yield: 4 to 6 servings

6 quail
all-purpose flour
½ cup sherry or white wine
1 small onion, minced
½ teaspoon salt

¼ teaspoon pepper
¼ teaspoon thyme
¼ teaspoon rosemary
½ cup margarine

Roll quail in flour and fry on all sides until browned. Combine rest of ingredients and bring to a boil. Pour over quail, cover, and bake at 350° for 45 minutes to 1 hour. Use quail juice as gravy over rice or dressing.

Dressing:

1 small onion, peeled
3 whole cloves
3 cups milk
3 cups fine bread crumbs
¾ teaspoon salt

garlic powder to taste
onion powder to taste
½ teaspoon paprika
6 tablespoons butter or
margarine, melted

Stick cloves in onion and place in a saucepan. Add milk and bring to boil. Strain and pour milk over bread crumbs; let mixture stand to absorb milk. Discard onion. Stir bread crumbs and add salt, garlic powder, onion powder, and paprika. Add additional milk to get desired thickness if necessary. Add butter and mix well. Serve on birds. Garnish with lemon slices and parsley if desired.

Note: Dressing is equally good with dove and makes an excellent stuffing for mushrooms.

Carolyn W. Glass

DUCK WITH CRANBERRY SAUCE
AND BRANDIED PEACHES

Do not prepare ahead   *Yield: 4 servings*

4 or 5 pound duck	1 (16-ounce) can peach halves,
salt and pepper	not drained
1 (7-ounce) can cranberry jelly	2 tablespoons brandy
¼ cup butter	

Preheat oven to 325⁰. Rub duck with salt and pepper, inside and out. Bake, covered, 20 minutes per pound. At the end of 30 minutes baking, remove duck from oven and pour off fat. Repeat this process 20 minutes later. *Pay particular attention to the exact cooking time!* While the duck bakes, melt cranberry jelly and butter in the top of a double boiler. Stir until blended; if necessary, remove container and place on direct heat to thoroughly blend. Pour mixture into a large skillet and keep it warm. When duck is baked, transfer to carving board and carve into thin slices, discarding skin. Place duck pieces into skillet and baste with sauce, making sure pieces are completely covered. Heat peaches in their juice, butter, and brandy. Transfer duck to hot serving platter, spoon on sauce, and arrange drained peaches around the duck.

Note: Very good flavor. Must be served immediately.

Anne F. Mitchell

⌒⬦⌒ SEAFOOD ⌒⬦⌒

BAKED BLUEFISH WITH SEAFOOD STUFFING

Yield: 4 to 6 servings

2½ pounds bluefish, dressed and split	1½ teaspoons salt
salt and pepper	⅛ teaspoon pepper
13 tablespoons butter or margarine, divided	7 tablespoons lemon juice, divided
1 small onion, chopped	1 teaspoon dried parsley
2 stalks celery, chopped	1 cup shrimp, cooked and chopped
⅓ cup mushrooms, chopped	½ cup crabmeat (optional)
1 (8-ounce) bag herb stuffing	1 tablespoon parsley

Lightly salt and pepper fish cavity. Melt 3 tablespoons butter; sauté onions and celery. In a separate saucepan, melt 1 tablespoon butter; sauté mushrooms. Combine with onions and celery; cook 2 minutes. Melt 3 tablespoons of butter and combine with stuffing, salt, pepper, 1 tablespoon lemon juice, parsley, shrimp, and crabmeat. Heat until butter is absorbed. Add onion mixture; stir well. Stuff fish, lightly salt and pepper and place on flat pan. Combine remaining butter, lemon juice, and parsley. Spoon mixture over top of the fish. Lightly salt and pepper over the butter mixture. Preheat oven to 400⁰ and bake for 30 minutes or until fish flakes.

Note: Outstanding when cooked on a charcoal grill.

Joanne M. Martin

CAUBLE'S FLOUNDER HOLLANDAISE

Yield: 2 servings

2 baby flounder or 1 large flounder	2 small summer squash
salt and pepper to taste	2 small zucchini
juice of ½ lemon	hollandaise sauce

Sprinkle flounder with salt, pepper, and lemon juice; place in a buttered baking dish. Preheat oven to 350⁰. Slice squash and zucchini into very thin, narrow strips. Place on top of fish. Cover dish and bake for 30 to 35 minutes at 350⁰. Remove from oven, uncover, and top with hollandaise sauce. Run under broiler until sauce bubbles; serve at once.

Phyllis D. Cauble

FLOUNDER IN FOIL

Yield: 6 servings

6 flounder filets
¼ cup salad oil
1 cup onion, chopped
⅓ cup green pepper, chopped
1 tablespoon all-purpose flour
½ cup clam juice
½ cup tomato juice

1 teaspoon Worcestershire
   sauce
dash Louisiana hot sauce
1 tablespoon capers
2 teaspoons garlic salt
½ teaspoon salt
1 teaspoon pepper

Heat oil in large skillet. Sauté onion and pepper until tender. Add flour and blend until smooth. Add juices, Worcestershire sauce, and hot sauce. Simmer about 5 minutes. Turn heat down; add capers, salt, and pepper. Preheat oven to 350°. Wash and dry filets; lay each on a generous square of aluminum foil. Spoon sauce over fish. Wrap foil loosely around each filet, place in baking dish and bake for 45 minutes at 350°.

Bess S. Cline

FLOUNDER COLBERT

Yield: 6 servings

6 flounder filets
½ cup butter
1 onion, chopped
½ cup all-purpose flour
½ cup tomato purée
1 pint fish stock
1 cup Burgundy wine
1 tablespoon lemon juice

1 teaspoon Worcestershire
   sauce
salt and pepper
all-purpose flour
2 eggs, beaten
1 cup milk
bread crumbs
1 cup vegetable oil

Sauté onions in butter. Blend in flour; add tomato purée, fish stock, wine, lemon juice, and Worcestershire sauce. Simmer 5 to 10 minutes. Season flounder filets with salt and pepper and roll in flour. Combine eggs and milk; dip filets in milk mixture, then roll in bread crumbs. Heat oil in large skillet; fry filets until golden brown. Serve filets on top of sauce, garnished with lemon slices. Delicious with broiled tomatoes and a green salad.

Susan L. Ingle

171

FLOUNDER CAGNEY

Yield: 2 to 4 servings

4 flounder filets
tomatoes, sliced
onions, sliced

salt and pepper to taste
parsley, chopped
¼ cup Parmesan cheese, grated

Place a layer of tomato and onion slices in a shallow baking dish. Salt and pepper filets and put them over tomatoes and onions. Top with parsley and Parmesan cheese. Bake at 400° for 20 minutes, until fish flakes easily.

Nancy F. Matheson

FLOUNDER WITH CRABMEAT SAUCE

Yield: 4 servings

2 large flounder filets
4 tablespoons butter or
  margarine
2 tablespoons all-purpose flour
1 cup milk

1 teaspoon dry mustard
1 teaspoon salt
dash of nutmeg
1 tablespoon parsley flakes
2 cups crabmeat

Melt butter and stir in flour. Remove from heat and add milk. Replace over heat and stir until thickened. Add remaining ingredients, except flounder. Broil flounder, skin side down, until it is almost done. Spread crab mixture on top and broil until hot and fish flakes.

Joanne M. Martin

SHRIMP INEZ

Yield: 4 servings

1½ pounds shrimp, shelled and
  deveined
¼ cup butter
1 clove garlic, chopped
½ teaspoon salt

1 teaspoon monosodium
  glutamate
½ cup snipped parsley
pepper to taste

Melt butter in large skillet. Add garlic, salt, and monosodium glutamate; saute until garlic is browned. Add shrimp; saute, stirring constantly, until pink. Add parsley and pepper; cook 1 minute.

Note: A lovely hors d'oeuvre, served in a chafing dish.

Dorothy Y. Menzies

172

SALMON LOAF

Yield: 6 to 8 servings

1 (15½-ounce) can salmon
1 (10¾-ounce) can cream of
celery soup
1 cup dry bread crumbs

2 eggs, beaten
½ cup onion, chopped
1 tablespoon lemon juice

Drain salmon, reserve ¼ cup liquid and add to soup. Mix salmon, soup, liquid, and all other ingredients together; pack into greased loaf pan. Bake at 375° for 1 hour; cool in pan 10 minutes. Turn out on platter and top with sauce.

Sauce:
1 (10¾-ounce) can cream of
celery soup

½ cup milk

Heat soup and milk together.

Onnie S. Golden

ISLAND SHRIMP AND NOODLES

Yield: 6 servings

1 (8-ounce) package spinach
noodles
2 to 3 pounds shrimp, peeled
and deveined
½ cup butter, clarified
1 (10¾-ounce) can cream of
mushroom soup
1 cup sour cream

1 cup mayonnaise
½ teaspoon Dijon mustard
1 tablespoon fresh or dried
chives, chopped
4 tablespoons dry sherry
½ cup sharp Cheddar cheese,
shredded

Prepare noodles according to package directions. Line a casserole with noodles and form into a nest. In a large skillet, sauté shrimp in clarified butter until pink and tender, about 5 minutes. Preheat oven to 350°. Cover noodles with shrimp. Combine soup, sour cream, mayonnaise, and mustard; add chives and sherry. Pour sauce over shrimp and top with shredded cheese. Bake for 30 minutes at 350°, until cheese is bubbly.

Camille M. Gardner

HILDA'S SEAFOOD CASSEROLE

Yield: 10 servings

1 large green pepper, chopped
  fine
1 small onion, chopped fine
1 cup celery, chopped fine
1 pound crabmeat
½ teaspoon salt
pepper to taste

1 tablespoon Worcestershire
  sauce
1 cup mayonnaise
4 hamburger buns, crumbled
1 pound shrimp, cooked and
  peeled

Preheat oven to 350°. Mix together green pepper, onion, celery, crab-meat, salt, pepper, Worcestershire sauce, and buns. Add mayonnaise and toss lightly. Put layer of mixture into a greased 9x13-inch casserole; lay shrimp on top and add balance of crab mixture. Bake for 30 minutes.

Note: This is also a good stuffing for fish.

Camille M. Gardner

SAUCY BAKED FISH

Yield: 4 servings

1 pound fish filets, fresh or
  frozen
¼ cup butter
½ cup onion, chopped
¼ cup green pepper, chopped
¼ pound fresh mushrooms,
  sliced

1 (8-ounce) can tomato sauce
2 tablespoons lemon juice
2 tablespoons vinegar
½ teaspoon thyme
⅛ teaspoon pepper

Grease a 6x12-inch baking dish. Place fish in dish. Melt butter in medium frying pan. Sauté onion, green pepper, and mushrooms until tender. Add tomato sauce, lemon juice, vinegar, thyme, and pepper. Simmer for 5 minutes. Preheat oven to 350°. Pour sauce over fish; bake 30 to 40 minutes, until fish flakes easily. Serve with rice or mashed potatoes.

Nell B. Walton

LOUISIANA STEAMED SHRIMP

Yield: 12 servings

5 pounds shrimp, in shell
1 cup salad oil
1 cup onion, chopped
1 cup green pepper, chopped

1 cup celery, chopped
½ cup green onions, chopped
½ cup parsley, chopped
3 cloves garlic, chopped

Heat oil in large, heavy pot. Add shrimp and stir until they are pink. Add chopped seasonings, cover pot and turn to medium heat. Cook 10 minutes, then add salt and pepper to taste. Cover and cook 10 minutes more. Serve with French bread. Sop up the juices on your plate with the French bread.

Beverly A. Guarino

SHRIMP NEWBURG

Yield: 10 servings

3 pounds shrimp, peeled,
   deveined and cooked
¾ cup butter or margarine
7 tablespoons all-purpose flour
4 cups milk

¾ cup catsup
2 tablespoons Worcestershire
   sauce
1 tablespoon salt
½ cup dry sherry

Melt butter and slowly add flour, stirring constantly to make a thick paste. Add milk, small amounts at a time, bringing mixture to a boil after each addition. Add catsup, Worcestershire sauce, and salt. When well blended, add shrimp and bring to a boil. Remove from heat; stir in sherry just before serving. Serve over rice, toast points, or in pastry shells. Lobster may be used instead of shrimp.

Roddy S. Dixon

HERB SEAFOOD CASSEROLE

Yield: 6 servings

1 pound raw shrimp, shelled
and cleaned
1 tablespoon chicken seasoned
stock base
1 cup boiling water
1 cup raw rice
1/4 cup butter or margarine
1 tablespoon arrowroot
1 1/2 cups milk

1/2 teaspoon dill weed, crushed
1 tablespoon shallot wine
vinegar
1 teaspoon Beau Monde
seasoning
1/2 teaspoon salt
pepper to taste
1 1/2 cups extra sharp Cheddar
cheese. shredded

Preheat oven to 350°. Combine all the ingredients in a 1 1/2-quart casserole. Bake for 30 minutes.

Anne M. Boyer

CREVETTE EN COQUILLE

Must prepare ahead

Yield: 4 to 6 servings

2 pounds shrimp, in shells
1 cup olive or corn oil
2 cloves garlic, minced
4 teaspoons dried rosemary,
lightly crushed

2 teaspoons dried oregano
2 large bay leaves, crumbled
3/4 teaspoon salt
1/8 teaspoon pepper
1 cup dry white wine

Combine unpeeled shrimp, oil, garlic, rosemary, oregano, and bay leaves in a bowl. Let stand at room temperature 2 hours. Turn mixture into a large skillet; sprinkle with salt and pepper. Cook over low heat, covered, about 20 minutes, stirring occasionally. Add wine; simmer uncovered 5 minutes. Transfer shrimp with slotted spoon to serving dish. Peel, eat, and enjoy.

Susanne M. Gunter

SHRIMP SCAMPI

Yield: 3 servings

1 pound shrimp in the shell
2 teaspoons garlic salt

juice of 1 lemon
2 tablespoons butter

Peel and devein shrimp. Place in shallow pan; sprinkle with garlic salt and lemon juice. Dot with butter. Broil on one side for 3 minutes; turn and broil 3 minutes more. Serve with grits and a big green salad.

Helen S. Moretz

TROUT BELIN

Yield: 4 servings

Stuffing:
¾ pound fresh or 1 (10-ounce)   4 shallots, finely chopped
   package frozen spinach   3 tablespoons butter
1 tablespoon chopped parsley   2 cups (½ pound) mushrooms,
1 teaspoon mixed herbs (chervil,   finely chopped
   tarragon, chives)   salt and pepper

Wash, drain, stem, and blanch fresh spinach in boiling water for 1 minute; drain. Defrost and drain frozen spinach. Chop spinach and mix with parsley and herbs. In a skillet, sauté shallots in butter until soft; add mushrooms, spinach, and seasonings. Cover the pan and cook gently 5 to 6 minutes. Cool.

4 fresh trout   3 tablespoons butter
¼ cup all-purpose flour,
   seasoned with ¼ teaspoon
   salt, pinch of pepper

Bone raw trout; fill with stuffing and reshape. Coat fish carefully in seasoned flour. In a skillet, melt 3 tablespoons butter and sauté trout over medium heat for 4 to 5 minutes on each side, or until fish is golden brown and flakes easily. Season lightly with salt and pepper and keep warm on serving platter.

Garnish:
1 tablespoon butter   2 teaspoons sugar
1 large orange, sliced

Wipe out skillet; melt butter and add orange slices. Sprinkle slices with half the sugar; turn and sauté briskly until browned. Sprinkle with remaining sugar, turn, brown other side and place 1 or 2 slices on each trout, or overlap slices around serving platter.

Sauce:
3 tablespoons butter   1 tablespoon parsley,
juice of 1 lemon   chopped
juice of 1 orange

Wipe out skillet; add butter and cook to a nut brown. Add juices and parsley all at once and pour over fish while still foaming. Garnish dish with watercress or other lettuce and serve.

Anne F. Mitchell

FISH AND CHIPS

Yield: 2 to 3 servings

1 pound fish filets
1 egg, beaten
⅓ cup milk
1 teaspoon salt
½ teaspoon pepper
¼ cup all-purpose flour

1 cup herb stuffing crumbs,
   crushed fine
potatoes, peeled and sliced
   for French fries
oil for frying

Pat filets dry, cut into thin strips. Combine egg, milk, salt, pepper, and flour. Dip filets in egg mixture; roll in crumbs. Fry fish and potatoes together in deep fat fryer or large skillet.

Susan L. Ingle

TANGY BAKED FISH FILETS

Yield: 4 servings

1 egg white
¼ cup mayonnaise
1 tablespoon spicy mustard

¼ teaspoon salt
freshly ground pepper to taste
4 fresh fish filets

Beat egg white until stiff. Fold in remaining ingredients except fish. Preheat oven to 400°. Place fish in a lightly greased shallow baking dish. Spread with meringue mixture. Bake 20 minutes, until puffed and golden brown.

Shirley L. Ballew

BEER BATTER SHRIMP

Yield: 4 servings

3 pounds shrimp
2¼ cups all-purpose flour
2 teaspoons paprika
2 cups beer
¼ teaspoon Louisiana hot sauce

½ teaspoon Worcestershire
   sauce
all-purpose flour
salt and pepper
fat for frying

Peel, split, and clean shrimp, leaving tails intact. Combine 2¼ cups flour and paprika. Add beer and mix well. Blend in sauces. Roll shrimp in some extra flour mixed with plenty of salt and pepper. Dip in batter and fry in deep fat heated to 375° for 2 or 3 minutes or until golden brown. Drain on paper towels.

Stevi S. Dozier

SHRIMP ORIENTAL

Yield: 4 servings

2 (4-ounce) cans sliced
  mushrooms
2 medium onions, sliced
1 tablespoon salad oil
1½ pounds shrimp, shelled
  and deveined
2 cups celery, sliced
1 (5-ounce) can water chestnuts,
  drained and sliced

1 green pepper, sliced
1½ teaspoons salt
⅛ teaspoon pepper
1 (14½-ounce) can beef bouillon
4 tablespoons soy sauce
2 to 3 tablespoons cornstarch

Sauté mushrooms and onions in salad oil for 5 minutes. Add shrimp, celery, water chestnuts, green pepper, salt, pepper, bouillon, and soy sauce; bring to a boil. Reduce heat immediately and simmer for 12 minutes, until vegetables are crisp but tender. Add cornstarch to a little water and combine with shrimp mixture for thickening. Serve over rice.

Carole J. Cumming

BAKED SHRIMP WITH FETA CHEESE

Yield: 4 servings

12 fresh raw jumbo shrimp,
  shelled and deveined
2 tablespoons butter
1 egg
¼ cup heavy cream
¼ cup feta cheese, crumbled

Louisiana hot sauce to taste
1 large tomato, peeled and
  sliced
juice of ½ lemon
1 tablespoon parsley, chopped
black pepper, freshly ground

Preheat oven to 400°. Cook shrimp in butter until both sides are pink. Transfer shrimp with a slotted spoon to a baking dish. Combine egg and cream; beat with a fork until well blended. Add cheese and continue mixing. Add hot sauce to taste; pour mixture over shrimp. Arrange tomato slices on top and bake until cheese mixture starts to bubble, about 10 minutes. Squeeze lemon juice on top, sprinkle with parsley and pepper.

Carolyn H. Walker

SHRIMP CREOLE I

Yield: 10 to 12 servings

4 pounds shrimp, shelled and
    deveined
¾ cup salad oil
3 heaping tablespoons all-
    purpose flour
1 bunch shallots or 1 large
    onion, chopped

½ small bulb garlic, sliced
1 teaspoon salt
½ teaspoon pepper
1 (12-ounce) can tomato paste
4 green peppers, sliced
4 cups stock from shrimp

Make roux with salad oil and flour; brown. Add onions and garlic; brown slightly. Add shrimp, salt, and pepper; stir until each shrimp is coated and does not stick to pan. Add tomato paste and sliced peppers; stir for 15 minutes over low heat. Add 1 cup of hot stock but do not stir. Turn heat to simmer. After 15 minutes, stir carefully with a fork. Don't let stock wash off the roux. Make a well at side of pan; carefully add rest of stock and simmer 1 hour.

Note: This takes time to prepare, but is well worth the effort.

Beverly A. Guarino & Anne F. Mitchell

SHRIMP CREOLE II

Yield: 6 servings

2 to 3 cups cleaned shrimp
5 slices bacon
½ cup onion, chopped
½ cup green pepper, chopped
¼ cup celery, chopped
2 cups tomatoes
½ cup chili sauce

1 teaspoon Worcestershire
    sauce
4 or more shakes Louisiana
    hot sauce
¼ teaspoon black pepper
1 teaspoon salt

Fry bacon; remove from pan. Sauté onion, green pepper, and celery in bacon fat. Add tomatoes, chili sauce, Worcestershire sauce, hot sauce, pepper, and salt. Cook slowly until thickened, stirring occasionally. If necessary, thicken mixture with 1 or 2 tablespoons all-purpose flour. Add shrimp about 30 minutes before serving. Simmer, stirring occasionally. Add crumbled bacon just before serving. Serve over hot rice.

Nancy C. Shuford

CRAB À LA QUEEN

Yield: 4 servings

1 (6½-ounce) package frozen
  crabmeat
1 (10¾-ounce) can cream of
  celery soup
1 (4½-ounce) can sliced
  mushrooms, drained

½ cup milk
1 tablespoon lemon juice
2 tablespoons dry sherry
4 tablespoons Parmesan cheese,
  grated

Combine soup, mushrooms, and milk. Bring to a boil, stirring constantly. Add crabmeat, lemon juice, and sherry. Place in a 1-quart casserole or individual baking dishes, top with cheese, and bake at 400° for 10 minutes. May be served over toast points or rice.

Note: Low in calories—163 per serving.

Shirley L. Ballew

SPINACH-CRAB CASSEROLE

Yield: 4 servings

1 (6½-ounce) can crabmeat
1 tablespoon lemon juice
1½ cups sharp cheese,
  shredded and divided
1 small onion, minced
1 (6-ounce) can tomato paste
1 cup sour cream

½ teaspoon salt
dash pepper
dash nutmeg
1 tablespoon dry sherry
1 (10-ounce) package frozen
  spinach, cooked and
  drained

Add lemon juice to crabmeat. Mix 1 cup cheese with onion, tomato paste, sour cream, seasonings, and sherry; pour over crabmeat. Add spinach, mix well, and turn into baking dish. Top with remaining cheese and bake at 350° for about 30 minutes, until hot and bubbly.

Winnie B. Hovey

OYSTERS HERMAN

Yield: 2 to 3 servings

1 pint oysters
salt and pepper
all-purpose flour
10 tablespoons butter, divided
¼ cup lemon juice

1 cup steak sauce
2 teaspoons Worcestershire
  sauce
½ cup sherry
2 tablespoons all-purpose flour

Salt and pepper oysters; dredge in flour. Fry oysters in 4 tablespoons butter on griddle or in a skillet. Add 4 tablespoons butter and continue cooking until brown and crisp. Set aside. Heat 2 tablespoons butter with lemon juice, steak sauce, Worcestershire sauce, and sherry; thicken mixture with 2 tablespoons flour to make a sauce. Place oysters on platter and cover with sauce; serve over rice or toast points.

Martha T. Kurad

MARINATED SHRIMP

Must prepare ahead   *Yield: 4 servings*

26 fresh mushrooms (or one
  8-ounce can)
1 green pepper, cut into large
  pieces
1 sweet onion, cut into wedges
1 pound shrimp, cooked and
  cleaned

½ cup cider vinegar
2 tablespoons lemon juice
1 teaspoon salt
1 teaspoon pepper
½ teaspoon garlic salt (optional)

Combine mushrooms, green pepper, onion, and shrimp. In small bowl, combine remaining ingredients. Pour over vegetable and shrimp mixture. Cover and marinate overnight in refrigerator.

Note: Easy, delicious and low calorie!

Kay J. Webber

OYSTERS TERRAPIN

Yield: 8 servings

1 pint oysters, drained
10 tablespoons butter, divided
2 small onions, chopped
1 pound mushrooms, sliced

2 tablespoons butter
2 tablespoons all-purpose flour
1 cup milk
toast points

Drain oysters. Sauté onions in 8 tablespoons butter; add mushrooms and cook 15 minutes. Combine with raw oysters and white sauce made with butter, flour, and milk. Serve on toast points for a delightful first course.

Peggy B. Shuford

QUICK OYSTERS ROCKEFELLER

Yield: 4 servings

16 large oysters with shells
rock salt
1 (10-ounce) package frozen
    spinach, cooked and drained
Worcestershire sauce,
    salt and pepper

butter
1 small onion, minced
parsley, minced
16 teaspoons bread crumbs

Preheat oven to 450°. Place oysters in shells on bed of rock salt in shallow pan. Mix cooked, drained spinach with Worcestershire sauce, salt, and pepper to taste. Spread spinach on oysters; dot each with butter, onion, parsley, and 1 teaspoon bread crumbs. Bake at 450° for 10 to 12 minutes.

Sally T. Blackwelder

TUNA PATTIES

Yield: 6 servings

1 (12 or 13-ounce) can tuna,
    well drained
1 cup bread crumbs
1 egg, slightly beaten
3/4 cup mayonnaise
1/2 cup onion, finely chopped

1/2 cup green pepper, finely
    chopped
1/2 cup celery, finely chopped
1 tablespoon Worcestershire
    sauce
1/4 cup corn oil

Mix tuna, bread crumbs, egg, mayonnaise, onion, pepper, celery, and Worcestershire sauce in a bowl. Heat oil over medium heat in a large skillet. Make tuna mixture into 6 patties and cook, turning once, about 4 minutes to a side, or until browned. Serve on hamburger buns with tartar sauce, or melt cheese on top for a tuna cheeseburger.

Ruth L. Hord

183

DEVILED CRAB

Yield: 5 servings

3 (7-ounce) cans crabmeat
1 teaspoon onion, grated fine
3 teaspoons butter
2 egg yolks beaten in 1 cup
    of water
1 teaspoon Worcestershire
    sauce
1 teaspoon parsley, chopped

1 teaspoon lemon juice
1 teaspoon dry mustard
⅛ teaspoon red pepper
⅛ teaspoon black pepper
½ teaspoon salt
½ teaspoon sugar
2 eggs, hard boiled and chopped
½ cup bread crumbs, divided

Sauté onion in butter; add crabmeat and egg yolks beaten with water. Simmer for about 10 minutes. Add Worcestershire sauce, parsley, lemon juice, and seasonings. Remove from heat; add ⅓ cup bread crumbs and eggs. Toss lightly and fill 10 greased shells or 5 individual casseroles. Sprinkle reserved bread crumbs on top; dot with butter. Bake at 350⁰ for 20 to 30 minutes.

Susan L. Ingle

OYSTER EGGPLANT CASSEROLE

Yield: 2 servings

1 pint oysters
¼ cup butter
½ cup onion, chopped
¼ cup green pepper, chopped
2 cloves garlic, chopped
1 large eggplant
½ cup parsley, chopped
1 cup canned tomatoes

2 bay leaves
1 teaspoon salt
½ teaspoon pepper
½ teaspoon thyme
⅔ cup oyster liquor
3 tablespoons butter
¾ cup bread crumbs
¼ cup sharp cheese, shredded

Drain oysters; reserve ⅔ cup oyster liquor. Cook onion, pepper, and garlic until tender in ¼ cup butter. Wash and cut eggplant in half. Scoop out pulp leaving ¼ inch thickness around shell. Turn shells upside down in cold water. Chop pulp. Add pulp and rest of ingredients to onion mixture. Cover and simmer 10 minutes. Preheat oven to 400⁰. Remove bay leaves from stuffing mixture; fill shells and bake at 400⁰ for 35 minutes.

Anne W. Jackson

LOBSTER HILLYER

Freezes well   *Yield: 12 to 16 servings*

9 lobster tails
¾ cup butter, melted
¾ cup all-purpose flour
3 pints light cream
1 tablespoon salt
2 tablespoons dill weed
¼ teaspoon pepper

2 tablespoons lemon juice
1½ cups ripe olives, pitted and
  sliced
¾ cup slivered almonds,
  toasted
½ cup dry white wine

Place the lobster tails in large pot of boiling water and cover. Cook until tender, about 20 minutes; drain. Cut each tail in half lengthwise and dice lobster meat. In a saucepan blend butter and flour. Season with salt, dill weed, and pepper. Add cream gradually to mixture, stirring constantly over low heat until thickened. Add lemon juice, olives, and lobster meat to sauce. At this point, lobster may be packed for freezing. To finish preparation, add almonds and wine. Heat and serve hot, over rice or toast points.

June P. Walter

COQUILLES ST. JACQUES

Yield: 4 to 6 servings

1 pound scallops
1 cup dry white wine
6 tablespoons butter
1 clove garlic, finely chopped
1 medium onion, finely chopped

½ pound mushrooms, sliced
3 tablespoons all-purpose flour
1½ cups light cream
salt and white pepper to taste
parsley, freshly chopped

Rinse scallops to remove any bits of sand or shell; dry. Add to large skillet with wine. Simmer 3 to 4 minutes, depending on size. Remove scallops and liquid from skillet; drain and reserve liquid. Melt butter in skillet; sauté garlic, onions, and mushrooms until tender. Sprinkle flour over mushroom mixture, stirring until flour is absorbed; slowly add cream, stirring constantly until thickened. Add salt, pepper, and 1 cup of reserved liquid, stirring until thickened. Add scallops and heat through. Sprinkle with fresh parsley; serve in patty shells, over toast points, or with rice.

Helen S. Moretz

SCALLOPS SAUTÉED WITH HERBS AND VEGETABLES

Yield: 6 servings

¼ cup each julienne strips of
    onions, carrots and celery
¼ cup sliced mushrooms
2 tablespoons butter
½ cup dry white wine
2 pounds bay or sea scallops
    (4 cups)
¼ cup butter
1 teaspoon spinach, finely
    chopped
1 teaspoon parsley, finely
    chopped

1 teaspoon each basil and
    tarragon leaves, finely
    chopped
1 large clove garlic, crushed
¼ teaspoon salt
⅛ teaspoon pepper
1 teaspoon all-purpose flour
1 tablespoon soft butter
6 puff pastry shells
parsley for garnish (optional)

Stir-fry julienne vegetables and mushrooms in a large frying pan in 2 tablespoons butter for 1 minute; add wine and simmer for 3 minutes. Remove mixture from pan and keep warm. Pat scallops dry. Cut sea scallops in thirds. Melt ¼ cup butter in frying pan over medium heat; add scallops. Cook and stir until scallops are almost done, about 3 minutes. Add vegetables, herbs, and seasonings. In a small bowl, blend flour and soft butter. Push scallops and vegetables to the side of pan; whisk in butter and flour. Cook and stir until slightly thickened. Spoon into puff pastry shells and sprinkle with additional parsley, if desired.

Shirley L. Ballew

PERFECT ESCALLOPED OYSTERS

Yield: 6 servings

1 pint oysters (reserve liquor)
2 cups cracker crumbs, medium
    coarse
½ cup butter, melted
½ teaspoon salt

dash pepper
¾ cup light cream
¼ cup oyster liquor
¼ teaspoon Worcestershire
    sauce

Drain oysters, saving ¼ cup liquor. Combine crumbs, butter, salt, and pepper. Spread half of crumb mixture in bottom of an 8-inch greased pan. Cover with oysters. Combine cream, oyster liquor, and Worcestershire sauce; pour over the oysters. Top with reserved crumb mixture. Bake at 350° for 40 minutes.

Winnie B. Hovey

STIR-FRIED SCALLOPS WITH MIXED VEGETABLES

Yield: 6 servings

1 pound scallops
½ cup bamboo shoots, thinly sliced
½ cup celery, thinly sliced
½ cup onions, thinly sliced
6 snow peas, stems removed
1 tablespoon cornstarch

2 teaspoons soy sauce
¼ cup cold water
3 tablespoons salad oil
½ teaspoon salt
½ cup chicken stock
½ teaspoon sugar

Quarter scallops, if large. Slice vegetables and set aside. Blend cornstarch, soy sauce, and cold water to a paste. Heat oil in wok or large frying pan. Add salt, then scallops, and stir-fry to coat with oil, about ½ minute. Add vegetables and stir-fry 2 minutes more. Add stock and sugar and heat quickly. Then cook, stirring constantly, over medium heat until vegetables are done (2 to 3 minutes.) Stir in cornstarch paste to thicken. Serve at once.

Note: Other vegetables may be substituted, such as tomatoes, parboiled green beans, parboiled carrots, water chestnuts, or green pepper rings.

Anne F. Mitchell

OYSTER CASSEROLE

Yield: 6 to 8 servings

1 quart oysters, drained
½ cup oyster liquor
½ cup butter
2 tablespoons all-purpose flour
1 teaspoon salt
½ teaspoon pepper
2 tablespoons green pepper, chopped

1 clove garlic, pressed
2 tablespoons onion, chopped
1 teaspoon Worcestershire sauce
1¼ cups cracker crumbs

Warm oysters in liquor over low heat. Melt butter; blend in flour, then add remaining ingredients, reserving ¼ cup of crumbs for topping. Combine mixture with oysters. Preheat oven to 375⁰. Grease an 11¾x7½x1¾-inch baking dish and place mixture in it. Top with reserved cracker crumbs and bake for 25 to 30 minutes.

Polly D. Walker

~ CRÊPES ~

STUFFED CRÊPES

Freezes well   *Yield: 24 crêpes*

Basic crêpes, page 90.
Filling:

½ cup butter or margarine
½ cup minced green onion
2 pounds (4 cups) cooked
   chicken or ham, cubed; or
   crabmeat, flaked

salt and pepper to taste
dash garlic powder (optional)
½ cup Vermouth

In a large skillet, melt butter. Add onion and chicken, tossing lightly. Cook a few minutes and add salt, pepper, and garlic powder. Stir in Vermouth and boil rapidly until liquid is almost evaporated. Scrape mixture into a bowl and set aside. Reserve skillet for preparing sauce.

Sauce:

⅔ cup Vermouth
¼ cup cornstarch
¼ cup milk
4 cups heavy cream

salt and white pepper to
   taste
2½ cups Swiss cheese,
   shredded and divided

Add Vermouth to skillet and boil rapidly until liquid is reduced to 2 tablespoons. Remove from heat. Combine cornstarch and milk, and add to Vermouth. Return skillet to low heat and slowly add cream; season with salt and pepper and cook until slightly thickened. Stir in 1½ cups cheese. Cook until melted and well blended.

Assemble:
butter

Preheat oven to 400°. Blend ½ sauce with filling mixture. Add seasonings if needed. Place a large spoonful onto each crêpe and roll. Place seam-side down into two 13x9x2-inch baking dishes. Spoon remaining sauce over crêpes and sprinkle with remaining cheese. Dot with butter. Bake 20 minutes, or until hot and bubbly.

Note: If crêpes are made ahead and refrigerated, remove from refrigerator 30 minutes before baking. Thaw frozen crêpes before baking.

Becky D. Burgess

CHICKEN OR TURKEY CRÊPE FILLING

Freezes well   *Yield: 12 servings*

5 tablespoons butter
5 tablespoons all-purpose flour
1/2 teaspoon salt
1/8 teaspoon pepper
1 cup cream
1 cup chicken broth
1/2 teaspoon Worcestershire
   sauce

2 tablespoons parsley, chopped
1 1/2 cups Swiss cheese,
   shredded and divided
3/4 cup white wine
2 cups chicken or turkey,
   chopped
1/2 cup olives, chopped

Melt butter. Blend in flour, salt, and pepper. Add cream, broth, and Worcestershire sauce. Cook until thickened, stirring constantly. Add parsley, 1 cup cheese, and wine, blending well. Transfer 1 cup sauce to a bowl. Add chicken and olives. Keep remaining sauce warm. Place 1 to 2 tablespoons of chicken mixture on each crêpe. Roll crêpes and place in a shallow baking dish. Pour remaining sauce over crêpes; sprinkle remaining cheese on top. Bake at 350° for 15 minutes.

Note: If freezing crêpes, add cheese topping just before baking.

Carolyn W. Lyerly

CHEDDAR SHRIMP CRÊPES

Yield: 6 servings

6 basic crêpes, page 90.

1 tablespoon butter
1/2 cup green onions with tops,
   sliced
1 cup mushrooms, sliced
1/4 cup butter
1/3 cup all-purpose flour

1/2 teaspoon salt
1/8 teaspoon white pepper
2 cups milk
1 cup Cheddar cheese, shredded
2 (6-ounce) packages frozen
   small shrimp, defrosted

In a skillet, melt 1 tablespoon butter on medium heat. Sauté onions and mushrooms. Add 1/4 cup butter, flour, salt, and pepper. Gradually stir in milk. Cook and stir until thickened. Add shredded cheese to skillet. Cook and stir over low heat until thickened. Mix 1 cup of sauce with shrimp. Fill each crêpe with 1/3 cup shrimp mixture, folding 2 sides over filling. Place crêpes, seam side down, in a buttered baking pan. Bake at 325° about 25 minutes. Serve topped with remaining sauce.

Carol H. Tuttle

189

SAUSAGE CRÊPE FILLING AND SAUCE

Freezes well   *Yield: 16 crêpes*

Basic crêpe recipe, page 90.

1 pound bulk sausage
¼ cup chopped onion
½ cup processed cheese,
    shredded

1 (3-ounce) package cream
    cheese
¼ teaspoon marjoram

Brown sausage; add onion and cook until tender. Drain. Add cheese, cream cheese, and marjoram, stirring until blended. Place 2 tablespoons filling down center of each crêpe; roll. Place seam-side down into a 11¾x7½-inch baking dish. Cover and chill. Preheat oven to 375⁰. Bake, covered, for 40 minutes.

Sauce:
½ cup sour cream
¼ cup butter or margarine,
    softened

Combine and spoon over crêpes. Continue baking for 5 minutes.

Note: Do not freeze crêpes with sauce.

Becky D. Burgess

SIDE DISHES

SIDE DISHES

192   ( ) Denotes: (HE) Hickory Entertains   (I) International   (M) Microwave Recipes

 # FRUITS

GOLDEN APPLES

Yield: 10 to 12 servings

1 cup sugar
2 cups water
8 firm apples, pared and halved
grated rind of 1 lemon

grated rind of 1 orange
juice of 1 lemon
juice of 1 orange

Boil sugar and water in wide pan or skillet until they spin a thread. Place apples in syrup. Add grated rinds. Cook at very low temperature until tender, turning carefully with a wooden spoon. Add lemon juice and orange juice. Cook until transparent. Place in a 2-quart glass serving dish. They will jell slightly and be golden. Good with pork or ham.

Note: Mrs. Menzies says this has been a family favorite for 40 years, yet no one will make it but her. She thinks the apples are worth every minute of trouble.

Dorothy Y. Menzies

RHUBARB AMBROSIA

Yield: 6 to 8 servings

5 cups rhubarb, cut into ½-inch
   pieces
1¾ cups sugar
1 tablespoon all-purpose flour
¼ teaspoon salt
1½ teaspoons grated orange
   rind

1 orange, sectioned, peeled
   and cubed
4 cups bread cubes
½ cup butter or margarine,
   melted
½ cup coconut, shredded or
   flaked

Preheat oven to 375°. Grease an 8x8x2-inch pan. Mix rhubarb, sugar, flour, salt, ¾ teaspoon orange rind, and orange. Add 2 cups bread cubes and ¼ cup melted butter. Mix well and put in pan. Combine remaining bread cubes, butter, orange rind, and coconut. Sprinkle over rhubarb mixture. Bake for 40 minutes or until browned. Serve warm.

Helen S. Joyce

BAKED FRUIT IN WINE

Yield: 4 servings

3 medium cooking apples
1 medium cooking pear
1 large lemon (½ thinly sliced
  and seeded, and the juice
  of the other half)
¾ cup fruity red wine

⅔ cup super fine sugar
½ stick cinnamon, broken in
  half
5 whole cloves
⅛ teaspoon salt
2 tablespoons butter

Preheat oven to 350°. Pare the apples and pear and cut into thick slices. Arrange in a single layer in a baking dish. Sprinkle with the juice of the unsliced lemon. Combine the wine, sugar, cinnamon, cloves, salt, and lemon slices. Heat, but do not boil, and stir until the sugar is dissolved. Pour this combination over the apples and pear, evenly spacing the lemon slices. Dot the top with butter. Bake covered until tender, about 40 to 50 minutes.

Note: This recipe can be doubled to serve eight persons or quadrupled to serve sixteen.

Josephine L. Hambrick

BAKED ORANGES

Yield: 12 servings

6 medium sized oranges
6 medium sized cooking apples
1 (16-ounce) can crushed
  pineapple

1½ cups sugar
3 tablespoons butter, melted
½ cup chopped nuts

Cut oranges in half. With a sharp knife, cut out pulp, leaving thin rind. Peel, core, and chop apples. Combine oranges, apples, pineapple, and sugar. Cook in large saucepan for several hours until *very* thick. Put mixture in orange cups and top with butter and nuts. Place in shallow pan with enough water to keep bottom of oranges from burning. Bake in preheated 325° oven for 30 minutes.

Note: Marvelous for Christmas or buffet.

Bess G. Geitner

RAW APPLESAUCE

Yield: 8 servings

4 medium sized apples   2 tablespoons lemon juice
¹/₂ cup honey

Wash and core apples. Do *not* peel. Cut up apples and add honey and lemon juice. Put in a blender or food processor. Process until well blended.

Note: Sweeter apples may need less honey. This is a "good for you" recipe, since no nutrients are lost through cooking.

Anne L. Moss

HONEY GRAPES

Yield: 6 servings

1¹/₂ pounds seedless grapes   3 tablespoons Cointreau
1 cup sour cream   3 teaspoons lemon juice
4 tablespoons honey   brown sugar

Wash grapes and let dry thoroughly. Mix sour cream, honey, Cointreau, and lemon juice well. Cover grapes thoroughly with above mixture. Sprinkle with brown sugar and chill in freezer for 15 to 30 minutes, or put in individual dessert dishes, sprinkle with brown sugar and chill in freezer.

Josephine L. Hambrick

PINEAPPLE SOUFFLÉ

Yield: 4 to 6 servings

¹/₂ cup sugar   2 eggs, beaten
¹/₂ cup butter, melted   4 slices bread, broken into
1 (10¹/₂-ounce) can crushed   pieces
    pineapple

Preheat oven to 350°. Combine all ingredients and pour into a 1¹/₂-quart casserole dish. Bake for 30 minutes.

Margaret F. Tallant

195

CRANBERRIES AMARETTO

Stores well   *Yield: 4 cups*

¹/₄ cup butter
1 pound fresh cranberries
2 cups sugar
juice of one lemon

grated peel of one lemon
3¹/₂ tablespoons orange
   marmalade
¹/₃ cup Amaretto liqueur

Spray inside of 2-quart saucepan with non-stick coating. Melt butter in pan and add cranberries, sugar, and lemon juice. Cook until berries are tender. Remove from heat. Add lemon peel, marmalade, and liqueur. Stir well.

Note: Serve with hot or cold pork or poultry. Serve as salad on lettuce with sour cream garnish. Great over vanilla ice cream. Will keep in refrigerator for several months.

Katty D. Lefler

 **PASTA**

BACON-NOODLE SKILLET

Yield: 6 servings

1 pound bacon
¹/₃ cup chopped green pepper
¹/₃ cup chopped onion
1 clove garlic, minced
1 teaspoon salt
¹/₂ teaspoon marjoram
¹/₂ teaspoon thyme

¹/₈ teaspoon pepper
1 (20-ounce) can stewed
   tomatoes
¹/₃ cup catsup
6-ounces raw wide egg noodles
1 cup longhorn cheese,
   shredded

Fry bacon to desired crispness; drain and crumble. Pour off drippings, reserving 2 tablespoons in skillet. Sauté green pepper, onion, and garlic in drippings. Add seasonings; cook for 5 minutes. Add tomatoes and catsup and bring to boil. Add noodles, cover, and simmer for 20 minutes. Stir in ¹/₂ bacon, top mixture with cheese, and add remaining bacon on top. Cover and heat for 5 minutes.

Lindy M. Dillow

FETTUCCINE VERDE

Yield: 6 servings

4 cups raw spinach
1 cup parsley
³/₄ cup Parmesan cheese, grated
¹/₂ cup walnuts
¹/₂ cup olive oil

1 clove garlic
¹/₂ teaspoon salt
¹/₄ teaspoon pepper
1 pound fresh spinach fettuccine

In the bowl of a processor or blender combine all ingredients except fettuccine. Process or blend until smooth. Cook fettuccine *al dente* about 5 minutes; drain well. Toss fettuccini with sauce in large serving dish until it is well coated. Garnish with additional cheese, if desired.

Note: Easy and truly delicious.

Dorothy Y. Menzies

FETTUCCINE WITH MUSHROOMS AND ZUCCHINI

Yield: 6 servings

¹/₂ pound mushrooms, thinly
   sliced
¹/₄ cup butter
1¹/₄ pounds zucchini
1 cup heavy cream
¹/₂ cup butter

2 tablespoons salt
1 tablespoon olive oil
1 pound fettuccine
³/₄ cup Parmesan cheese, freshly
   grated
¹/₂ cup chopped parsley

Melt butter in deep skillet and sauté mushrooms for 2 minutes. Add zucchini, cream and remaining butter. Boil and simmer for 3 minutes. In a large pot, boil 7 quarts water. Add salt, olive oil, and fettuccine. Boil 7 minutes and drain. Add fettuccine, Parmesan cheese, and parsley to ingredients in skillet. Toss gently and transfer to serving platter. Serve with extra Parmesan cheese.

Note: A wonderful luncheon dish, Sunday night supper, or as the second course in an Italian dinner.

Anne F. Mitchell

197

FETTUCCINE WITH CHEESE

Yield: 6 servings

1 pound fettuccine noodles	1 cup Gruyere cheese, shredded
1 cup butter, melted	¾ cup heavy cream
1 cup Parmesan cheese, freshly grated	freshly ground pepper

Cook pasta *al dente* in boiling salted water, then drain. Place hot, drained pasta in a heat-proof casserole over low heat. Add butter, cheeses, and cream, tossing after each addition. Sprinkle with pepper and serve.

Note: Better than potatoes with beef.

Judy B. Smith

LASAGNA

Yield: 10 to 12 servings

1 pound ground beef	1 (15-ounce) can tomato sauce
½ pound sausage	1 (28-ounce) can tomatoes
1 onion, chopped	1 tablespoon salad oil
2 garlic cloves, minced	1 (24-ounce) carton cottage
1 cup Burgundy wine	cheese
1 teaspoon oregano leaves	2 (6-ounce) packages mozzarella
1 teaspoon basil	cheese
1 teaspoon sugar	1 (1½-ounce) can Parmesan
1 teaspoon salt	cheese
1 (12-ounce) can tomato paste	1 pound box lasagna noodles

Brown beef, sausage, onion, and garlic in Dutch oven. Add wine, spices, tomato paste, tomato sauce, tomatoes, and salad oil. Cook slowly for 30 minutes. Cook noodles according to package directions; drain. Line 13x10x2-inch lasagna pan with noodles, layer meat sauce and cheeses; repeat. Bake uncovered at 300° for 30 minutes or until bubbly.

Note: For smaller amount: use ½ pound noodles, (6-ounces) tomato paste, (8-ounces) tomato sauce, and (16-ounces) tomatoes. To increase recipe, use an extra ½ pound ground beef and extra cheese. Bake in 2 pans. Buy 12-ounces of mozzarella cheese in a ball and shred in food processor. If beef is not lean, do not add salad oil.

Frances R. Hilton

MY VEGETABLE LASAGNA

Yield: 8 to 10 servings

1 (8-ounce) box lasagna noodles
   cooked

Sauce:

4 tablespoons olive oil, divided	1½ teaspoon salt
1 large onion, chopped	½ teaspoon pepper
1 large green pepper, chopped	½ teaspoon oregano
3 carrots, chopped	¼ teaspoon basil
4 cloves garlic, chopped	⅛ teaspoon rosemary
½ pound eggplant, peeled and diced	1 bay leaf
	hot pepper sauce to taste
1 egg beaten	1 cup red wine
¾ pound mushrooms, sliced	1 pound ricotta cheese
1 quart canned tomatoes, chopped	2 cups cooked spinach, drained
	¾ pound mozzarella cheese, sliced
½ cup parsley, minced (or ¼ cup dried)	1 cup Parmesan cheese, grated

In 3 tablespoons olive oil, sauté onion, green pepper, carrots, and garlic until soft. Toss eggplant with egg. Add mushrooms and eggplant to oil and simmer 5 minutes. Add remaining oil if needed. Combine tomatoes, parsley, salt, pepper, spices, and herbs with vegetable mixture. Add several dashes of hot pepper sauce and wine. Simmer, uncovered, for 1 hour, stirring frequently. Remove bay leaf. Preheat oven to 350°. Spoon ⅓ of tomato sauce in the bottom of a greased 13x9x2-inch pan. Cover with ½ noodles, followed by ⅓ sauce, all of the ricotta, all of the spinach, ½ mozzarella and ½ Parmesan. Layer remaining ingredients as follows: noodles, sauce, mozzarella and Parmesan. Bake for 40 to 50 minutes, or until light brown and bubbly. Let stand a few minutes before cutting.

Note: Well worth the preparation time. A really different entrée.

Anne F. Mitchell

199

RAVIOLI AL RICOTTA

May prepare ahead   *Yield: Approximately 6 servings*

Filling:

⅛ cup finely chopped onions,   ½ cup mozzarella cheese,
   sautéed in 1 tablespoon   grated
   butter   freshly ground nutmeg
1 egg, slightly beaten   salt to taste
1 pound ricotta cheese
½ cup Parmesan cheese,
   freshly grated

Mix together the onions, egg, cheeses, nutmeg and salt; then refrigerate until ready for use.

Dough:

4 cups unbleached flour   4 teaspoons olive oil
4 eggs   ½ teaspoon salt

Place flour on work surface, making a well in the center. Add remaining ingredients in the well. Begin to mix with a fork, gradually incorporating all the flour. Knead for 10 minutes until smooth and elastic. Cover and allow to rest for 10 minutes. Divide dough into 4 equal parts and lightly roll out each part to ⅛-inch thickness in a rectangular shape. Using a pastry cutter, cut the dough into strips 4-inches wide. Place a rounded teaspoon of filling in center of strip, 3-inches apart, along half the strip. Fold each strip over in half lengthwise, covering the mounds of filling. To seal, press edges together with tines of fork and press gently between mounds to form rectangles about 2-inches long. Cut apart with pastry cutter. Dry on board for 1 hour or longer before cooking. *(This process can be much simpler with a hand cranked pasta machine.)* To cook, bring 5-quarts of water to rapid boil. Add 1 tablespoon salt. Add a few ravioli at a time to the water and boil, uncovered, approximately 10 minutes or until tender. Drain well and serve with your favorite tomato sauce.

Emily N. Garrett
(The Apron String—A kitchen specialty shop)

TAGLIATELLE VERDI

Yield: Approximately 6 servings

1 cup fresh spinach leaves, washed and completely dried	2 teaspoons olive oil
	2¼ cups unbleached flour
	1 teaspoon salt
3 large eggs	

Using metal blade, mince spinach in food processor by pulsing machine until the spinach is finely chopped. Add the eggs and oil and process the mixture for 10 seconds. Reserve ½ cup of the flour and add the remaining flour and salt. Process until the dough forms a ball. Stop the machine and check the dough by touching it quickly. The dough should not be the least bit sticky. Add the reserved flour by the tablespoon until it is dry enough and smooth. Wrap the dough in plastic and let it rest 30 minutes. Using a pasta machine, roll and cut the dough into tagliatelle (fettucine), or roll and cut by hand. Have ingredients for sauce ready, then cook pasta in boiling salted water (no oil) only until it is *"al dente"* or slightly firm to the bite. Immediately proceed with the following sauce and serve.

Sauce:

6 slices bacon, diced	1 cup heavy cream
½ cup pine nuts	freshly ground nutmeg
¾ cup Parmesan cheese, freshly grated	freshly ground pepper
	salt

In a four quart pot, sauté the bacon pieces until crisp. Drain, but do not wash the pot. Toast the pine nuts in 350° oven until slightly brown (approximately 10 minutes). Add nuts to bacon. Add hot drained pasta to above mixture along with the cheese, cream, nutmeg, pepper, and salt. Toss until the pasta is coated and serve immediately.

Mary Ann K. Forehand
(The Apron String—A kitchen specialty shop)

MACARONI MOUSSE

Yield: 6 servings

1 cup macaroni, cooked and
  drained
1½ cups hot milk
1 cup soft bread crumbs
¼ cup butter or margarine,
  melted
1 pimento, chopped
1 tablespoon parsley, chopped

1 tablespoon onion, grated
1½ cups sharp Cheddar cheese,
  shredded
¼ teaspoon salt
⅛ teaspoon pepper
dash of paprika
3 eggs, well beaten

Pour milk over bread crumbs. Add butter, pimento, parsley, onion, cheese, salt, pepper, and paprika. Add eggs; blend thoroughly. Place macaroni in a 6x10-inch well-greased baking dish. Pour in the bread mixture. Bake in a 325° oven for 50 minutes, or until it is firm and holds its shape when turned out on serving dish. May be served from casserole if desired.

Note: An old recipe which gives macaroni and cheese a new flavor.

Caroline B. Bumbarger

 RICE

WILD RICE CASSEROLE

Yield: 6 servings

1½ cups wild rice
4 (10½-ounce) cans beef
  bouillon
1 cup butter or margarine
1 cup chopped onion

1 cup chopped green pepper
1 cup sliced mushrooms
1 cup heavy cream
salt and pepper to taste

Wash rice and cook it in beef broth until most of the liquid is absorbed. Melt butter and sauté onion, pepper, and mushrooms. Add cream, salt, and pepper to vegetables. Place rice in a 2½-quart casserole, pour cream mixture over rice, and blend. Bake at 350° for 20 minutes.

Carolyn W. Lyerly

BIBER'S RED RICE

R
I
C
E

Yield: 6 to 8 servings

1 cup raw long-grain rice
2 cups water, slightly salted
4 strips bacon

1 large onion, chopped
1 (14½-ounce) can tomatoes
salt and pepper to taste

Cook rice in water. In a large skillet, fry bacon while rice cooks. Drain bacon on paper, reserving drippings. Sauté onions in the drippings. Add tomatoes and cook until mixture thickens, chopping tomatoes finely as they cook. Stir often! When rice is cooked, drain well. Add rice to sauce, add salt and pepper, and crumble bacon over top.

Note: Enjoyed by 4 generations, this dish is very good with ham or fried chicken.

Joanne M. Martin

COMPANY RICE

Yield: 10 to 12 servings

6 tablespoons butter or
 margarine
1 medium onion, chopped
½ medium green pepper,
 chopped
1 cup raw long-grain rice
1 (4-ounce) jar mushroom
 pieces

1 (4-ounce) jar pimentos, diced
1 (4-ounce) can water chestnuts,
 chopped
1 teaspoon parsley flakes
½ teaspoon salt
½ teaspoon pepper
1 (10½-ounce) can beef bouillon
7-ounces water

Preheat oven to 375°. In a large skillet, melt butter and sauté onion and green pepper. Add rice, stirring until rice loses its color; do not brown. Remove from heat. Add mushrooms, pimentos, water chestnuts, parsley, salt, and pepper. Stir until blended and pour in the bouillon and water. Carefully pour mixture into a 13x9x2-inch casserole; cover. Bake for 20 minutes. Remove cover and continue baking for an additional 20 minutes.

Note: For convenience, prepare ahead, refrigerate, and cook before serving.

Sylvia H. Bowman

203

ST. PAUL'S RICE

Yield: 8 servings

1 pound hot sausage
1 large green pepper, chopped
1 stalk celery, diced
2 (2-ounce) packages dried
    chicken noodle soup

½ cup raw long-grain rice
4½ cups water
½ cup slivered almonds

Preheat oven to 350°. Break sausage into spoon-size pieces and brown over low heat. Drain meat on paper reserving drippings in skillet. Sauté green pepper and celery in 3 tablespoons drippings. In a large pot, combine soup mix, rice, and water, stir well, and let it come to a boil. Boil 7 minutes and add sausage, pepper, and celery. Put mixture into a 2-quart casserole and bake, covered, for 1 hour. Remove cover and sprinkle with almonds the last 30 minutes.

Variations: Add ½ cup mushrooms and 1 teaspoon Worcestershire sauce, or 1 (8-ounce) can water chestnuts.

Sherry S. Abernethy, Sally M. Fox & Shirley B. Clarke

GREEN AND GOLD RICE

Yield: 8 servings

1 medium size onion, chopped
1 tablespoon margarine
1 (13¾-ounce) can cheese soup
1 (6-ounce) roll, or jar, sharp
    cheese
½ teaspoon garlic powder
1 (8-ounce) can sliced
    mushrooms, undrained

2 (10-ounce) packages frozen
    chopped broccoli, cooked
    and drained
3 cups hot, cooked rice, (quick
    or long-grain)
1 (3-ounce) can French fried
    onion rings

Sauté chopped onion in margarine. Add cheese soup, sharp cheese, and garlic powder. Cook over low heat until cheese melts. Add mushrooms, broccoli and rice. Turn into a 10x6x2-inch glass casserole. Top with onion rings. Bake at 350° for 20 minutes or until hot and bubbly.

Jane S. Monroe

DIRTY RICE

Freezes well   *Yield: 6 to 8 servings*

1 pound uncooked ground beef   ½ cup chopped celery
1 cup raw long-grain rice   1 can water
1 cup chopped green onions   cayenne pepper to taste
1 (10¾-ounce) can mushroom   black pepper to taste
   soup   parsley to taste

Combine all ingredients. Bake at 300° for 1½ hours in a 2-quart casserole.

Lou Ellen J. Goodwin

BAKED STEAMED RICE

Yield: 6 servings

½ cup margarine   1 cup raw rice
1 medium onion, chopped   1 (2½-ounce) can chopped
1 can beef consommé, undiluted   mushrooms
1 can chicken broth, undiluted

Sauté chopped onion in melted margarine until tender. Combine consommé, broth, rice, and mushrooms and pour into a 1½-quart casserole dish. Cover and bake at 350° for 1 hour.

Helen S. Joyce

GREEN RICE

Yield: 6 servings

4 tablespoons butter or   ½ cup parsley, finely chopped
   margarine   ¼ cup chives, finely chopped
¼ cup Parmesan cheese, grated   1 teaspoon salt
3 cups cooked long-grain rice   ¼ teaspoon pepper

Melt butter in a saucepan. Add Parmesan cheese; mix. Blend in rice, stirring until butter is absorbed. Add parsley, chives, salt and pepper. Heat for 5 minutes.

Anne F. Mitchell

CURRIED RICE

Yield: 6 servings

3-ounces butter or margarine
2 large onions, chopped
3 tablespoons curry powder
2 tablespoons all-purpose flour

1½ cups chicken stock
1 cup cream
½ cup milk
3 cups cooked rice

Melt butter in a large skillet. Sauté onions over moderate heat until they are golden. Blend in curry powder and flour, stirring to form a smooth paste. Gradually add stock, cream, and milk. Mix well, stirring until sauce thickens. Add rice; stir until all the liquid is absorbed. Cook for 10 minutes.

June P. Wilfong

HERB RICE

Yield: 6 servings

1 cup raw long-grain rice
2 cups cold water
2 beef bouillon cubes
½ teaspoon salt
½ teaspoon rosemary

½ teaspoon marjoram
½ teaspoon thyme
1 teaspoon chives
1 tablespoon butter or
    margarine

Combine all ingredients in a saucepan. Cook over high heat until mixture boils; reduce heat. Stir once, cover, and simmer for 14 minutes, or until liquid is absorbed.

Note: This is a basic recipe. Vary according to your preferences and other dishes you plan to serve. White wine may be substituted for water. Use ½ chicken broth and ½ water, omitting the beef bouillon, and vary the herbs. Minced garlic may be added as rice cooks.

Jane S. Monroe

SAFFRON RICE

Yield: 6 servings

¼ teaspoon saffron, crumbled
2 tablespoons olive or salad oil
2 tablespoons butter or
    margarine

1½ cups raw long-grain rice
1½ teaspoons salt

Mix saffron with 1 tablespoon hot water; set aside. In a saucepan, heat oil and butter. Add rice and salt; cook, stirring occasionally, for 5 minutes. Add saffron mixed with water and 3 cups additional water. Bring to boil; reduce heat and simmer, covered, for 15 to 20 minutes, or until liquid is absorbed.

Sylvia H. Bowman

RICE OLIVE CASSEROLE

Yield: 6 servings

1 cup raw long-grain rice
1 cup New York State cheese,
    diced
1 (2-ounce) jar stuffed olives,
    sliced and drained

1 cup tomatoes
½ cup salad oil
½ cup chopped onion
1 cup water
salt and pepper to taste

Preheat oven to 350°. Combine all ingredients. Bake in a 1½ to 2-quart casserole for 1 hour. Do not be alarmed by soupy appearance as liquid is absorbed as casserole cooks.

Note: If recipe is doubled, add 15 minutes to cooking time.

Nikki I. Gillespie

 **VEGETABLES**

ARTICHOKE-TOMATO CASSEROLE

Yield: 6 to 8 servings

½ cup bread crumbs
1 (14-ounce) can artichokes
5 large tomatoes, quartered or
   canned tomatoes

salt to taste
⅓ cup Parmesan cheese, grated
6-ounces sharp Cheddar
   cheese, shredded

Preheat oven to 350°. Butter a 2-quart oblong dish and place a thin layer of bread crumbs on bottom. Cut artichokes in half and arrange artichokes and tomatoes over bread crumbs. Salt to taste. Sprinkle Parmesan, then sharp cheese over top. Bake at 350° for 30 minutes.

Mary Kathryn F. Hemphill

ASPARAGUS CASSEROLE

May prepare ahead   *Yield: 4 to 6 servings*

1½ cups butter-flavored cracker
   crumbs, divided
½ cup margarine

1 (15-ounce) can tall asparagus
½ cup almonds, slivered and
   toasted

Sauce:
4 teaspoons margarine
3 teaspoons all-purpose flour
1½ cups milk
1 (8-ounce) carton pasteurized
   process sharp cheese
   spread

½ teaspoon salt

Melt margarine; mix with 1 cup crackers crumbs. Line a 2-quart casserole with a layer of crumbs; add asparagus, then almonds. Preheat oven to 450°. Heat sauce and pour over all. Sprinkle reserved crumbs on top. Bake at 450° for 10 to 15 minutes.

Della Marie V. McKinnon

SPINACH ARTICHOKE CASSEROLE

Yield: 6 servings

2 (10-ounce) packages frozen
  chopped spinach, thawed
1 (8-ounce) package of cream
  cheese
8 tablespoons margarine
1 tablespoon lemon juice

salt and pepper to taste
1 (14-ounce) can artichoke
  hearts, drained and halved
4 ounces sharp cheese, grated
¼ cup corn flake crumbs

Preheat oven to 350°. Cook spinach about 3 minutes; drain. Add cream cheese, margarine, and lemon juice; mix until blended. Season with salt and pepper. Lightly grease a 1½-quart casserole and place artichokes on bottom. Spread spinach mixture on top; cover with cheese and corn-flake crumbs. Bake at 350° for 30 minutes.

Anne M. Boyer

BLACK BEANS IN RUM

May prepare ahead

Yield: 8 servings

1 pound black beans
1 large onion, chopped
2 cloves garlic, finely minced
3 stalks celery
1 carrot, minced
1 small herb bouquet*

salt
freshly ground pepper
3 tablespoons butter
2 jiggers dark rum, divided
1 (8-ounce) carton commercial
  sour cream

Soak beans overnight in cold water. The next day, add onion, garlic, celery, carrot, herb bouquet, salt, and pepper to taste. Simmer slowly until beans split. Preheat oven to 350°. Place beans and juice in a bean pot or casserole. Add butter and 1 jigger rum. Cover and bake until beans are tender. (Baking time is indefinite as black beans vary). When done, add remaining rum. Serve piping hot with cold sour cream.

Note: For a small herb bouquet, use dried or fresh basil, thyme, parsley, etc. tied into a small square of cheese cloth.

Marianna M. Raugh

209

GREEN BEANS À la SUISSE

Yield: 6 servings

4 cups green beans, French
   sliced and cooked
2 tablespoons butter, melted
2 tablespoons all-purpose flour
1/4 teaspoon salt
1/4 teaspoon pepper

1 teaspoon onion, grated
1 teaspoon sugar
1 cup sour cream
1/2 pound Swiss cheese, chopped
1 1/2 cups corn flakes, crushed
2 tablespoons butter, melted

Preheat oven to 350°. Into butter stir flour, salt, pepper, onion, and sugar. Add sour cream gradually. Fold in beans; heat thoroughly. Pour into greased 1 1/2-quart casserole. Place cheese on top of beans and add corn flakes mixed with melted butter. Bake for 20 minutes.

Peggy E. Hill

BEAN-TOMATO BAKE

May prepare ahead   *Yield: 6 to 8 servings*

1 cup onions, chopped
2 tablespoons vegetable oil
1 large tomato, chopped
1 cup celery, diced
1/2 cup green pepper, chopped
1 tablespoon parsley
1/2 teaspoon salt

1/4 teaspoon pepper
1/4 teaspoon garlic powder
1/2 teaspoon sugar
2 (16-ounce) cans French green
   beans
3/4 cup sharp cheese, grated
3/4 cup bread crumbs

Preheat oven to 325°. Sauté onion in oil. When browned, add tomato, celery, and green pepper. Season with parsley, salt, pepper, garlic powder, and sugar. Simmer 30 minutes. Cook beans 10 minutes. Place alternating layers of beans and tomato mixture in buttered casserole dish. Top with cheese, then bread crumbs. Bake in 325° oven for 25 minutes.

Joanne M. Martin

HERBED GREEN BEANS

May prepare ahead   *Yield: 6 servings*

2 tablespoons olive oil
1½ pounds green beans, cut
   in pieces
4 green onions, (or 1 small
   onion), finely chopped

½ cup parsley, chopped
¼ teaspoon thyme
1 cup Italian canned tomatoes
salt and pepper to taste

Pour oil in bottom of a heavy saucepan and add the beans, onions, parsley, thyme, tomatoes, salt, and pepper. Cover and simmer slowly for 20 to 30 minutes, or until tender.

Sylvia H. Bowman

LIMA BEAN AND CORN CASSEROLE

Must prepare ahead   *Yield: 8 servings*

2 cups lima beans, fresh or
   frozen
2 cups corn, fresh or frozen
½ cup onion, chopped
¼ cup pimento, chopped

½ cup sharp cheese, shredded
2 cups cream sauce
1 cup soft bread crumbs
3 tablespoons butter or
   margarine, melted

Cook lima beans and corn. Set aside with onion and pimento.

Cream Sauce:
4 tablespoons butter or
   margarine
4 tablespoons flour
2 cups evaporated milk,
   undiluted

½ teaspoon salt
½ teaspoon pepper

Preheat oven to 350°. Prepare cream sauce by melting butter in pan, stirring flour into melted butter, then adding milk and seasonings. Stir until sauce is thick; add cheese. Combine lima beans, corn, onion, pimento, sauce, and seasonings; place in a greased 1½-quart casserole. Sprinkle bread crumbs over the top and drizzle butter over the bread crumbs.

Note: This is better when prepared overnight. This is easily multiplied; can multiply by 10 without any problem.

Alice B. Davidson

**V
E
G
E
T
A
B
L
E
S**

211

BROCCOLI WITH POPPY SEED SAUCE

Yield: 6 to 8 servings

2 (10-ounce) packages broccoli
  spears
3 tablespoons butter
3 tablespoons onion, finely
  chopped
1½ cups sour cream
2 teaspoons vinegar

2 teaspoons sugar
1½ teaspoons poppy seed
1 teaspoon paprika
½ teaspoon salt
⅛ teaspoon cayenne pepper
¼ cup chopped pecans

Prepare broccoli according to package directions. In small saucepan, sauté onions in melted butter until golden; remove saucepan from heat. Stir in sour cream, vinegar, sugar, poppy seed, paprika, salt, and cayenne pepper. Drain broccoli and arrange on a heated platter. Pour sour cream mixture over broccoli. Sprinkle with pecans.

Carolyn W. Lyerly

LIMA BEAN PURÉE

May prepare ahead   *Yield: 4 to 6 servings*

2½ cups dried limas, (or
  frozen Fordhook limas)
¼ cup butter
1 onion, finely chopped

juice of ½ lemon
½ teaspoon cumin, ground
½ teaspoon coriander, ground
salt and pepper to taste

Cover beans with water, bring to a boil, and simmer, covered, for 45 minutes or until tender. Drain and reserve liquid. In a skillet melt butter and cook onion until soft. Add to the beans and work mixture through a sieve, or purée in a food processor with a little of cooking liquid, (1 or 2 tablespoons). Return the purée to pan and add lemon juice, cumin, coriander, salt, and pepper. Reheat, adding enough of the reserved liquid to make a mixture that falls fairly easily from a spoon. Pile in a serving dish.

Katty D. Lefler

SNOW-CAPPED BROCCOLI SPEARS

Yield: 6 servings

2 (10-ounce) packages frozen
  broccoli spears
1 tablespoon butter or
  margarine, melted
2 egg whites

¼ teaspoon salt
½ cup mayonnaise or salad
  dressing
Parmesan cheese, grated

Preheat oven to 350°. Cook broccoli according to package directions and drain well. Arrange stem ends toward center of an oven proof platter or 9-inch pie plate. Brush with butter. In a small bowl, beat egg whites and salt until stiff peaks form. Gently fold in mayonnaise. Spoon mixture in center of broccoli and sprinkle with Parmesan cheese. Bake at 350° for 12 to 15 minutes.

Note: An elegant and pretty dish. Sauce becomes puffy as it bakes.

Grace W. Menzies

BRUSSELS SPROUTS

May prepare ahead   *Yield: 8 servings*

2 tablespoons butter
2 teaspoons all-purpose flour
¾ cup warm chicken broth
¼ teaspoon salt
pinch of white pepper

¼ teaspoon basil
3 pounds Brussels sprouts
1½ cups water chestnuts,
  sliced

Melt butter in double boiler; blend in flour and cook, stirring until bubbly. Add chicken broth gradually, stirring until smooth. Add spices and keep warm over hot water. Cook sprouts in boiling, salted water until tender; drain well. Stir chestnuts into sauce and pour over sprouts.

Lou Ellen J. Goodwin

ALMOND CABBAGE CASSEROLE

May prepare ahead   *Yield: 4 to 6 servings*

1 medium head of cabbage,   1 cup Cheddar cheese, grated
   shredded   1 (10¾-ounce) can mushroom
1 (2-ounce) jar of pimento,   soup
   chopped   red pepper
1 (2¼-ounce) package slivered   buttered cracker crumbs
   almonds

Preheat oven to 350°. Boil cabbage in water with salt and butter; drain.
Combine pimento, almonds, cheese, mushroom soup, and a dash of red
pepper and mix with cabbage. Place in a greased 2-quart casserole and
cover with buttered cracker crumbs. Bake at 350° for 30 minutes.

Toni Y. Coleman

CARMELIZED ONIONS IN SQUASH

Yield: 4 servings

2 small acorn squash   2 tablespoons butter or
½ cup sugar   margarine
2 large onions, sliced, separated ½ teaspoon orange peel, finely
   into rings, or chopped   shredded

Preheat oven to 350°. Cut squash in half lengthwise. Remove seeds and
strings. Place squash, cut side down, in a shallow baking dish. Bake at
350° for 30 minutes. Turn squash over and bake 15 to 20 minutes, or until fork tender. While squash bakes, heat sugar in a heavy skillet over
medium heat without stirring until it begins to melt. Heat and stir 3
minutes, or until it is golden brown. Add onions, butter, and orange
peel. Continue cooking and stirring for 7 minutes or until onions are
tender and glazed. Liquid should resemble corn syrup. To serve, spoon
onions and syrup into each squash half. Serve at once.

*Note: A delicious salt-free dish. The orange peel adds a very different
flavor.*

Dorothy Y. Menzies

KAY'S RED CABBAGE WITH APPLES

May prepare ahead   *Yield: 6 to 8 servings*

2 heads red cabbage, shredded   2 or 3 apples, peeled and sliced
2 to 4 tablespoons margarine,   1 onion, grated
   or butter   juice of one lemon
½ cup molasses   ½ cup red wine

Melt butter in Dutch oven on top of stove; add cabbage and molasses, and brown over medium heat, stirring constantly. Add apples, onion, lemon juice, and salt to taste. Simmer covered 1 to 2½ hours, stirring occasionally. Add wine after 1½ hours, and cook until tender.

Kay I. Showfety

SCALLOPED CABBAGE

Freezes well   *Yield: 8 to 10 servings*

1 large head of cabbage   1 (8-ounce) package of stuffing
1 cup Cheddar cheese, shredded   mix
1 (10¾-ounce) can cream of
   mushroom soup

Steam cabbage until tender; cut in bite-size pieces and place in an 8-inch square glass casserole. Sprinkle cheese on top. Place soup on top of cheese, then add stuffing mix: Bake at 350° for 30 to 45 minutes.

Variation: Substitute 1½ cups of white sauce for mushroom soup and 1 teaspoon of sugar and buttered cracker crumbs to cover top of cabbage.

Jan S. Mullis

CARROT VICHY

Yield: 8 servings

3 bunches carrots   1 teaspoon sugar
1 cup butter   ⅓ cup cognac
salt

Preheat oven to 300°. Slice carrots in thin slices. Melt butter in 2-quart casserole and add salt, sugar, cognac, and carrots. Cover and place in a 300° oven for 1 hour. Watch carefully to see that this does not brown.

Alice L. Bost

CARROT LOAF

Yield: 12 servings

3 eggs
1 cup evaporated milk
3 cups carrots, cooked
2 cups soft bread crumbs

2 tablespoons butter, melted
¾ teaspoon onion, grated
1½ teaspoons salt
¼ teaspoon pepper

Preheat oven to 350°. Mix all ingredients and pour into greased and floured 2-quart mold. Set in pan of hot water and bake at 350° for 35 minutes.

Note: Serve hot with green peas in center.

Sally M. Fox

CARROT RING

May prepare ahead   *Yield: 8 servings*

2 cups carrots
1 cup saltine crackers, crumbled
1 cup milk
3 eggs, beaten
⅓ cup butter, melted

1 teaspoon onion, finely
   chopped
salt and pepper to taste
pinch of nutmeg

Boil carrots in salt water for 30 minutes. Sieve or use food processor and add all other ingredients to carrots. Pour in well greased 3-quart ring mold. Place mold in pan of water and cook until firm, 30 minutes.

Note: This is nice with peas in center for serving.

Ann B. Whitener

JERRI'S ONION CASSEROLE

May prepare ahead   *Yield: 8 to 10 servings*

4 cups white onions, sliced
1 (10¾-ounce) can cream of
   mushroom soup

1 cup almonds, slivered
½ cup cornflake crumbs
½ cup margarine

Preheat oven to 350°. Arrange layers of onions, soup, and nuts in a 1-quart casserole dish. Top with crumbs. Melt margarine and pour on top. Bake uncovered for 1 hour at 350°.

June P. Wilfong

CELERY ALMONDINE

May prepare ahead   *Yield: 8 to 10 servings*

2 bunches celery, sliced ½-inch thick
8 tablespoons butter
4 tablespoons all-purpose flour
2 cups milk
1 cup celery water
salt to taste
1 cup slivered almonds, divided
4 tablespoons dry bread crumbs
butter

Cover celery with boiling, salted water. Lay leaves on top. Cook 10 to 15 minutes after water reaches boiling point. Discard leaves, reserve 1 cup of liquid, and drain celery. Melt butter; stir in flour. Gradually add milk and cook slowly until smooth. Stir in celery water; add salt if needed. In a casserole dish, layer as follows: ½ sauce, ½ celery, ½ almonds, remaining celery and remaining sauce. Top with bread crumbs, dot with butter, and sprinkle on remaining almonds. Bake at 350° for 30 minutes.

Margaret Ann W. Campbell

GREEN PEAS WITH LETTUCE AND ONIONS

Yield: 6 servings

¼ cup sweet butter
2 large white onions, finely chopped
1 medium head Romaine lettuce, divided
2 (17-ounce) cans petite peas, drained
salt and pepper to taste
½ teaspoon sugar
4 sprigs parsley
2 tablespoons butter
parsley, finely chopped

Melt butter in a large saucepan; add onions, cover, and simmer over low flame until the onions are transparent and soft. It is important to conserve as much moisture as possible. Wash lettuce and shred center leaves but leave outer leaves whole. Place shredded lettuce on top of the onions. Drain peas and place on top of lettuce. Add salt, pepper, sugar, and parsley. With the whole leaves, cover the pea mixture. Cover tightly and cook slowly for 30 to 40 minutes. If the peas do not seem to have enough moisture, add a little water. Remove from flame and discard whole lettuce leaves. Add butter and a little finely chopped parsley to serve.

Katty D. Lefler

GLORIOUS PEAS

Freezes well   *Yield: 8 to 10 servings*

2 cups fresh mushrooms, sliced   salt and pepper
1 tablespoon butter   3 teaspoons cornstarch
1 (14½-ounce) can tomatoes   2 (17-ounce) cans petite peas
1 small onion, chopped   3 slices bacon
1 teaspoon chili powder

Preheat oven to 350°. Sauté mushrooms in butter; combine with tomatoes, onions, chili powder, and salt and pepper to taste; simmer for about 30 minutes. Mix cornstarch with a little water. Add to tomato mixture, cooking and stirring until thickened. Drain peas and place in casserole. Mix mushrooms with peas and add tomato mixture. Cut bacon into 2-inch pieces and distribute over casserole. Bake at 350° for 20 to 30 minutes, or until bacon is done.

Note: I met this old friend at the Caso de Campo in the Dominican Republic recently; it's the identical recipe I've been cooking for 45 years!

Dorothy Y. Menzies

EGGPLANT CASSEROLE

Yield: 6 servings

1 medium eggplant   1 tablespoon brown sugar
3 tablespoons butter, melted   2 whole cloves
2 tablespoons all-purpose flour ½ bay leaf
2 cups tomato, chopped   1 (6-ounce) package mozzarella
1 small onion, chopped   cheese, sliced
1 teaspoon salt   Parmesan cheese, grated

Peel and cube eggplant; cook in boiling water for 10 minutes. Drain. Melt butter in a skillet and blend in flour. Add tomatoes, onion, salt, sugar, cloves, and bay leaf; cook for five minutes. Place eggplant in a greased 2-quart casserole. Pour sauce over eggplant and top with mozzarella cheese. Sprinkle with Parmesan cheese. Bake at 350° for 30 minutes.

Nancy P. Shuford

CONFETTI CORN PUDDING

Yield: 6 servings

3 eggs, slightly beaten
2 (5.33 ounce) cans evaporated
  milk
2 tablespoons sugar
1 teaspoon salt
1 (17-ounce) can cream style
  corn

2 tablespoons butter, melted
2 tablespoons onion, minced
¼ cup green pepper
1 cup pimento

Mix all ingredients and add to milk. Bake in a buttered 2-quart casserole for one hour at 350° or until done. Turn off oven and let stand for 30 minutes.

Sally M. Fox

MUSHROOM CASSEROLE

Must prepare ahead　　　　　　　　　　　　*Yield: 6 servings*

2 eggs, beaten
1 (10¾-ounce) can cream of
  mushroom soup
1½ cups milk
salt and pepper
1 pound mushrooms, sliced
¼ cup butter

⅓ cup onion, chopped
⅓ cup green pepper, chopped
⅓ cup celery, chopped
8 slices extra thin bread
Parmesan cheese, grated
paprika

Mix eggs with soup and milk to make a smooth sauce. Season with salt and pepper. Sauté mushrooms in butter and add onion, pepper, and celery; stir fry several minutes. Remove from heat. Preheat oven to 325°. Place 4 slices of bread on bottom of greased 1-quart casserole dish. Cover bread with mushroom mixture and place remaining 4 slices of bread on top. Pour sauce over all and sprinkle with Parmesan cheese. Garnish with paprika. *Let stand for 1 hour.* Bake at 325° approximately 1 hour.

Sally T. Blackwelder

OREGANO SQUASH CASSEROLE

May prepare ahead   *Yield: 6 to 8 servings*

8 to 10 yellow squash
1 onion, chopped
2 tablespoons butter
1/2 cup processed American
   cheese, cut in pieces

1 teaspoon salt
2 teaspoons ground oregano
1/4 cup sour cream
1/4 cup almonds, slivered

Cook squash with onion in boiling salted water until tender; drain thoroughly. Add butter and mash thoroughly. Add cheese, salt, oregano, sour cream, and almonds. Mix well and bake at 350° for 30 minutes.

Nancy F. Matheson

PARMESAN TATERS

Yield: 8 servings

8 potatoes
1/2 cup Parmesan cheese, grated
1/2 cup all-purpose flour

1 teaspoon salt
1 teaspoon pepper
8 tablespoons margarine

Preheat oven to 375°. Wash potatoes, leaving peeling on; cut in quarters. Roll in cheese, flour, salt, and pepper mixture and place in a 9x13x2-inch casserole. Melt butter and add to potatoes. Bake at 375° for 20 minutes. Turn potatoes and bake 20 minutes more or until tender.

Vicki V. Bowman

TOMATO GRUYÉRE

3 tomatoes
1 garlic clove, chopped
1 tablespoon basil
1 tablespoon parsley

1/2 cup bread crumbs
1/2 cup Gruyère or Parmesan
   cheese, freshly grated
butter

Cut each tomato in half and scoop out some of the meat. *Do not peel.* Sprinkle each half with a mixture of bread crumbs, parsley, garlic, and basil. Top with freshly grated Gruyère or Parmesan cheese and a dot of butter. Wrap in foil and grill for 15 or 20 minutes.

Anne Byrd
"Keeping Pace with Anne Byrd"
Published and Copyrighted by Pace Publications
(Used with permission by the Author.)

GLORIFIED ONIONS

Must prepare ahead   *Yield: 8 to 10 servings*

5 to 6 medium onions, sliced   ½ cup mayonnaise
½ cup vinegar   1 teaspoon celery salt
1 cup sugar   1 teaspoon celery seed,
2 cups water   (optional)

Slice onions thin and soak in vinegar, sugar, and water in the refrigerator for 2 to 4 hours. Drain well and toss with mayonnaise, celery salt, and celery seed.

Note: Delicious served with crackers as an hors d'oeuvre or stuffed in a tomato as a salad.

Sherry S. Abernethy

STEAMED SQUASH MEDLEY

May prepare ahead   *Yield: 6 to 8 servings*

1 pound small zucchini   1 tomato, peeled and chopped
1 pound small yellow crookneck   2 leaves mint
   squash, sliced in half   2 cloves garlic, minced
   lengthwise   salt and pepper to taste
1 medium onion, finely chopped   ¼ cup olive oil

Cut the zucchini in half crosswise, then each piece almost through lengthwise, forming little fans. Place zucchini and squash in a large skillet with oil; add the onion, tomato, mint, garlic, salt, and pepper. Cover and simmer for 15-20 minutes, or until vegetables are barely tender. Remove cover and cook down rapidly to reduce juices.

Note: This is a beautiful dish on a platter—all red, green, and yellow.

Catherine H. Yeager

221

YELLOW SQUASH PUFFS

Yield: 4 servings

¾ pound yellow squash, sliced
1 egg, beaten
⅓ cup all-purpose flour
⅓ cup cornmeal

1 teaspoon baking powder
½ teaspoon salt
1 medium onion, grated
vegetable oil, 3½ inches

Cook squash, covered, in boiling water 10 to 15 minutes or until tender. Drain; mash 1 cup of squash and combine with egg. Stir well. Combine flour, cornmeal, baking powder, and salt. Add squash mixture and onion; stir until blended. Drop squash mixture by level tablespoon into hot oil. Cook until golden brown, turning once. Drain well on paper towels.

Ginger E. Starnes

SWEET POTATO AND APPLE CASSEROLE

Must prepare ahead   *Yield: 6 servings*

2 pounds sweet potatoes,
  cooked
1½ pounds cooking apples
⅔ cup light brown sugar
6 tablespoons butter

½ cup apple cider or juice
3 tablespoons maple syrup
1 tablespoon lemon juice
1 teaspoon cinnamon
½ teaspoon ginger

Preheat oven to 325°. Cook potatoes; cool, skin, and slice ¼-inch thick. Peel apples; quarter, core, and slice ¼-inch thick. Keep apples in cool water with a little juice to keep from discoloring. In a small saucepan, bring sugar, butter, cider, syrup, lemon juice, cinnamon, and ginger to a boil. Lower heat and let mixture boil slowly for 10 minutes. Drain apples, pat dry. Arrange apples and sweet potatoes in a 9x13x2-inch casserole. Cover with sauce and bake at 325° for 25 to 30 minutes, basting occasionally.

Note: McIntosh is the kind of apple to use in this recipe. If you use Winesap or Cortland, increase cooking time to 12 to 20 minutes.

Marian M. Johnson

BAKED SQUASH RING

Yield: 4 to 5 servings

3 cups yellow squash, diced
¼ cup butter, melted
¼ cup milk
3 eggs, well beaten
1 teaspoon salt

⅛ teaspoon white pepper (or
    dash hot sauce)
¼ cup buttered bread crumbs
1 tablespoon onion, minced
a pinch of fine herbs

Preheat oven to 350°. Cook squash in a small amount of water, un-covered, until tender. Force through a sieve or food processor. Add but-ter, milk, eggs, salt, white pepper, bread crumbs, onion, and herbs; blend well. Turn into a 1½-quart well buttered ring mold and set in a pan of hot water. Bake at 350° for 45 minutes or until inserted knife comes out clean.

Note: This is pretty served with peas in center.

Anne F. Mitchell

TOMATO PIE

Yield: 6 to 8 servings

9-inch pie crust, partially baked
3 medium tomatoes, cored,
    peeled and thickly sliced
salt and pepper to taste
½ teaspoon dried basil (or
    tarragon)

¼ cup chives, chopped (may use
    dried)
½ cup mayonnaise
1 cup sharp Cheddar cheese,
    shredded

Preheat oven to 350°. Line cooled pie crust with tomatoes, covering bot-tom completely. Sprinkle tomatoes with salt, pepper, basil, and chives. In a small bowl, thoroughly combine mayonnaise and cheese. Carefully spread mixture evenly over tomato slices, making sure you seal edges of pie crust completely. Bake for 30 to 35 minutes, or until bubbly. Serve at once.

Note: A perfect entrée for a summertime luncheon, or as accompaniment for any grilled meat. You may use 6 tart shells approximately 2-inches in diameter instead of pie shell. Divide ingredients among shells and bake for 20 to 25 minutes.

Camille M. Gardner

223

SPINACH ROLL

Partially prepare ahead   *Yield: 8 servings*

3 boxes frozen chopped spinach   ¹/₄ teaspoon nutmeg
5 eggs, separated   salt and pepper to taste
6 tablespoons butter, melted

Preheat oven to 375⁰. Butter a jellyroll pan and cover with wax paper. Cook spinach in almost no water until just done. Drain and squeeze to extract as much water as possible. Beat egg yolks until lemon yellow and fluffy. Add butter, nutmeg, salt, and pepper and stir gently into the spinach. Beat egg whites until stiff and fold into the spinach mixture. Spread on wax paper to cover pan. Bake in a 375⁰ oven for 15 to 18 minutes until top springs back when touched. Turn over onto a damp tea towel and quickly peel off the paper. If not using immediately, roll up in towel and refrigerate.

Duxelles Filling:
1¹/₂ pounds fresh mushrooms   1 tablespoon flour
¹/₄ pound butter   salt and pepper to taste

Preheat oven to 350⁰. Cook mushrooms in butter, sprinkling with flour, stirring until a rich brown. Season to taste with salt and pepper. When ready to serve, unroll and fill, then roll up; wrap in foil and heat through in a 350⁰ oven.

Note: Other fillings to use—minced chicken and ham, cooked shrimp or anything creamed. As a main dish serve with hollandaise sauce; omit the sauce when served as a side dish.

Anne F. Mitchell

CURRIED BRUSSELS SPROUTS

Yield: 4 servings

1 (10-ounce) package Brussels   ¹/₂ teaspoon curry powder
   sprouts   paprika
1 teaspoon salt
¹/₂ cup mayonnaise (or salad
   dressing)

Cook Brussels sprouts in salted water, about 3 minutes, so that they are still crisp. Drain and add mayonnaise mixed with curry. Sprinkle with paprika. Serve immediately.

Shirley B. Clarke

LILLY'S STUFFED POTATOES

Freezes well   *Yield: 6 servings*

6 medium-sized baking potatoes   ⅓ cup mayonnaise
2½ cups milk, heated   ¼ pound extra sharp Cheddar
½ tablespoon salt   cheese, shredded

Bake potatoes at 350⁰ for 1½ hours or until done. Scoop out pulp while
still hot; reserve jackets. Add milk, a little at a time, to potatoes and mix
well. Beat potatoes until creamy and all lumps disappear. Use electric
beaters if potatoes remain lumpy. Add salt and mayonnaise. The mixture may look "soupy" but it will thicken. If potatoes are large, more
milk and mayonnaise may need to be added to potato mixture. Stuff
jackets with whipped potatoes and sprinkle cheese on top. Place in an
ungreased baking dish and bake 325⁰ for 15 minutes or until heated
through.

Note: Freeze stuffed potatoes uncooked and thaw before ready to heat.

Anne M. Boyer

SPINACH PIE

May prepare ahead   *Yield: 4 to 6 servings*

3 eggs   ¼ cup butter or margarine
1 pound cottage cheese   3 tablespoons all-purpose flour
⅓ pound Cheddar cheese,   ½ teaspoon salt
    shredded   ⅛ teaspoon pepper
1 (10-ounce) package frozen
    spinach, thawed and
    chopped

Preheat oven to 350⁰. Beat eggs and set aside. Mix cottage cheese,
Cheddar cheese, spinach, butter, flour, salt, and pepper and add to
beaten eggs. Pour into a greased 1-quart casserole and bake one hour at
350⁰.

Roddy S. Dixon

225

SNOWY MASHED POTATOES

Yield: 12 servings

12 medium potatoes
8 ounces cream cheese
1 (8-ounce) carton sour cream
2 teaspoons salt
¼ cup chives

½ teaspoon paprika
1 tablespoon butter
⅛ teaspoon pepper
garlic salt

Preheat oven to 350°. Cook potatoes until tender, drain, and beat with electric mixer. Add cream cheese, sour cream, salt, pepper, garlic salt, and chives; beat until light. Pour into a 9x13x2-inch casserole; sprinkle with paprika and dot with butter. Bake at 350° for 30 minutes.

Note: may add 1 tablespoon beef bouillon granules, 3 tablespoons grated cheese and additional cheese on top.

Elaine T. Young, Alice B. Davidson, & Beverly R. Hyatt

VEGETABLE TRIO WITH ZIPPY SAUCE

Yield: 12 to 16 servings

1 cup mayonnaise
2 hard-cooked eggs, chopped
3 tablespoons lemon juice
2 tablespoons onion, minced
1 teaspoon Worcestershire
    sauce
1 teaspoon prepared mustard
¼ teaspoon garlic salt

dash hot pepper sauce
2 (10-ounce) packages frozen
    French style beans
1 (10-ounce) package frozen
    peas
1 (10-ounce) package frozen
    baby lima beans

Combine ingredients except vegetables. Heat and stir over low heat just until hot. Cook vegetables according to package directions. Drain well and mix together. Pour hot sauce over vegetables.

Note: Tasty vegetable combo. Perfect for your next buffet dinner.

Bess G. Geitner & Mary Kathryn F. Hemphill

SAUTÉED ZUCCHINI

Yields: 6

8 tablespoons butter	salt and pepper to taste
8 medium zucchini, grated	
1 to 2 tablespoons dill weed, dried	

Melt the butter in a sauté pan. Add the zucchini and dill. Toss over medium heat for about 5 minutes or until just tender. Season and serve.

Anne Byrd
"Keeping Pace with Anne Byrd"
Published and Copyrighted by Pace Publications
(Used with permission by the Author.)

VEGETABLE TRIO

Yield: 6 to 8 servings

2 (15-ounce) cans asparagus	2 eggs, hard-boiled and sliced
1 (2½-ounce) can mushrooms	salt and pepper to taste
1 (14-ounce) can artichokes	paprika
1 (2½-ounce) package sliced almonds	

Sauce:

2 tablespoons butter	1 cup cream
2 tablespoons all-purpose flour	¾ pound sharp Cheddar cheese, shredded
2 tablespoons asparagus juice	

Preheat oven to 350°. Make white sauce with butter, flour, asparagus juice, and cream. Add cheese and stir until melted. Set sauce aside. Combine asparagus, mushrooms, artichokes, almonds, and eggs; salt and pepper to taste. Put ½ of vegetable mixture in a greased 2-quart casserole and cover with ½ of the sauce. Repeat layers of vegetables and sauce. Sprinkle top with paprika and bake for 30 minutes or until hot and bubbly.

Lou Ellen J. Goodwin

ITALIAN ZUCCHINI CRESCENT PIE

Yield: 6 servings

4 cups zucchini, thinly sliced
1 cup onion, coarsely chopped
1/2 cup margarine or butter
1/2 cup parsley, chopped
1/2 teaspoon salt
1/2 teaspoon pepper
1/4 teaspoon garlic powder
1/4 teaspoon oregano leaves

1/4 teaspoon sweet basil leaves
2 eggs, well beaten
2 cups mozzarella cheese, shredded
1 (8-ounce) can refrigerated crescent dinner rolls
2 teaspoons mustard

Preheat oven to 375°. In skillet, cook zucchini and onion in margarine until tender, about 10 minutes. Stir in parsley and seasonings. In large bowl, blend eggs and cheese; then stir in vegetable mixture. Separate rolls into 8 triangles and place in ungreased 11-inch quiche pan, 10-inch baking dish, or 12x8-inch dish. Press over bottom and up sides to form crust. Spread crust with mustard and pour vegetable mixture into crust. Bake for 18 to 20 minutes, or until knife inserted comes out clean. If crust becomes too brown, cover with foil during last 10 minutes of baking. Let stand 10 minutes before serving. Cut into desired sizes, depending on whether serving as appetizer or vegetable.

Judy M. Bost

ZUCCHINI CASSEROLE

May prepare ahead   *Yield: 6 servings*

1 medium zucchini, cut in quarters
10 plum tomatoes or 5 or 6 regular tomatoes
1 tablespoon all-purpose flour

1 tablespoon sugar
salt and pepper to taste
2 tablespoons onion, minced
Parmesan cheese, grated

Preheat oven to 350°. Cut zucchini into quarter-inch slices and halve these. Cut tomatoes in pieces and place with zucchini in a 2-quart casserole. Mix flour, sugar, onion, salt, and pepper and sprinkle over vegetables. Top with Parmesan cheese and bake for 45 minutes.

Note: Canned tomatoes can be substituted. If using canned tomatoes, use some of the juice.

Susie D. Patton

228

DESSERTS

I
N
D
E
X

( ) Denotes: (HE) Hickory Entertains   (I) International   (M) Microwave Recipes

( ) Denotes: (HE) Hickory Entertains   (I) International   (M) Microwave Recipes

 CAKES

THE PERFECT PREPARED PAN

½ cup vegetable shortening   ½ cup all-purpose flour
½ cup vegetable oil

Combine all ingredients in a blender or food processor; process until smooth. Pour mixture into a pint jar, cover, and refrigerate. Mixture keeps up to six months. Brush on pans with a pastry brush as needed. Cakes will be easy to remove from pans every time.

AMARETTO CAKE

Freezes well   *Yield: 12 to 16 servings*

1 cup butter, at room
  temperature
2½ cups sugar
6 eggs, at room temperature
1 cup sour cream
1 teaspoon vanilla extract
1 teaspoon orange extract

1 teaspoon lemon extract
2 teaspoons almond extract
3 cups sifted all-purpose flour
¼ teaspoon baking soda
½ teaspoon salt
½ cup Amaretto liqueur

Preheat oven to 325⁰. Grease and flour a 10-inch tube or bundt pan. Cream butter and sugar until fluffy. Add eggs one at a time, beating well after each addition. Beat in sour cream, then extracts. Sift together sifted flour, soda, and salt; gradually add to creamed mixture. Add Amaretto and beat well. Pour into prepared pan and bake 1 hour and 15 minutes or until cake tests done. Cool 5 minutes in pan, then turn out on wire rack and cool. Glaze.

Glaze:
1 cup orange marmalade
½ cup apricot preserves

¼ cup Amaretto liqueur
1 cup chopped almonds, toasted

Heat marmalade and preserves with Amaretto until melted. Drizzle over cooled cake, and sprinkle with almonds.

Shirley L. Ballew

BLACK FOREST CAKE

Must refrigerate   *Yield: 18 servings*

4 (1-ounce) squares
   unsweetened chocolate
1³/₄ cups all-purpose flour
1³/₄ cups sugar
1¹/₄ teaspoons baking soda
1 teaspoon salt
¹/₄ teaspoon baking powder
²/₃ cup margarine, softened

1¹/₄ cups water
1 teaspoon vanilla extract
3 eggs
Chocolate Filling
Cream Filling
chocolate curls (optional)
cherry pie filling (optional)

Preheat oven to 350°. Brush sides and bottoms of four 9-inch layer pans with margarine. Melt chocolate and cool. In large mixer bowl, combine all ingredients except eggs. Beat on low speed to blend. Beat for 2 minutes at medium speed, scraping sides. Add eggs. Beat 2 minutes more. Pour ¼ batter into each prepared pan. Bake 15 to 18 minutes, or until cakes test done. Cool in pan 5 minutes. Remove layers from pans and cool thoroughly. Prepare fillings and assemble.

Chocolate Filling:
1¹/₂ (4-ounce) bars sweet
   chocolate

³/₄ cup margarine, softened
¹/₂ cup pecans, crushed

Melt chocolate in top of double boiler over hot water. Cool. Blend in margarine. Stir in nuts.

Cream Filling:
2 cup heavy cream, whipped
1 tablespoon sugar

1 teaspoon vanilla extract

Add sugar and vanilla to whipped cream. Beat to blend. To assemble: Place one layer on serving plate; cover with ½ Chocolate Filling. Top with second layer; cover with ⅓ Cream Filling. Repeat with remaining 2 layers. Spread remaining ⅓ Cream Filling around sides of cake. Garnish with chocolate curls or spoon cherry pie filling over top of cake just before serving. Refrigerate until ready to serve.

Dee E. Hodges

APPLE DAPPLE CAKE

Freezes well *Yield: 12 to 16 servings*

3 eggs
2 cups sugar
1½ cups vegetable oil
3 cups all-purpose flour
1 teaspoon baking soda
1 teaspoon salt

1 teaspoon cinnamon
2 teaspoons vanilla extract
3 cups apples, diced
1 cup nuts, chopped
1 cup coconut, grated (optional)

Preheat oven to 350°. Grease and flour a 10-inch tube or bundt pan or a 9x13x2-inch sheet pan. Beat eggs, sugar, and oil until fluffy. Combine flour, soda, salt, and cinnamon. Add to egg mixture. Mix in vanilla, apples, nuts, and coconut. Pour into prepared pan. Bake tube cake 1 hour 15 minutes; sheet cake 45 minutes or until cake tests done. Let cake cool 5 minutes and turn out on serving plate. Ice while still warm.

Icing:
½ cup margarine
1 cup brown sugar

¼ cup milk
1 teaspoon vanilla extract

Place margarine, sugar, and milk in saucepan. Bring to a boil and boil 2½ minutes. Remove from heat; add vanilla. Pour over warm cake.

Sarah S. Raney & Elaine S. Zerden

HOT MILK CAKE

Freezes well *Yield: 16 servings*

4 eggs, separated
2 cups sugar
2 cups all-purpose sifted flour
3 teaspoons baking powder

½ teaspoon salt
1 teaspoon vanilla extract
1 cup milk
½ cup butter (no substitute)

Preheat oven to 375°. Grease and flour three 9-inch layer pans. Beat egg whites until stiff peaks form; add egg yolks and beat until light lemon color. Beat in sugar gradually until well blended. Resift flour with baking powder and salt; add to egg mixture. Stir in vanilla. In a saucepan, bring milk and butter to a boil; pour into batter and mix thoroughly. Pour into prepared pans. Bake 30 minutes or until cakes test done. Frost with your favorite frosting. Excellent with Pineapple Filling, page 256, and Lemon Frosting, page 253.

Della Marie V. McKinnon

234

GREEK WALNUT TORTE

Must prepare ahead   *Yield: 8 to 12 servings*

9 eggs, separated
1 cup sugar
3 cups walnuts, ground
1/2 cup packaged dry bread
    crumbs
1 tablespoon orange rind, grated
2 teaspoons lemon rind, grated
1 teaspoon ground cinnamon

1/2 teaspoon ground cloves
1/2 teaspoon salt
2 teaspoons baking powder
1 teaspoon vanilla extract
1/2 cup water
Brandy Butter Cream
2/3 cup walnuts, coarsely broken

Make torte the day before, or very early on the day it is to be served. Preheat oven to 350°. Line bottoms of three 8-inch layer cake pans with waxed paper. In medium mixer bowl, beat egg yolks and sugar at high speed with electric mixer until very thick and light in color. Combine ground walnuts, bread crumbs, orange rind, lemon rind, cinnamon, cloves, salt, and baking powder. Mix vanilla and water with egg yolk mixture and stir into walnut mixture. In large mixer bowl, beat egg whites at high speed until stiff and dry. Fold gently into walnut mixture until thoroughly combined. Pour into prepared pans. Bake 30 minutes or until tester comes out clean. Cool cakes in pans on racks. When cool, loosen cakes around edges and turn out of pans; remove paper. If torte is to be served the next day, wrap cooled layers and store at room temperature. Several hours before serving, prepare Brandy Butter Cream. Fill and frost layers; lightly press broken walnuts into frosting on top of torte.

Brandy Butter Cream:
1/2 cup butter or margarine
1/8 teaspoon salt
1 (16-ounce) box powdered
    sugar

1 egg
1 teaspoon vanilla extract
2 tablespoons brandy

In small mixing bowl, beat butter at medium speed until creamy. Beat in salt and sugar; add egg, vanilla and brandy. Beat until fluffy.

Dorothy Y. Menzies

C
A
K
E
S

BROWNSTONE FRONT CAKE

Freezes well   *Yield: 16 servings*

3 tablespoons cocoa
½ cup warm water
1 teaspoon baking soda
1 cup butter
2 cups sugar
4 eggs

1 teaspoon vanilla extract
3 cups all-purpose flour
1 teaspoon baking powder
1 teaspoon salt
1 cup buttermilk

Preheat oven to 350°. Grease and lightly flour three 9-inch layer pans. Combine cocoa, warm water, and soda in a 1 cup measure. Set aside. Cream butter; add sugar gradually; beat until light and fluffy. Add eggs, one at a time, beating well after each addition. Add vanilla. Stir in cocoa mixture. Sift flour, baking powder, and salt. Add to creamed mixture alternately with buttermilk, beginning and ending with flour mixture. Mix well after each addition. Pour into prepared pans. Bake 30 to 35 minutes. Cool in pans for 5 minutes. Turn out of pans and cool completely.

Frosting:
1 cup butter (no substitute)
3 cups sugar

1 cup evaporated milk
1 teaspoon vanilla extract

In a heavy medium saucepan, over low heat, melt butter; add sugar and milk. Bring to a boil. Boil for 3 minutes, stirring constantly. Reduce heat to simmer; cook 1 hour, stirring occasionally; remove from heat. Beat with an electric mixer on high speed until cool and spreading consistency. Add vanilla; blend well. Spread on cooled layers and sides.

Shirley L. Ballew

PUMPKIN CAKE

Freezes well   *Yield: 16 servings*

2½ cups sugar
1¼ cups vegetable oil
4 eggs
1 (16-ounce) can pumpkin
2 cups self-rising flour
1 teaspoon cinnamon

1 teaspoon allspice
1 teaspoon baking powder
1 teaspoon salt
1 teaspoon vanilla extract
1 cup nuts, chopped

Preheat oven to 350°. Grease and flour a 10-inch bundt or tube pan. Combine sugar and oil. Add eggs one at a time, beating well after each addition. Beat in pumpkin. Mix together flour, cinnamon, allspice, baking powder, and salt. Add to pumpkin mixture. Blend well. Add vanilla and nuts. Pour into prepared pan and bake 1 hour. Remove from oven and let stand 10 minutes before removing from pan. Cool. Butter sauce may be poured or brushed over cake; however, it is excellent plain.

Butter Sauce:
¹/₂ cup sugar   ¹/₄ cup butter
1 tablespoon cornstarch   1 teaspoon vanilla extract
¹/₄ cup buttermilk

Combine sugar and cornstarch in heavy saucepan. Add buttermilk, butter, and vanilla. Bring to a boil. Boil 1 minute, stirring constantly. Pour warm, *not hot*, over cooled cake or brush on cake with pastry brush.

Margaret F. Tallant

BLACKBERRY JAM CAKE

Yield: 14 to 16 servings

1 cup butter, softened   ¹/₈ teaspoon salt
2 cups sugar   1 teaspoon ground cloves
4 eggs, at room temperature   1 cup milk
3 cups sifted cake flour   1 teaspoon lemon extract
3 teaspoons baking powder   1 teaspoon lemon zest
1 teaspoon ground cinnamon   1 cup seedless blackberry jam

Preheat oven to 350°. Grease and lightly flour three 9-inch layer pans. Cream butter and sugar until light and fluffy in a large bowl. Add eggs one at a time, beating well after each addition. Sift flour, baking powder, cinnamon, salt, and cloves together 3 times. Add flour mixture alternately with milk to cream mixture, beginning and ending with flour mixture. Add lemon extract and lemon zest; fold in blackberry jam. Mix well. Pour batter into prepared pans. Bake 20 to 25 minutes or until cake tests done. Ice with 7-Minute Frosting.

Note: The originator of this cake said, "You will never eat a better cake," and it is true. Hint: Zest is the outer rind of the lemon or orange. It contains none of the white which is bitter.

Dorothy Y. Menzies

237

BEST EVER POUND CAKE

Freezes well   *Yield: 16 to 20 servings*

1 cup butter (no substitute),
    at room temperature
3 cups sugar
6 eggs

3 cups all-purpose flour
1 cup heavy cream
1 tablespoon vanilla extract
2 teaspoons lemon extract

Preheat oven to 300°. Grease and lightly flour a 10-inch tube or bundt pan. Cream butter and sugar until fluffy. Add eggs one at a time, beating thoroughly after each addition. Add flour and cream alternately, a total of 6 additions each. Add flavorings, mixing well. Pour batter into prepared pan and bake 1 hour and 35 to 45 minutes or until cake tests done. Cool 30 minutes in pan before inverting onto plate. May be glazed, but it is not necessary.

Ruth L. Hord

FAVORITE POUND CAKE

Freezes well   *Yield: 16 servings*

1 cup butter (no substitute)
½ cup vegetable shortening
3 cups sugar
6 eggs
3 cups all-purpose flour

½ teaspoon baking powder
1 cup milk
2 teaspoons vanilla extract
2 teaspoons lemon extract
1 teaspoon almond extract

Preheat oven to 325°. Grease and flour a 10-inch tube or bundt pan. Cream butter and shortening; gradually add sugar until light and fluffy. Add eggs one at a time, beating well after each addition. Combine flour and baking powder; add to creamed mixture alternately with milk and extracts. Beat well after each addition. Pour into prepared pan and bake 1½ hours or until cake tests done. Cool in pan 5 minutes before removing to rack to cool completely.

Virginia H. Speagle & Mary F. Teeter

Variations: CHOCOLATE POUND CAKE: Add ½ cup cocoa to flour and baking powder. Increase milk to 1¼ cups. Omit lemon and almond extract. Increase vanilla extract to 1 tablespoon. Mix and bake as above. Can glaze or frost with favorite chocolate frosting.

BROWN SUGAR POUND CAKE: Substitute sugar with 1 pound light brown sugar and 1 cup sugar. Omit lemon extract. Can add 1 cup nuts, chopped. Mix and bake as above. Good plain or with caramel frosting.

Duart J. Johnston

CHRISTMAS POUND CAKE

Freezes well   *Yield: 16 servings*

½ cup pecans, finely chopped
1 (8-ounce) package cream
   cheese
1 cup butter, softened
1¾ cups sugar
1 tablespoon vanilla extract
1 tablespoon brandy flavoring
5 eggs

2½ cups all-purpose flour
½ teaspoon baking powder
1 tablespoon cornstarch
½ teaspoon salt
½ cup candied red and green
   cherries
½ cup candied pineapple
½ cup pecans, chopped

Preheat oven to 325°. Heavily grease bottom and sides of a 10-inch tube pan and sprinkle evenly with ½ cup finely chopped pecans. Cream together cream cheese, butter, sugar, and flavorings. Add eggs one at a time, beating after each addition. Sift flour, baking powder, cornstarch, and salt together. Combine with candied fruit and ½ cup chopped pecans. Fold into batter; mix well. Pour over nuts in prepared pan. Bake 30 minutes; reduce oven temperature to 300° and bake 1½ hours. Cool 10 minutes in pan and turn out on rack to cool.

Patti C. Owens

BRANDY SOUR CREAM POUND CAKE

Freezes well   *Yield: 30 servings*

1½ cups butter
3 cups sugar
6 large eggs
1 cup sour cream
3 cups all-purpose flour

½ teaspoon baking soda
⅛ teaspoon salt
1 teaspoon vanilla extract
1 teaspoon almond extract
2 tablespoons brandy

Preheat oven to 325°. Grease and flour a 10-inch bundt or tube pan and a 5x9x3-inch loaf pan. Cream butter and sugar until light in a large mixer bowl. Add eggs, one at a time, beating well after each addition. Stir in sour cream. Place measured flour into sifter with soda and salt, and sift 3 times. Add flour mixture, ½ cup at a time, to butter mixture; blend well after each addition with mixer at lowest setting. Add extracts and brandy (not extract). Mix well. Pour into prepared pans. Bake bundt cake for 1 hour and loaf cake 45 to 50 minutes. Cool cakes in pans 10 minutes before turning out on racks.

Judy F. Flowers

COLD OVEN POUND CAKE

Freezes well   *Yield: 12 to 16 servings*

1½ cups butter   ¼ teaspoon baking powder
3 cups sugar   1 cup milk
6 eggs   2 teaspoons lemon juice
3 cups all-purpose flour

Have all ingredients at room temperature. Grease well a 10-inch tube pan. In large mixer bowl, cream butter and sugar until smooth and creamy. Add eggs one at a time, beating well after each addition. Sift flour and baking powder together. Add to creamed mixture alternately with milk. Beat well. Add lemon juice and beat for 10 minutes at medium speed of electric mixer. Pour into prepared pan. Place in *cold oven;* turn oven on to 350°. Bake for 1 hour and 20 minutes or until cake tests done.

Deda E. Helms & Greta W. Garth

PRALINE CHEESECAKE

Must prepare ahead, freezes well   *Yield: 12 to 16 servings*

1¼ cups graham cracker   1 (5½-ounce) can evaporated
  crumbs   milk
¼ cup sugar   2 tablespoons all-purpose flour
¼ cup pecans, chopped, toasted   1½ teaspoons vanilla extract
¼ cup butter, melted   3 eggs
3 (8-ounce) packages cream   1 cup pecan halves, toasted
  cheese, softened   Praline Sauce
1 cup brown sugar, firmly
  packed

Preheat oven to 350°. Butter bottom and sides of a 9-inch spring-form pan. Combine graham cracker crumbs, sugar, pecans, and butter. Press crumbs over bottom and 1½-inches up sides of prepared pan. Bake for 10 minutes. Cool. Beat cream cheese, brown sugar, milk, flour, and vanilla until well blended. Add eggs one at a time, beating well after each addition. Continue beating until light and fluffly. Pour over prepared crust and bake for 50 to 55 minutes or until set. Cool 30 minutes. Loosen and remove rim. Cool completely. Arrange pecan halves on top. Refrigerate overnight to mellow. Several hours before serving prepare Praline Sauce.

Praline Sauce:
1 cup dark corn syrup   2 tablespoons brown sugar
¼ cup cornstarch   1 teaspoon vanilla extract

Combine syrup, cornstarch, and brown sugar in heavy saucepan. Heat and stir until thickened and bubbly. Remove from heat; add vanilla. Serve sauce over each serving or brush on top of pecans.

Grace W. Menzies

BLACKBOTTOM AMARETTO CHEESECAKE

Must prepare ahead, freezes   *Yield: 12 servings*

1½ cups chocolate wafers   1 cup sugar
   (about 30 wafers)   4 eggs
1 cup blanched almonds, lightly   ⅓ cup heavy cream
   toasted   ¼ cup Amaretto liqueur
⅓ cup sugar   1 teaspoon vanilla extract
6 tablespoons cold butter, cut   1 cup sour cream
   into 6 pieces   1 tablespoon sugar
3 (8-ounce) packages cream   1 teaspoon vanilla extract
   cheese, at room
   temperature

Preheat oven to 300°. Butter sides and bottom of a 9½ inch spring-form pan. Using food processor, place broken chocolate wafers, almonds, and ⅓ cup sugar in work bowl. Pulse to combine; add butter and process until very fine crumbs are formed. Pat mixture on the bottom and 1½ inches up sides of prepared pan. Bake 5 minutes. Cool. Reset oven to 375°. Cut cream cheese into 24 pieces; place in work bowl with 1 cup sugar; with steel blade, process until well blended. Add eggs one at a time, processing 1 minute after each addition. Add heavy cream, liqueur, and 1 teaspoon vanilla. Process until mixture is very light, about 5 minutes. Pour over baked shell. Bake 50 minutes, or until cake has almost set. Cool on rack for 5 minutes. Combine sour cream, 1 tablespoon sugar, and 1 teaspoon vanilla. Spread mixture evenly over cake. Return to oven and bake 5 minutes. Cool to room temperature. Cover lightly and chill for 24 hours. To serve, garnish with blanched, slivered, toasted almonds around top edge.

Shirley L. Ballew

TOFU CHEESECAKE

Must prepare ahead   *Yield: 6 to 8 servings*

1 9-inch graham cracker crust
1 tablespoon cornstarch
2 tablespoons water
2 pounds tofu, cut up

½ teaspoon salt
½ cup lemon juice
½ cup honey
2 teaspoons vanilla extract

Preheat oven to 350°. Prepare graham cracker crust. Dissolve cornstarch in water. Combine all ingredients in a blender or food processor and blend until creamy. Pour filling over crust and bake for 40 minutes or until top is golden brown and cake has jelled. Cool to room temperature and refrigerate overnight before serving. Top with fruit if desired.

Note: This is a creamy, low-cost, low-fat version of cheesecake.

Barbara A. Garlitz

RICOTTA CHEESECAKE

Must prepare ahead, freezes   *Yield: 8 to 10 servings*

½ cup graham cracker crumbs
½ cup butter, melted
1½ cups sugar
4 eggs
2 (8-ounce) packages cream
    cheese (at room
    temperature)
1 (16-ounce) carton ricotta
    cheese (at room
    temperature)

1 tablespoon lemon juice
2 teaspoons vanilla extract
3 tablespoons all-purpose flour
3 tablespoons cornstarch
2 cups sour cream

Preheat oven to 325°. Generously butter a 9-or 10-inch springform pan and sprinkle with cracker crumbs to cover bottom and sides. Combine melted butter and sugar. Beat in eggs one at a time, beating well after each addition. Add cheeses, lemon juice, vanilla, flour, cornstarch, and sour cream. Beat until smooth and well blended. Pour into prepared pan. Bake 1 hour; turn off oven. Leave cake in oven for 1 more hour. Remove and cool to room temperature. Cover and refrigerate overnight or up to 3 days before serving.

Lynne G. Leffler

PEACHES AND CREAM CHEESECAKE

Yield: 6 to 8 servings

¾ cup all-purpose flour
1 teaspoon baking powder
½ teaspoon salt
1 (3-ounce) package vanilla
  pudding (not instant)
3 tablespoons butter, softened
1 egg
½ cup milk
1 (16-ounce) can sliced peaches,
  drained and juice reserved

1 (8-ounce) package cream
  cheese, softened
½ cup sugar
3 tablespoons reserved peach
  juice
1 tablespoon sugar
½ teaspoon cinnamon

Preheat oven to 350°. In a bowl, combine flour, baking powder, salt, vanilla pudding, butter, egg, and milk; beat 2 minutes with mixer. Pour into 9 or 10-inch pie pan; cover batter with sliced peaches. In a small bowl, combine cream cheese, ½ cup sugar, and reserved peach juice; beat 2 minutes; spoon mixture over peaches. Combine 1 tablespoon sugar and cinnamon; sprinkle over top of pie. Bake 30 minutes. Cool before serving. May be refrigerated.

Barbara A. Garlitz

HOT FUDGE PUDDING CAKE

Do not prepare ahead   *Yield: 9 servings*

1 cup all-purpose flour
¾ cup sugar
2 tablespoons cocoa
2 teaspoons baking powder
¼ teaspoon salt
½ cup milk

2 tablespoons shortening or
  butter, melted
1 cup nuts, finely chopped
1 cup brown sugar
¼ cup cocoa
1¾ cups hot water

Preheat oven to 350°. Combine flour, sugar, 2 tablespoons cocoa, baking powder, and salt in large bowl. Stir in milk and shortening. Mix well. Add nuts. Pour into one 9x9x2-inch ungreased square pan. Combine brown sugar and ¼ cup cocoa; sprinkle over batter in pan. Pour hot water evenly over mixture in pan. Bake for 45 minutes. While hot, cut into squares; invert each square onto an individual serving plate and spoon sauce over each square. Serve warm, with whipped cream or ice cream topping.

Rebecca B. Simpson

243

CHOCOLATE DELIGHT
Cake and Icing made all together

Freezes well   *Yield: 16 servings*

2 (8-ounce) packages cream
   cheese
1 cup butter or margarine, at
   room temperature
2 (1-pound) boxes powdered
   sugar

2 (4-ounce) bars sweet
   chocolate
¼ cup hot water
1½ teaspoons vanilla extract

Cream cheese and butter until well blended; gradually add sugar. Combine chocolate and hot water; heat until chocolate is melted; add to cheese mixture. Add vanilla and beat well. Remove 3 cups of mixture; set aside to frost cake. To remaining mixture add:

¼ cup butter or margarine
3 eggs
2¼ cups all-purpose flour

1 teaspoon soda
1 cup buttermilk

Cream butter into mixture; add eggs one at a time, beating well after each addition. Add flour and soda alternately with buttermilk. Beat until thoroughly mixed. Grease and flour three 9-inch layer pans; divide batter equally between pans. Place in a preheated oven at 350° for 25 to 30 minutes or until cakes test done. Cool 10 minutes in pans before removing to racks to cool completely. Frost with reserved mixture between layers and on top and sides of cake. Cake is more moist if refrigerated.

Nancy F. Matheson & Carolyn W. Lyerly

HUMMINGBIRD CAKE

May prepare ahead, refrigerate   *Yield: 16 servings*

3 cups all-purpose flour
2 cups sugar
1 teaspoon salt
1 teaspoon soda
1 teaspoon ground cinnamon
3 eggs, beaten
1½ cups salad oil

1½ teaspoons vanilla extract
1 (8-ounce) can crushed
   pineapple, undrained
2 cups chopped pecans or
   walnuts, divided
2 cups chopped bananas
Cream Cheese Frosting

244

Preheat oven to 350°. Grease and flour three 9-inch layer pans. Combine dry ingredients in a large mixing bowl; add eggs and salad oil, stirring until dry ingredients are moistened. *Do not beat.* Stir in vanilla, pineapple, 1 cup chopped nuts, and bananas. Spoon batter into prepared pans and bake for 25 to 30 minutes or until cakes test done. Cool in pans 10 minutes; remove from pans and cool completely. Spread frosting between layers and on top and sides of cake. Sprinkle with 1 cup chopped nuts. Can refrigerate.

Cream Cheese Frosting:

2 (8-ounce) packages cream cheese, softened
1 cup butter or margarine, softened

2 (16-ounce) boxes powdered sugar
2 teaspoons vanilla extract

Combine cream cheese and butter; cream until smooth. Add powdered sugar; beat until light and fluffy. Stir in vanilla. Yield: enough for a 3-layer cake.

Kay B. Melton

RICHMOND BLACKBOTTOMS

Yield: Forty-five to forty-eight 1½-inch cupcakes

1 (8-ounce) package cream cheese
1 egg, beaten
1⅓ cups sugar, divided
⅝ teaspoon salt, divided
1 (6-ounce) package chocolate morsels

1½ cups all-purpose flour
¼ cup cocoa
1 teaspoon baking soda
1 cup water
⅓ cup vegetable oil
1 tablespoon vinegar
1 teaspoon vanilla extract

Preheat oven to 350°. Combine cream cheese, egg, ⅓ cup sugar, and ⅛ teaspoon salt. Beat well; stir in chocolate morsels. Set aside. Sift flour, 1 cup sugar, cocoa, soda, and ½ teaspoon salt into mixing bowl. Add water, oil, vinegar, and vanilla. Beat well. Place mini-cupcake paper liners into 1½-inch muffin pans. Fill each liner half full with cocoa mixture. Drop about ¾ teaspoon of the cream cheese mixture on top of cocoa mixture. Bake 20 to 25 minutes.

Dee E. Hodges

245

FRESH COCONUT HOLIDAY CAKE

Yield: 16 servings

3 cups sifted cake flour
3 teaspoons baking powder
¼ teaspoon salt
1 cup butter
1 (16-ounce) box powdered
    sugar

4 eggs, separated
1 cup milk
1 teaspoon vanilla extract
1 cup freshly grated coconut
Custard Filling
Butter Cream Frosting

Preheat oven to 375°. Grease two 9-inch cake pans and line pans with waxed paper; lightly grease and flour lined pans. Sift together cake flour, baking powder, and salt; set aside. Cream butter; add sugar gradually, beating until light and fluffy. Add egg yolks one at a time, beating well after each. To creamed mixture, add sifted dry ingredients alternately with milk, mixing well after each addition. Add vanilla and coconut. Fold in stiffly beaten egg whites. Pour batter into prepared pans and bake for 30 minutes or until cakes test done. Allow cakes to cool 5 to 10 minutes in pans. Remove to racks and split each layer in half, making 4 thin layers. Cool.

Custard Filling:
⅓ cup all-purpose flour
⅛ teaspoon salt
⅔ cup sugar
2 cups milk, scalded

3 egg yolks
1 tablespoon butter
1 teaspoon vanilla extract
grated fresh coconut

In heavy saucepan, combine flour, salt, and sugar; add scalded milk. Cook over medium heat until mixture begins to thicken. In small bowl mix egg yolks, butter, and vanilla. Add to milk mixture; continue cooking until thickened. Pour mixture through sieve. Spread mixture between cake layers and sprinkle tops of each layer with coconut. Frost top layer and sides with frosting. Keep any extra custard to add to frosting.

Sweet Butter Cream Frosting:
3 tablespoons all-purpose flour
½ cup milk
1½ cups milk

1 cup butter
1 cup sugar
1½ teaspoons vanilla extract

Combine flour and ½ cup milk to make a paste. In heavy saucepan scald 1½ cups milk. Add paste and cook until thickened. Strain. Cream butter and gradually add sugar; beat well. Add milk mixture and any remaining custard. Beat very well and frost cake. Sprinkle generously with grated coconut.

Bess G. Geitner

MILK CHOCOLATE CAKE

Yield: 16 servings

2¼ cups sugar, divided
3 tablespoons water
2 (1-ounce) squares
 unsweetened chocolate,
 melted
¾ cup butter
1 teaspoon vanilla extract
4 eggs, separated

2¼ cups sifted cake flour
1 teaspoon cream of tartar
½ teaspoon soda
½ teaspoon salt
1 cup milk
Cream Filling
Chocolate Cream Cheese
 Frosting

Preheat oven to 350º. Lightly grease and flour three 9-inch layer pans. Combine ¼ cup sugar, water, and melted chocolate; set aside. Cream butter and add remaining 2 cups sugar gradually, beating until light and fluffy. Add vanilla, then egg yolks one at a time, beating well after each addition. Add chocolate mixture and blend thoroughly. Sift flour, cream of tartar, soda, and salt together; add alternately with milk, beginning and ending with flour mixture. Beat until smooth. Beat egg whites until stiff but not dry; fold gently into batter until well blended. Pour into prepared pans; bake 25 to 30 minutes, or until cakes test done.

Cream Filling:

½ cup sugar
3 tablespoons all-purpose flour
⅛ teaspoon salt

1½ cups milk
2 eggs, beaten
½ teaspoon vanilla extract

In top of a double boiler, mix ¼ cup sugar, flour, and salt. Add ½ cup milk, stir until smooth. Pour in remaining 1 cup milk and cook over boiling water for 10 minutes until smooth and thickened. Combine remaining ¼ cup sugar and eggs. Add hot mixture slowly, stirring constantly. Return to double boiler and cook for 5 more minutes. Cool and add vanilla. Spread between cooled layers.

Chocolate Cream Cheese Frosting:

¼ cup butter or margarine
1 (8-ounce) package cream
 cheese
3 (1-ounce) squares
 unsweetened chocolate,
 melted

dash salt
3 cups sifted powdered sugar
⅓ cup heavy cream
1 teaspoon vanilla

Cream butter. Add cheese, chocolate, and salt. Add sugar alternately with cream, beating thoroughly after each addition. Add vanilla. Spread on top and sides of cake.

Winnie B. Hovey

PINEAPPLE CARROT LAYER CAKE

Freezes well   *Yield: 16 to 18 servings*

2 cups all-purpose flour
2 teaspoons baking powder
1½ teaspoons soda
2 teaspoons cinnamon
1 teaspoon salt
1½ cups vegetable oil
2 cups sugar

4 eggs
2 cups raw carrots, grated
1 (8.5-ounce) can crushed
   pineapple, undrained
½ cup pecans, chopped
   (optional)

Preheat oven to 350°. Grease and flour three 9-inch layer pans. Sift together flour, baking powder, soda, cinnamon, and salt. Set aside. Combine oil and sugar in large mixer bowl. Add eggs one at a time, beating after each addition. Add sifted dry ingredients; mix well. Stir in carrots, pineapple, and pecans. Pour into prepared pans. Bake 35 to 40 minutes. *Do not overbake.* Frost with Pineapple Icing.

Pineapple Icing:
¼ cup butter, softened
1 (8-ounce) package cream
   cheese, softened
1 (16-ounce) box powdered
   sugar

1 teaspoon vanilla extract
1 (8.5-ounce) can crushed
   pineapple, well drained
1 cup pecans, finely chopped
   (optional)

Combine all ingredients and mix well. Spread between layers and on top and sides of a 9-inch, 3 layer cake.

Roddy S. Dixon

MY FAVORITE RUM CAKE

Freezes well   *Yield: 16 servings*

1 cup pecan pieces
1 (18.5-ounce) package yellow
   cake mix
1 (3¾-ounce) package instant
   vanilla pudding mix

4 eggs
¾ cup cold water
¼ cup vegetable oil
¼ cup dark rum

Preheat oven to 325°. Grease and flour a 10-inch tube or bundt pan. Sprinkle pecans evenly over bottom of pan. In large mixer bowl, combine all other ingredients. Beat on medium speed of electric mixer for 2 minutes. Pour into prepared pan. Bake for 50 minutes. Cool in pan for 15 minutes. Invert on serving plate. Prick cake with long-tined fork. Glaze.

Glaze:
1 cup sugar
1/2 cup butter or margarine
1/2 cup water

1/4 cup plus 1 tablespoon
   dark rum

In saucepan, combine sugar, butter, and water. Bring to a boil and boil 5 minutes, stirring constantly. Remove from heat and add rum. Spoon hot glaze over warm cake.

Pat Y. Tolbert

GRANDMOTHER'S CHRISTMAS CAKE

Yield: 12 servings

Raisin Filling
1/2 cup butter
1 cup sugar
2 eggs
1 3/4 cups sifted cake flour
2 1/2 teaspoons baking powder

1/2 teaspoon salt
1/2 cup milk
1 teaspoon vanilla
rind of an orange, grated
7-Minute Frosting

Preheat oven to 350°. Grease and lightly flour two 8 or 9-inch layer pans. Cream butter; add sugar gradually and beat until light and fluffy. Add eggs one at a time; beat well after each addition. Resift flour with baking powder and salt. Add flour mixture, in 4 equal parts, alternately with milk to creamed mixture. Mix in vanilla and orange rind. Pour batter into prepared pans and bake for 25 minutes or until cake pulls away from sides of pan. Cool on racks.

Raisin Filling:
2 1/2 cups raisins
1 1/2 cups pecans
4 tablespoons orange juice

2 eggs
1/2 cup sweet wine or bourbon

Grind raisins and pecans together; moisten with orange juice. Beat eggs; add wine or bourbon; combine with raisin mixture and let stand several hours to mellow. Taste; add more wine or bourbon if desired. Spread between layers. Frost top and sides of cake with 7-Minute Frosting.

Note: Grind raisins and nuts in a food processor or meat grinder.

Dorothy Y. Menzies

249

COCONUT PECAN PUMPKIN CAKE

Freezes well   *Yield: 16 servings*

2 cups sugar
1 (16-ounce) can pumpkin
1 cup vegetable oil
4 eggs, beaten
2 cups all-purpose flour
1 teaspoon salt

2 teaspoons baking soda
2 teaspoons baking powder
2 teaspoons ground cinnamon
1/2 cup flaked coconut
3/4 cup chopped pecans

Preheat oven to 350°. Grease and flour three 9-inch layer pans. Combine sugar, pumpkin, oil, and eggs; beat 1 minute at medium speed of electric mixer. Combine flour, salt, soda, baking powder, and cinnamon; add pumpkin mixture. Beat 1 minute at medium speed. Stir in coconut and pecans. Pour batter into prepared pans. Bake for 25 to 30 minutes or until cakes test done. Cool in pans 10 minutes; remove from pans and cool completely. Spread with frosting.

Frosting:
1 cup butter or margarine, softened
2 (8-ounce) packages cream cheese, softened
1 (16-ounce) box powdered sugar

2 teaspoons vanilla extract
1/2 cup chopped pecans
1 cup flaked coconut

Combine butter and cream cheese; beat until light and fluffy. Add sugar and vanilla, mixing well. Stir in pecans and coconut. Spread between layers and on top and sides of three layer cake.

Bobbi H. Dickinson

CHOCOLATE BOURBON CAKE

Must prepare ahead, freezes   *Yield: 16 to 18 servings*

1 pound dry macaroons (about 4 dozen)
1 cup bourbon
1 dozen double lady fingers, split
2 cups butter (no substitute)
1 cup sugar

1 cup powdered sugar
12 eggs, separated
4 ounces unsweetened chocolate, melted
1 teaspoon vanilla extract
1 cup pecans, chopped
1 1/2 cups heavy cream, whipped

Break and soak the macaroons in bourbon. Line a 10-inch springform pan around sides and bottom with split lady fingers. Cream butter and sugars until light and fluffy. Beat egg yolks until light and blend into butter mixture. Beat in chocolate; add vanilla and pecans. Beat egg whites until stiff but not dry; fold into chocolate mixture. Alternate layers of chocolate mixture and soaked macaroons ending with chocolate layer, in lined pan. Chill overnight, or freeze. If frozen, defrost overnight in refrigerator. Remove sides of pan. Decorate with whipped cream. Slice and serve.

Donna G. Gerrard

ORANGE DATE NUT CAKE

Yield: 12 to 16 servings

1 cup sugar	1 cup buttermilk
3/4 cup butter	1 (8-ounce) package chopped
3 eggs	dates
3 cups all-purpose flour	1 cup pecans, chopped
1/2 teaspoon salt	1 teaspoon vanilla extract
1 1/2 teaspoons baking soda	grated rind of 2 oranges

Preheat oven to 350º. Grease a 10-inch tube or bundt pan. Cream sugar and butter until fluffy. Add eggs one at a time, beating well after each addition. Mix together flour, salt, and soda. Add dry ingredients alternately with buttermilk to creamed mixture. Blend well. Fold in dates, nuts, vanilla, and grated orange rind. Mix thoroughly. Pour into prepared pan and bake 1 hour. Glaze while hot in pan. Let cake cool 1 hour after glazing in pan, then remove.

Glaze:

juice of 2 oranges	1 cup sugar

Squeeze juice from oranges; add sugar; bring to a boil, then simmer until transparent. Pour over hot cake.

Elaine S. Zerden & Sara D. Burgess

Variation: Cake can be baked in 1 1/2-inch muffin tins. Bake for 15 minutes. Remove from tins and dip in glaze while warm. Makes 6 to 7 dozen.

Della Marie V. McKinnon

DOROTHY'S CHOCOLATE CAKE

Refrigerate   *Yield: 16 servings*

1 cup cocoa
2 cups boiling water
1 cup butter or margarine,
  softened
2½ cups sugar
4 eggs
1½ teaspoons vanilla extract

2¾ cups all-purpose flour
2 teaspoons baking soda
½ teaspoon baking powder
½ teaspoon salt
Filling
Frosting
pecan halves (optional)

Preheat oven to 350°. Grease and flour three 9-inch round cake pans. Combine cocoa and boiling water, stirring until smooth; set aside to cool. Combine butter, sugar, eggs, and vanilla; beat at high speed of electric mixer until light and fluffy (about 5 minutes). Combine dry ingredients; add to sugar mixture alternately with cocoa mixture, beating at low speed of electric mixer and beginning and ending with flour mixture. Do not overbeat. Pour batter into prepared pans. Bake for 25 to 30 minutes or until a wooden pick inserted in center comes out clean. Cool in pans 10 minutes; remove from pans, and cool completely. Spread filling between layers, and spread frosting on top and sides. Garnish with pecans, if desired. Serve at once, or refrigerate until ready to serve.

Filling:
1 cup heavy cream   ¼ cup powdered sugar
1 teaspoon vanilla extract

Beat cream and vanilla until foamy; gradually add powdered sugar, beating until peaks hold their shape. Chill.

Frosting:
1 (6-ounce) package semisweet   1 cup butter or margarine
  chocolate morsels   2½ cups powdered sugar,
½ cup light cream   sifted

Combine chocolate morsels, cream, and butter in a saucepan; cook over medium heat, stirring until chocolate melts. Remove from heat; add powdered sugar, mixing well. Set saucepan in ice, and beat until frosting holds its shape and loses its gloss. Add a few more drops of cream if needed to make icing spreading consistency.

Dorothy Y. Menzies

ZUCCHINI CAKE

Freezes well   *Yield: 12 to 16 servings*

½ cup plus 1 tablespoon butter
2 cups sugar
3 eggs
3 (1-ounce) squares
   unsweetened chocolate,
   melted
2 teaspoons vanilla extract
2 teaspoons orange rind, grated

½ cup milk
2 cups zucchini, coarsely grated,
   drained
2½ cups all-purpose flour
2½ teaspoons baking powder
1½ teaspoons baking soda
1 teaspoon salt
1 teaspoon cinnamon

Preheat oven to 350°. Grease a 10-inch bundt pan. Cream butter and sugar until light in a large mixing bowl. Add eggs one at a time, beating well after each addition. Add melted chocolate, vanilla, orange rind, and milk. Blend thoroughly. Stir in grated zucchini. Sift flour with baking powder, baking soda, salt, and cinnamon. Add to zucchini mixture and mix well. Turn batter into prepared pan. Bake 60 to 65 minutes or until cake pulls away slightly from sides of pan and feels firm when touched. Cool slightly in pan, then turn out and let cool completely.

Susan L. Ingle

Variation: A lunch box favorite. Cake is just as good made with unsweetened cocoa or carob. Follow instructions on cocoa or carob box to substitute for the chocolate. Zucchini can be grated in food processor or blender; if using blender add a little bit of orange juice for moisture. Drain in a sieve before adding to batter.

FROSTING
LEMON BUTTER FROSTING

Yield: 1½ cups

⅓ cup butter, melted
2 tablespoons lemon juice
rind of one lemon, grated

2 cups powdered sugar
few drops yellow food coloring

Combine all ingredients in small mixer bowl and beat until smooth. Spread over top and side of Hot Milk Cake.

Della Marie V. McKinnon

253

BIRTHDAY CAKE ICING

Yield: covers one 3 layer cake

2½ cups sugar
3 tablespoons light corn syrup
½ cup water
4 egg whites

pinch of cream of tartar
⅓ to ½ cup powdered sugar
candy thermometer

Combine sugar, syrup, and water in a heavy saucepan, bring to a boil and boil until mixture reaches 240° on a candy thermometer. (If weather is humid, cook syrup to 242°.) While syrup is cooking, in large bowl of electric mixer, beat egg whites with cream of tartar until very stiff. Add syrup; continue beating at high speed until firm peaks form; stir in powdered sugar. Spread over layers.

Note: A candy thermometer is a must for this recipe.

Martha T. Kurad

CARAMEL ICING

Yield: 2 cups

2 cups brown sugar
1 cup sugar
1 cup sour cream

pinch of salt
1 tablespoon butter
1 teaspoon vanilla extract

In a heavy saucepan, combine sugars, sour cream, and salt. Cook over low heat, stirring constantly, to 238° or until a soft ball forms when dropped into a cup of cold water. Remove from heat; add butter and vanilla. Place pan in ice and cool to lukewarm without stirring. When cool, beat with electric mixer until thickened. Spread between layers and on top and sides of a two layer 8- or 9-inch cake.

Dorothy Y. Menzies

COLONNADE ICING

Freezes well   *Yield: 8 cups*

4½ cups sugar
1 cup water
6 tablespoons light corn syrup
6 egg whites

½ cup powdered sugar
1 teaspoon vanilla, almond, rum,
    brandy, peppermint, or any
    flavor you like

In a heavy saucepan, combine sugar, water, and corn syrup; cook over medium heat to a soft ball stage or 238° on a candy thermometer. (When testing in cold water, remove frosting from heat, to prevent overcooking.) Add slowly to egg whites which have been beaten stiff but not dry, beating thoroughly until the icing is like cream. Add powdered sugar and flavoring.

Note: This is a soft-on-the-inside, crusty on-the-outside icing that never fails. Left-overs may be refrigerated or frozen. To use, heat over warm water in double boiler to lukewarm or spreading consistency.

Bess G. Geitner

FUDGE FROSTING

Yield: 2 cups

2 (1-ounce) squares
    unsweetened chocolate
⅔ cup milk
2 cups sugar
½ teaspoon salt

2 tablespoons light corn syrup
2 tablespoons butter or
    margarine
1 teaspoon vanilla extract

In a heavy saucepan, break chocolate into small pieces, add milk and heat until chocolate melts. Add sugar, salt, and syrup; stir until mixture comes to a boil. Cook until a soft ball forms in cold water, or 238° on a candy thermometer. Remove from heat; add butter and vanilla. Place pan in ice to cool to lukewarm. Beat with electric mixer until spreading consistency.

Dorothy Y. Menzies

DUART'S MARSHMALLOW ICING
(SEVEN MINUTE)

Yield: 2 cups

1 large egg white
1 cup sugar
3 marshmallows, diced
2 tablespoons light corn syrup

¼ teaspoon cream of tartar
¼ teaspoon salt
⅓ cup boiling water

In a large double boiler mix together egg whites, sugar, marshmallows, corn syrup, cream of tartar, and salt. Add boiling water. Place over boiling water and beat constantly at high speed until stiff (about 7 to 10 minutes). Spread on cake. This icing will not get crusty.

Sally T. Blackwelder

PINEAPPLE FILLING

Yield: 2 cups

1 cup sugar
8 tablespoons all-purpose flour
¼ teaspoon salt
1 (8-ounce) can crushed
    pineapple

4 tablespoons lemon juice
2 egg yolks
2 tablespoons butter

In a heavy saucepan, blend sugar, flour, salt, and pineapple. Add lemon juice and egg yolks. Cook over medium heat, stirring constantly until filling becomes very thick. Add butter; beat and cool. Use as a filling for Hot Milk Cake and frost with Lemon Butter Frosting.

Della Marie V. McKinnon

ORANGE COCONUT FILLING

Yield: topping for 13x9x2-inch cake

1 egg
½ cup sugar
1 cup orange juice

1 tablespoon cornstarch
rind of ½ orange, grated
fresh grated coconut

In a heavy saucepan, combine egg, sugar, juice, cornstarch, and rind; cook until thickened. Spread over cake and sprinkle with coconut.

Della Marie V. McKinnon

MARIE'S YUMMY LEMON FILLING

Yield: 1 cup

2 eggs
1 cup sugar
juice and grated rind of 2
   large lemons

2 tablespoons butter

Beat eggs in top of double boiler until fluffy. Add sugar and blend well. Add juice and rind. Cook over boiling water until thickened, stirring constantly (about 15 to 20 minutes). Add butter and stir until melted. Remove from heat and cool. Serve hot or store in refrigerator in glass container up to 2 to 3 weeks.

Note: This filling served warm over stale pound cake makes it a delight. Cooled, it is perfect for cake filling. It is wonderful as a sauce for a fruit compote or fruit salad.

Sally T. Blackwelder

ROBERT E. LEE CAKE FILLING

1 large coconut, grated
juice and grated rind of 3
   large oranges
juice and grated rind of 3
   large lemons

3 cups sugar
¾ cup coconut milk
3 egg whites, beaten

Drain coconut and reserve milk. Grate coconut. Juice and grate rind of oranges and lemons. Strain juices. In a heavy saucepan, combine sugar and coconut milk (add enough water to make ¾ cup). Cook until it forms a soft ball in cold water, or 238° on a candy thermometer. Pour over beaten egg whites. Beat until thoroughly mixed. Cool a few minutes. Pour juices and rind over mixture. Mix thoroughly. Pour by tablespoons over layers of a yellow or white layer cake. Pierce layers, to aid in thoroughly soaking each layer. When soaked, sprinkle with coconut. Use all mixture for a 3 layer cake and pat coconut around sides.

Note: This is a very old recipe and is delicious.

Dorothy Y. Menzies

DESSERTS

AMARETTO BAVARIAN DESSERT

Must prepare ahead   *Yield: 16 servings*

1 (16-ounce) angel food cake
5 cups hot milk
1¾ cups sugar
¼ cup all-purpose flour
5 eggs, well beaten

pinch of salt
1 tablespoon unflavored gelatin
¼ cup cold milk
¼ cup Amaretto or sherry
prepared whipped topping

Remove brown crust from cake and break into small pieces in large mixing bowl. Heat milk in a 3-quart heavy saucepan. When hot, beat in sugar, flour, eggs, and salt. Cook over low heat, stirring constantly, until mixture coats spoon. Remove from heat and quickly add gelatin softened in cold milk. Stir until well blended. Add Amaretto. Fold mixture into cake pieces. Spray a 10-inch bundt pan with vegetable coating. Pour cake mixture into pan and chill overnight. To serve, unmold and frost with prepared whipped topping.

Joanne M. Martin

LEMON CUPS

Yield: 8 servings

2 tablespoons butter, melted
1 cup sugar
4 tablespoons all-purpose flour
pinch of salt
5 tablespoons lemon juice

grated rind of 1 lemon
3 eggs, separated
1½ cups milk
½ cup heavy cream, whipped

Preheat oven to 350º. Cream butter with sugar, flour and salt. Add lemon juice and rind. Set aside. Beat egg yolks well, and add milk. Add to creamed mixture and mix well. Fold in stiffly beaten egg whites. Pour into greased oven-proof custard cups; place in a pan of hot water. Bake for 45 minutes. When baked, each dessert will have custard on the bottom and cake on top. Serve warm or chilled; topped with whipped cream.

Nancy S. Spivey

BANANAS FOSTER

Yield: 4 to 6 servings

¼ cup butter
½ cup light brown sugar, firmly
   packed
4 ripe bananas, peeled and
   sliced lengthwise

dash nutmeg
¼ cup banana liqueur
½ cup white rum
1 pint French vanilla ice cream

In a flat chafing dish or large skillet, melt butter and brown sugar. Add bananas in a single layer and sauté until tender. Sprinkle with nutmeg. Pour banana liqueur over all. In a small saucepan warm rum. With a long tapered match ignite rum and pour over bananas. Remove from heat and baste until flame burns out. Serve immediately topped with ice cream.

Sylvia H. Bowman

COFFEE MOLD

Must prepare ahead   *Yield: 16 servings*

1 (10-ounce) package
   marshmallows
1 cup strong hot coffee
3 tablespoons rum

1 pint heavy cream, whipped
2 (3-ounce) packages lady
   fingers, split

Melt marshmallows in top of double boiler; add coffee while melting. Cool. When cool, add rum. When thoroughly cooled, add whipped cream. Line buttered 6-cup mold with lady fingers. Cover with ½ of the coffee mixture. Add another layer of lady fingers and then remaining coffee mixture. Refrigerate overnight.

Frosting:
1 pint heavy cream, whipped   1 cup almonds, toasted

Unmold dessert on serving plate. Frost with whipped cream and garnish with almonds. Refrigerate until ready to serve.

Joanne M. Martin

BISQUE TORTONI

Yield: ½ gallon

½ gallon all natural vanilla
   ice cream
12 macaroons, crumbled
¼ cup cream sherry
1 (6-ounce) jar red maraschino
   cherries

1 (6-ounce) jar green
   maraschino cherries
¾ cup slivered almonds

While ice cream is softening, soak macaroon crumbs in sherry. Quarter and drain cherries. Blend soaked crumbs, cherries, and almonds into soft ice cream. Return to ice cream carton and refreeze. A pretty and easy holiday dessert.

Note: If frozen, macaroons will crumb quickly in food processor.

Nancy C. Shuford

CHOCOLATE NUT CRUMBLE

Must prepare ahead

Yield: 6 to 8 servings

1½ cups vanilla wafer crumbs
½ cup chopped nuts
½ cup butter
1 cup powdered sugar
3 egg yolks
1½ (1-ounce) squares semi-
   sweet chocolate, melted

½ teaspoon vanilla extract
3 egg whites, stiffly beaten
½ pint heavy cream, whipped
·6 to 8 red maraschino cherries

Mix crumbs and nuts. Put ½ mixture in the bottom of an 8x8x1-inch pan. Cream butter and powdered sugar. Add egg yolks, melted chocolate, and vanilla; mix well. Fold in egg whites. Pour chocolate mixture over crumbs and top with remaining crumbs. Chill overnight. Top with whipped cream and cherries when ready to serve.

Note: This recipe comes from one of the best cooks in North Carolina. It is a grand company dessert; easy, delicious, light, and needs to be prepared ahead.

Susan L. Ingle

CAPRICE TORTE
(PROCESSOR)

May prepare ahead   *Yield: 12 to 15 servings*

1²/₃ cups blanched almonds   4 egg yolks
7-ounces unsweetened   ¹/₄ teaspoon salt
   chocolate, cut in pieces   1 teaspoon vanilla extract
1 cup butter   4 egg whites
1 cup plus 2 teaspoons sugar

Preheat oven to 300°. Prepare an 8-inch spring-form pan by lining with foil, then butter well. Set aside. In work bowl of food processor with *steel knife*, grind almonds finely. Remove to mixing bowl. Add chocolate to work bowl and process until finely chopped. Add to almonds. In work bowl cream butter and sugar. Add egg yolks, salt, and vanilla. Process to combine. Stir into almond and chocolate mixture. Beat egg whites until stiff, but not dry, and fold into almond mixture; Pour into prepared pan. Bake for 40 minutes. Cool on a rack. Remove foil and decorate with powdered sugar or whipped cream.

Anne F. Mitchell

CARROT TORTE

Yield: 10 to 12 servings

1 cup sugar   juice of ¹/₂ lemon
1 cup carrots, cooked and   juice of ¹/₂ orange
   mashed   raspberry jam
1 cup grated almonds, blanched   whipped cream
6 eggs, separated

Combine sugar, carrots, almonds, egg yolks (mixing well after adding each yolk) and juices. Beat egg whites until stiff but not dry. Add to mixture and pour into oiled 8-inch spring form pan without center spout. Bake at 350° for 45 minutes. Allow to cool. Spread on layer of jam or preserves and cover with whipped cream.

Donna G. Gerrard

SALLY'S HOT SHERRIED FRUIT CRÊPES

May prepare ahead   *Yield: 85 crêpes*

2½ cups butter, melted
10 tablespoons all-purpose flour
2½ cups sugar
5 (16-ounce) cans pears,
  chopped, drained, reserve
  juice
5 (16-ounce) can peaches,
  chopped, drained, reserve
  juice
5 (20-ounce) cans pineapple
  chunks, drained, reserve
  juice

3 (16-ounce) cans seedless
  grapes, halved, drained,
  reserve juice
5 (16-ounce) cans apricots,
  chopped, drained, reserve
  juice
1 cup reserved juice
5 cups dry sherry
85 prepared crêpes (Basic
  crêpes, page 90)
cinnamon and sugar

Place butter in a large saucepan over medium heat. Stir in flour and sugar until smooth. Mix juices from all drained fruits; add 1 cup of mixed juice and the sherry to sugar mixture slowly, stirring constantly until smooth and thickened. Remove from heat and divide sauce into 2 equal parts. Add fruits to one part in a *large* bowl and cool. Prepare crêpes. Fill crêpes with fruit mixture, tucking ends under carefully. Place in shallow buttered baking dishes and "ice" with remaining sauce. Cover and refrigerate until ready to bake. One half hour before serving, sprinkle tops with a light cinnamon and sugar mixture; bake at 350° for 20 to 30 minutes.

Note: This recipe can be divided by 5 to serve 15 people. This is delicious for brunch served with sausage-egg casserole, hot brioche, and a green salad or fresh asparagus.

Sally T. Blackwelder

APRICOT-ALMOND SAUCE FOR CRÊPES

Yield: 4 servings

8 Dessert Crêpes, page 90.

½ cup apricot preserves   2 ounces orange Curaçao
½ cup butter   slivered almonds, toasted

Preheat oven to 350°. Combine preserves, butter, and Curaçao; cook until thickened. To assemble dessert, fold 8 crêpes twice, place on a silver platter and heat 5 minutes. Pour warm sauce over crêpes and sprinkle with almonds.

Note: Use the same liqueur for sauce and crêpes. Cook Extra crêpes as directed, stack between layers of waxed paper, and freeze for another time.

Anne F. Mitchell

MOUSSE AU CHOCOLAT

Must prepare ahead   *Yield: 6 servings*

6 (1-ounce) squares semi-sweet   5 egg whites at room
  chocolate   temperature
1 tablespoon strong coffee   ¼ teaspoon cream of tartar
1 tablespoon orange-flavored   orange peel, cut into thin strips
  liqueur   6 mint sprigs

Melt chocolate with coffee in a double boiler over hot (not boiling) water. Remove from heat and beat in the liqueur until mixture is smooth. Beat egg whites and cream of tartar until stiff, but not dry. Beat 2 or 3 tablespoons of the beaten egg white into chocolate mixture to loosen it up. Fold in remaining egg whites gently and thoroughly, until no streaks of white remain. Spoon into 6 demi-tasse cups, individual souffle cups, pots-de-creme cups, or wine glasses. Refrigerate at least 2 hours. Decorate with chopped thin peel of orange and mint sprigs.

Note: This is wonderful and only 158 calories each serving.

Anne F. Mitchell

**D
E
S
S
E
R
T
S**

CHOCOLATE SOUFFLÉ

Yield: 8 servings

2 (1-ounce) squares
  unsweetened chocolate
2 cups milk
½ cup sugar
⅓ cup all-purpose flour

½ teaspoon salt
2 tablespoons butter or
  margarine
1 teaspoon vanilla extract
4 eggs, separated

Heat chocolate and milk in top of double boiler, beating until chocolate melts and mixture is well blended. Combine sugar, flour, and salt. Add small amount of chocolate mixture, stirring until smooth. Return to double boiler and cook for 5 minutes, or until thick, stirring often. Add butter and vanilla. Cool slightly. Beat egg whites until stiff. Then beat yolks until thick and lemon-colored. Stir yolks into chocolate mixture. Fold in whites. Pour into a buttered 1½-quart soufflé dish or casserole. Set into pan of hot water and bake at 350° for 1¼ hours, or until firm.

June P. Wilfong

DIETER'S CITRUS SOUFFLÉ

Must prepare ahead   *Yield: 4 to 6 servings*

1 tablespoon unflavored gelatin
¼ cup cold water
2 cups skimmed milk
4 egg yolks

artificial sweetener to taste
½ cup lemon juice
2 tablespoons grated lemon peel
8 egg whites, stiffly beaten

Dissolve gelatin in cold water. Bring milk to boil; add egg yolks and beat. Cook over medium heat until mixture has thickened. Add gelatin and cool. Add sweetener, lemon juice and peel. As mixture begins to congeal, fold in egg whites. Pile into a soufflé dish and refrigerate.

Variation: For orange or lime soufflé, use corresponding juice and peel in place of lemon.

Lindy M. Dillow

DIVINE CHOCOLATE MOUSSE CAKE

Must prepare ahead   *Yield: 12 to 16 servings*

Meringues:
5 egg whites   1 3/4 cups powdered sugar
pinch of cream of tartar   1/3 cup unsweetened cocoa
3/4 cup sugar   parchment paper

Preheat oven to 300°. In a large bowl, beat egg whites with cream of tartar until soft peaks form. Beat in sugar, 2 tablespoons at a time and continue beating until it holds very stiff peaks. Sift together powdered sugar and cocoa, and add to mixture. Set parchment paper on baking sheets. Using an inverted 8-inch square cake pan as a guide, trace 3 squares onto paper. Divide meringue on the squares, spreading evenly to the edges. Bake, alternating baking sheets if necessary for even baking, for 1 hour and 15 minutes. Transfer to racks and cool.

Chocolate Mousse:
13-ounces semi-sweet chocolate   3 cups heavy cream, well chilled
7 egg whites   1 1/2 teaspoons vanilla extract
1/4 teaspoon cream of tartar

In a double boiler over water, melt chocolate. Let cool until lukewarm. Beat egg whites and cream of tartar until stiff peaks form. In another bowl, beat cream and vanilla until it holds stiff peaks. Fold the chocolate carefully into the egg whites. Then fold in cream. Makes 9 cups.

Assemble:
Put 1 meringue on cake stand and spread it thickly with chocolate mousse. Top with second meringue, spread thickly with mousse and top with third meringue. Transfer remaining filling to pastry bag fitted with decorative tip and decorate top of cake with rows of overlapping figure eights. Chill cake, lightly covered, for 4 hours or overnight. Cake may be kept refrigerated for up to 48 hours.

Note: So spectacular and sinfully delicious you will be tempted to eat the whole thing!

Anne F. Mitchell

265

KAHLÚA MOUSSE

Prepare ahead, freeze   *Yield: 8 servings*

¼ cup superfine sugar
1 tablespoon cognac
3 tablespoons Kahlúa
3 (1-ounce) squares semi-sweet
chocolate

1 (1-ounce) square unsweetened
chocolate
2 egg whites, stiffly beaten
2 cups heavy cream, whipped
shaved semi-sweet chocolate

In heavy saucepan, combine sugar, cognac, and Kahlúa; simmer over very low heat until sugar is dissolved, but not brown. Melt the semi-sweet and unsweetened chocolate in top of a double boiler. Add sugar syrup and stir until smooth. When mixture is thoroughly cooled, fold in beaten egg whites. (If chocolate mixture is too stiff to fold, add 1 tablespoon Kahlúa.) Gently fold the egg whites and chocolate mixture into the whipped cream. Freeze. Can be kept several days. To serve, garnish with the shaved chocolate.

Note: To make superfine sugar, place granulated sugar in blender or food processor and process until very fine.

Josephine L. Hambrick

LUSCIOUS PEACH PUDDING

Must prepare ahead   *Yield: 10 servings*

3 cups fresh peaches, diced
½ cup butter or margarine,
melted
2 eggs, well beaten

1 cup sugar
1 (8-ounce) carton prepared
whipped topping, divided
vanilla wafers

Cover diced peaches and set aside. Combine melted butter, eggs, and sugar in mixing bowl. Beat on medium speed for 4 or 5 minutes. Fold in ⅔ of whipped topping and stir in peaches. In greased 2-quart dish, cover bottom with vanilla wafers, top with ½ peach mixture; repeat. Top with remaining whipped topping. Refrigerate at least one hour before serving.

Lynn L. Lyerly

COLD CITRUS SOUFFLÉ

Yields: 6-8

Liquid and Yolks:
1 package gelatin   5 egg yolks
¼ cup rum

Flavorings:
1½ cups sugar   zest of one lemon
¼ cup lemon juice   zest of two limes
¼ cup lime juice

Cream and whites:
2 cups whipping cream   ¼ teaspoon cream of tartar (if
5 egg whites   not using a copper bowl)
1 tablespoon sugar   ⅛ teaspoon salt

Prepare a 1-quart soufflé dish by putting a collar around it and wiping it with an oiled paper towel. Sprinkle the gelatin on the ¼ cup of liquid in a small saucepan.

Beat the egg yolks until frothy. Gradually add the ½ cup of sugar. Continue beating until the mixture is thick and mousse-like (refers to that point when the mixture becomes very thick and creamy like a mousse, with the yolks a pale yellow). Fold in the remaining flavorings.

Whip the cream until it is the same consistency as the egg yolks and sugar. Beating until the cream is stiff will make it hard to incorporate.

Check the gelatin. It should look like grainy jello. Place the gelatin over extremely low heat to melt.

Meanwhile, whisk the whites, salt and optional cream of tartar to the soft peak stage. Add the 1 tablespoon sugar and whisk to moist, stiff peaks.

Pour the melted gelatin into the yolk mixture. Fold in the egg whites. Finally, fold in the whipped cream.

Pour the mixture into a prepared soufflé dish. Refrigerate for at least 3 hours to set. If freezing, refrigerate for 1 hour. Then wrap and freeze.

Note: If the gelatin gets too hot, it may fail to gel or will become stringy and clump together. It must be melted over extremely low heat. Periodically, remove the pan from the heat and place it on your hand. If the pan is too hot for your hand, it is too hot for the gelatin. If your gelatin is too hot you will not forget it!

Anne Byrd
"Omelettes & Souffles"
(Used with permission of the Author.) ISB#0-941034-08-9

LEMON BISQUE

Must prepare ahead, freeze   *Yield: 6 to 8 servings*

3 tablespoons cornstarch
1 cup sugar
pinch of salt
rind of 1 lemon, grated
1 cup boiling water

juice of 2 lemons
2 eggs, separated
½ pint whipping cream, whipped
8 to 12 graham crackers,
    crushed and divided

Mix cornstarch, sugar, salt, and rind. Add boiling water, stirring to blend. Cook in double boiler until clear. Cool. Beat egg yolks and lemon juice and add to mixture. Fold in whipped cream. Beat egg whites until stiff; fold into mixture. Spread ⅔ crumbs in bottom of 8x5x3-inch loaf pan. Fill with lemon mixture and sprinkle remaining crumbs on top. Freeze; do not stir.

Joanne M. Martin

ROWENA'S PLUM PUDDING

Yield: 6 servings

1 cup suet, finely chopped
1 cup molasses
4 cups all-purpose flour
1 teaspoon cinnamon
½ teaspoon nutmeg

1 teaspoon soda
1 cup milk
2 cups candied mixed fruit
sauce

Combine suet and molasses. Add flour, spices, soda, and milk. Stir in candied fruit. Pour mixture into greased 2-quart mold, filling to 1-inch from top. Cover mold tightly and place in large kettle; fill kettle with water to cover ½ to ⅔ of mold. Cover kettle and steam for 3 hours. Unmold and serve hot topped with sauce.

Sauce:
4 cups powdered sugar
¼ cup butter

3 eggs, separated
brandy, to taste

Cream sugar and butter. Beat egg yolks and combine with sugar mixture. Beat well, then add brandy. Beat egg whites until stiff and fold into mixture.

Alice L. Bost

BAVARIAN STRAWBERRY CUSTARD CAKE

Must prepare ahead   *Yield: 12 to 14 servings*

1 cup sugar
2 tablespoons all-purpose flour
4 egg yolks
2 cups milk
dash salt
1 tablespoon unflavored gelatin
¼ cup cold water
1 teaspoon vanilla extract

4 egg whites
2 cups heavy cream, whipped,
   divided
1 (1-pound) angel food cake,
   broken in bite size pieces
2 to 3 cups fresh strawberries,
   sliced and sweetened

In top of double boiler, over hot water, combine sugar, flour, egg yolks, milk, and salt. Cook until thickened, stirring constantly. Dissolve gelatin in water; add to custard. Stir in well. Add vanilla and cool. (You may put pan in bowl of ice and stir to hasten cooling.) When thoroughly cooled, whip 1 cup of cream. Beat egg whites until stiff; fold cream and egg whites into custard. In a large bowl, gently fold cake pieces into custard. Pour into a 12-inch tube pan. Chill for at least 24 hours. At serving time, turn out on serving plate. Whip remaining cream, sweeten slightly. Frost cake with whipped cream. Garnish generously with strawberries.

Nancy C. Shuford

POT DE CRÈME

Must prepare ahead   *Yield: 6 to 8 servings*

2 cups heavy cream
4 egg yolks
5 tablespoons sugar
⅛ teaspoon salt

1 tablespoon orange rind, grated
2 tablespoons Grand Marnier
heavy cream, whipped (optional)

Place cream in top of double boiler and bring it almost, but not quite, to a boil. Meanwhile, beat the egg yolks, sugar, and salt until light and lemon colored. Gradually add cream to the yolks, stirring with a wire whisk. Return mixture to double boiler and place over low heat; stir with a wooden spoon until the custard thickens and coats the spoon. Immediately set in cold water to stop the cooking action. Pour custard into individual pot de crème or custard cups. Chill and top with grated rind and a small amount of whipped cream, if desired.

Nancy S. Johnson

LEMON ANGEL MERINGUES

Must prepare ahead   *Yield: 8 to 10 servings*

Meringues:

4 egg whites, at room
   temperature
¼ teaspoon cream of tartar

1 cup sugar
pinch of salt

Preheat oven to 250°. Lightly oil a teflon cookie sheet. In large bowl, combine egg whites and cream of tartar. Beat on high speed until soft peaks form. Gradually add sugar and salt. Continue beating until meringue is very stiff, about 10 minutes or until sugar is completely dissolved. Spread meringue into 3-inch "nests" on prepared pan. Bake 1 hour. Turn oven off and allow meringues to cool in oven for 1 hour. Do not open door. Carefully loosen meringues with spatula before completely cooled.

Filling:

4 egg yolks
½ cup sugar
2 tablespoons lemon peel

¼ cup lemon juice
1 cup heavy cream, divided

Beat egg yolks in top of double boiler until light lemon colored and thickened. Gradually beat in sugar. Blend in lemon peel and juice. Cook over hot, not boiling, water, stirring constantly for 5 to 8 minutes until thickened. Completely cool. Whip ¾ cup of heavy cream until soft peaks form. Fold into cooled lemon mixture. Spoon mixture into meringue shells. Cover tightly with foil and chill for at least 12 hours before serving. To serve, whip remaining heavy cream and add a dollop to each filled meringue.

Nancy C. Shuford

FAVORITE PEACH DESSERT

Must prepare ahead   *Yield: 6 servings*

1 cup sugar
⅓ cup cream sherry
juice of one lemon
¼ cup light rum
4 egg yolks
pinch of salt
pinch of nutmeg

1 tablespoon unflavored gelatin
¼ cup cream sherry
½ cup sour cream
2 fresh peaches, sliced
4 egg whites
fresh peaches, sliced, garnish

In top of double boiler, combine sugar, ⅓ cup sherry, lemon juice, rum, egg yolks, salt, and nutmeg. Over boiling water, stirring constantly, cook until the consistency of heavy cream. Dissolve gelatin in ¼ cup of sherry. When thoroughly dissolved, add to custard mixture; blend well. In food processor or blender combine ½ cup custard, sour cream, and 2 sliced peaches. Process until well blended. Mix with remaining custard and chill until the consistency of raw egg whites (about 30 minutes). Beat egg whites until stiff, but not dry. Fold into chilled custard. Pour into 1½-quart chilled mold rinsed with ice water. Refrigerate several hours; preferably overnight. To serve; unmold and top with sliced fresh peaches for garnish.

Ruth F. Deaton

GRAND MARNIER SOUFFLÉ
WITH HOT STRAWBERRY SAUCE

Must prepare ahead, freeze   *Yield: 8 servings*

1 quart vanilla ice cream, slightly softened	1 cup heavy cream, whipped
24 macaroons, crumbled	4 teaspoons powdered sugar
4 tablespoons Grand Marnier	4 tablespoons toasted almonds
	hot strawberry sauce

Combine ice cream, crumbled macaroons, and Grand Marnier. Fold in whipped cream. Spoon into a 6-cup mold. Sprinkle surface with powdered sugar and almonds. Cover with plastic wrap. Freeze until firm, 4 to 5 hours or overnight. Loosen edges and wrap with warm towel for 4 to 5 seconds. Turn out on a chilled platter and serve with hot strawberry sauce.

Hot Strawberry Sauce:

1 quart fresh strawberries (or 2 [10-ounce] packages frozen strawberries)	sugar, to taste
	4 tablespoons Grand Marnier

Hull fresh berries and cut in half. Mix sauce just before serving. Put berries in a saucepan with sugar (about 1 cup for fresh berries.) Simmer until soft but not mushy. Remove from heat and add Grand Marnier. Serve warm over frozen soufflé.

Anne F. Mitchell

271

FROZEN STRAWBERRY DELIGHT

Must prepare ahead   *Yield: 10 to 12 servings*

1 cup all-purpose flour   ½ cup butter, melted
¼ cup brown sugar, firmly   ½ cup pecans, chopped
  packed

Preheat oven to 350°. Mix all ingredients together and spread evenly in an 8-inch square pan. Bake 20 minutes, stirring occasionally. Press ⅔ of the crumbs into 9-inch spring-form pan. Reserve the remainder for topping.

Filling:
1 (10-ounce) package frozen   2 egg whites
  strawberries, thawed   1 cup heavy cream, whipped
1 cup sugar   sliced fresh strawberries,
2 teaspoons lemon juice   optional

In large mixer bowl, combine strawberries, sugar, lemon juice, and egg whites. Beat on high speed until stiff peaks form, about 10 minutes. Fold in whipped cream. Spoon mixture on top of crumbs and top with the remaining crumbs. Freeze until firm. Garnish with fresh strawberries, if desired.

Judy F. Flowers & Nancy C. Shuford

WINE JELLY

Must prepare ahead   *Yield: 10 cups*

4 tablespoons unflavored gelatin   ⅔ cup brandy or bourbon
2 cups cold water   juice of 1 lemon
6 cups boiling water   2 cups sugar
2½ cups sherry or white wine   1 pint heavy cream, whipped

Sprinkle gelatin over cold water and let stand. Add boiling water, stirring to dissolve gelatin. Add sherry, brandy, lemon juice, and sugar. Taste before mixture congeals; more sherry and/or sugar can be added, if desired. Refrigerate. (Dessert will not completely congeal.) To serve, pass jelly in a glass bowl, topped with whipped cream.

Note: Excellent for a holiday dessert.

Sara C. Shores

 **ICE CREAMS**

FOUR FRUIT ICE
(Processor)

Yield: 8 servings

1 (8-ounce) can peeled apricots	1½ cups fresh orange juice
3 bananas, cut into 2-inch pieces	½ cup fresh lemon juice
	1 cup sugar
½ cup sugar	¼ cup water

Drain and reserve juice from apricots. Place apricots, bananas and ½ cup sugar in work bowl of food processor. With *steel blade,* process until smooth. Add orange and lemon juices. Process to blend. Combine remaining cup of sugar and water in heavy saucepan; boil to a syrup. Pour syrup over fruit mixture in work bowl. Process to mix. Add reserved apricot juice. Process thoroughly. Pour into bowl and freeze. Stir occasionally during freezing. Serve in stemmed glasses with a plain cookie.

Note: This is from Josephine Grimes—one of Hickory's greatest cooks.

Nancy F. Matheson

SORBET AUX FRAISES (STRAWBERRY ICE)

Yield: 4 to 6 servings

2 pints fresh strawberries	juice of 2 lemons, strained
2 cups powdered sugar	2 egg whites, well beaten
2½ cups water	

Wash and hull berries. Reserve 6 berries for garnish. Combine berries, sugar, water, and lemon juice in a blender until smooth. Pour into 3 freezer trays and freeze. After 1 hour, break up the mixture in a large mixing bowl and beat until nearly smooth. Refreeze. Beat again every hour until mixture is frozen. Then break up the ice well and blend in the egg whites. Refreeze. To serve: stir well and serve in parfait or sherbet glasses with strawberries as garnish.

Sally T. Blackwelder

273

I
C
E

C
R
E
A
M
S

BUTTER PECAN ICE CREAM

Yield: 6 servings

1 cup light brown sugar, firmly
    packed
½ cup water
dash salt
2 eggs, beaten
2 tablespoons butter

1 cup milk
1 teaspoon vanilla extract
1 cup heavy cream, whipped
½ cup toasted pecans, finely
    chopped

Combine sugar, water, and salt in top of double boiler. Cook until sugar is melted. Pour a small amount of mixture over beaten eggs and return eggs to sugar mixture. Stir and cook over hot, not boiling, water until thickened. Add butter. Cool; add milk and vanilla. Whip cream until thickened and fold into cooled mixture. Stir in pecans. Pour into half-gallon ice cream churn and freeze until firm, according to manufacturer's directions.

Note: This recipe doubles or triples nicely.

Kay I. Showfety

VANILLA ICE CREAM

Yield: 4 quarts

4 eggs, well beaten
½ pint whipping cream
1 cup sugar
2 tablespoons vanilla extract

2 (14-ounce) cans sweetened
    condensed milk
1½ quarts milk

Combine eggs, cream, sugar, and vanilla in a bowl and mix well. Add sweetened condensed milk and stir well. Add rest of milk, stir again, pour mixture into churn container and freeze according to manufacturer's instructions.

Variation: For chocolate ice cream, add ½ (16-ounce) can chocolate syrup and substitute 1 tablespoon chocolate flavoring for vanilla extract. Add chocolate chips to vanilla ice cream before freezing for chocolate chip ice cream.

Brenda K. Cline

274

LEMON ICE CREAM

Yield: 1½ gallons

1 quart whipping cream
1 quart half and half
1 pint milk
4 cups sugar

juice of 8 lemons (about ¾ cup)
1 tablespoon lemon rind, grated
2 teaspoons lemon extract

Combine all ingredients in a large mixing bowl; mix well. Pour mixture into container of a 1½ gallon churn and freeze according to manufacturer's instructions. Let ripen 30 minutes; place in freezer to harden.

Kay I. Showfety

WINIFRED'S BUTTER PECAN ICE CREAM

Yield: 1 gallon

3 tablespoons butter, melted
(no substitute)
1 cup chopped pecans
3 eggs
1½ cups sugar
pinch of salt
1 (14-ounce) can sweetened
condensed milk
1 (13-ounce) evaporated milk

1 (3⅝-ounce) package butter
pecan instant pudding mix
4 tablespoons coffee creamer
¼ cup hot water
1 teaspoon vanilla extract
2 teaspoons butter flavoring
1 teaspoon maple flavoring
milk

Preheat oven to 325°. Mix butter with nuts; spread out on pan and toast for 15 minutes. Watch carefully and stir often so they will brown evenly. Remove and cool. Cream eggs and sugar well. Add salt and stir in condensed milk, evaporated milk, and instant pudding. Dissolve coffee creamer in hot water and add to mixture along with vanilla and flavorings. Mix well and pour into ice-cream container. Add enough milk to bring mixture to ⅔ full. Mix well. Put dasher in place and on either side add pecans (prevents nuts from settling to bottom of container). Freeze according to manufacturer's directions.

Catherine H. Yeager

275

PECAN ICE CREAM LOG WITH
WARM BOURBON SAUCE

Must prepare ahead, freeze   *Yield: 12 servings*

7-ounces pecans, finely ground
   (about 1¾ cups)
3 tablespoons unsweetened
   cocoa
8 eggs, separated
½ teaspoon cream of tartar
1½ cups sugar, divided
1 teaspoon vanilla extract

⅔ cup powdered sugar
2 tablespoons unsweetened
   cocoa
1½ quarts coffee, vanilla, or
   caramel ice cream
warm bourbon sauce
toasted chopped pecans

Position rack in center of oven and preheat to 350°. Butter a 15x10x1-inch jelly roll pan and line with waxed paper; oil paper lightly. Mix pecans with 3 tablespoons cocoa in small bowl; set aside. Beat egg whites until foamy. Add cream of tartar and beat until soft peaks form. Gradually add ½ cup granulated sugar and beat until stiff but not dry. In large bowl combine egg yolks with remaining granulated sugar and vanilla and beat until thickened and pale yellow. Beat in 1 cup egg whites. Gradually fold in nut mixture alternately with remaining egg whites being careful not to over fold; some streaks of egg whites should show. Spread batter evenly in prepared pan. Bake until edges of cake shrink from pan and top springs back when lightly touched, about 15 to 20 minutes. Remove from oven; cool in pan. Loosen edges of cake with knife. Combine powdered sugar with remaining cocoa and sift about half over surface of cake; cover with towel, place a board or bottom of another jelly roll pan on top and invert cake onto work surface. Gently peel off waxed paper. *To assemble:* Soften ice cream slightly, and spread to within 1-inch of long edges of cake. Drizzle some of bourbon sauce over top. Using towel as aid, roll cake into long cylinder (cake may crack in several places, but this will not matter.) Secure ends with long picks and freeze until firm. If desired, sift additional powdered sugar and cocoa mixture over top, or brush with sauce and roll in pecans. Return to freezer. To serve, remove from freezer, place on serving platter and let stand at room temperature 10 minutes. Slice diagonally into pieces ¾-inch thick. Pass remaining bourbon sauce separately.

Warm Bourbon Sauce:

1½ cups dark corn syrup
¾ cup sugar
¾ cup brown sugar, firmly
   packed

⅔ cup evaporated milk
3 tablespoons corn oil
dash salt
¼ to ⅓ cup bourbon

Combine ingredients except bourbon in medium saucepan and mix well. Place over medium heat and stir constantly until mixture comes to a boil. Let boil, stirring occasionally, 5 minutes. (Milk will look curdled.) Remove from heat and let cool 15 minutes. Transfer to blender, add bourbon and mix until smooth. Reheat before serving. Sauce will keep 1 month in refrigerator.

Note: Compliments over this unique dessert are ample reward for the preparation time.

I C E C R E A M S

ICE CREAM SUPREME

Yield: 8 servings

½ gallon all-natural vanilla ice
  cream
3-ounces Crème de Cocao

3-ounces bourbon or
3-ounces blackberry brandy
3-ounces scotch

Soften ice cream to a mushy stage. Combine with either pair of liqueur-liquor ingredients in a *silver* pitcher and keep in freezer at least 3 hours or until ready to serve.

Ruth F. Deaton

WORLD'S EASIEST STRAWBERRY ICE CREAM

Yield: 1 quart

2 cups buttermilk
1½ cups strawberry jam (or
  any fruit jam)

Stir buttermilk into jam. Pour into refrigerator tray and freeze until firm. Cut up frozen mixture and place in chilled mixer bowl. Whip with electric mixer until fluffy. Return to tray and freeze firm.

Catherine H. Yeager

ZABAGLIONE ICE CREAM

Yield: 5 cups

2 cups heavy cream
2 cups milk
¾ cup sugar
6 egg yolks, slightly beaten
½ to 1 cup sweet Marsala wine

½ teaspoon vanilla extract
grated peel from half of a lemon
pinch cinnamon
Amaretti cookies, page 301.

Combine cream, milk, and sugar in a saucepan. Place on moderate heat and stir occasionally until mixture is hot. Gradually add hot milk to egg yolks, whisking constantly. Pour back into saucepan and return to heat. Stir constantly over moderate heat until mixture coats the back of the spoon. Strain into a glass container and refrigerate until cool. Add wine, vanilla, lemon peel, and cinnamon; pour into ice cream maker. Freeze according to manufacturer's instructions. When ready to serve, top with crumbled Amaretti cookies.

Emily N. Garrett and Mary Ann K. Forehand
(The Apron String—A kitchen specialty shop)

PASTRY

NEVER FAIL PIE CRUST

Yield: 4 crusts

3 cups all-purpose flour
1 teaspoon baking powder,
   (optional)
1 teaspoon salt
1 tablespoon sugar

1¼ cups vegetable shortening,
   (or 1 cup lard)
1 egg, beaten
1 tablespoon vinegar
4 to 5 tablespoons cold water

Sift together flour, baking powder, salt, and sugar. With pastry blender, cut shortening into dry ingredients until mixture resembles coarse meal. In a measuring cup, beat egg; add vinegar and water. Add egg mixture to flour until dough becomes moist and forms a ball. Divide dough into 4 parts; roll each crust out on lightly floured board. For baked pie shell, bake 10 to 12 minutes at 425⁰.

Anita G. Anderson

PROCESSOR PIE CRUST

Yield: 2 crusts

2⅔ cups all-purpose flour
½ teaspoon salt
6 tablespoons butter, chilled
6 tablespoons shortening,
   chilled

½ cup cold water
steel blade

Combine all ingredients, except water; pulse until mixture resembles coarse meal. With machine on, gradually add water through feed tube until sufficiently moist. Turn machine off just before ball forms. Divide dough; roll out on lightly floured board.

Shirley L. Ballew

279

CHOCOLATE WAFER PIE SHELL
(Food Processor)

May be made in food processor   *Yield: one 9-inch pie shell*

5 tablespoons cold butter, sliced   1 tablespoon sugar
18 thin chocolate wafers,   ⅛ teaspoon ground cinnamon
  broken into pieces

Preheat oven to 300°. Place butter in bottom of work bowl. Add remaining ingredients; process 3 to 4 seconds, stopping to scrape down sides of bowl. Continue processing until cookies are finely ground. Press mixture firmly and evenly against sides and bottom of a 9-inch pie plate or springform pan. Bake 5 minutes. Cool.

Judy B. Smith

PIES

APPLE PIE WITH CANDIED CRUST

Serve warm   *Yield: 8 servings*

4 to 5 cups apples, sliced   ½ teaspoon salt
2 teaspoons lemon juice   ⅛ teaspoon nutmeg
1 cup all-purpose flour   ½ cup butter
1 cup brown sugar

Preheat oven to 350°. Slice apples; sprinkle with lemon juice. Fill a greased 10-inch pie pan with sliced apples. Mix flour, sugar, salt, and nutmeg. Cut in butter with pastry blender or food processor. Cover apples with mixture to form top crust of pie. Bake 50 to 60 minutes.

Note: This is delicious served hot out of the oven.

Barbara A. Garlitz

MO'S BROWN BAG APPLE PIE

Yield: 8 servings

4 large apples, sliced into
    salted water and drained
1 cup sugar, divided
3 tablespoons all-purpose flour
1 (9-inch) deep dish pie shell,
    unbaked

½ cup all-purpose flour
½ cup butter
1 (10-ounce) brown paper bag

Preheat oven to 375°. Slice apples into salted water. Combine ½ cup sugar and 3 tablespoons flour. Drain apples; toss with sugar and flour mixture; pour into unbaked pie shell. In a bowl, combine remaining ½ cup sugar and ½ cup flour; cut in butter with pastry blender until mixture resembles a coarse meal. Place this mixture in the center of pie; put pie in brown paper bag. (The bag may be closed with a paper clip.) Bake 60 minutes. Remove pie from bag immediately after baking. (Top should be golden brown.) Cool before serving.

Carole J. Cumming

CHOCOLATE AMARETTO PIE

May be prepared a day ahead

Yield: 6 to 8 servings

1 (9-inch) chocolate wafer pie
    shell, page 280
¼ cup Amaretto liqueur
2 teaspoons unflavored gelatin
½ cup sour cream, room
    temperature
1½ cups heavy cream

1 cup powdered sugar
¾ cup toasted almonds, finely
    ground
semi-sweet chocolate, shaved
    (optional)
toasted almonds, chopped
    (optional)

Prepare chocolate wafer pie shell. Combine liqueur and gelatin in small heat-resistant cup and mix until softened. Place cup in simmering water and heat until gelatin is completely liquefied, about 2 to 3 minutes. Transfer gelatin to large bowl; add sour cream, blending well. Stir in cream and powdered sugar; whip until stiff. Fold in ground almonds and spoon into shell. If desired, decorate with shaved chocolate and toasted almonds. Refrigerate at least 2 hours or until set.

Note: This pie tastes even better made the day before it is served.

Shirley L. Ballew

BRANDY ALEXANDER PIE

Yield: 6 to 8 servings

Pie Shell:

1⅓ cups graham cracker crumbs	¼ cup unsalted butter, melted
	¼ cup sugar

Preheat oven to 350°. Combine graham cracker crumbs, butter, and sugar; press mixture on bottom and sides of buttered 9-inch, deep dish glass pie plate. Bake 10 minutes. Cool shell on wire rack.

Filling:

4 teaspoons unflavored gelatin	¼ cup crème de cacao
½ cup cold water	dash of cream of tartar
⅔ cup sugar, divided	dash of salt
3 large eggs, separated	2 cups heavy cream, divided
dash of salt	in half and whipped
¼ cup brandy	chocolate curls

In top of double boiler, sprinkle gelatin over cold water to soften for 10 minutes. Add ⅓ cup sugar, egg yolks that have been slightly beaten, and salt. Cook over boiling water stirring until mixture begins to thicken. Remove from heat; transfer mixture to large bowl; add brandy and crème de cacao. Set bowl in ice and stir mixture constantly until chilled and thickened; remove from ice. (Do not allow mixture to completely set up.) In another bowl, beat 3 egg whites at room temperature with cream of tartar and salt until stiff; gradually add remaining ⅓ cup sugar. In a chilled bowl, beat 1 cup heavy cream until stiff. Fold beaten egg whites and whipped cream into brandy mixture. Pour filling into pie shell; chill, loosely covered, for 3 hours or until set. Decorate pie with remaining 1 cup whipped cream and chocolate curls.

Janet E. Schoonderwoerd

WONDERFUL FUDGE PIE

Yield: 8 servings

¾ cup butter
3 (1-ounce) squares
   unsweetened chocolate
3 eggs
1½ cups sugar

¾ cup all-purpose flour
1½ teaspoons vanilla extract
1½ teaspoons instant coffee
3 tablespoons chocolate syrup
coffee or vanilla ice cream

Preheat oven to 325°. Melt butter with chocolate over low heat, stirring occasionally until smooth. Beat eggs with mixer at high speed for 5 minutes or until very thick; beat in sugar until color is light. Blend in flour, vanilla extract, and the chocolate mixture. Pour filling into greased, 9-inch, glass pie plate. Bake 30 minutes; cool. Mix instant coffee and chocolate syrup. Serve pie with ice cream topped with chocolate coffee syrup.

Judy B. Smith

FRENCH SILK PIE

Yield: 6 to 8 servings

1 (9-inch) pie shell, baked
½ cup butter, softened
¾ cup sugar
1 (1-ounce) square unsweetened
   chocolate, melted

1 teaspoon vanilla extract
2 eggs
1 cup heavy cream, whipped
grated chocolate for garnish

In a small bowl, cream butter; beat in sugar until mixture is fluffy. Add chocolate and vanilla. Add eggs one at a time, beating for 5 minutes after each addition. *This step is very important for the pie to be a success.* Pour into baked pie shell; cover with whipped cream and grated chocolate if desired. Serve or may be refrigerated for several hours before serving.

Renee W. Cline

BLACK BOTTOM ICE CREAM PIE

Must prepare ahead, freeze   *Yield: 6 servings*

1 (9-inch) prepared graham-
cracker or chocolate pie
crust
1 (6-ounce) package semi-sweet
chocolate morsels

½ cup heavy cream
½ teaspoon vanilla extract
1 pint chocolate ice cream
1 quart vanilla ice cream

Chill crust. Over low heat, in heavy saucepan combine chocolate morsels and heavy cream; stir occasionally until chocolate melts. Add vanilla. Chill sauce thoroughly. Spread softened chocolate ice cream over chilled crust, freeze. When frozen, top with ¾ of chocolate sauce; return to freezer until sauce has frozen. Soften vanilla ice cream and spread over frozen sauce. Drizzle with remaining sauce. Freeze. To serve, remove pie from freezer about 5 minutes before slicing.

Stevi S. Dozier

CRANBERRY-NUT PIE

Freezes well   *Yield: 8 servings*

1 (9-inch) pie shell, unbaked
3 eggs, slightly beaten
⅔ cup sugar
dash of salt
¾ cup dark corn syrup

⅓ cup unsalted butter, melted
1 cup cranberries, coarsely
chopped
1 cup pecan halves

Preheat oven to 350°. Beat eggs slightly; add sugar and salt, stirring until blended. Add corn syrup, butter, cranberries, and nuts, mixing well. Pour filling into pie shell and cover edges with foil. Bake 25 minutes; remove foil and bake an additional 25 minutes or until filling is set. Cool thoroughly before serving.

Note: This is a nice dessert for the Thanksgiving or Christmas holidays.

Judy C. West

FRESH GRAPE PIE

Yield: 6 servings

1 double-crust pie pastry,
  page 279.
5½ cups North Carolina
  Muscadine grapes, washed
  and drained
1 cup sugar
¼ cup all-purpose flour

⅛ teaspoon salt
1 teaspoon lemon peel, grated,
  (optional)
1 tablespoon orange peel, grated
  (optional)
2 tablespoons butter, cubed

Preheat oven to 350°. Line a 9-inch pie pan with pastry shell; reserve additional pastry for top crust. Wash grapes; drain. Remove skin from each grape by pressing between thumb and forefinger; reserve skins. In medium saucepan, bring pulp to boil over medium heat, stirring constantly; boil 2 minutes. Press pulp through sieve to remove seeds. Add skins to pulp; mix well. In small bowl, combine sugar, flour, and salt; add grape pulp, lemon peel, and orange peel. Pour filling into bottom crust; dot with butter. Roll out reserved pastry; cover pie with top crust. Bake 40 to 45 minutes. Serve warm.

Note: This pie may also be made with Scuppernong grapes.

Dorothy Y. Menzies

GRASSHOPPER PIE

Must be frozen   *Yield: 8 servings*

1 (9-inch) chocolate wafer pie
  shell, page 280.
6 chocolate wafers, crushed and
  reserved

¼ cup crème de menthe
1 (7-ounce) jar marshmallow
  cream
2 cups heavy cream, whipped

Prepare chocolate wafer pie shell. Crush 6 chocolate wafers; set aside. Gradually add crème de menthe to marshmallow cream; blend well. Fold in whipped cream and blend carefully. Pour filling into prepared chocolate wafer shell. Sprinkle reserved chocolate wafer crumbs over top of pie; freeze. Let pie stand at room temperature 10 minutes before serving.

Judy B. Smith

GRANDMOTHER'S LEMON CURD PIE

Yield: 6 servings

1 (9-inch) deep dish pie shell, baked	¾ cup buttermilk
1¼ cups sugar	1 teaspoon lemon extract
2 tablespoons all-purpose flour, rounded	¼ teaspoon cream of tartar
	3 tablespoons sugar
3 eggs, separated	½ teaspoon vanilla extract

Preheat oven to 325°. In saucepan, combine sugar and flour, blending well; add slightly beaten egg yolks and buttermilk. Cook over medium heat, stirring constantly until thick like pudding. Add lemon extract; pour into baked pie shell. Beat 3 egg whites with cream of tartar until they hold a soft shape; gradually add 3 tablespoons sugar and vanilla extract, beating meringue until shiny and stiff. Cover pie with meringue; bake 15 minutes or until lightly browned.

Note: Grandmother's original recipe called for 2 or 3 eggs, depending on the price of eggs or who was coming to dinner.

Winnie B. Hovey

ANY FRUIT PIE

Yield: 6 to 8 servings

2 (16 to 20 ounce) cans fruit, drained (peaches, apples, or blackberries)	1 egg
	½ cup butter, melted
	1 teaspoon vanilla extract
2 tablespoons all-purpose flour	3 slices bread, crust removed
1 cup sugar	ice cream or whipped topping

Preheat oven to 350°. Thoroughly drain fruit; put into greased 9-inch pie pan. Combine flour and sugar; add egg, melted butter, and vanilla; pour over fruit. Tear bread slices into small pieces and put over filling. Bake 30 minutes. Serve with ice cream or whipped topping.

Note: Bread may be cut to form lattice work on top of pie.

Carolyn W. Glass

MABEL'S MARSHMALLOW PIE

Must prepare ahead   *Yield: 12 servings*

24 marshmallows
½ cup milk
2 eggs, beaten
1 cup heavy cream, whipped
12 graham crackers, crushed

½ cup butter, melted
1 (1-ounce) square bitter
   chocolate, shaved
½ cup pecans, chopped

In top of double boiler, melt marshmallows in milk. Add eggs and cook until custard consistency. Let mixture cool. Fold in cream. Make crust of graham crackers and butter in an 8x12x2-inch dish. Pour custard over crumbs. Sprinkle chocolate and nuts over top. Refrigerate overnight.

Mary Kathryn F. Hemphill

TWO WAY PIE

Yield: 12 servings

2 (9-inch) pie shells, baked
4 egg yolks, slightly beaten
1½ cups sugar
4 tablespoons all-purpose flour,
   heaping
2 cups water, boiling

¼ cup fresh lemon juice
1 tablespoon lemon rind, grated
2 (1-ounce) squares
   unsweetened chocolate,
   melted
4 tablespoons butter, divided

In a bowl, combine egg yolks, sugar, and flour; gradually add boiling water and stir until blended. Divide filling into two saucepans. In one pan, add lemon juice and grated rind. In second pan, add melted chocolate. Add 2 tablespoons butter to each saucepan. Cook over low heat, stirring constantly, until fillings thicken. Pour each mixture into baked pie shell; cool while preparing meringue.

Meringue:
4 egg whites
¼ teaspoon cream of tartar

½ cup sugar
1 teaspoon vanilla extract

Preheat oven to 325°. Beat egg whites with cream of tartar until they hold a soft shape; gradually add sugar, beating meringue until shiny and stiff; add vanilla extract. Swirl meringue over both fillings. Bake 15 to 18 minutes or until top is lightly browned. Cool before serving.

Frances C. Watson

LEMON-APRICOT CREAM PIE

Yield: 6 servings

1 (9-inch) pie shell, baked

Apricot purée:

8 ounces dried apricots   ⅓ cup granulated sugar
water to cover

In saucepan, cover dried apricots with water. Bring to gentle boil; simmer, uncovered 30 minutes. Add sugar; cook 5 minutes, stirring to dissolve sugar. Cool. Drain cooled apricots carefully, discarding liquid. Purée apricots in blender, processor or sieve. Sweeten if desired. Reserve apricot purée. (This may be made day before and refrigerated.)

Lemon Filling:

5 eggs   4 tablespoons butter, sliced
1 cup sugar   1 cup heavy cream, whipped
rind of large lemon, grated   ¼ cup powdered sugar
juice of 2 large lemons   1 teaspoon vanilla extract
dash of salt

In double boiler, combine eggs and sugar; beat until light in color. Add lemon rind and juice; blend well. Add salt and butter, continuing to stir constantly over gently simmering water until mixture thickens. Remove from heat; beat with wire whisk until smooth; cool completely. Spread apricot purée over bottom and sides of baked pie shell. Pour cooled lemon filling over purée; refrigerate 3 hours. Before serving, whip heavy cream until stiff; add powdered sugar and vanilla extract; beat thoroughly. Spread whipped cream over pie to completely cover filling.

Note: The filling for this pie will be gooey when sliced but delicious!

Anne F. Mitchell

TRADITIONAL PUMPKIN PIE

Yield: 12 servings

2 (9-inch) deep-dish pie shells,
  unbaked
3 eggs, slightly beaten
2 cups pumpkin, cooked and
  mashed
½ cup light corn syrup
½ cup brown sugar, packed
½ teaspoon salt
2 teaspoons cinnamon
¾ teaspoon ginger
¾ teaspoon nutmeg
½ teaspoon cloves
1½ cups heavy cream or
  evaporated milk
1½ teaspoons vanilla extract
heavy cream, whipped and
  sweetened to taste

Preheat oven to 350°. Thoroughly combine eggs, pumpkin, corn syrup, and brown sugar; add salt, cinnamon, ginger, nutmeg, and cloves. Stir in heavy cream and vanilla extract. Pour filling into unbaked pie shells. Edges of pastry may be covered with foil to prevent over browning. Bake 60 minutes or until knife inserted in center comes out clean. Cool. Serve with sweetened whipped cream.

Carole J. Cumming

PUMPKIN ICE CREAM PIE

Must prepare ahead, freeze   *Yield: 8 servings*

1 (9-inch) pie shell
1 quart vanilla ice cream,
  softened
¾ cup canned pumpkin
¼ cup honey
½ teaspoon ground cinnamon
¼ teaspoon ground ginger
⅛ teaspoon nutmeg
⅛ teaspoon ground cloves
¼ teaspoon salt
⅓ cup pecans, chopped
whipped cream (garnish)
pecan halves (garnish)

Bake and cool pie shell. Combine ice cream, pumpkin, honey, cinnamon, ginger, nutmeg, cloves and salt. Blend well and pour into pie shell. Sprinkle with chopped pecans. Freeze until serving time. To serve, garnish with whipped cream and pecan halves.

Betty Lou M. Bumbarger

FAVORITE STRAWBERRY PIE

Yield: 8 servings

1 (9-inch) pie shell, baked
1 cup sugar
3½ tablespoons cornstarch
dash of salt
1 cup strawberries, crushed
½ cup butter
¼ cup water

1 (3-ounce) package cream
  cheese, softened
1 cup whole strawberries
1 cup heavy cream, whipped
¼ teaspoon almond extract
2 tablespoons powdered sugar

Combine sugar, cornstarch, salt, crushed strawberries, butter, and water in heavy saucepan; cook over medium heat until thick and transparent, stirring constantly. Cool. Spread softened cream cheese on bottom of baked pie shell. Stand whole strawberries in cream cheese to cover bottom of pie completely. Pour and spread cooled sauce over strawberries. Whip cream until stiff; add almond extract and powdered sugar; spread over pie. Chill several hours before serving.

Carolyn W. Lyerly

FRESH STRAWBERRY PIE

Yield: 6 to 8 servings

1 (9-inch) pie shell, baked
1 quart fresh strawberries,
  divided
1 cup sugar

3 tablespoons cornstarch
dash of salt
1 cup heavy cream, whipped
  and sweetened to taste

Refrigerate half the strawberries; crush remaining strawberries and bring to a boil over medium heat. Combine sugar, cornstarch, and salt; stir into hot strawberry mixture. Cook, stirring constantly until thickened, about 10 minutes. (The consistency should be like a thick jam.) Cool. Spread chilled whole strawberries in baked pie shell; pour cooled strawberry filling over top. Refrigerate uncovered for several hours. To serve, top with sweetened whipped cream.

Note: Blueberries may also be used for this delicious pie.

Susan L. Ingle

PECAN PIE

Yield: 6 to 8 servings

3 eggs, slightly beaten	dash of salt
1 cup sugar	1/4 teaspoon lemon juice
1 cup white corn syrup	1 cup pecan halves
1/4 cup butter, melted	1 (9-inch) pie shell, unbaked

Preheat oven to 350°. Thoroughly combine eggs, sugar, corn syrup, butter, salt, and lemon juice; stir in pecans. Pour filling into unbaked pie shell. Bake 40 minutes; reduce heat to 300° and bake 10 minutes more, until filling is set.

Note: Lemon juice is the secret ingredient to this delicious pecan pie.

Frances R. Hilton

RUM RAISIN PIE

Yield: 6 servings

1 (9-inch) deep-dish pie shell, unbaked	1 1/2 cups raisins
2 eggs	3/4 cup butter, melted
1 cup sugar	1 tablespoon vinegar
1 1/2 cups coconut, shredded	1/3 cup brandy or rum
1 1/2 cups pecans, chopped	1 teaspoon vanilla extract
	pecan halves to decorate

Preheat oven to 325°. Mix all ingredients, reserving pecan halves to decorate top of pie. Pour filling into unbaked pie shell. Bake 40 minutes or until filling is set.

Lindy M. Dillow

LEMON CHESS PIE

Yield: 6 servings

6 tablespoons butter, melted	2 tablespoons lemon juice
3 eggs, beaten	1 teaspoon vanilla extract
1 1/2 cups sugar	1 (9-inch) pie shell, unbaked

Preheat oven to 350°. Melt butter; cool; add eggs and sugar. Mix well; add lemon juice and vanilla. Pour filling into unbaked pie shell. Bake 45 to 55 minutes until top is golden and filling is set. (Do not overbake.) Cool before serving.

Joanne F. Underdown

FRUIT COBBLER

Yield: 8 servings

½ cup butter or margarine
1 cup all-purpose flour
1 cup sugar
2 teaspoons baking powder
1 cup milk

4 cups fruit, cut up and
  sweetened to taste
  (strawberries, peaches,
  or blueberries)

Preheat oven to 350°. Melt butter in bottom of 13x9x2-inch baking pan in the oven. In a bowl, combine flour, sugar, and baking powder; add milk to dry ingredients and mix well. Pour batter over melted butter. (Do not stir.) Put sweetened fruit on top. Bake 60 minutes or until golden brown. Serve warm or cold.

Note: This is delicious with vanilla ice-cream on top.

Carolyn W. Glass & Ann A. Moser

SHERRY PIE

Must prepare ahead   *Yield: 6 to 8 servings*

Crust:
½ cup margarine
1 cup all-purpose flour

¼ cup brown sugar
½ cup pecans, chopped

Preheat oven to 375°. Combine margarine, flour, and brown sugar; blend well; add pecans. Place mixture into bottom of a 9-inch pie pan. Bake 15 minutes, stirring occasionally. While hot press mixture into pie pan, reserving 3 tablespoons for topping. Chill.

Filling:
8 ounces miniature
  marshmallows

½ cup sherry
1 cup heavy cream, whipped

In top of double boiler, combine marshmallows and sherry. Heat until marshmallows are completely melted. Remove from heat; cool. Gently fold whipped cream into marshmallow mixture; mound into pie shell. Sprinkle reserved crumbs on top. Refrigerate overnight for flavors to blend.

Jean L. Hefner

THREE-FRUIT PIE

Yield: 18 servings

3 (9-inch) pie shells, baked
6 bananas, sliced
orange juice to cover bananas
1 (16½-ounce) can sour red
    pitted cherries, drained and
    juice reserved
1 (20-ounce) can crushed
    pineapple, drained and
    juice reserved

2 cups sugar
½ cup cornstarch
1 teaspoon vanilla extract
1 teaspoon red food coloring
1 cup pecans, chopped
2 cups heavy cream, whipped

Put sliced bananas into bowl and cover with orange juice; let soak. Thoroughly drain juices from cherries and pineapple, adding enough water to make 2 cups of liquid; add sugar and cornstarch to liquid, mixing well. Cook over medium heat, stirring occasionally until mixture thickens; add vanilla and food coloring. Cool completely. Drain sliced bananas and place in bottom of baked pie shells. Add well-drained cherries and pineapple to cooled liquid mixture; add nuts; pour over bananas in pie shells. Top with whipped cream; chill.

Note: The canned fruits must be drained thoroughly to make this filling successful. Recipe makes 3 pies.

June V. Brehm

ENGLISH LEMON BUTTER TARTS

Yield: 16 servings

16 tart shells, baked
6 eggs
½ cup butter, sliced
2 cups sugar
juice and grated rind of 2
    lemons

1 cup heavy cream, whipped
2 to 3 tablespoons powdered
    sugar, sifted
½ teaspoon almond extract

Beat eggs; add butter, sugar, lemon juice, and grated rind. Cook in double boiler over hot water, stirring often until thickened. Pour mixture into baked tart shells; cool. Whip cream; add powdered sugar and almond extract. Spread over tarts before serving.

Note: This filling will keep for a week in a jar in the refrigerator.

Kay B. Melton

293

JEFFERSON DAVIS TARTS

Yield: 18 servings

18 tart shells, baked
½ cup butter
2 cups light brown sugar
4 egg yolks
2 tablespoons all-purpose flour
1 teaspoon cinnamon
½ teaspoon allspice

1 teaspoon nutmeg
1 cup heavy cream
½ cup dates, chopped
½ cup raisins
½ cup pecans, chopped
whipped cream, sweetened to
    taste

Preheat oven to 325°. Cream butter and sugar; beat in egg yolks. Add flour, spices, heavy cream, dates, raisins, and pecans; mix well. Spoon filling into baked tart shells. Bake 45 minutes. Serve with sweetened whipped cream.

Nancy P. Shuford

WINNER'S CIRCLE PIE

Yield: 6 to 8 servings

1 (9-inch) deep-dish pie shell,
    unbaked
½ cup pecans, chopped
3 tablespoons bourbon
¼ cup margarine, melted
1 cup sugar

3 eggs
¾ cup butter-flavored pancake
    syrup
1 teaspoon vanilla extract
¼ teaspoon salt
¼ cup chocolate morsels

Preheat oven to 375°. Soak pecans in bourbon; set aside. In a mixing bowl, combine margarine, sugar, and eggs, beating until fluffy. Add syrup, vanilla, salt, and chocolate morsels; blend well. Pour filling into pie shell; sprinkle with bourbon soaked pecans. Bake 45 to 55 minutes, until filling is set.

Note: If crust browns too quickly, cover pastry edges with foil toward end of baking time.

Betty Lou M. Bumbarger

CANDIES &
COOKIES

INDEX

CANDIES AND COOKIES

( ) Denotes: **(HE) Hickory Entertains**   **(I) International**   **(M) Microwave Recipes**

296

 **CANDY**

ALMOND TOFFEE

Yield: 8 to 10 dozen

2 cups butter
2 cups margarine
4 cups sugar
⅔ cup water
4 tablespoons light corn syrup

2 pinches salt
2 teaspoons vanilla
2 cups coarsely ground almonds
2 (8-ounce) milk chocolate bars
1 cup finely ground almonds

Combine butter, margarine, sugar, water, corn syrup, salt and vanilla in a Dutch oven. Cook over medium high heat until candy thermometer registers 290⁰. Let stand for approximately 15 minutes; then add coarse almonds. Pour into two 15x10x1-inch jelly roll pans lined with aluminum foil. Cool. Melt chocolate bars slowly in the top of a double boiler. Quickly spread the chocolate over the candy. Sprinkle the finely ground almonds on top of the chocolate. Refrigerate until hardened. Break into pieces.

Roddy S. Dixon

MRS. GLASS'S DATE FINGERS

Yield: 5 dozen

½ cup butter
1 cup brown sugar
1 (8-ounce) package chopped
    dates

2 cups oven-toasted rice cereal
1 cup chopped nuts
½ cup coconut
powdered sugar

Combine butter, sugar, and dates in a saucepan. Cook over low heat until well dissolved; stir constantly while melting. Remove from heat and add cereal, nuts, and coconut; blend thoroughly. Cool completely and shape into balls or fingers. Roll in powdered sugar. Put on waxed paper to set. Store in a tightly covered tin.

Carolyn W. Glass

297

DIVINITY

Yield: 30 pieces

2 cups sugar
½ cup water
½ cup light corn syrup
1 egg white, beaten stiff

pinch of salt
1 teaspoon vanilla
30 pecan halves

Combine sugar, water, and corn syrup in a saucepan. Cook over low heat to soft ball stage (240°). Beat egg white until stiff peaks form. Slowly pour the sugar-water-corn syrup mixture over the stiffly beaten egg white, beating constantly. Beat until the mixture is stiff and cool. Add salt and vanilla. Drop from 2 spoons onto a buttered plate or parchment paper. Place a pecan half on top of each piece.

Katharyn L. Aderholdt

FUDGE

Yield: 10 dozen

4 cups sugar
1 cup margarine
1 (13-ounce) can evaporated
  milk
3 (6-ounce) packages semi-
  sweet chocolate chips

2 cups miniature marshmallows
nuts (kind and amount to taste)
1 tablespoon vanilla

Combine sugar, margarine, and milk in a large, heavy saucepan. Bring to a boil and cook 14 minutes, or until a ball forms in cold water. Pour over chocolate chips and marshmallows in the large bowl of an electric mixer; work fast because the candy sets up quickly and will not be smooth otherwise. Mix well; add nuts and vanilla. Pour into a buttered 13x9x2-inch baking pan; cool and cut into squares.

Frances R. Hilton

HAYSTACKS

Yield: 4 dozen

1 (12-ounce) package
  butterscotch chips
1 (3-ounce) can Chow Mein
  noodles

1 cup salted peanuts

Melt butterscotch chips in top of double boiler over boiling water. Remove from heat and stir in Chow Mein noodles and peanuts. Drop by teaspoon on waxed paper. Let cool for approximately 20 minutes.

Carol H. Tuttle

PEANUT BUTTER BALLS

Freezes well

Yield: 10 dozen

1/2 cup margarine or butter,
  softened
1 cup smooth peanut butter
1 cup crunchy peanut butter
1 (16-ounce) box powdered
  sugar

3 cups oven-toasted rice cereal
3 (6-ounce) packages semi-
  sweet chocolate chips
1/10 pound of paraffin

Combine butter, peanut butters, sugar, and cereal. Mix with your hands until well combined. Make balls 3/4-inch in diameter. Chill on a baking sheet. Melt chocolate chips and paraffin in the top of a double boiler. Dip chilled balls in the chocolate mixture; place the chocolate covered balls on a baking sheet lined with waxed paper. Cool; put in containers in the freezer.

Note: These keep for several weeks in the refrigerator or may be eaten straight from the freezer.

Chris R. Bates

PEANUT BUTTER CANDY

Yield: 3 dozen

2 cups sugar
3 tablespoons butter
1 (5.33-ounce) can evaporated
  milk

1 cup miniature marshmallows
1 (12-ounce) jar crunchy peanut
  butter
1 teaspoon vanilla

Combine sugar, butter, and evaporated milk in an iron frying pan. Boil for 5 minutes, stirring constantly. Remove from heat and add marsh-mallows, peanut butter, and vanilla; beat well. Pour into a well-greased 9-inch square pan. Mark off squares; cut when firm.

Katharyn L. Aderholdt

PEG'S PRALINES

Yield: 6 dozen

2 cups sugar
1 cup light brown sugar
1/2 cup milk
1/2 cup sweetened condensed
  milk

1/4 cup butter
1/4 teaspoon salt
3 cups chopped pecans

Combine all ingredients, except nuts, in a large saucepan. Over medium heat bring slowly to a full rolling boil, being careful not to scorch. Use a wooden spoon to stir. Add nuts and continue boiling until candy reaches 232° on candy thermometer. Remove from heat; stir only enough to give a creamy look. Spoon out on buttered baking sheets or on brown paper. Cool. Store in a tightly covered tin.

Peggy E. Hill

COOKIES

AMARETTI

Yield: 3 dozen

3/4 cup blanched almonds
1 1/4 cups sugar, divided
1/2 teaspoon almond extract

2 egg whites
sugar crystals

Preheat oven to 350°. Grease a cookie sheet. Chop and pulverize almonds. Mix with half of the sugar and the extract; set aside. Beat egg whites until very stiff. Add almond mixture to the egg whites; mix well. Shape into 1-inch balls or cookies and place on prepared pan 1-inch apart. Sprinkle with sugar crystals, if available. Bake for 5 minutes or until lightly browned.

Shirley L. Ballew

APRICOT PECAN BARS

Yield: 2 1/2 dozen

2/3 cup dried apricots
1/2 cup butter or margarine,
   softened
1/4 cup sugar
1 cup all-purpose flour
1/3 cup all-purpose flour
1/2 teaspoon baking powder

1/4 teaspoon salt
1 cup brown sugar
2 eggs, well beaten
1/2 teaspoon vanilla
1 cup chopped pecans (optional)
powdered sugar

Rinse apricots and cover with water. Boil for 10 minutes, drain, cool and chop or process in food processor. Meanwhile, preheat the oven to 350°. Mix butter, 1/4 cup sugar, and 1 cup flour until crumbly; pack into a greased 11x7x1 1/2-inch pan. Bake for 25 minutes until light brown; remove from oven. Sift together 1/3 cup flour, baking powder, and salt. Gradually beat brown sugar into eggs. Add flour mixture and combine well. Mix in vanilla, pecans, and apricots. Spread over baked layer and bake for 30 minutes. Cool in pan, cut into bars, and roll in powdered sugar.

Nancy F. Matheson

BABE RUTH BARS

Yield: 2 dozen

1 cup light corn syrup
1 cup sugar
1½ cups smooth peanut butter
4 cups oven toasted rice cereal

1 (6-ounce) package semi-
  sweet chocolate chips
1 (6-ounce) package
  butterscotch chips

Combine syrup and sugar in a saucepan and bring to a full boil; remove immediately from the heat. Mix in peanut butter and cereal. Press into a buttered 13x9x2-inch baking pan. Melt the chocolate chips and the butterscotch chips in the top of a double boiler; spread as icing over the first mixture. Cool and cut into 2x2-inch squares.

Janice S. Thornton

GRAMMIE'S BROWNIES

Must prepare ahead   *Yield: 2 dozen*

1 cup butter
4 (1-ounce) squares semi-sweet
  chocolate
2 cups sugar
4 eggs, lightly beaten

1 cup all-purpose flour
¼ teaspoon salt
2 teaspoons vanilla
2 cups chopped pecans

Preheat oven to 325°. Grease a 13x9x2-inch pan. Melt butter and chocolate in a saucepan over low heat. Add sugar; stir. Add beaten eggs and stir mixture again. Add flour, salt, vanilla, and pecans and stir well. Pour into prepared pan and bake for 40 minutes. Allow to stand over-night before cutting. These brownies are very moist, not cake-like.

Roddy S. Dixon

CUT-OUT SUGAR COOKIES

Yield: 6 dozen

½ cup butter, softened
¾ cup sugar
¾ teaspoon vanilla
1 egg, lightly beaten

2 cups all-purpose flour
½ teaspoon baking soda
pinch of salt

Preheat oven to 375°. Grease cookie sheets. Cream together butter and sugar. Add vanilla and egg; beat until smooth. Sift flour, soda, and salt together; blend into creamed mixture. (The dough will be stiff.) Roll out on a lightly floured board; cut into desired shapes. Bake for 10 to 12 minutes.

Roddy S. Dixon

MARIE'S CRÈME DE MENTHE BROWNIES

Must prepare ahead   *Yield: 5 dozen*

4 (1-ounce) squares
   unsweetened chocolate
1 cup butter or margarine
4 eggs, lightly beaten

2 cups sugar
½ teaspoon salt
1 teaspoon vanilla
1 cup all-purpose flour

Preheat oven to 350°. Grease heavily a 13x9x2-inch baking pan. Melt chocolate and butter; cool slightly. Beat eggs and add to chocolate mixture. Gradually add sugar, salt, vanilla, and flour; beat for 1 minute. Pour into prepared pan and bake 20 to 25 minutes. They will be fudgy—do not overbake. Let cool.

Filling:
½ cup butter or margarine,
   softened
4 cups powdered sugar

¼ cup crème de menthe
¼ cup evaporated milk

Cream butter and sugar. Add crème de menthe and milk and mix well. Spread over base and chill.

Topping:
1 (6-ounce) package semi-
   sweet chocolate chips
3 teaspoons water

4 tablespoons butter or
   margarine

Combine all ingredients over low heat in a saucepan; melt. Spread topping over filling; refrigerate until topping begins to set up. Cut into 1x2-inch bars and leave in pan. Freeze. Serve frozen.

Kay I. Showfety

ONE-PAN BROWNIES

Yield: 2 dozen

¾ cup butter (no substitute)   3 tablespoons cocoa
1½ cups self-rising flour   ½ cup chopped pecans
1½ cups sugar   1 teaspoon vanilla
3 eggs, lightly beaten

Preheat oven to 350°. Grease a 13x9x2-inch baking pan. Melt butter. Add flour, sugar, eggs, cocoa, pecans, and vanilla; combine well with a fork. Do not use a mixer. Bake for 25 to 30 minutes. Cool completely before icing.

Icing:
6 tablespoons butter, softened   dash of salt
1 (16-ounce) box powdered   ¼ cup light cream
   sugar   1½ teaspoons vanilla
3 tablespoons cocoa

Combine butter, sifted powdered sugar, cocoa, and salt; mix well. Gradually add the cream and vanilla.

Sylvia W. Kercher

BUTTER CHEWS

Yield: 4 dozen

¾ cup butter or margarine,   1 cup chopped pecans
   softened   1 cup coconut
3 tablespoons sugar   1 teaspoon vanilla extract
2 cups all-purpose flour   1½ cups powdered sugar
5 eggs, well beaten   ¼ cup lemon juice
1 (16-ounce) box light brown
   sugar

Preheat oven to 350°. Grease a 13x9x2-inch baking pan. Combine butter, sugar, and flour; mix well. Press batter in the bottom of the prepared pan and bake for 15 minutes. Beat eggs well; add brown sugar, pecans, coconut, and vanilla; blend well. Pour over first mixture. Return to oven and bake for 25 to 30 minutes. Mix powdered sugar and lemon juice; pour over warm cookies. Cool and cut into squares.

Mary F. Teeter

BUTTER WAFERS

Yield: 5 dozen

2 cups all-purpose flour
1 cup sugar
½ teaspoon cinnamon
½ teaspoon allspice
¾ cup butter or margarine,
    softened

1 large egg, lightly beaten
1½ teaspoons vanilla extract
1 tablespoon milk

Preheat oven to 400°. Sift together flour, sugar, cinnamon, and allspice. Add butter and blend well. Combine egg, vanilla extract, and milk and stir into mixture. Mix well to form a dough; shape in ½-inch balls. Place 2 inches apart on an ungreased cookie sheet; flatten to 1/16-inch thickness. You may sprinkle colored sugar in the center of each cookie if desired. Bake for 6 to 8 minutes or until lightly brown. Cool on a wire rack.

Nancy S. Johnson

CARAMEL LAYER SQUARES

Yield: 2½ to 3 dozen

1 (14-ounce) package light
    caramels
⅓ cup evaporated milk
1 (18½-ounce) box German
    chocolate cake mix

¾ cup butter, melted
⅓ cup evaporated milk
1 cup chopped nuts
1 (12-ounce) package semi-
    sweet chocolate chips

Preheat oven to 350°. Grease and flour a 13x9x2-inch baking pan. In the top of a double boiler, melt caramels and ⅓ cup evaporated milk. In a large bowl, place dry cake mix, melted butter, and ⅓ cup evaporated milk. Mix by hand to form a stiff dough; stir in nuts. Press ¾ of the dough into the prepared pan. Bake for 10 minutes. Remove from oven and sprinkle chocolate chips on baked crust. Spread melted caramel mixture over the chocolate chips, using a knife. Sprinkle the remaining ¼ of the cake mixture over the top. (It will not spread or cover the top.) Bake for 20 minutes. Cool completely before cutting into squares.

Carole J. Cumming

CHEESE CAKE BARS

Freezes well   *Yield: 4 dozen*

1 cup melted butter or   ½ cup sugar
   margarine   1 cup all-purpose flour
1½ cups well crushed graham   1 cup chopped nuts
   crackers

Preheat oven to 350°. Combine all ingredients and mix well. Press into an ungreased 13x9x2-inch pan and bake for 12 minutes.

Filling:
2 (8-ounce) packages cream   2 eggs, lightly beaten
   cheese, softened   1 teaspoon lemon peel
⅔ cup sugar   2 tablespoons lemon juice

Cream together cream cheese and sugar. Add eggs, lemon peel, and lemon juice and mix well. Pour over baked crust and bake for 20 to 25 minutes. Cool and cut into squares.

Anita G. Anderson

CREAM CHEESE CRESCENTS

Must prepare ahead   *Yield: 5 dozen*

1 cup butter, softened   ¾ cup finely chopped walnuts
1 (8-ounce) package cream   ⅓ cup sugar
   cheese, softened   1½ teaspoons cinnamon
2 cups all-purpose flour   powdered sugar
¼ teaspoon salt

Cream together butter and cream cheese. Stir flour and salt together; add to creamed mixture, mixing well. Shape dough in 8 balls, wrap each ball in plastic wrap, and chill for at least 2 hours. Preheat oven to 350°. On a lightly floured surface roll each ball in an 8-inch circle; cut in 8 wedges. Combine walnuts, sugar, and cinnamon; sprinkle ¼ teaspoon of this mixture over each wedge of dough. Starting at wide edge of dough, roll up each wedge, shaping it into a crescent. Place point side down on ungreased cookie sheet. Bake for 12 minutes or until lightly browned. Cool and dust with powdered sugar.

Kay I. Showfety

DATE PECAN BARS

Must prepare ahead   *Yield: 6 to 7 dozen*

1 cup butter, softened
2 cups sugar
3 eggs, lightly beaten
1 teaspoon baking soda
2 teaspoons water
1 (8-ounce) package chopped
   dates

3 cups all-purpose flour
1 teaspoon cinnamon
1 teaspoon nutmeg
1/4 teaspoon ground cloves
dash salt
1 cup chopped pecans

Cream butter and sugar until light and fluffy. Add eggs one at a time, beating well after each addition. Combine baking soda and water, add to creamed mixture, and beat. Add dates to above mixtures.

Sift together flour, cinnamon, nutmeg, cloves, and salt. Gradually add the flour mixture to the creamed mixture. Blend in the nuts. Chill the dough 5 to 6 hours or overnight.

Preheat oven to 350°. Grease a cookie sheet. On a lightly floured surface, roll dough into rolls the length of the cookie sheet and 3/4-inch in diameter. You should have 3 rolls. Press down to flatten to 1/4-inch. Sprinkle with sugar. Bake for 10 minutes. While hot, make diagonal slices, 1 to 1 1/2-inches long. Cool on rack before storing in airtight containers.

Linda P. Frye

HERMITS

Yield: 4 dozen

1 cup butter, softened
1 1/2 cups brown sugar
2 eggs, lightly beaten
1/2 teaspoon baking soda
1/2 cup buttermilk

2 1/2 cups all-purpose flour,
   divided
1 cup golden raisins
1/2 cup pecan halves

Preheat oven to 375°. Grease a cookie sheet. Cream butter and sugar in food processor. Add eggs and process. Add soda to buttermilk and set aside. Add 1 1/2 cups flour to processor. Process. Add buttermilk and remaining flour. Add raisins, processing on and off once. Add pecans, processing on and off once. Drop by teaspoonful on greased cookie sheet 2-inches apart. Bake 10 minutes or until golden brown. Remove from pan immediately.

Mary Hazel W. Abernethy

EASY MACAROONS

Yield: 4 dozen

2 (7-ounce) packages coconut   2 teaspoons vanilla
1 (15-ounce) can sweetened
    condensed milk

Preheat oven to 325°. Grease a cookie sheet. Mix all ingredients together and combine well. Drop by teaspoon on prepared cookie sheet. Bake 10 to 20 minutes on the upper rack of the oven. Remove from cookie sheet immediately.

Note: If macaroons fall apart, shape them into desired form. When cool, they are firm.

Carolyn W. Glass

OATMEAL CAKES

Yield: 2 dozen

1 cup butter or margarine,   1 teaspoon baking soda
    softened   1 teaspoon salt
1 cup brown sugar   1 teaspoon cream of tartar
½ cup sugar   3 cups quick-cooking oatmeal
3 eggs, well beaten   1 teaspoon vanilla
1½ cups all-purpose flour

Preheat oven to 350°. Grease cookie sheet. Cream together butter and sugars. Add eggs and beat until light and fluffy. Sift together flour, soda, salt, and cream of tartar; blend into creamed mixture. Stir in oatmeal and vanilla by hand, mixing well. Drop by teaspoon on prepared cookie sheet. Bake for 12 to 15 minutes. While still warm, put the flat side of 2 cookies together with the following filling.

Cream Filling:
½ cup butter or margarine,   2 cups powdered sugar
    softened   1 teaspoon vanilla
½ cup shortening

Mix all ingredients together with mixer or food processor.

Elaine A. Myers

OATMEAL COOKIES

Yield: 3 dozen

½ cup butter, softened
½ cup sugar
1 egg, lightly beaten
¼ cup all-purpose flour
⅛ teaspoon baking powder
⅛ teaspoon salt
1 cup English walnuts or
    pecans, chopped

1 cup chopped dates
½ cup coconut
¼ cup candied or drained
    maraschino cherries,
    chopped
1 cup quick-cooking oatmeal

Preheat oven to 375°. Grease a cookie sheet. Cream together butter and sugar. Add egg; mix well. Stir together flour, baking powder, and salt; add to creamed mixture and blend. Add nuts, dates, coconut, cherries, and oatmeal; mix thoroughly. Drop by teaspoon on prepared cookie sheet. Bake 10 to 12 minutes. Remove from cookie sheet immediately.

Nancy C. Shuford

OATMEAL-CORNFLAKE DROP COOKIES

Yield: 6 to 8 dozen

1 cup shortening
1 cup brown sugar
1 cup sugar
2 eggs, lightly beaten
1½ cups all-purpose flour
1 teaspoon baking soda
½ teaspoon salt

½ teaspoon vanilla
2 cups quick-cooking oatmeal
1 cup cornflakes or oven-toasted
    rice cereal
1 cup pecans, chopped
1 (6-ounce) package semi-
    sweet chocolate chips

Preheat oven to 350°. Grease cookie sheets. Cream together shortening and sugars; add beaten eggs. Mix flour, soda, and salt together; add to creamed mixture. Stir in vanilla, oatmeal, cornflakes, pecans, and chocolate chips and mix well. Drop by teaspoons onto cookie sheet and bake for 10 minutes or until lightly browned.

Variation: Omit chocolate chips, add one cup raisins and a teaspoon each of cinnamon, nutmeg, and ginger.

Judy B. Smith

OATMEAL-PEANUT BUTTER COOKIES

Yield: 6 dozen

1¾ cups all-purpose flour
½ teaspoon salt
1 teaspoon baking soda
½ cup butter, softened
1 cup sugar
1 cup brown sugar
½ cup chunky peanut butter

2 eggs, lightly beaten
¼ cup milk
1 teaspoon vanilla
2½ cups quick-cooking oatmeal
½ cup raisins
½ cup semi-sweet chocolate
  chips

Preheat oven to 350°. Stir flour, salt, and soda together; set aside. Beat butter, sugars, and peanut butter together until creamy. Blend in eggs, milk, and vanilla. Stir in flour mixture. Add oatmeal, raisins, and chocolate chips; mix well. Drop by tablespoon 2 inches apart on ungreased cookie sheet. Bake for 12 to 15 minutes.

Linda P. Frye

THUMBPRINT COOKIES

Yield: 4 dozen

1 cup butter, softened
3 heaping tablespoons sugar
2¾ cups all-purpose flour

2 teaspoons almond flavoring
jelly or jam
powdered sugar

Preheat oven to 350°. Grease a cookie sheet. Cream together butter and sugar. Add flour and flavoring, mixing well. Shape in 1-inch balls. Press down the center of each ball with your thumb. Fill the dent with a small amount of jelly or jam, such as guava. Bake for approximately 15 minutes or until golden. Cool and roll in powdered sugar. Store in tightly covered tins.

Variations: You may place a pecan half on top of the jelly or jam. Also, chopped nuts can be added to the dough.

Sylvia H. Bowman

PECAN BARS

Yield: 4 dozen

½ cup butter, softened
½ cup margarine, softened
1 cup sugar
1 egg, separated

2 cups all-purpose flour
2 teaspoons vanilla
½ cup chopped pecans

Preheat oven to 350°. Grease a 15x10x1-inch jelly roll pan. Cream butter, margarine, and sugar until light and fluffy. Add egg yolk and beat well. Add flour and then vanilla. Spread batter in prepared pan. Beat egg white until stiff; spread egg white on top of batter. Sprinkle nuts on top. Bake for 30 minutes or until very lightly browned on top and edges. Do not overbake. Allow to cool slightly and cut in squares.

Caroline R. LaTorre

ICED SPICE BARS

Yield: 4 dozen

1½ cups all-purpose flour
1 cup sugar
½ cup milk
½ cup vegetable oil
2 eggs, lightly beaten
1 teaspoon salt

1 teaspoon baking soda
1 teaspoon cinnamon
1 teaspoon cloves
½ cup chopped pecans or
    walnuts
½ cup raisins

Preheat oven to 375°. Grease a 15x10x1-inch jelly roll pan. Combine flour, sugar, milk, vegetable oil, eggs, salt, soda, cinnamon, and cloves; mix well. Stir in nuts and raisins. Turn batter into prepared pan, spreading evenly. Bake until golden, about 20 minutes. Cool bars in pan on rack for 10 minutes. Cool completely before icing.

Icing:
4 tablespoons butter or
    margarine, melted
1 (16-ounce) box powdered
    sugar

1 tablespoon vanilla
milk

Place melted butter in a bowl. Gradually add the powdered sugar and vanilla; beat well. Add enough milk to make the right consistency. Ice the bars and cut into squares.

Judy B. Smith

311

C
O
O
K
I
E
S

SCOTCH SHORTBREAD

Yield: 12 to 16 squares

½ cup unsalted butter, softened   ⅛ teaspoon salt
¼ cup sugar   powdered sugar
1¼ cups all-purpose flour

Preheat oven to 325°. Line a 8-inch square pan with waxed paper. Cream
butter and sugar until light and fluffy. Add flour and salt, mixing well.
Turn batter into prepared pan and bake for 20 minutes or until lightly
browned. Let shortbread cool in pan. Dust heavily with powdered sugar
and cut into squares.

Note: Good served with syllabub as a holiday tradition.

Judy C. West

VIENNESE CRESCENTS

Yield: 6 dozen

1 cup butter, softened   2¼ cups all-purpose flour
¾ cup sugar   1½ teaspoons vanilla
1 cup ground or finely chopped   powdered sugar
    pecans

Preheat oven to 325°. Cream together butter and sugar. Add pecans,
flour, and vanilla; knead to a smooth dough. Shape about 1 rounded
teaspoon at a time into small crescents. Bake on an ungreased cookie
sheet for 15 to 17 minutes. Cool for 1 minute. While still warm, roll
cookies in sifted powdered sugar. Cool completely on racks and roll
again.

Nancy C. Shuford

POTPOURRI

POTPOURRI

I
N
D
E
X

( ) Denotes: (HE) Hickory Entertains   (I) International   (M) Microwave Recipes

POTPOURRI

BOUQUET GARNI

2 to 3 sprigs parsley
1 sprig thyme

1 bay leaf

Tie herbs together with string or place into a cheesecloth bag. Put herb bouquet into stews and sauces during cooking period to enhance flavor.

Anne F. Mitchell

BISCUIT MIX

Stores well

Yield: about 10 cups

8 cups all-purpose flour
4 teaspoons salt
4 tablespoons baking powder

1½ cups dry milk
1½ cups shortening

Combine all ingredients and mix together until the mixture is crumbly. Store in a tightly covered container in refrigerator. Use in any recipe calling for biscuit mix.

Joyce S. Trado

EASY GRANOLA

Stores well

Yield: 15 servings

7¾ cups regular oats, uncooked
1¼ cups flaked coconut
¾ cup brown sugar, firmly
    packed
1 cup wheat germ
1 cup chopped pecans
½ cup salted sunflower seeds

½ cup sesame seeds
1½ teaspoons salt
¾ cup vegetable oil
⅓ cup water
1½ teaspoons vanilla
½ to 1 cup raisins

Combine oats, coconut, brown sugar, wheat germ, pecans, sunflower seeds, sesame seeds, and salt. In another bowl, combine oil, water, and vanilla, stirring well. Pour liquid over dry mixture; toss gently to coat. Divide mixture into two 15x10x1-inch jellyroll pans. Bake at 250⁰ for 35 to 40 minutes, stirring every 10 minutes. Remove from oven and cool. Stir in raisins and store in airtight containers. Serve as a cereal or a delicious snack.

Jan S. Mullis

315

HOMEMADE SWEETENED CONDENSED MILK

Stores well   *Yield: 1 ¼ cups*

1 cup instant dry milk   ⅓ cup boiling water
⅔ cup sugar   3 tablespoons margarine, melted

Combine all ingredients in blender container. Process until mixture is smooth and the consistency of commercial sweetened condensed milk. Store in refrigerator until needed.

Joyce S. Trado

BEER MUSTARD

May prepare ahead   *Yield: 1 cup*

½ cup dry mustard   pinch of turmeric
½ cup stale beer

Combine ingredients and stir until well blended. Chill until ready to serve. *A hot mustard*—good with Chinese food or when used as a spread for hot dogs.

Joyce S. Trado

MARIE'S HOMEMADE MUSTARD

Prepare ahead   *Yield: 2 cups*

½ cup all-purpose flour, sifted   ½ cup dry mustard
¼ cup sugar   ½ cup cider vinegar
⅛ teaspoon salt

Combine dry ingredients. Slowly add vinegar and beat with a whisk until smooth. (If mixture is too stiff, add more vinegar.) Keep mustard tightly sealed in refrigerator. *This mustard is hot!* For a milder mustard, add ½ cup prepared mustard.

Note: The further ahead you make this mustard, the better the flavor. I make it 2 weeks before using.

Variation: For horseradish mustard, add 3 tablespoons prepared horseradish.

Sally T. Blackwelder

316

MAYONNAISE

May prepare ahead   *Yield: 1 quart*

yolks of 6 eggs   2 tablespoons sugar
1 quart vegetable oil, chilled   2 teaspoons salt
juice of 2 lemons   2 teaspoons prepared mustard
5 teaspoons vinegar   1 teaspoon red pepper

Put 6 yolks in a mixer bowl or food processor. Add oil in small amounts, slowly, alternating oil and lemon juice until about 1 pint of oil has been used. Then add vinegar and follow with sugar, salt, mustard, and red pepper. Continue beating until all oil is used and the mayonnaise is of thick consistency. Refrigerate; will keep indefinitely.

Duart J. Johnston

BLENDER SOUR CREAM

Yield: 1½ cups

1 (12-ounce) carton cottage   2 tablespoons lemon juice
   cheese

Mix cottage cheese and lemon juice in blender and blend well. A very good imitation sour cream.

Charlene A. Bronnenberg

TACO SEASONING MIX

Stores well   *Yield: 6 ounces*

2 teaspoons dried instant   ½ teaspoon ground cumin
   minced onion   ½ teaspoon oregano
1 teaspoon salt   ½ teaspoon cornstarch
½ teaspoon crushed dried red   ¼ teaspoon cayenne pepper
   pepper
½ teaspoon instant minced
   garlic

Combine all ingredients and blend well. Store in airtight container.

Note: Makes the equivalent of 1 envelope of commercial seasoning mix. Always a welcomed gift for people who enjoy Mexican food.

Joyce S. Trado

BASIC ROUX

2 tablespoons butter,   2 tablespoons flour
   shortening, or bacon   seasonings
   drippings   stock

Melt butter in a skillet. Remove skillet from heat and add flour, stirring well to blend. Return skillet to heat and stir constantly until mixture is a medium or dark brown color, being careful not to burn. Gradually add seasonings and stock as required for your recipe, stirring constantly until mixture is smooth. Roux is required for a wide variety of sauces and gravies.

Sylvia H. Bowman

HOMEMADE CURRY POWDER

Stores well   *Yield: 2 cups*

1-ounce pepper   1 to 3-ounces cayenne pepper
1-ounce ginger   1 to 2-ounces ground cardamon
1-ounce dry mustard   1 to 2-ounces cumin seed
3-ounces coriander seed   1 to 2-ounces cinnamon
3-ounces turmeric

Sift all ingredients together and store in tightly capped bottles.

Note: Adds a distinctive touch to any dish requiring curry powder. A good gift idea for the discerning cook.

Joyce S. Trado

ALL-PURPOSE CREOLE SEASONING MIX

Stores well   *Yield: 2 pounds*

1 (26-ounce) box table salt   1-ounce garlic powder
1½-ounces ground black pepper   1-ounce chili powder
2-ounces ground red pepper   1-ounce monosodium glutamate

Mix together all ingredients. Use as you would salt; when salty enough do not add other seasonings until tasting. Makes an unusual gift.

Joyce S. Trado

APPLE MARMALADE

Yield: 3 pints

2 oranges, quartered, seeded,
and thinly sliced
6 medium-sized apples, peeled,
cored, and coarsely chopped

2 cups water
3 tablespoons lemon juice
5 cups sugar
paraffin, melted

Place the oranges, apples, water, and lemon juice in a saucepan. Boil gently for 15 minutes; add sugar and cook until mixture comes to a rolling boil or reaches 220° on a candy thermometer. Cook 10 more minutes, stirring constantly and put into hot sterilized jars. Seal.

Chris R. Bates

MOTHER'S FAVORITE STRAWBERRY JAM

Must prepare ahead   *Yield: 2 to 4 pints*

1 quart strawberries
4 cups sugar

2 tablespoons vinegar
paraffin, melted

Wash and decap strawberries. Put in a saucepan. Add sugar and cook 2 hours on medium to low heat at a slow boil, stirring occasionally. Add vinegar and stir. Remove from heat and let stand overnight. Remove skim from top and discard. Put in jars and seal. *Delicious!*

Carolyn W. Glass

BRANDIED PEACH JAM

Yield: 4 to 6 half-pints

3 cups (or 3 pounds) fresh
peaches, peeled and
chopped
1 tablespoon lemon juice
¼ teaspoon grated lemon peel

1 (1¾-ounce) package powdered
pectin
5 cups sugar
1 cup brandy

Combine peaches, lemon juice, lemon peel, and pectin: bring to full boil, stirring frequently. Add sugar and boil hard for 1 minute, stirring constantly. Remove from heat and stir in brandy. Seal in clear jars and process in water bath for 10 minutes.

Note: For Amaretto Peach Jam, reduce sugar to 4½ cups and add ½ cup Amaretto instead of brandy.

Joyce S. Trado

319

JERUSALEM ARTICHOKE PICKLES

Must prepare ahead   *Yield: A lot*

1 pint onions
1 quart Jerusalem artichokes
1 pint green tomatoes
6 green peppers
1 head cabbage
1 bunch celery
2 dill pickles
1/2 cup salt

1 cup all-purpose flour
3 cups sugar
1 1/2 tablespoons celery seed
1 1/2 tablespoons mustard seed
1 tablespoon dry mustard
2 tablespoons turmeric
1 quart vinegar

Chop onions, artichokes, tomatoes, peppers, cabbage, celery, and pickles. Combine with salt and let stand 24 hours. Rinse and drain. Combine flour, sugar, celery seed, mustard seed, dry mustard, turmeric, and vinegar; cook until thick, but do not boil. Combine vegetables and sauce. Heat thoroughly, but do not boil. Put in sterile jars and seal.

Camille M. Gardner

MOTHER'S SMALL WHITE CUCUMBER PICKLES

Yield: 10 to 12 pints

6 quarts small white cucumbers
    (10 pounds)
1 quart white onions (2 pounds)
3/4 cup salt
crushed ice (about 16 pounds)

2 1/2 pints vinegar
6 cups sugar
1 tablespoon turmeric
2 tablespoons mustard seed
1 teaspoon celery seed

Place a layer of cucumbers and onions in a large container and salt them. Cover with crushed ice. Alternate layers until cucumbers, onions, salt, and ice are gone, ending with ice. Let this stand 3 hours. Rinse off all the salt and drain vegetables. Dry with towels until all possible juice is removed. Bring vinegar, turmeric, mustard seed, and celery seed to a boil. Add dry cucumbers and onions and bring to a boil again. Pack·in hot, sterilized jars. Seal.

Peggy G. Bissette

SPICY PINEAPPLE PICKLES

Must prepare ahead   *Yield: 6 to 8 servings*

1 (20-ounce) can chunk   ½ cup vinegar
   pineapple   5 or 6 whole cloves
⅔ cup sugar   3 or 4 whole allspice, optional
dash salt   2 sticks cinnamon

Drain pineapple and put into refrigerator dish. Combine sugar, salt, vinegar, cloves, allspice, and cinnamon; bring to a boil. Simmer about 10 minutes. Pour over pineapple chunks in the refrigerator dish; let cool before returning to refrigerator. Best if prepared several days in advance.

Note: Can be tinted for the holiday season.

Mary H. Allran

PUMPKIN CHIPS

Must prepare ahead   *Yield: 12 pints*

12 pounds pumpkin   9 lemons, sliced
10 pounds sugar

Cut pumpkin in strips. Remove rind and slice thinly. Add sugar and sliced lemons; soak overnight. Next day boil about 3 hours or until thickened. Put into hot sterilized jars. Seal.

Isabel F. Whaley

YELLOW SQUASH PICKLES

Yield: 5 quarts

4 quarts squash, thinly sliced   1½ teaspoons celery seed
6 medium white onions, sliced   1 teaspoon turmeric
¼ cup coarse pickling salt   3 cups cider vinegar
5 cups sugar   1½ teaspoons mustard seed

Add salt to sliced squash and onions. Cover with ice. Mix thoroughly and let stand 3 hours. Drain; combine sugar, celery seed, turmeric, vinegar, and mustard seed. Pour over squash mixture. Heat to a boil. Place into hot, sterilized jars and seal.

Nancy F. Matheson

REFRIGERATOR OR FREEZER PICKLES

Must prepare ahead   *Yield: 4 pints*

2 quarts cucumbers   ³/₄ teaspoon salt
2 medium onions   ³/₄ teaspoon celery seed
1¹/₂ cups water   ¹/₂ teaspoon garlic salt
1³/₄ cups cider vinegar   ¹/₂ teaspoon onion salt
1¹/₂ cups sugar (or 1 cup honey)   ¹/₂ teaspoon celery salt

Thinly slice cucumbers and onions; put into 4 sterilized pint jars. Combine water, vinegar, sugar, salt, celery seed, garlic salt, onion salt, and celery salt. Boil for 1 minute and pour over cucumbers and onions. Seal. Let stand in the refrigerator for 12 hours before eating or freezing.

Note: Be sure to allow ¹/₂-inch head space at the top of each jar for sealing.

Pat Y. Tolbert

WATERMELON RIND PICKLES

Must prepare ahead   *Yield: 4 pints*

4 pounds watermelon rind   9 cups sugar
¹/₂ cup air slack lime   2 whole cloves
1 gallon water   6 sticks of cinnamon
green food coloring   6 blades mace
1 (1-ounce) can ginger root   1¹/₄ pints vinegar
1 pint water

Pare watermelon rind, making sure to remove all the pink melon. Soak overnight in lime water; then soak in clear water for 1 hour. Cook in the clear water, adding enough ginger root to make strong ginger tea. Add the food coloring, cook the ginger root until tender, and remove the root from the ginger tea. Bring this syrup to a boil, cooking until the rind becomes clear (about 45 minutes). Rind should be tender. Let stand for 24 hours. Remove spices. Return to boiling point; pack into hot, sterilized jars and seal.

Sis H. Gregg

322

AUNT BELLE'S CHOW-CHOW

Must prepare ahead   *Yield: 8 quarts*

3 quarts green tomatoes   1 cup salt
3 quarts bell peppers (green)   9 cups brown sugar
3 quarts bell peppers (red)   5 tablespoons dry mustard
3 quarts cabbage   3 tablespoons turmeric
3 quarts onion   1 gallon vinegar
12 stalks celery   1 cup all-purpose flour
2 dozen small white cucumber
    pickles

Slice or chop tomatoes, peppers, cabbage, onion, celery, and pickles.
Add salt and mix well. Let stand overnight, then drain and rinse. Make a
syrup of the sugar, mustard, turmeric, vinegar, and flour. Bring the syrup
to a boil, add vegetables, and bring to a boil again. Pack hot into sterilized jars and seal.

Sis H. Gregg

DELICIOUS MARINATED CABBAGE

Yield: 1½ quarts

1 head cabbage, grated fine   1 teaspoon mustard seed
    in blender   1 tablespoon salt
1 medium onion, diced   1 cup sugar
1 medium green pepper, diced   1 cup vinegar
1 teaspoon celery seed   ½ cup oil

Mix cabbage, onion, and pepper. Combine celery seed, mustard seed,
salt, sugar, vinegar, and oil; bring to a boil. Pour over cabbage mixture.
Put into containers and refrigerate. Will keep for weeks.

Note: Good with barbecue and black-eyed peas.

Carolyn W. Glass

323

PEACH CHUTNEY

Yield: 4 to 5 pints

4 pounds peaches, peeled and
  chopped
2 quarts vinegar, divided
4 cups sugar
2 tablespoons white mustard
  seed (If you can't get it,
  use yellow.)

1 tablespoon ground dried chili
  pepper
1 clove garlic
1½ cups raisins
1 pound preserved ginger with
  syrup, chopped

Add 1 quart vinegar to peaches. Boil for 20 minutes. In second pan combine 1 quart vinegar and sugar, boiling until it is a thick syrup. Pour off most of the fruit liquid and add it to the vinegar sugar syrup; boil until thickened. Combine this mixture with peaches, mustard seed, chili pepper, garlic, and raisins; cook 30 minutes. Add chopped ginger and its syrup and cook 10 minutes longer. Place in hot sterilized bottles and seal.

Note: The flavor is improved if bottles are placed in the sun for several days, but it is not necessary.

Martha T. Kurad

CORN RELISH

Must prepare ahead   *Yield: 3 cups*

1 (17-ounce) can whole kernel
  white corn, drained
½ green pepper, finely chopped
1 whole pimento, finely chopped
5 stalks celery, finely chopped
1 large onion, finely chopped

⅔ cup corn oil
2½ tablespoons wine vinegar
2½ teaspoons salt
1 teaspoon pepper
1½ teaspoons dry mustard

Mix corn, pepper, pimento, celery, and onion. Combine corn oil, vinegar, salt, pepper, and mustard and pour over vegetable mixture. Place in a tightly closed container and marinate 24 hours before using. Drain before serving; reserve liquid to pour over leftover relish.

Note: A delicious salad may be made with ½ cup of the Corn Relish folded into a basic tomato aspic.

Carolyn W. Glass

GINGER PEARS

Yield: 18 jelly glasses

9 pounds pears, pared and
   cooked
12 cups sugar
juice of 4 lemons

rind of 2 lemons
3-ounces crystallized ginger
paraffin, melted (optional)

Cut pears into thin slices. In a large kettle, combine pears and sugar, cooking over low heat until sugar melts and syrup forms. Stir constantly. Simmer until pears are clear, stirring occasionally. Add lemon juice and rind. Cut ginger into small pieces and add to mixture; simmer until thick. (This may take 1 hour.) Put into sterilized jelly glasses and cover with a thin layer of paraffin or seal in sterilized pint jars while hot.

Note: Food processor speeds slicing process. Excellent with most meats, especially lamb, ham, or chicken.

Martha T. Kurad

PEAR RELISH

Yield: 10 pints

6 medium-sized peppers (3 red,
   3 green)
1 peck pears (15 pounds)
5 medium onions

2 tablespoons pickling spices
4 cups sugar
1 tablespoon turmeric

Grind peppers, drain and discard juices. Grind pears and onions, retaining juices. Combine peppers, pears, onions, spices, sugar, and turmeric; cook for 30 minutes. Put in hot sterilized jars. Seal.

Becky H. Henry

LEMON-ONION SAUCE

May prepare ahead   *Yield: 6 to 8 servings*

¼ pound butter
1 small onion, chopped

1½ tablespoons fresh lemon
juice

Melt butter in a skillet. Sauté onions until clear, but not brown. Add lemon juice. Serve over broccoli, asparagus, or French style green beans.

Note: Add 1 to 2 tablespoons water when reheating if sauce is prepared ahead.

Polly D. Walker

BLEU CHEESE SAUCE

May prepare ahead   *Yield: 6 servings*

¼ cup butter or margarine
2 tablespoons all-purpose flour
1½ cups milk

1 (2-ounce) package bleu
cheese, crumbled

In a saucepan, melt butter, add flour, and then milk. Cook until thick, stirring constantly. Add bleu cheese. Reheat if prepared ahead. Delicious on baked potatoes.

Doris B. Fuller

PESTO SAUCE

Yield: 1 cup

3 cups fresh basil leaves,
loosely packed
¾ cup olive oil
¼ cup pine nuts
3 garlic cloves
1 teaspoon salt

2 tablespoons butter
½ cup Parmesan cheese,
freshly grated
3 tablespoons Romano cheese,
freshly grated

Put all ingredients except cheeses into blender or food processor; process until smooth. Pour sauce into a small bowl; add cheeses and mix well. Adjust seasoning, if necessary. Serve at room temperature over hot pasta.

Susan L. Ingle

SALSA DE JITOMATE

1 small onion, chopped
3 cups Italian plum tomatoes
1 clove of garlic, minced

salt to taste
½ teaspoon oregano
2 tablespoons vegetable oil

Combine onion, tomatoes, garlic, salt and oregano in a blender and blend until smooth. In saucepan heat with oil. Simmer fifteen minutes.

Camille M. Gardner

HERB MAYONNAISE DRESSING

Yield: 1½ cups

1 cup mayonnaise
½ teaspoon lemon juice
¼ teaspoon salt
¼ teaspoon paprika
¼ cup parsley, minced
1 tablespoon onion, grated
1 tablespoon chives

⅓ teaspoon curry powder
½ teaspoon Worcestershire
    sauce
1 clove garlic, minced
1 tablespoon capers
½ cup heavy cream, whipped,
    or ½ cup sour cream

Combine all ingredients except whipped cream. Gently fold in whipped cream. Serve on vegetables or use as a dip.

Note: Delicious with shrimp. Add more lemon juice to taste and ½ teaspoon of celery seed.

Camille M. Gardner

327

PARMESAN SAUCE

Yield: ½ cup

2 tablespoons butter, melted
   and cooled
4 tablespoons mayonnaise
2 tablespoons Parmesan cheese,
   grated

¼ teaspoon Worcestershire
   sauce
1½ tablespoons fresh onion
   juice

Add remaining ingredients to butter. Stir well to blend.

Note: Make sauce at least an hour before serving. Delicious over baked potatoes and other vegetables.

Mary Ruth W. Burns

HOT DOG CHILI

May prepare ahead   *Yield: 24 servings*

1 pound ground beef
1 cup water
1 medium onion, chopped
1 cup catsup
1 teaspoon salt

¼ teaspoon black pepper
¼ teaspoon red pepper
1 tablespoon prepared
   mustard

Cook beef over low heat until it is done. Add remaining ingredients and cook over low heat for 45 minutes. Top hot dogs with chili.

Nellie W. Barnes

HORSERADISH DRESSING

Yield: 1¼ cups

¾ cup heavy cream
3 to 4 tablespoons lemon juice
¼ tablespoon salt
2 tablespoons grated
   horseradish

2 tablespoons sour cream
pinch of cayenne
⅛ teaspoon paprika

Beat heavy cream until stiff. Add the other ingredients slowly, beating constantly.

Note: Delicious with cold meat, especially roast beef.

Josephine L. Hambrick

LINDSEY'S CHICKEN MARINADE

May prepare ahead   *Yield: 6 servings*

¼ cup red wine vinegar
2 tablespoons vegetable oil
2 tablespoons soy sauce
2 tablespoons catsup

¼ teaspoon grated onion or
   onion powder
¼ teaspoon pepper
½ teaspoon salt

Combine ingredients, stirring until mixture is well blended. Pour over meat and marinate 12 to 24 hours. Although marinade is delicious with all meats, it is especially good with grilled chicken. Baste chickens with marinade several times as they cook.

Joanne M. Martin

ORIENTAL MEAT MARINADE

May prepare ahead   *Yield: 1 cup*

4-ounces naturally brewed
   soy sauce
3-ounces olive oil
¼ teaspoon garlic salt

⅛ teaspoon garlic powder
1 tablespoon Beau Monde
   seasoning
salt and pepper to taste

Combine ingredients in large bowl. Pour marinade over beef and marinate for at least 1½ hours on each side. If possible, marinate longer or overnight.

Note: A wonderful marinade for an eye of the round roast.

Anne F. Mitchell

TANGY CHICKEN MARINADE

May prepare ahead   *Yield: 6 to 8 servings*

½ cup lime juice
¼ cup vegetable oil
1 teaspoon tarragon

1 teaspoon onion salt
¼ teaspoon pepper

Combine ingredients, stirring well to blend. Brush over 2 chickens and marinate 2 to 3 hours. Baste chickens several times with marinade as they cook.

Sylvia H. Bowman

MARINADE FOR GRILLED BEEF SHORT RIBS

Must prepare ahead   *Yield: 1 ¼ cups*

1 cup flat beer
¼ cup vegetable oil
1 onion, diced
½ teaspoon sage or thyme

¼ teaspoon garlic powder, or
   more to taste
1 tablespoon salt

Combine all ingredients and stir well to blend. Pour over ribs and marinate overnight. Grill ribs over hot coals for 1 hour, basting several times with marinade. If desired, bake ribs in 350⁰ oven for 20 minutes and finish cooking them for 20 minutes over coals.

Note: Place ribs and sauce in a tightly sealed plastic bag to marinate. Turn bag over several times during marinating period to distribute marinade.

Lindy M. Dillow

MUSTARD SAUCE

Yield: 1 ¾ cups

1 cup brown sugar, packed
⅓ cup dry mustard
2½ teaspoons all-purpose flour
½ cup vinegar

1 beef bouillon cube
2 eggs
¼ cup sherry

Combine sugar, dry mustard, and flour in a double boiler. Add vinegar, bouillon cube, and eggs. Blend well and cook until thickened. Remove from heat and add sherry. Serve with ham, or use as a glaze for baked ham.

Ernestine K. Grimes

TARTAR SAUCE

Yield: 1 cup

1 cup mayonnaise
1 tablespoon onion, minced
1 tablespoon sweet pickle relish

1 tablespoon parsley, finely
   chopped
1 tablespoon capers (optional)

Mix all ingredients; chill.

Susan L. Ingle

MOTHER'S HAMBURGER SAUCE

Yield: 1 cup

½ cup butter or margarine
2 cups onions, sliced
½ cup catsup
2 tablespoons brown sugar
2 tablespoons vinegar

2 teaspoons Worcestershire
   sauce
2 teaspoons prepared mustard
salt to taste

Melt butter and sauté onions. Add catsup, brown sugar, vinegar, Worcestershire sauce, mustard, and salt. Simmer 5 minutes and serve.

Connie H. Abernethy

ANNE'S CURRY SAUCE

May prepare ahead   *Yield: 4 to 6 servings*

¼ cup vegetable oil
2 cups onions, finely chopped
2 cloves garlic, finely chopped
1 tablespoon paprika
1½ teaspoons gingeroot, grated
1½ teaspoons coriander
1 teaspoon salt
½ teaspoon cardamon
1 teaspoon ground turmeric

1 teaspoon ground cumin
1 teaspoon ground cinnamon
1 teaspoon red pepper, or to
   taste
¼ teaspoon pepper
⅛ teaspoon ground cloves
1 cup yogurt or buttermilk
3-ounces tomato paste
1½ cups chicken stock

In a deep skillet, heat oil over low heat. Add onions and cook for about 5 minutes. Add garlic and cook until tender. Add paprika, gingeroot, coriander, salt, cardamon, turmeric, cumin, cinnamon, red pepper, pepper, and ground cloves. Stir well to blend. Gradually stir in yogurt, tomato paste, and stock; continue to stir until thickened.

Note: Add cooked chicken, shrimp, beef, or lamb and simmer 10 minutes before serving over a bed of rice. See page 358.

Anne F. Mitchell

331

SPECIAL DIP FOR BROILED STEAK STRIPS

Yield: 2 cups

1 pound butter
juice of 3 lemons
1/2 cup Worcestershire sauce
1 teaspoon browning and
    seasoning meat sauce

1 clove garlic, minced
1 tablespoon freshly ground
    pepper
1/2 teaspoon dry mustard
1/4 teaspoon hot sauce

Mix all ingredients in the top of double boiler. Heat over boiling water but do not boil sauce. Serve as soon as thoroughly heated as a dip for steak.

Roddy S. Dixon

THE PERFECT FONDUE POT SAUCE

Must prepare ahead   *Yield: 6 servings*

1 1/2 cups Burgundy
1 cup beef broth
1 small onion, thinly sliced
3 sprigs of parsley
1 teaspoon salt

1/2 teaspoon margarine
1/8 teaspoon pepper
1/8 teaspoon garlic powder
1/2 bay leaf

Combine all ingredients in fondue pot. Simmer for 5 minutes. Cover and let stand for at least 2 hours. Heat to boiling before you put fondue pot on lighted base when ready to fondue your beef.

Peggy B. Shuford

EASY BAKED HAM SAUCE

Yield: 6 servings

1 (10-ounce) jar crab apple jelly
1 teaspoon dry mustard
1/4 teaspoon ground cloves

1/4 teaspoon ground cinnamon
2 tablespoons cider vinegar

Combine ingredients in a saucepan. Cook over low heat until mixture is thoroughly heated. Serve hot over baked ham.

Ruth F. Deaton

ORANGE CURRY DIP FOR CHICKEN LEGS

May prepare ahead   *Yield: 1½ cups*

1 cup orange marmalade	1 tablespoon Worcestershire
⅓ cup vinegar	sauce
4 tablespoons sugar	1 teaspoon salt
2 tablespoons brown sugar	½ teaspoon ground ginger
1½ tablespoons curry powder	

Combine marmalade, vinegar, sugars, curry powder, Worcestershire sauce, salt, and ginger in a saucepan. Bring to a boil, then simmer, stirring constantly, until marmalade is melted and sauce is blended. Serve warm or cold.

Phyllis D. Cauble

BUTTERSCOTCH SAUCE

Yield: 6 to 8 servings

1½ cups brown sugar, packed	½ tablespoon lemon juice
¼ cup water	½ cup chopped nuts
4 tablespoons butter or	
margarine	

Boil sugar, water, and butter to *almost* a soft-ball stage. Add lemon juice. Just before serving, add nuts, stirring well to blend. Good over either ice cream or plain cake.

Dorothy Y. Menzies

ROSEMARY'S PINEAPPLE-RUM TOPPING

Yield: 12 to 15 servings

3 (12-ounce) jars pineapple	1 cup rum
topping	½ cup chopped crystallized
1 cup chopped pecans	ginger

Combine all ingredients, stirring well to blend. Spoon on servings of vanilla ice cream. Stores well in refrigerator for several days.

Joanne M. Martin

MARY'S CHOCOLATE SAUCE

Yield: 8 servings

2½ (1-ounce) squares
  unsweetened chocolate
½ cup water
½ cup sugar

1 (14-ounce) can sweetened
  condensed milk
1 tablespoon vanilla

Melt chocolate in water over low heat. Add sugar and cook until a drop of the mixture forms a soft ball when dropped in a glass of cool water. Remove from heat. Beat in condensed milk and vanilla. Cool and place in refrigerator.

Note: Stores well. Rich and delicious over homemade ice cream. An old family favorite.

Joanne M. Martin

HARD SAUCE

Yield: ½ cup

½ cup butter (no substitute)
1 cup powdered sugar

brandy, bourbon, or vanilla to
  taste

Cream butter until softened. Gradually add sugar, beating until smooth. Flavor as desired. A dollop of hard sauce is delicious on steamed puddings.

Anne F. Mitchell

MRS. GLASS'S SHERRY SAUCE

May prepare ahead   *Yield: 2 cups*

2 cups brown sugar
1 cup sugar
½ cup butter
½ cup hot water

2 eggs, well beaten
juice of 1 lemon
1 cup sherry

In a saucepan, combine brown sugar, sugar, butter, and hot water. Cook, stirring until melted and sauce comes to a slow boil. Remove from heat. Using a hand mixer, slowly pour eggs into hot mixture. Return to low heat and add lemon juice and sherry. Keep sauce in refrigerator until you are ready to serve it. Delicious hot or cold over ice cream or angel food cake.

Carolyn W. Glass

INTERNATIONAL CUISINE

I
N
D
E
X

( ) Denotes: (HE) Hickory Entertains   (I) International   (M) Microwave Recipes

 # AUSTRALIA

AUSTRALIAN CHICKEN BREASTS

Yield: 4 servings

2 ounces hazelnuts (filberts)
4 chicken breasts, skinned and
    boned
2 tablespoons seasoned flour
1 egg yolk

1 tablespoon cooking oil
1 or 2 slices of bread,
    crumbed (enough to coat
    chicken)
½ cup clarified butter

Place 2 ounces of hazelnuts in a small baking dish. Roast in a 450⁰ oven with the oven door ajar. Remove them from the oven when they are fragrant and chop them finely. A blender is helpful for this. Set aside. Flatten the chicken breasts. (A bottle is a handy flattening tool.) Coat with seasoned flour. Beat the egg yolk and oil together with a fork and brush on chicken filets. Next, dip filets in bread crumbs, and brown them in clarified butter in a medium-large skillet over medium heat until lightly browned, but thoroughly cooked.

Sauce:
2 teaspoons arrowroot
8 ounces chicken stock
¼ cup butter
salt and pepper to taste

1 teaspoon lemon juice
4 ounces cream
1 ounce brandy

Mix 2 teaspoons of arrowroot with an equal amount of cold chicken stock. Bring remainder of chicken stock to a boil in a medium saucepan and blend in arrowroot mixture carefully but thoroughly. Add ¼ cup butter and 2 to 3 teaspoons of the ground nuts, salt, and pepper to taste. Add lemon juice to freshen, then add the cream and brandy. Stir well and serve.

Lindy M. Dillow

⌒ AUSTRIA ⌒

FRIEDA'S VIENNESE GOULASH

Yield: 8 servings

2 teaspoons marjoram	2 pounds onions, sliced
1 teaspoon caraway seeds	1 tablespoon sweet Hungarian
1 teaspoon lemon zest (lemon	paprika
peel), finely chopped	2 pounds beef, cut in 1-inch
1 teaspoon lemon juice	cubes
1 clove garlic	2 cups water, divided
¾ cup butter	salt to taste
1 teaspoon tomato paste	¼ cup flour

Crush together marjoram, caraway seeds, lemon rind, and garlic. Add lemon juice. In a 4-quart, heavy pot combine butter, tomato paste, and seasoning. Add onions and sauté, stirring constantly until golden. Add paprika and cook ½ minute more, stirring constantly. Add beef, 1 cup water, and salt to taste. Cover tightly and simmer until beef is tender, about 1½ hours. Add a little more water during cooking only if necessary. Just before serving, add ½ cup water and let sauce boil up once. If more sauce is preferred, sprinkle goulash with ¼ cup flour just before the water is added at the end and add one more cup water. Serve with spätzle, noodles, or boiled potatoes.

Marianna M. Raugh

FRIEDA'S SEMMEL KNÖDEL (FLOUR DUMPLINGS)

Yield: Approximately 10 servings

1 tablespoon vegetable oil	3 cups all-purpose flour, sifted
1 onion, finely chopped	salt to taste
2 eggs, well beaten	1 cup bread cubes
2 tablespoons parsley,	6 tablespoons butter, melted
finely chopped	boiling salted water
¾ cup milk	

Sauté onion in oil until golden; add parsley and cook 1 minute. Set aside. Stir eggs into milk and mix with sifted flour. Add salt and bread cubes; then sauté in butter until crisp. Cool for 30 minutes. Shape dough into dumplings the size of a baseball; press hard so dough will hold together. Boil in salted water for 15 minutes, or until Semmel Knodel rise to the top. Serve with Viennese Goulash or sauerkraut and pork roast with gravy.

Anne F. Mitchell

CHINA

BEEF MANDARIN

Yield: 4 servings

3 tablespoons vegetable oil
1 (10-ounce) package frozen pea
  pods
1 pound sirloin tips, cut into
  thin, 3-inch strips
1/2 teaspoon onion powder
1 teaspoon monosodium
  glutamate
1/2 teaspoon salt
1/4 teaspoon garlic powder

1 (1-ounce) package brown
  gravy mix
1 cup water
2 tablespoons each of brown
  sugar and soy sauce
1 (4 1/2-ounce) jar sliced
  mushrooms, drained
hot cooked rice
Mandarin orange sections

Heat oil in a heavy skillet. Add pea pods and sauté 2 minutes. Remove pea pods and add steak strips and seasonings. Cook, stirring constantly, just until redness disappears. Sprinkle gravy mix over meat, add water, brown sugar, and soy sauce. Cook and stir until thickened. Stir in mushrooms and pea pods. Cook until just heated through. Serve on hot rice and garnish with mandarin orange segments, if desired.

Winnie B. Hovey

CHINESE HOT-SOUR SOUP

May prepare ahead

Yield: 4 to 5 servings

1/4 pound lean pork
3 or 4 black mushrooms,
    soaked in 1 1/2 cups water
2 cakes tofu (bean curd)
1 scallion
1 egg
2 tablespoons cornstarch
1/4 cup water
5 cups stock

1 cup mushroom soaking water
1 tablespoon sherry
2 tablespoons rice wine vinegar
    or white vinegar
3/4 to 1 teaspoon salt
1 teaspoon soy sauce
1/4 teaspoon pepper
few drops sesame oil

Sliver mushrooms, pork, and tofu; mince scallion. Beat egg lightly. Blend cornstarch and cold water to a paste. Bring stock and mushroom liquid to a boil. Add pork and mushrooms; simmer covered 10 minutes. Add tofu and simmer, covered, for 3 minutes more. Stir in sherry, vinegar, salt, soy sauce, and pepper. Thicken with cornstarch paste. Slowly add beaten egg, stirring gently, once or twice. Remove from heat; sprinkle with sesame oil and minced scallion. *If preparing ahead, omit the addition of beaten egg until time to serve.*

Anne F. Mitchell

339

PEANUT COATED MANDARIN ORANGE CHICKEN

Yield: 8 servings

6 whole chicken breasts,
   skinned and boned
3 egg whites
6 tablespoons cornstarch
½ cup light corn syrup
1 cup mandarin oranges,
   puréed

1½ teaspoons salt
2 teaspoons sherry
¼ teaspoon pepper
2 cups peanuts, chopped
1 cup peanut oil
sweet and sour sauce—recipe
   below

Cut chicken breasts into 1-inch strips. Combine egg whites, cornstarch, salt, pepper, and sherry. Dip chicken strips into egg-white mixture, then into corn syrup, and then into the puréed mandarin oranges. Finally coat with peanuts. Fry in 1 cup of peanut oil, in a wok or skillet, over medium heat until thoroughly cooked, about 2 minutes.

Sweet and sour sauce:
¾ cup water
¼ cup brown sugar
¼ cup light corn syrup
½ cup rice vinegar
1 tablespoon plus ½
   teaspoon cornstarch
1 tablespoon soy sauce

1 tablespoon sherry
¼ cup water
garnish: 2 cups pineapple
   chunks, 2 medium
   carrots, parboiled, cut
   into ¼-inch flower shapes

Bring water to a boil. Add corn syrup and stir in sugar, cooking another minute; add vinegar; cook 1 more minute. Blend cornstarch, soy sauce, sherry, and cold water to make a paste. Stir paste into the cooked mixture and continue cooking until sauce thickens. Pour sauce over chicken and garnish with pineapple and carrots.

Note: This recipe won third place in a national oriental cooking contest sponsored by a well-known cornstarch and corn syrup company.

Anne F. Mitchell

LION'S HEAD (SEE-JEE-TAO)

May prepare ahead   *Yield: 4 servings*

4 to 6 dried black mushrooms,
    soaked in water, minced
1 pound pork, ground with
    some fat
10 water chestnuts, minced
2 scallion stalks, minced
2 slices fresh ginger root,
    minced
1 egg, lightly beaten
4¹/₂ teaspoons cornstarch,
    divided

1 teaspoon sugar
¹/₂ teaspoon salt
dash of pepper
1 tablespoon sherry
3 to 4 cups oil for deep-frying
1 head Chinese cabbage, leaves
    separated and cut in 4-inch
    sections
2 tablespoons oil
1¹/₄ cups chicken stock, divided,
    1 cup heated

Blend beaten egg with 1½ teaspoons cornstarch, sugar, salt, pepper, and sherry. Blend with pork, water chestnuts, scallions, ginger, and mushrooms. This should be done lightly with a wooden spoon. Meat will lose juice if mixed too long. Divide mixture into 4 parts; with moistened hands form each into 9 large meatballs. Using a wire basket in hot oil, deep-fry meatballs until golden, about 5 minutes. Drain on paper towel. Heat remaining 2 tablespoons of oil, add cabbage and stir-fry about 2 minutes to soften slightly. Use cabbage to line sides and bottom of heavy pan or earthenware casserole. Place meatballs over cabbage. Pour heated stock over this and simmer covered until done, about 1½ hours. Arrange cabbage on a serving platter with meatballs on top. Blend tablespoon of cornstarch and remaining cold stock to a paste; add to liquids in pan and cook, stirring to thicken. Pour sauce over meatballs and serve.

Note: This dish gets its name because the meatballs and sliced cabbage suggest the head of a lion with its mane. Lion's head keeps well and may be made in advance and reheated. This is one of my favorite Chinese dishes!

Anne F. Mitchell

CHINESE CASHEW CHICKEN

Yield: 4 servings

4 chicken breast halves, boned
  and skinned
2 tablespoons oil
1 tablespoon cornstarch
¼ cup soy sauce
¼ cup water
¼ teaspoon salt
⅛ teaspoon pepper
¼ pound fresh mushrooms,
  sliced

1 cup celery, bias cut to
  ¼-inch
1 clove garlic, minced
1 (8-ounce) can of water
  chestnuts, drained
½ cup green onions, sliced
1 medium tomato, chopped
½ cup cashews
1 (6-ounce) package frozen
  pea pods

Cut chicken into 1-inch cubes. Heat oil in wok or electric frying pan to 350°. Combine cornstarch, soy sauce, water, salt, and pepper in a small bowl; stir and set aside. Add chicken, mushrooms, celery, and garlic to oil and stir-fry until chicken turns white; about 3 minutes. Stir in chestnuts and green onions; stir-fry 3 minutes. Stir in cornstarch mixture and cook, stirring constantly for 2 minutes. Stir in tomato and cashews; cook 2 minutes. Add pea pods and serve over rice.

Note: I have substituted bell pepper and carrots for water chestnuts. I have also used green peas instead of pea pods.

Nell B. Walton

ESTONIA

TÜRGIOAD (GREEN BEANS)

Must prepare ahead   *Yield: 5 to 6 servings*

3 cups green beans, snapped
1½ cups water, lightly salted
2 tablespoons butter or
  margarine

¼ teaspoon fresh dill, chopped,
  or dash of dill weed
salt to taste

Bring water to boil. Add beans and bring again to boil. Cook gently, covered, for 10 to 15 minutes, depending on tenderness desired. Drain; season with butter, dill, and additional salt to taste.

Helgi K. Shuford

KAPSARULLID (ESTONIAN CABBAGE ROLLS)

Freezes well   *Yield: 14 to 16 servings*

1 large head of cabbage, washed
  and separated
1½ pounds chuck, ground
1 to 2 medium onions, chopped
2 medium potatoes, cooked and
  mashed
1 egg
1 cup beef bouillon, or beef
  broth

2 slices bread, shredded
1½ teaspoons salt
¼ teaspoon pepper
2 tablespoons butter or
  margarine
sauce

Cut off about 1 inch from base of cabbage leaves. Place cabbage in a saucepan in boiling, salted water to cover. Cook, covered, about 3 minutes or until leaves have wilted. Remove cabbage from water and drain. Set aside. Combine chuck with onions, potatoes, egg, beef bouillon, bread, salt, and pepper; mix well. Lay cabbage leaves flat and place a tablespoon of the meat mixture in the center of each leaf. Fold sides of leaf over top of stuffing; then fold ends. Heat butter in pan; add cabbage rolls and brown lightly on all sides. Place in a deep pan such as a roaster with seamside down.

Sauce:

2 cups beef broth or
    bouillon, diluted
2 tablespoons tomato purée
salt to taste
1 tablespoon flour

¼ cup or more water, cold
2 tablespoons sour cream
1 tablespoon butter
crab apples

Make a paste of water and flour, set aside. Pour on top of cabbage rolls, a mixture of beef broth, tomato purée, and salt. Cover and simmer on top of stove or in a medium-slow oven (300°) for about 1 hour. Remove cabbage to platter and keep warm. Add to the liquid in roaster the flour-paste mixture and cook ½ minute. Add sour cream and butter and heat, mixing thoroughly. *Do not boil.* Pour some of sauce over cabbage and pass rest in a dish. Garnish with crab apples and parsley.

Note: Serve with mashed potatoes.

Helgi K. Shuford

PIRUKAS (STUFFED PASTRIES)

Must prepare ahead   *Yield: 8 to 10 servings*

Pastry:

2½ cups all-purpose flour   ½ cup sour cream
1 teaspoon salt   2 eggs, beaten separately
¾ cup butter, chilled   2 teaspoons milk

Sift the flour with salt. Using a pastry blender, cut in the butter until mixture resembles coarse meal. Add the sour cream and 1 egg and work in until the dough is pliable. Cover with waxed paper and chill for 1 hour. Beat remaining egg and milk together to be used for sealing pastries.

Small Individual Pastries:
Preheat oven to 375⁰. Divide the dough into 3 parts. Keep 2 parts of dough in refrigerator while working with the 1. Roll out dough on floured board. Cut into circles 3½ to 4 inches in diameter. Drop a teaspoon of filling on each circle. Baste the edges with egg-milk mixture. Fold over to form a semi-circle and pinch edges together. Brush with egg-milk mixture. Bake for 10 to 15 minutes or until golden brown.

Large Rectangular Loaf Pastry:
Preheat oven to 375⁰. Butter a 14x8-inch pan. Divide the dough in half with 1 part slightly larger than the other. On floured board roll out dough into 2 rectangles approximately 13x6-inches. Place smaller rectangle into pan, top with filling, and moisten edges with egg-milk mixture. Drape larger rectangle on top, pinch edges, and seal. Cut off any excess dough. Prick top to allow steam to escape. With excess dough, make decorative strips. Brush with egg-milk mixture. Arrange strips, attractively, on dough. Brush again with egg-milk mixture. Bake for 35 to 40 minutes or until golden brown.

Rice and Egg Filling:

1¼ cups rice, cooked   4 hard-boiled eggs, chopped
2 tablespoons butter, melted   salt and pepper to taste
1 tablespoon dill, chopped

Add enough water to rice so that it is 2½-inches above rice level. Bring to boil, reduce heat and simmer, covered, for 15 minutes. Drain, rinse with cold water and drain again. Combine rice with butter, dill, eggs and season with salt and pepper. Chill until time to fill the pastries.

Ground Beef Filling:

4 tablespoons butter, divided
½ cup mushrooms, finely chopped
¼ cup onions, finely chopped
1½ pounds chuck, ground
¾ cup sharp Cheddar or Swiss cheese, grated
¼ cup milk
1 teaspoon dill, or 1 tablespoon parsley, chopped
salt and pepper to taste
2 tablespoons sour cream
1 teaspoon Worcestershire sauce

Melt 2 tablespoons of the butter in a sauce pan; add mushrooms and cook for 5 minutes or until browned. In a large skillet melt remaining butter and sauté the onions. Add beef and cook until browned. Mix together with cheese, milk, dill, mushrooms, sour cream, and Worcestershire sauce. Season with salt and pepper. Chill.

Note: Serve the large rectangular loaf pastry in thick slices with cranberry sauce and a green vegetable for lunch. The Ground Beef Filling is best for the rectangular loaf. The small pastries are excellent with soup or a tossed salad. They are great traditional favorites on the Estonian Smorgasbord table.

Helgi K. Shuford

KAMPOTT (FRUIT COMPOTE)

Must prepare ahead   *Yield: 6 servings*

3 cups water, boiling
½ cup sugar
1 cinnamon stick
1 cup prunes, pitted
1 cup apricots, dried
1 cup apples, dried
1 cup pears, dried
½ teaspoon potato starch
½ cup water, cold
whipped cream or ice cream

In a large pan bring water to boil and add sugar, cinnamon stick, and prunes; then add apricots, apples, and pears. Boil gently, covered, for about 25 minutes. Remove from heat. Dissolve the potato starch in ½ cup of water; then slowly add this to the fruit and boil another minute. Chill. Serve in individual bowls with whipped cream or ice cream.

Helgi K. Shuford

INTERNATIONAL

KARTULISALAT (POTATO SALAD)

Must prepare ahead   *Yield: 10 to 12 servings*

6 large potatoes, unpeeled,
  boiled, sliced, or cubed
2 tablespoons salad oil
2 tablespoons vinegar
2 tablespoons sugar
¼ teaspoon salt
½ cup celery, chopped
¼ cup red onions, chopped
½ cup cucumbers, chopped
4 hard-cooked eggs, separated
½ cup mayonnaise

¾ cup sour cream
¼ teaspoon horseradish
  (optional)
1 teaspoon dry mustard
1 teaspoon sugar
½ teaspoon fresh dill,
  chopped or ¼ teaspoon
  dill weed, dried
salt to taste
parsley
egg slices

Mix together the oil, vinegar, sugar, and salt to make salad dressing. Peel and slice or cube potatoes while still hot, then pour dressing over them. Marinate for 2 to 3 hours. Add the celery, onions, cucumbers, and chopped egg whites to potatoes. Press the egg yolks through a sieve and mix with the mayonnaise, sour cream, horseradish, mustard, and sugar. Fold gently into salad. Season with the dill and salt. Chill for several hours or overnight before serving. Garnish with egg slices and parsley.

Helgi K. Shuford

 **FRANCE**

RATATOUILLE

Yield: 6 to 8 servings

2 cups yellow squash, cubed
⅓ teaspoon cumin seed
2 cups eggplant, peeled and
  cubed
½ teaspoon oregano
2 cups onion, sliced
2 green peppers, sliced

½ teaspoon marjoram
3 or 4 tomatoes, sliced
½ teaspoon dill weed, or seeds
¾ to 1 teaspoon seasoned salt
½ to 1 teaspoon garlic powder
⅓ cup salad oil

In an 8 to 10-cup casserole, with lid, layer vegetables: squash on the bottom, sprinkle with cumin seed; eggplant, sprinkle with oregano; onions and green pepper, sprinkle with marjoram. Combine salt, garlic powder, and salad oil. Pour over all. Cover and bake ½ hour at 350°. Add a layer of tomatoes and sprinkle with dill weed. Bake 15 minutes more.

Joyce S. Trado

346

BRAISED FILLET OF BEEF CHASSEUR (FRANCE)

May partially prepare ahead   *Yield: 4 servings*

Espagnole sauce:

3 tablespoons oil

2 tablespoons onion, finely diced

2 tablespoons carrots, finely diced

1 tablespoon celery, finely diced

1½ tablespoons flour

2 teaspoons tomato paste

1 tablespoon chopped mushrooms

2½ cups well-flavored brown stock

bouquet garni

salt and pepper

This may be prepared the day before. Sauté onion, carrots, and celery in oil until tender. Add flour and stir until brown. Add tomato paste, mushrooms, stock, bouquet garni, salt, and pepper. Simmer until thickened, stirring and straining occasionally.

Beef:

2 to 2½ pound fillet of beef

1 tablespoon oil

1 large onion, sliced

2 large carrots, sliced

½ pound mushrooms

1 tablespoon butter

1 shallot, finely chopped

½ cup white wine

1 teaspoon tomato paste

Preheat oven to 350°. Tie beef with string at 2-inch intervals to keep it in shape during browning. Heat oil in heavy casserole. Put in beef and brown on all sides. Remove from pot, reduce heat, and add onion and carrots. Cover pot and cook gently for about 10 minutes or until vegetables absorb the oil and begin to brown. Return beef to pot and pour over Espagnole sauce. This part can be prepared ahead of time, but do not cook further until ready to serve or meat will be done. Cover with foil and a tight-fitting lid and bring to a boil. Braise in heated oven for about 25 to 35 minutes for rare beef. Use a meat thermometer to accurately judge time. Trim mushroom stems level with the caps and sauté caps quickly in the butter until tender. Stir in shallots and cook for about 1 minute, then add wine and continue cooking until reduced by half. Stir in tomato paste. Remove beef from pot and keep warm. Strain sauce onto mushroom mixture, bring just to a boil, and taste for seasoning. Carve beef in ½-inch slices and arrange down the center of a hot platter. Lift mushrooms from sauce with a slotted spoon and arrange them at each side of the beef. Moisten beef with 2 to 3 tablespoons sauce and serve the rest separately.

Note: Suggested wines—a major Burgundy such as Morey St. Denis (French) or Pinot Noir (California).

Anne F. Mitchell

LA CHOUCROUTE GARNIE

Meats (the more the better):
bacon—about ½ pound slab, cut crosswise but not through the rind
smoked pork butt or shoulder or pork loin or spare ribs
sausages—several kinds such as Alsatian or German knockwurst
sauerkraut—enough to cover all meats
2 carrots, halved
2 small onions, studded with cloves

6 juniper berries
8 peppercorns, coarsely ground
lard
1 cup meat stock or consommé for every 2 pounds of sauerkraut used
½ cup white wine for every 2 pounds of sauerkraut used
1 jigger of gin, Kirsch, or vodka for every 2 pounds of sauerkraut used

Wash sauerkraut in several changes of cold water; press out *all* liquid and fluff out. Using a deep pot, big enough to hold all ingredients with 2 inches to spare, place bacon rinds or a little lard on the bottom. Place carrots and onions on bottom, too. Now add the first round of kraut, at least 1-inch thick. Sprinkle with juniper berries and peppercorns. Add all meats (except bacon and knockwurst) in layers. Cover meats with a top layer of kraut at least 1-inch deep. For every 2 pounds of kraut, take 1 cup canned consommé or stock, mix with ½ cup white wine and pour into choucroute. Toss in a jigger or 2 of liquor. Cover with tight-fitting lid (tight it must be), and put in 275° oven for no less than 3 and no more than 5 hours. Electric fry cooker is perfect. Do not stir or disturb. If it cooks too fast and dries out, add wine or stock or water. There should be no excess liquid when done. When done, the texture of the kraut must be absolutely melting and succulent. Two and one-half hours before serving, add bacon, excavating a place for it. One half hour before serving, bury the knockwurst. Take a big, handsome serving dish, make a great mound of choucroute and arrange the meats and sausages on top and around. Let there be quantities of hot, mealy boiled potatoes and some good mustard, both essential.

Note: The amount of ingredients varies according to the number of people served.

Dorothy Y. Menzies

348

CASSOULET (FRANCE)

Yield: 8 to 10 servings

4 cups small, dried pea beans
2 quarts water
1 tablespoon salt
2 cloves garlic, minced
2 carrots, quartered
2 onions, studded with cloves
1 bouquet garni (parsley, celery,
    bay leaf, and thyme in
    cheesecloth)
½ cup diced salt pork
2 tablespoons duck drippings
    or cooking oil

1½ pounds lean pork, cubed
1 pound lamb, cubed
2 Bermuda onions, chopped
1 (8-ounce) can tomato sauce
1 cup chopped shallots
1 cup celery, thinly diced
1 cup dry white wine
1 garlic or Polish sausage
1 roasted duck, cut in bite-
    size pieces

Combine beans, salt, and water in large kettle and let stand overnight, or boil 2 minutes and soak 1 hour. Add garlic, carrots, onions with cloves, bouquet garni, salt pork. Cook gently 1 hour. Skim off foam. Heat drippings or oil in skillet. Add meats and sauté until brown. Transfer to bean mixture. Sauté onion, shallots, and celery in remaining drippings until tender. Add tomato sauce and wine and simmer 5 minutes. Add to beans. Add garlic sausage, cover, and simmer until all are tender, about 1 hour, adding water if necessary. Skim off excess fat and remove bouquet garni. Transfer to large earthenware casserole. Add roast duck and bake, uncovered, in 350° oven for 35 minutes.

Catherine H. Yeager

 **GERMANY**

GRANDMOTHER'S SAUERBRATEN

Must prepare ahead   *Yield: 6 servings*

3 pounds round steak
1 tablespoon salt
½ teaspoon pepper
2 onions, thinly sliced
1 carrot, thinly sliced
1 stalk celery, chopped
4 whole cloves
4 peppercorns
2 cups red wine vinegar

2 bay leaves
3 cups water
2 tablespoons oil
6 tablespoons butter or
   margarine
5 tablespoons flour
1 tablespoon sugar
10 ginger cookies, crushed

Season meat with salt and pepper. Place in large bowl. Combine onions, carrot, celery, cloves, peppercorns, vinegar, bay leaves, and water. Pour over meat and cover. Refrigerate for 4 days. After 4 days, remove from refrigerator and drain the meat from marinade mixture. Brown the meat in oil. Add marinade to browned meat and bring to a boil. Lower heat and cook for 3 hours. In separate pan, melt butter and add flour and sugar. Brown to a dark color, pour over meat, and cook 1 hour. Remove meat from pan and cut into serving-size pieces. Add crushed ginger cookies to mixture in pan and stir until thickened, approximately 2 minutes. Remove from heat and pour over meat.

Pat Y. Tolbert

PFANNKUCHEN OR GERMAN PANCAKE

Yield: 2 servings

4 egg yolks, beaten
2 tablespoons arrowroot or
   cornstarch
¼ cup lukewarm milk
¼ cup lukewarm water

¾ teaspoon salt
1 tablespoon sugar
grated rind of 1 lemon
4 egg whites, stiffly beaten
2 tablespoons butter

Combine egg yolks, arrowroot, milk, water, salt, sugar, and lemon rind. Stir until smooth. Fold in egg whites. Melt butter in a heavy, 10-inch skillet. When skillet is hot, pour in pancake batter. Cook over low to medium heat, partly covered, for about 5 minutes. Another method is to cook the batter in this manner until partly set, and then place the skillet in a preheated 400° oven until it is puffed and firm. Serve at once with one of the following: 1) powdered sugar and cinnamon, 2) lemon sauce and powdered sugar, 3) covered with jam or jelly and then rolled, or 4) wine sauce, rum sauce, or fruit sauce.

Note: It should puff up well, but may fall when served.

Lindy M. Dillow

INTERNATIONAL

GERMAN SWEET SOUR TONGUE

Yield: 6 to 8 servings

1 beef tongue	5 rounded tablespoons all-purpose flour
4 celery stalks	
1 bay leaf	4 tablespoons vinegar
2 teaspoons salt	1½ teaspoons cinnamon
3 cups broth from tongue	¼ teaspoon ground cloves
5 tablespoons molasses	¾ cup raisins
5 tablespoons butter	

Cook tongue in water to cover with celery, salt, and a bay leaf for several hours or until tender. In iron frying pan, melt butter and add flour. Stir over low heat until roux is a dark brown. My grandmother says this German recipe owes its flavor to the roux being dark brown, almost burned. When it has reached this point, slowly add broth, stirring with wooden spoon, until thickened. Add molasses, seasonings, vinegar, and raisins. Cook, stirring occasionally, until sauce is thick and dark. Adjust sweet and sour sauce, adding salt if necessary. Peel heavy skin from tongue and slice. Add to sauce and simmer 15 or 20 minutes more. Serve with boiled potatoes.

Note: This was Mrs. Menzies' great-grandmother's recipe. It came from Hessen-Cassel in what was then the middle of Prussia. It probably was an original variation of sauerbraten, but is much richer.

Dorothy Y. Menzies

GRANDMOTHER'S GERMAN CABBAGE

Yield: 6 servings

1 large head red cabbage,
   thinly sliced
2 onions, thinly sliced
1 apple, cored and thinly sliced
½ cup red currant jelly
1 bay leaf

½ teaspoon salt
¼ teaspoon pepper
¼ pound butter
2 ham knuckles
¼ cup water
6 tablespoons cider vinegar

Mix together cabbage, onions, apple, jelly, bay leaf, salt, and pepper. Melt butter and place in heavy casserole with tight-fitting lid. Add cabbage mixture, ham knuckles, and water to melted butter. Cover and cook on low heat for 2½ hours. Remove from heat, add vinegar, and serve.

Pat Y. Tolbert

 GREECE

GREEK EASTER SOUP

Yield: 4 to 6 servings

Lamb Stock:
2 pounds lamb bones
1 small onion
2 stalks celery

salt and pepper
water

Prepare 8 cups of lamb stock using 2 pounds lamb bones with some meat on them, onion, celery, salt, pepper, and water. Strain lamb broth after it has simmered for 2 hours.

8 cups lamb broth
½ cup rice
4 eggs, well beaten
juice of 2 lemons

3 tablespoons minced dill
    or parsley
salt and white pepper

Bring broth to a boil and cook rice in it until tender. Remove from heat. Slowly pour about 1 cup of hot soup into eggs, beating constantly. Slowly pour egg mixture back into remaining hot soup, beating constantly. Heat, but do not boil. Stir in lemon juice, add dill or parsley, and season with salt and pepper to taste.

Anne F. Mitchell

GREEK SPINACH PIE

Yield: 18 servings

½ package (1-pound size) prepared phyllo or strudel pastry leaves (16 sheets, 12x15-inches)
¼ cup butter, melted
½ cup onion, finely chopped
3 (10-ounce) packages frozen, chopped spinach, thawed and drained
3 eggs

½ pound feta cheese, crumbled
¼ cup parsley, chopped
2 tablespoon fresh dill, chopped, or 1½ teaspoons dill weed, dried
1 teaspoon salt
⅛ teaspoon pepper
¾ cup butter, melted

Preheat oven to 350º. Let pastry leaves warm to room temperature according to package directions. Sauté onion in ¼ cup melted butter in medium skillet 5 minutes, or until golden. Add spinach to onion, stirring to combine; remove from heat. Beat eggs in a large bowl. Stir in cheese, parsley, dill, salt, pepper, and spinach-onion mixture; mix well. Brush a 13x9x2-inch baking pan lightly with some of the ¾ cup melted butter. In bottom of baking pan, layer 8 phyllo leaves (see note) one by one, brushing top of each with some of the melted butter. Spread evenly with spinach mixture. Cover with 8 more leaves, brushing each one with melted butter; pour any remaining butter over top. Using scissors, trim off any uneven edges of pastry. Cut through top layer of pastry to form 18 rectangles, about 3x2-inches each. Bake 30 to 35 minutes or until top crust is puffy and golden.

Note: Keep unused pastry leaves covered with damp paper towels to prevent them from drying out.

Renie W. Cline

GREEK MOUSSAKA

Yield: 8 to 10 servings

1 medium eggplant
1 pound ground beef or lamb
½ cup onion, chopped
1 clove garlic, minced

1 (8-ounce) can tomato sauce
¼ teaspoon cinnamon
½ teaspoon salt
cheese sauce—recipe below

Peel and slice eggplant. Soak in salted water for ½ hour. Brown ground meat; remove with slotted spoon. Brown onion and garlic in drippings. Add tomato sauce, cinnamon, salt, and meat; simmer 10 minutes. Drain eggplant; cook in microwave oven until soft, or brush with vegetable oil and broil in single layer until brown, turning and doing opposite side. Layer eggplant and meat sauce in a 2-quart casserole, ending with the meat sauce. Top with cheese sauce. Bake for 45 minutes at 350°. Leftovers are good reheated and served in pita bread pouches as a sandwich.

Cheese Sauce:

2 tablespoons butter or
    margarine
2 tablespoons flour
¼ teaspoon nutmeg
1 (5¾-ounce) can evaporated
    milk
¼ cup water

½ teaspoon chicken broth
    granules
1 egg, beaten
1 cup cottage cheese, small
    curd
¼ to ½ cup parmesan cheese

Melt butter; add flour and nutmeg. Cook and stir until bubbly. Stir in milk, water, and chicken granules, stirring constantly over low heat until mixture thickens and boils, about 1 minute; cool slightly. Slowly, add 1 cup of sauce to beaten egg and mix well; then put back in sauce. Cook, stirring constantly for 1 minute. Remove from heat and stir in both kinds of cheese. Can force through a fine sieve or smooth in a blender, if desired.

Joyce S. Trado

GARIDES ME SALISA
(Shrimp with Tomato Sauce and Feta Cheese)

Yield: 4 servings

6 tablespoons olive oil
¼ cup onion, finely chopped
4 medium fresh ripe tomatoes, or 1½ cups canned tomatoes, peeled, chopped and drained
½ cup dry white wine
2 tablespoons parsley, finely chopped

½ teaspoon oregano, crumbled
1 teaspoon salt
freshly ground black pepper
¼ cup feta cheese, cut in ¼-inch cubes
1½ pounds raw shrimp, shelled

In a heavy 10 to 12-inch skillet or shallow casserole, heat oil over moderate heat until a light haze forms. Add onion, stirring frequently. Cook for 5 minutes, or until soft and transparent, not brown. Stir in tomatoes, wine, 1 tablespoon parsley, oregano, salt, and pepper. Bring to a boil and cook briskly, uncovered, until the mixture thickens to a light purée. Add the shrimp and cook over moderate heat 5 minutes. When shrimp are pink and firm to the touch, stir in the cheese. Taste for seasoning and sprinkle top with remaining parsley.

Lou Ellen J. Goodwin

 HOLLAND

JAN HAGEL

Yield: 2 dozen cookies

1 cup butter, softened (no substitute)
1 cup sugar
1 egg, separated

2 cups sifted all-purpose flour
½ teaspoon cinnamon
¼ cup almonds, sliced (or any chopped nuts)

Preheat oven to 300°. Cream butter and sugar. Add egg yolk and mix. Sift flour and cinnamon and add gradually to the creamed mixture. Mix thoroughly. Turn dough out onto a 15½x12-inch cookie sheet. Pat the dough with hands to ⅛-inch thickness. (You may need to put part of the dough onto another cookie sheet.) Brush with unbeaten egg white to which a teaspoon of water has been added. Sprinkle with almonds or nuts. Bake 20 minutes. Cut into 1-inch by 2-inch bars.

Janet E. Schoonderwoerd

STAMPPOT VAN ZUURKOOL MIT SPEKEN WORST
(Sauerkraut with Potatoes, Bacon, Sausage)

Yield: 6 to 8 servings

2 pounds red boiling potatoes
    (about 8 medium), peeled
    and cubed
6 slices bacon, diced
3 small onions, chopped
½ pound fresh mushrooms,
    sliced
3 tablespoons butter

1 (16-ounce) can sauerkraut,
    drained, rinsed
white pepper to taste
1 pound smoked, no garlic,
    ready-to-eat sausage, cut in
    1-inch pieces
chopped parsley for garnish

Put potatoes and ½ cup water in 3-quart casserole. Cover with plastic wrap and microcook on *high* 10 minutes, or until fork tender. Mash with potato masher until smooth. Cook bacon in 2-quart casserole on *high* 3 minutes, or until light brown; stir into potatoes. Put onions, mushrooms, and butter in same dish used for bacon. Microcook 3 minutes; stir and microcook 2 minutes. Stir into potato mixture; stir in sauerkraut. Season with white pepper. Put sausage over potato mixture; microcook 7 minutes or until heated through. Garnish with parsley.

Janet E. Schoonderwoerd

 INDIA

INDIAN BUTTERMILK FRUIT SOUP

Must be chilled ahead   *Yield: 4 servings*

1 cup orange juice
¼ teaspoon orange rind, grated

¼ cup sugar
3 cups buttermilk

Chill all the ingredients separately. At serving time, combine them and serve at once.

Note: Lemon juice or any fruit flavoring may be added instead of orange juice.

Helen M. Brooks

INDIAN KOFTAH CURRY

Yield: 6 to 8 servings

Meatballs:

1 pound beef, finely ground
1 medium onion, finely minced
4 cloves garlic, minced
2 potatoes, peeled, boiled,
   and mashed
2 fresh green chili peppers,
   finely minced
1 egg

1 teaspoon salt
⅛ teaspoon each of pepper,
   ground cardamon seeds,
   ground cinnamon, and
   cloves
vegetable oil for browning
   meatballs

Mix all ingredients thoroughly in a large mixing bowl. Form into balls about the size of walnuts. Brown the meatballs in oil and set aside.

Sauce:

1 medium onion, chopped
3 medium tomatoes, chopped
1 teaspoon ground coriander
½ teaspoon each of ground
   turmeric, red pepper, and
   ginger

½ teaspoon ground cumin seed
1 tablespoon of oil in which
   meatballs were browned

Fry these ingredients lightly for 5 minutes and then add:

1 cup coconut milk
½ teaspoon salt

approximately 2 teaspoons
   of lemon juice

Stir to blend. Add the meatballs and simmer gently for about ½ hour.

Note: For those who consider highly seasoned food a treat, this is delicious and inexpensive fare for parties; a one-dish dinner to serve over rice, with chutney and a salad.

Lindy M. Dillow

INDIAN TANDOORI CHICKEN

Must prepare ahead   *Yield: 8 servings*

3 cups plain yogurt
6 cloves garlic, crushed
1½ tablespoons fresh ginger,
    grated
¾ cup fresh lime juice
2 tablespoons ground coriander
1 tablespoon ground cumin seed

1 teaspoon cayenne pepper
1 teaspoon powdered anise
2 (2-pound) roasting chickens
lime wedges
1 large onion, sliced in wedges
    and stewed

Mix yogurt, garlic, lime juice, and spices. Rub chickens inside and out with this mixture. Place chickens in a large bowl or non-metal container, and pour the rest of the marinade over them. Cover, and marinate in the refrigerator for 24 to 48 hours. Turn the chickens at least once if not fully covered by marinade. Preheat oven to 375°. Remove chickens from the marinade; place in a large roasting pan or 13x9x2-inch baking pan and roast in oven for about 1 hour or until done. Baste with marinade during roasting. Disjoint and serve with a wedge of lime and some stewed onion. Rice, a salad, and fresh fruit for dessert go well with this.

Note: Very spicy! Not for the timid palate.

Lindy M. Dillow

SAMBALS FOR CURRY DISHES

Chutney
Chopped Peanuts
Chopped Bacon
Grated Coconut
Chopped Onions
Chopped Eggs
Chopped Bananas
Raisins Soaked In Wine
Chopped Tomatoes
Chopped Pickles

Chopped Pineapple
Chopped Hot Peppers
Chopped Ginger Root
Chopped Apple
Chopped Dates
Chopped Mango
Chopped Avocado
Chopped Kumquats
Chopped Green Peppers
Chopped Mint

Any or all of these may be used with curry entrées.

PORK TEKO TEKO (INDONESIAN)

Yield: 4 servings

1 whole pork filet, uncut
salt and pepper
bacon, enough to wrap pork
 (6 to 8 slices)
toothpicks
1 medium onion, diced
½ pound mushrooms, sliced
2 tablespoons butter

2 tablespoons arrowroot
½ to 1 cup chicken stock
½ cup white wine
dash of cayenne pepper
squeeze of lemon juice
lemon slices and parsley for
 garnish

Skewer pork filet lengthwise and season with salt and pepper. Wrap bacon slices around filet, overlapping ends, and fasten with toothpicks where necessary to hold. Broil 8 to 10 minutes on each side, about 10 inches from broiler. Sauce: Sauté onion and mushrooms in butter; top with arrowroot. Add stock and wine. Sprinkle with cayenne pepper and lemon juice. Drizzle sauce over broiled meat and garnish with lemon slices and parsley.

Lindy M. Dillow

 **ITALY**

ITALIAN WALNUT BROCCOLI

Yield: 8 servings

3 (10-ounce) packages chopped
 broccoli
½ cup butter
4 tablespoons all-purpose flour
1½ tablespoons powdered
 chicken stock base

2 cups milk
⅔ cup water
6 tablespoons butter
⅔ of an 8-ounce package of
 herb stuffing mix
⅔ cup chopped walnuts

Cook broccoli until barely tender. Drain, and place in a buttered 9x13x2-inch casserole. In a small saucepan, melt ½ cup butter. Remove from heat and blend in flour and chicken stock base. Gradually add milk. Return to heat and cook, stirring until smooth and boiling. Pour over broccoli. Heat together water and remaining butter, and when butter is melted, add stuffing mix and walnuts. Top broccoli with this mixture. To serve: bake at 400° for 20 to 30 minutes.

Anne F. Mitchell

FAVORITE OLD COUNTRY ITALIAN MEATBALLS

Yield: 6 to 8 servings

1½ pounds ground beef
¼ pound ground pork
1 cup fine, dry bread crumbs
1 to 2 cloves garlic, minced
½ cup milk
½ cup Parmesan cheese, grated
⅓ to ½ cup onion, minced
1 egg, beaten
1 tablespoon parsley, minced
½ teaspoon salt

¼ teaspoon pepper
⅛ teaspoon each: ground cinnamon, ground allspice, and ground nutmeg
¼ teaspoon lemon juice
¼ teaspoon each: basil and oregano
⅛ teaspoon red pepper
¼ cup olive oil

Thoroughly mix all ingredients except olive oil. Shape mixture into 1-inch balls; brown in hot olive oil in a large skillet. Remove and drain on paper towels. Serve with any good spaghetti sauce over pasta.

Lindy M. Dillow

BASIC ITALIAN SAUCE FOR MANICOTTI, LASAGNA, SPAGHETTI, AND LINGUINI

Yield: 1 quart

1 (16-ounce) can tomato purée (Italian if possible)
2 (8-ounce) cans peeled tomatoes with basil
1 (6-ounce) can tomato paste
¼ cup olive oil, (a good, light oil)

4 cloves garlic, chopped
½ cup very dry red wine
½ teaspoon each: red pepper, crushed; basil, oregano, sugar, salt, and pepper

Using a large stockpot, lightly brown garlic in olive oil. Add purée and slightly crushed tomatoes, tomato paste, wine, and spices. Simmer at least 2 hours. (If this sauce tends to be too thin, add more tomato paste; if too thick, add more wine.)

Note: An Italian friend gave me this recipe and told me that Italian mamas make their basic sauce on Monday for use all week.

Susie D. Patton

VEAL SCALLOPINE

Yield: 6 to 8 servings

1½ to 2 pounds veal steak, ½ inch thick	½ teaspoon sugar
1 teaspoon salt	¼ cup all-purpose flour
1 teaspoon paprika	¼ cup fat
½ cup salad oil	1 medium onion, sliced
¼ cup dry red wine	1 green pepper, in strips
1 clove garlic, split	¼ pound sliced mushrooms
1 teaspoon prepared mustard	1 (10-ounce) can chicken bouillon
¼ teaspoon nutmeg	6 stuffed olives, sliced

Cut veal into serving pieces. Make sauce of salt, paprika, oil, wine, garlic, mustard, nutmeg, and sugar. Combine well. Marinate veal 15 minutes; remove garlic. Lift veal from sauce. Dip in flour; brown well in hot fat. Add onion, green pepper, and mushrooms. Combine chicken bouillon with sauce and pour over veal. Cook, covered, slowly until veal is tender, approximately 45 minutes. Turn occasionally; add olives 5 minutes before serving.

Kay J. Webber

MEXICO

CHILIES RELLENOS CON QUESO

Yield: 6 servings

6 large dried chilies anchos or 1 (7-ounce) can green chilies	All-purpose flour for dredging
	¼ cup vegetable oil
6 ½-inch slices Monterey Jack or mozzarella Cheese	3 large eggs, separated
	Salsa de Jitomate (see page 327)

Place dried chilies in a bowl; add scalding water to cover and let stand until soft. Leave stems; make a slit down sides and gently remove seeds. Place cheese inside each chili; dust lightly with flour. Beat egg yolks until thick and lemon colored; then beat egg whites until they stand in soft peaks. Fold yolks into whites and carefully dip each chili into egg mixture until coated. Fry one at a time in hot oil, turning once. Cook until golden brown; then drop into simmering tomato sauce and cook five minutes.

SOPAIPILLAS

Dough freezes well   *Yield: 32*

4 cups all-purpose flour
1½ teaspoons salt
1 tablespoon sugar
1 teaspoon baking powder
1 tablespoon vegetable oil

1 (¼-ounce) package dry yeast
¼ cup lukewarm water
1¼ cups warm milk
fat for frying
honey

Combine dry ingredients; add vegetable oil and stir into mixture. Dissolve yeast in lukewarm water and add to milk. Make a well in center of dry ingredients; add liquid and work into dough. Grease a bowl, add dough and knead 15-20 times, then set aside for approximately 10 minutes. Divide dough into 8 portions. Roll each into a 12-inch circle, making certain dough is rolled thinly, ¼-inch thick. Cut each circle into 4 triangular pieces or squares. Fry, 1 or 2 at a time, in about 3-inches of hot fat (420⁰) until puffy and brown on both sides. Drain on paper towels. Serve with honey.

Helen M. Brooks

MEXICAN TORTILLA BELLENO

Yield: 4 to 6 servings

12 tortillas
hot cooking oil

cheddar cheese, grated

Filling:
2 tablespoons cooking oil
1 pound ground beef
½ cup onion, chopped
1 clove garlic, minced
1 cup ripe olives, chopped
1 cup canned tomatoes, drained
½ cup raisins, chopped

½ teaspoon chili powder
1 teaspoon ground cinnamon
⅛ teaspoon ground cloves
1 teaspoon sugar
1 teaspoon salt
2 tablespoons vinegar

Lightly brown ground meat, onion, and garlic in oil. Add other ingredients (which may be chopped in a food processor) and simmer 20 minutes.

Sauce:

1 tablespoon cooking oil
1/4 cup onion, chopped
1 clove garlic, minced
2 (8-ounce) cans tomato
    sauce
1/4 cup green pepper, chopped

1 teaspoon chili powder
1/4 cup celery, chopped
1/4 teaspoon oregano
1/8 teaspoon thyme
1/2 cup condensed beef bouillon

Sauté the onion and garlic in oil until transparent. Add remaining ingredients. Simmer 20 minutes. To Assemble: Dip each tortilla in hot oil long enough to soften. Put filling on it and roll up; place in greased shallow baking dish (such as 9x13x2-inch.) After all tortillas are filled and rolled, pour half of the sauce over them and sprinkle with grated cheddar cheese. Bake at 350° for 20 minutes. Serve with remaining sauce.

Martha T. Kurad

～ NORWAY ～

NORWEGIAN JULEKAGE

2 (1/4-ounce) packages dry yeast
1/2 cup lukewarm water
2 cups milk, scalded
1/2 cup butter
2/3 cup sugar
1/2 teaspoon crushed cardamon

2 teaspoons salt
8 cups all-purpose flour
2 eggs, beaten
1 cup candied fruit
1 cup raisins

Dissolve yeast in lukewarm water. Pour scalded milk over butter, sugar, cardamon, and salt. When lukewarm, add yeast and about 1/2 of the flour and beaten eggs. Beat well with beater for several minutes. Add fruit and raisins and enough flour to make a soft dough. Turn out onto a floured board, cover with towel and let dough "rest" for 15 minutes. Knead smooth, adding as little flour as possible. Place in a greased bowl, turning dough to grease all sides. Cover and set in a warm place to rise. When dough has risen to double in bulk, punch down and let rise once more until double in bulk. Shape into round loaves or Christmas trees made of small bun-size pieces. Let rise until double in bulk and bake at 350° for 35 to 40 minutes. Frost with light icing and decorate with cherries and nuts or colored sugar.

Note: This is an authentic Norwegian recipe—A great gift idea.

Anita G. Anderson

363

NORWEGIAN SWEET SOUP

1 cup prunes
1 cup dried apricots
1 cup currants
1 quart water
1 quart mixed fruit juices
3 apples, peeled and diced
1 (16-ounce) can dark sweet
    cherries, undrained

³/₄ cup sugar
¹/₂ cup lemon juice
¹/₂ cup orange juice
1 tablespoon orange rind
¹/₂ cup quick cooking tapioca

Simmer first 5 ingredients together for ¹/₂ hour. Add last 7 ingredients and simmer 1 hour. Delicious served cold or warm with whipped cream as a garnish. (Keeps several weeks in refrigerator.)

Anita G. Anderson

RUSSIA

RUSSIAN COLD BORSCHT

Yield: 6 to 8 servings

7 to 8 cups chicken consommé,
    divided
1 cup uncooked beets, cut in
    julienne strips
2¹/₂ cups uncooked beets,
    finely chopped
1 cup carrots, finely chopped
1 cup onions, finely chopped
1 tablespoon red-wine vinegar

salt to taste
2 egg yolks, raw
1 tablespoon sugar
1¹/₂ cups sour cream
2 tablespoons fresh lemon juice
1 cucumber, cut into
    ¹/₄-inch dice
¹/₄ cup fresh dill, minced

Pour consommé, except for 1 cup, into a large soup kettle. Place the remaining cup of consommé into a small saucepan and add the julienned beets. Simmer, covered, about 10 minutes over medium heat. Strain into kettle containing the larger amount of consommé. Reserve julienned beets. Bring consommé to boiling point; add chopped, uncooked beets, carrots and onions; stir in the vinegar. Cook, covered, 15 to 20 minutes over medium heat. Strain into a bowl, and discard vegetables. Chill thoroughly. In a soup tureen, beat egg yolks, sugar, sour cream, and lemon juice until smooth. Gradually stir in chilled broth to make a smooth paste. If lumpy, strain again. Chill for 15 to 20 minutes more. At serving time add reserved beets and the cucumber, and sprinkle with dill.

Robin L. Mills

POTATOES ALEXANDRE (RUSSIA)

Yield: 8 servings

8 large, white baking potatoes
2 tablespoons butter
1 cup sour cream
2 tablespoons chives, chopped
¼ teaspoon nutmeg, or more
    to taste

salt and pepper
1 pound caviar
8 lemon wedges
dill or parsley sprigs

Preheat oven to 400°. Bake potatoes 45 to 60 minutes, depending upon size. When potatoes are done, cut a slice from the top. This slice should be about ¼-inch thick, but large enough to remove the potato pulp. Spoon the pulp into a saucepan. Keep potato skins warm in oven. Place saucepan over low heat, add butter, sour cream, chives, nutmeg, salt, and pepper. Stir rapidly with a spoon to blend. If desired, add more butter or sour cream. Stuff the potato shells with potato mixture. Top each potato with equal amounts of caviar and garnish with a lemon wedge and dill sprigs.

Margaret Ann W. Campbell

RUSSIAN CREAM

Yield: 5 to 6 servings

1 envelope unflavored gelatin
½ cup cold water
1 cup coffee cream

½ cup sugar
1 cup sour cream
1 teaspoon vanilla

Sprinkle 1 envelope (which is 1 tablespoon) unflavored gelatin over ½ cup cold water. Combine and heat 1 cup of coffee cream and ½ cup sugar in a double boiler. Cream should be quite hot, but not actually scalded. Stir in softened gelatin until it is dissolved. Chill until partially thickened—the consistency of unbeaten egg white. Stir in sour cream and vanilla. Turn into 5 or 6 individual molds or small dessert dishes which have been rinsed with cold water. Chill until firm.

Note: For approximately 8 servings, increase sugar to ¾ cup, sour cream to 1½ cups. This is a bland but very good dessert.

Lindy M. Dillow

RUSSIAN BLACK BREAD

May prepare ahead   *Yield: 2 loaves*

4 cups rye flour, unsifted
3 cups all-purpose flour, unsifted
1 teaspoon sugar
2 teaspoons salt
2 cups whole bran cereal
2 tablespoons caraway seed, crushed
2 teaspoons instant coffee
2 teaspoons onion powder
½ teaspoon fennel seed, crushed

2 (¼-ounce) packages dry yeast, undissolved
2½ cups water
¼ cup vinegar
¼ cup dark molasses
1 (1-ounce) square chocolate, unsweetened
¼ cup margarine
1 teaspoon cornstarch
½ cup cold water

Preheat oven to 350°. Combine the rye flour and all-purpose flour. Mix thoroughly in a large bowl, 2⅓ cups flour mixture, sugar, salt, cereal, caraway seed, coffee, onion powder, fennel seed, and yeast. Combine 2½ cups water, vinegar, molasses, chocolate, and margarine in a saucepan and place over low heat until liquids are warm. Margarine and chocolate do not need to melt. Add to dry ingredients gradually and beat for 2 minutes with electric mixer at medium speed, scraping bowl occasionally. Add ½ cup flour mixture and beat at high speed for 2 minutes, scraping bowl occasionally. Stir in enough remaining flour mixture to make a soft dough. Turn out onto a lightly floured board. Cover dough with bowl and let rest for 15 minutes. Knead for 10 to 15 minutes or until smooth and elastic. Dough may be sticky. Place in a greased bowl and turn dough to grease all sides. Cover and let rise in warm place for about 1 hour or until doubled in bulk. Punch down. Turn out onto a lightly floured board and divide in half. Shape each half into a ball about 5-inches in diameter. Place each ball in the center of a greased 8-inch round cake pan. Cover and let rise in a warm place, for about 1 hour or until doubled in bulk. Bake for 45 to 50 minutes or until done. Combine the cornstarch and ½ cup cold water in a saucepan. Bring to boil over medium heat, stirring constantly. Cook, stirring constantly for 1 minute. Brush over tops of loaves. Return bread to oven and bake for 2 to 3 minutes or longer until glaze is set. Remove from pans and cool on wire racks.

Nancy F. Matheson

JAPAN

JAPANESE SUKIYAKI

Yield: 4 to 6 servings

1 pound sirloin or round steak, sliced paper thin into 2x¼-inch strips
1 tablespoon peanut oil (plus ¼ teaspoon sesame oil, optional)
½ pound mushrooms, thinly sliced
10 scallions, cut into 1½-inch lengths
3 celery stalks, diagonally sliced
1 large onion, thinly sliced
1 (5-ounce) can of bamboo shoots, drained
1 cup bean sprouts
3 cups raw spinach leaves, washed
2 cakes tofu, cut into 12 pieces each

1 cup carrots, julienne cut, optional
4 to 5 stalks Napa cabbage, cut into 1-inch strips, optional
3 tablespoons sugar
⅓ to ½ cup good soy sauce (tamari may be used)
¾ to 2 cups beef or rich chicken broth
⅓ cup sake or dry sherry
¼ teaspoon monosodium glutamate, optional
4 to 6 cups hot cooked rice
1 raw egg yolk per person, optional
fresh grated horseradish, optional

Arrange raw meat, bean curd, and vegetables decoratively on a large platter, keeping each separate. (This dish is designed to be cooked at the table for guests! It can, however, be cooked in a large skillet on the stove.) Heat an electric skillet or very large frying pan to medium heat. Brown the meat in the oil and push to one side. Combine broth, soy, sake, sugar, and monosodium glutamate in a pitcher. Add ½ of broth mixture to skillet and then add vegetables, (those that must cook longest-add first); keep each vegetable separate. Simmer 5 minutes, uncovered. Add broth when necessary. Add the bean curd (Tofu) and cook 1 minute. Serve on hot plates with bowls of rice. Egg yolk, soy sauce, and grated white radish may be served as dips.

Lindy M. Dillow & Anne F. Mitchell

367

 **SPAIN**

SPANISH PAELLA VALENCIANA

Yield: 6 servings

6 pieces of chicken
1½ to 2-pounds lobster, optional; substitute crab claws
1½ pounds raw shrimp in their shells
6 hard-shelled clams or a 7 or 8-ounce can of clams and juice
6 mussels
3 chorizos or substitute ½ pound other garlic-seasoned smoked pork sausage
2 teaspoons salt
freshly ground pepper

¾ cup olive oil
2-ounces lean, boneless pork, cut into ¼-inch cubes
1 medium onion, chopped
2 to 3 garlic cloves, chopped
1 medium red or green pepper, cut into strips
2 large tomatoes, peeled, seeded, and finely chopped
3 cups raw rice
¾ teaspoon ground saffron
6 cups boiling water or chicken stock
½ cup fresh peas or ½ cup frozen peas, defrosted
2 lemons, cut into 6 wedges

In Spain a paella may be simple or elaborate. Vary the combination of chicken, meats, and shellfish to suit your taste. Cooked green string beans or artichoke hearts may be added or substituted for the peas. If using a lobster, split into pieces. Shell the shrimp, leaving the tails intact. Devein the shrimp. If using clams and mussels, wash with a stiff brush. Set the shrimp, clams, and mussels aside. Place the sausages in a skillet and prick them in 2 or 3 places. Add enough cold water to cover them completely and bring to a boil over high heat. Reduce heat to low and simmer for 5 minutes. Drain on paper towels and slice into ¼-inch rounds. Pat the chicken dry with paper towels and season it with 1 teaspoon salt and a few grindings of pepper. In a skillet heat ¼ cup olive oil over high heat until a light haze forms above it. Add the chicken, skin side down, and brown well, turning the pieces with tongs and regulating the heat to avoid burning. As the pieces brown, remove to a plate. Add the lobster and cook over high heat for 2 to 3 minutes or until the shell turns pink. Set lobster aside and add the sausages to the pan. Brown on both sides and then spread on paper towels to drain. Remove fat from pan and add ½ cup olive oil. Heat until a light haze forms; add the pork and brown quickly on all sides over high heat. Add onions, garlic, pepper strips, and tomato, stirring constantly. Cook briskly until most of the liquid in pan evaporates and the mixture is thick enough to hold its shape lightly in a spoon. Set aside. About ½ hour before you plan to serve the paella, preheat oven to 400°. In a 14-inch paella pan or a skillet or casserole at least 14 inches in diameter and 2 to 2½-inches deep, combine the onion-tomato mixture, rice, remaining 1 teaspoon salt and saffron. Pour in the boiling water and, stirring constantly, bring to a boil over high heat. Remove the pan from the heat immediately. Taste to correct seasonings. Arrange the chicken, lobster, sausage, shrimp, clams on top of the rice and scatter the peas at random over the whole. Set the pan on the bottom rack of the oven and bake, uncovered, 25 to 30 minutes, or until all liquid has been absorbed by the rice and it is tender. Do not stir at all. When the paella is done, remove it from the oven and drape a towel over it. Let it rest 5 to 8 minutes. Then, garnish the paella with the lemons and serve at table.

Anne F. Mitchell

SWEDEN

SWEDISH RUSKS

Yield: 3 dozen servings

1 cup margarine	1 teaspoon salt
1¾ cups sugar	1 cup sour cream
2 eggs	1 cup chopped or sliced
2 teaspoons almond extract	almonds
5 cups all-purpose flour	1 teaspoon ground cardamon
1 teaspoon soda	

Preheat oven to 350°. Cream margarine and sugar, add eggs, beat well. Blend in almond extract. Sift dry ingredients together. Add to creamed mixture, alternating with sour cream. Add almonds. Divide dough into 8 equal parts. Shape into 15-inch rolls and place 4 on each of 2 ungreased cookie sheets. Bake for about 30 minutes until lightly browned. Remove rolls from pans and cut into ¾ inch slices at an angle. Place rusks on pan flat side down and toast until lightly browned. Can be stored tightly covered in tin container for several weeks.

Anita G. Anderson

 MOROCCO

MOROCCAN COUSCOUS

Yield: 4 to 6 servings

6 cups couscous (2¼ pounds)
3 pounds lamb, cut in pieces
1 tablespoon salt
1½ teaspoons ground pepper
2 pinches of saffron
¼ teaspoon ground turmeric
6 large Spanish onions,
   quartered

1 cup sweet butter
1 teaspoon coriander or 3 sprigs
   fresh
2 cinnamon sticks
1½ teaspoons ground cinnamon
1 cup honey or sugar
¼ pound black raisins

Place the lamb, 2 teaspoons of the salt, 1 teaspoon of pepper, a pinch of saffron, turmeric, 1 quartered onion, 3 tablespoons of the butter, coriander, and cinnamon sticks in bottom of a Dutch oven. Melt the butter over low heat, add 2 quarts of water, and bring to a boil. Cover and simmer 1 hour. Slice the remaining onions, place in a heavy casserole with 2½ cups water, cover tightly, steam 5 minutes. Remove cover, drain onions. After lamb has cooked for 1 hour, transfer 1 cup of broth to casserole. Add more water to lamb if necessary. Put onions, ground cinnamon, ½ teaspoon pepper, 1 teaspoon salt, 5 tablespoons butter, and honey in the casserole. Mix well and cook, uncovered, 5 minutes. Add raisins and simmer, covered, for 30 minutes. Follow package directions for cooking couscous. Cook lamb 30 minutes more, adding water if necessary. Remove cover from casserole and cook until all the liquid has evaporated and the onions have become a thick glaze. This part can be made ahead. Thirty minutes before serving, bring lamb broth to a boil. Steam couscous for 20 minutes over broth in a colander. Reheat onion glaze. Blend remaining butter and a pinch of saffron and add to couscous the last 5 minutes of steaming. Place couscous on platter and toss. Make a well in the center and place drained lamb in it and cover with glazed onions. Strain broth and moisten the couscous. Serve at once.

Note: This is a sweet couscous; just delicious!

Anne F. Mitchell

MICROWAVE
DELIGHTS

MICROWAVE

( ) Denotes: (HE) Hickory Entertains   (I) International   (M) Microwave Recipes

 # MICROWAVE

STUFFED MUSHROOMS CATAWBA

Yield: 12 large mushrooms

12 large fresh mushrooms
3 tablespoons butter, melted
⅓ cup seasoned bread crumbs

dash of salt
dash of red pepper
½ cup cooked shrimp, chopped

Wipe mushrooms with a damp paper towel to clean. Remove and reserve stems. Microwave butter 30 to 40 seconds on *high* in a flat baking dish to melt. Dip caps in butter and place top side down in dish. Chop stems and combine with remaining ingredients. Fill mushroom caps. Cover with waxed paper. Microwave on *high* 3 to 4 minutes. Serve warm.

SMOKED COCKTAIL SAUSAGE

Yield: 20 servings

Hot sauce

2 tablespoons instant dry
   minced onion
1 tablespoon brown sugar
2 teaspoons dry mustard
½ cup water
¼ cup olive oil
1 cup catsup
2 tablespoons tarragon vinegar
2 tablespoons red wine vinegar
3 drops commercial liquid
   smoke

2 tablespoons Worcestershire
   sauce
1 tablespoon chili powder
2 teaspoons paprika
1 teaspoon salt
1 teaspoon black pepper
1 teaspoon oregano
1 clove garlic, crushed
1 bay leaf

Combine all ingredients in a 2-quart glass casserole. Microwave on *high* 5 minutes or until sauce begins to bubble.

1 pound miniature smoked
   cocktail sausages or
   1 pound smoked link
   sausage, cut into bite-
   size rounds

Add smoked sausage to hot sauce in a 2-quart glass casserole. Let sit in sauce until serving time. Just before serving, microwave on *high* 4 minutes until heated through, stirring once. After heating, place sausages and sauce in chafing dish over low flame; serve.

MOCK OYSTER DIP

Yield: 5 cups

1 (10-ounce) package frozen
chopped broccoli
6 tablespoons butter
1⅓ cups onions, minced
1 (10¾-ounce) can cream of
mushroom soup, undiluted
1 (4-ounce) can mushrooms,
drained and minced

1 (6-ounce) package garlic-
flavored cheese spread, cut
into pieces
¼ teaspoon hot pepper sauce
¼ teaspoon salt

Pierce broccoli package and place on paper plate. Microwave on *high* 5 to 6 minutes. Drain well and set aside. Microwave butter in a 2-quart casserole on *high* 30 seconds to melt. Stir in onions. Cover with plastic wrap and microwave on *high* 5 to 6 minutes. Stir well once. Add soup, mushrooms, cheese spread and hot sauce. Cover with plastic wrap and microwave on *medium-high* 5 to 6 minutes or until cheese melts. Stir in cooked broccoli and salt. Mix well. Serve warm as a dip. Good with corn chips.

MINI-MEATBALLS

Yield: 35 meatballs

1 pound extra-lean ground chuck
½ teaspoon salt
¼ teaspoon pepper
¼ teaspoon garlic salt
¼ teaspoon oregano
1 egg

1 tablespoon onion, finely
chopped
¼ cup dry bread crumbs
1 (8-ounce) can tomato sauce,
divided

Combine all ingredients except ½ cup tomato sauce. Shape into ½-inch meatballs. Place in a 12x8-inch baking dish. Spoon reserved tomato sauce over meatballs. Cover with plastic wrap. Microwave on *high* 8 to 9 minutes, rotating dish ¼ turn every 2 minutes. Let stand, covered, 2 to 3 minutes before serving. Serve hot.

Tip:
Ground meats can be browned in a plastic colander placed in a glass casserole. Pour drippings from casserole and place browned meat in casserole and continue with recipe.

ORIENTAL CHICKEN LIVERS

Must prepare ahead   *Yield: 12 livers*

12 chicken livers   6 slices bacon, cut in half
5 ounces soy sauce   1 cup firmly packed brown sugar
3 water chestnuts, cut in
  quarters

Marinate chicken livers in soy sauce overnight. Insert ¼ water chestnut
in each liver. Wrap with ½ slice bacon; roll in brown sugar. Let stand in
soy sauce for one more hour. Drain. Place on large microwave-proof
plate, cover with a paper towel. Microwave on *medium-high* 3 minutes.
Turn each piece over. Microwave on *medium-high* 3 more minutes. Turn
each piece over again; microwave on *high* for 1 minute. Turn each piece
once more and microwave on *high* 1 minute. Let stand 5 minutes. Serve
hot.

CRABMEAT SUPREME

Must prepare ahead   *Yield: 4 cups*

2 (8-ounce) packages cream   2 teaspoons hot mustard
  cheese   ¼ cup dry white wine
2 (6½-ounce) cans crabmeat,   2 tablespoons powdered sugar
  drained   ½ teaspoon salt
1 clove garlic, minced   ⅛ teaspoon pepper
½ cup mayonnaise

Place cheese in a 3-quart casserole. Microwave on *high* 1½ to 2 minutes
to soften cheese. Add remaining ingredients and mix well. Chill several
hours or overnight. When ready to serve, microwave on *high* 5 to 6
minutes. Stir once. Serve hot as a dip with crackers, melba toast rounds,
or breadsticks.

Tip:
Timing is important in microwave cooking. Timing will depend on
many variables: food temperature, shape, composition, and quantity. In-
creasing or decreasing the size of a recipe will affect the cooking time.
Increase or decrease timing to agree with changes in a recipe.

CAULIFLOWER SOUP

Yield: 8 cups

1 medium head cauliflower
1 cup onion, chopped
1/2 cup celery, chopped
3 1/2 cups chicken stock
1/2 cup water
1 teaspoon salt

1 teaspoon celery salt
1/4 teaspoon white pepper
1 teaspoon Worcestershire
    sauce
1 1/2 cups light cream

Rinse, then place whole cauliflower on a small paper plate. Cover cauliflower and plate with plastic wrap. Microwave on *high* 4 minutes. Turn cauliflower and plate over and microwave on *high* 4 more minutes. Keep covered and set aside. Place onion and celery in a 3-quart casserole, cover with plastic wrap; microwave on *high* 3 minutes. Add chicken stock, water, salt, celery salt, white pepper, and Worcestershire sauce. Cut cauliflower in flowerets and add to liquid. Cover and microwave on *high* 8 minutes. Pour small amount of the hot mixture into a blender or food processor and purée; continue processing until all is blended. Return soup to the 3-quart casserole. Stir in light cream and microwave on *high* 2 minutes or until hot. Serve. Garnish with chives and paprika.

CHILI TOPPED WITH CHEESE

Yield: 7 cups

1 pound ground beef
1 medium onion, coarsely
    chopped
1 green pepper, coarsely
    chopped
1 stalk celery, coarsely chopped
1 clove garlic, minced
1 (16-ounce) can stewed
    tomatoes

1 (6-ounce) can tomato paste
3/4 cup canned beef broth
2 teaspoons chili powder
1/2 teaspoon dried whole oregano
1/2 teaspoon salt
1/2 teaspoon pepper
1 bay leaf
1 1/2 cups shredded sharp
    Cheddar cheese

Combine ground beef, onion, pepper, celery, and garlic in a 3-quart casserole. Cover with casserole lid. Microwave on *high* for 6 to 9 minutes or until the beef is browned, stirring twice to crumble beef; drain well. Add stewed tomatoes, tomato paste, beef broth, chili powder, oregano, salt, pepper, and bay leaf; mix well. Cover and microwave on *high* for 10 minutes; stir once. Cover and microwave on *medium* for 30 to 35 minutes. Spoon into serving bowls and immediately sprinkle with cheese.

FRENCH ONION SOUP

Yield: 8 servings

8 yellow onions
¼ pound butter
6 cups beef stock
1 cup sherry
salt

pepper
8 slices day old French bread
1 cup Muenster cheese,
    shredded

Peel and slice yellow onions into thin slices. Put butter and onions into a baking dish. Microwave on *high* for 10 minutes, stirring at least three times. The onions should be very soft and a brownish color. Add the beef stock and sherry. Microwave on *medium-high* for 10 minutes, stirring twice. Salt and pepper to taste. In each soup bowl or cup, place a piece of bread topped with a spoonful of cheese. Pour hot soup over bread and serve.

FLUFFY GOLDEN OMELET

Yield: 1 serving

2 tablespoons butter or
    margarine, divided
¼ cup green pepper, chopped
¼ cup onion, chopped
1 tablespoon pimento, chopped
2 eggs, separated, at room
    temperature

1 tablespoon sour cream
1 tablespoon mayonnaise
dash of salt
dash of pepper

Place 1 tablespoon butter, green pepper, onion, and pimento in a 1-quart casserole; cover with plastic wrap and microwave on *high* for 3 to 3½ minutes. Set aside. Beat egg whites until stiff peaks form. Combine egg yolks, sour cream, mayonnaise, salt, and pepper; beat well. Gently fold egg whites into yolk mixture. Place remaining butter in an 8-inch pie plate. Microwave on *high* for 30 to 45 seconds or until melted. Spread melted butter over plate. Pour egg mixture into pie plate. Microwave on *medium* for 3 minutes or until partially set; lift edges with spatula so uncooked portion spreads evenly. Microwave on *medium* 2 minutes or until center is almost set. Spread vegetable mixture over half of omelet. Loosen omelet with spatula and fold in half. Gently slide the omelet onto a warm serving plate.

Note: Omelet can be kept warm, in a very low conventional oven, up to 30 minutes.

WILTED SPINACH SALAD

Yield: 4 servings

1½ pounds fresh spinach	4 green onions, chopped
6 slices bacon	2 hard boiled eggs, chopped

Wash and dry spinach thoroughly. Remove tough stems and bad leaves. Tear into bite-size pieces. Put aside. Cut bacon into one-inch pieces. Place in a glass measure. Microwave on *high* for 3 minutes, covered with a paper towel. Stir once. Remove bacon and reserve drippings for dressing. Add onions and bacon to spinach. Set aside.

Dressing:

6 tablespoons bacon drippings	1 tablespoon sugar
3 tablespoons red wine vinegar	salt and pepper to taste

In a 1-cup glass measure, measure reserved bacon drippings and add vegetable oil to make 6 tablespoons. Combine with vinegar, sugar, salt, and pepper to taste. Just before serving, microwave on *high* 30 seconds. Pour immediately over salad. Garnish with chopped eggs and serve.

To cook eggs: Place 2 tablespoons water in a small measure. Microwave on *high* 1 minute. Break 2 eggs into the water immediately. Pierce yolks well with a pick or fork. Microwave 1½ minutes on *high.* If the eggs are not hard cooked, cook 30 seconds longer. Drain; cool, chop eggs.

BOEUF BOURGUIGNONNE

Yield: 4 servings

1 to 1½ pounds round steak	¼ teaspoon pepper
3 tablespoons all-purpose flour	⅓ cup red wine
2 teaspoons instant beef bouillon	¼ cup water
1 tablespoon onion flakes	1 onion, sliced
½ teaspoon salt	½ cup canned mushrooms, drained

Cut steak into serving pieces. Combine flour, instant bouillon, onion flakes, salt, and pepper. Dredge steaks with flour mixture; place in glass 2-quart casserole. Add wine and ¼ cup water; cover with glass lid or plastic wrap. Microwave on *high* for 3 minutes. Turn steaks over. Microwave on *high* for about 2 minutes or until no longer pink. Scatter onion and mushrooms over top of steaks; cover. Microwave on *medium* for 15 minutes or until tender.

CRAB STUFFED CHICKEN BREASTS

Yield: 6 servings

6 chicken breasts, skinned
   and boned
salt and pepper to taste
3 tablespoons butter
½ cup onion, chopped
½ cup celery, chopped
3 tablespoons dry white wine
1 (7½-ounce) can crab meat,
   drained, flaked, cartilage
   removed

½ cup herb-seasoned stuffing
   mix
paprika
1 envelope Hollandaise sauce
   mix
⅔ cup milk
½ cup Swiss cheese, shredded
2 tablespoons dry white wine

Place chicken, boned side up, on cutting board; cover with plastic wrap. Pound lightly to flatten each to about 8x6-inches. Remove wrap. Sprinkle with a little salt and pepper. Set aside. In a mixing bowl combine butter, onion, and celery. Microwave, covered, on *high* for 2 minutes, stirring once. Stir in 3 tablespoons wine, crab, and stuffing mix. Divide stuffing among chicken breasts. Roll up like a jelly roll, pressing to seal well. Place seam side down in a 12x7½x2-inch baking dish, so rolls do not touch. Sprinkle with paprika. Microwave, covered, on *medium-high* for 20 minutes or until done, giving dish one-half turn once. Cover to keep warm. In a 2-cup glass measure, blend sauce mix and milk. Add cheese. Microwave, uncovered, on *high* 3 minutes or until mixture boils, stirring after 1 minute, then every 30 seconds. Stir in remaining 2 tablespoons wine. Spoon sauce over chicken. Serve warm.

Tips:
Microwave food the minimum suggested cooking time, then test for doneness. Cook longer if needed. A few seconds of overcooking will dry out and toughen foods.

Salting food to be microwaved on the surface has a tendency to dehydrate foods and can cause a tough product. If salt is mixed or dissolved in the cooking liquid, it can be added during preparation. Salt foods near the end of cooking or after cooking is completed.

When cooking meat remember that bones conduct heat. If the bone is on one side of the meat, that side will cook faster. Boneless cuts of meat take longer cooking time, but cook more evenly.

STUFFED ONIONS

Yield: 10 servings

10 medium onions
2 tablespoons butter
1 pound ground round beef
1 clove garlic, minced
1/2 cup mozzarella cheese,
  shredded
2 teaspoons snipped parsley
1/4 teaspoon pepper

1 teaspoon all-purpose
  seasoning
1 egg, beaten
1/2 cup beef broth soup,
  undiluted
1/3 cup tomato sauce
1 bay leaf
mozzarella cheese, garnish

Peel and slice off root end and top of onions. Place onions in a large flat dish. Dot tops with butter (do not add water or salt). Cover tightly with plastic wrap and microwave on *high* 25 minutes. Rotate dish once. Drain and hollow each onion. Set aside, covered, in same dish. Place meat and garlic in a plastic colander over a 2-quart mixing bowl. Cover with waxed paper and microwave on *high* 4 minutes. Stir meat once, so it will not lump. Discard meat drippings and return meat to mixing bowl. Add cheese, parsley, seasonings, and egg. Divide mixture evenly among hollowed onions. Mix beef broth, tomato sauce, and bay leaf in a 2-cup measure. Microwave on *high* 1 minute and pour over stuffed onions. Cover with waxed paper. Microwave on *high* 5 minutes or until heated through. To garnish, sprinkle mozzarella cheese over top after cooking.

HOT CHICKEN SALAD

Yield: 6 servings

2 or 3 chicken breasts, cut
  in bite-size pieces
1 (10½-ounce) can creamed
  chicken soup
1 teaspoon Worcestershire
  sauce
2 tablespoons onion, minced
1 cup celery, diced

3 hard cooked eggs, diced
1/3 cup pecans, chopped
1/2 cup mayonnaise
3/4 teaspoon salt
3/4 teaspoon curry powder
1 cup potato chips, crushed
paprika

In a 2-quart glass casserole microwave chicken on *high* for 4 minutes. Stir often. Add remaining ingredients except for potato chips and paprika. Microwave on *high,* covered, for 5 to 7 minutes. Rotate dish ¼ turn; sprinkle with chips and paprika. Microwave on *high,* uncovered, 5 to 7 minutes. Let stand 5 minutes. Crisp top under broiler if desired. Serve on toast or toasted English muffins.

MANICOTTI FLORENTINE

Freezes well   *Yield: 4 servings*

1 (8-ounce) package manicotti
    shells or 10 prepared
    crepes
1 (10-ounce) package frozen
    chopped spinach, defrosted
1 (12-ounce) carton dry cottage
    cheese

1 egg, slightly beaten
2 tablespoons seasoned bread
    crumbs
1 cup Parmesan cheese, grated
1 teaspoon salt
⅛ teaspoon pepper

Follow package directions for cooking manicotti shells. Drain. Or prepare crepes from favorite recipe. Set aside. Squeeze spinach dry and mix in a bowl with cottage cheese, egg, bread crumbs, Parmesan cheese, salt, and pepper. Blend well and stuff manicotti shells or crepes with mixture. Place stuffed shells in a 7x11-inch baking dish. Prepare sauce.

Sauce:

1 pound ground round beef
1 cup onions, chopped
1 (1½-ounce) package spaghetti
    sauce mix
1 (16-ounce) can herb tomato
    sauce

½ cup fresh mushrooms, sliced
3 large thin slices mozzarella
    cheese

Place meat and onion in a plastic colander over a 2-quart glass mixing bowl. Cover with waxed paper. Microwave on *high* for 4 minutes, stirring once to break up lumps. Discard liquid and transfer meat to bowl. Add spaghetti sauce mix, tomato sauce and mushrooms. Cover with waxed paper. Microwave on *high* for 5 minutes, stirring once. Place cheese slices over stuffed shells. Pour sauce over cheese slices; cover with waxed paper. Microwave on *high* for 7 minutes, rotating dish every 2 minutes ¼ turn. Let stand 5 minutes before serving. Serve hot.

Tip:

Fresh herbs are easily dried in a microwave oven. Spread ½ cup fresh herbs between paper towels. Microwave on *high* 2 minutes or until dried.

To scald ½ cup cold milk in a 1-cup measure, heat on *high* 1 to 1½ minutes.

CHICKEN-ASPARAGUS DIVAN

Yield: 4 servings

1 pound fresh asparagus
6 teaspoons water
3 cups cooked chicken, diced
6 teaspoons butter
2 small onions, chopped
1/2 cup celery, chopped
6 teaspoons all-purpose flour

1 1/2 cups milk
2 chicken bouillon cubes
1/4 teaspoon dry mustard
salt and pepper to taste
1 cup Swiss cheese, shredded
1 teaspoon parsley, chopped

Place asparagus in a dish with thicker stalks toward outer edge. Add water; cover with plastic wrap. Microwave on *high* 5 to 7 minutes, rotating dish 1/2 turn after 3 minutes. Top with chicken and set aside. In a bowl melt butter; add onions and celery. Microwave 2 minutes on *high*. Stir in flour, milk, bouillon cubes, mustard, salt, and pepper. Mix well. Microwave on *high* 2 minutes or until thickened, stirring several times. Add cheese. Stir and pour over chicken and asparagus. Cover and microwave on *high* 2 to 3 minutes. Garnish with parsley.

Note: Broccoli can be substituted for asparagus; a beautiful company dish.

Anne C. Brock

CANNELONI WITH RICOTTA

Yield: 6 servings

1 tablespoon cooking oil
1 cup onions, chopped
1 carrot, chopped
1 stalk celery, chopped
1 (28-ounce) can whole
  tomatoes, drained and
  pureed

1/2 teaspoon salt
1/8 teaspoon pepper
1/8 teaspoon nutmeg
12 large cannelloni *or* manicotti
  pasta shells
Ricotta filling

Place oil, onions, carrot, and celery in a 2-quart casserole covered with plastic wrap or tight fitting lid. Microwave on *high* for 5 minutes, stirring once. Add tomatoes, salt, pepper, and nutmeg. Cover and microwave on *high* 10 minutes, stirring once. Set aside covered. Boil pasta in microwave or use conventional method according to package directions. Drain.

Ricotta filling:
1 cup mozzarella cheese, shredded
1½ cups cooked ham, diced
1 (16-ounce) carton ricotta cheese
2 eggs
⅛ teaspoon nutmeg
1 teaspoon salt
½ teaspoon pepper
½ teaspoon basil
½ cup Parmesan cheese, grated
1 tablespoon butter, melted

Combine cheese, ham, ricotta, eggs, nutmeg, salt, and pepper in a mixing bowl. Stuff pasta with ham mixture and place in a buttered 7x11-inch baking dish. Pour sauce over cannelloni. Sprinkle with basil, Parmesan cheese, and butter. Microwave on *high* 6 minutes until cheese melts. Serve hot.

ORIENTAL PORK

Yield: 5 servings

1 pound pork tenderloin
1 tablespoon cornstarch
3 tablespoons soy sauce
1 teaspoon instant chicken bouillon
4 cups thin-sliced Chinese cabbage
1 (6-ounce) package frozen pea pods
½ cup bamboo shoots, drained
⅔ cup water chestnuts, drained and sliced

Cut pork into bite-size pieces, trimming fat. Combine with cornstarch, soy sauce, and bouillon in a 2-quart glass casserole. Microwave on *high* for 6 minutes or until meat is done, stirring once. Add vegetables. Microwave on *high* 6 to 10 minutes until done. Stir every 3 minutes to insure even cooking. Serve over rice if desired but count the extra calories! *173 calories per serving.*

Cathi H. Dillon

Tips:
Microwave cooking is a dieting natural. Few vitamins are lost during preparation. High calorie oils are not necessary. Using their own juices for cooking fish, poultry, vegetables and fruits make excellent choices for the diet conscious.

Make several small slashes in plastic wrap used to tightly wrap or cover food. This lets some steam escape.

SHRIMP THERMIDOR BAKE

Yield: 4 servings

¼ cup onion, chopped
¼ cup celery, chopped
2 tablespoons water
1 (10¾-ounce) can Cheddar
  cheese soup
½ cup skim milk
2 tablespoons dry sherry

¾ pound fresh or frozen shelled
  shrimp, cooked
2 tablespoons chopped parsley
dash of hot pepper sauce
¾ cup bread crumbs
dash of paprika
1 tablespoon butter, melted

In a glass bowl, combine onion and celery in water; cover with waxed paper. Microwave on *high* 3 to 4 minutes or until tender. Stir in soup, milk, sherry, shrimp, parsley, and hot pepper sauce. Spoon mixture into 4 individual baking dishes. Toss together bread crumbs, paprika, and butter. Sprinkle around edges of each dish. Microwave 4 to 6 minutes on *high* or until heated through; rearrange dishes after 3 minutes.

Anne C. Brock

TROUT AMANDINE

Yield: 6 servings

2 pounds trout fillets or other
  fish fillets, fresh or frozen
red pepper

2 tablespoons margarine, melted
Sauce

Defrost fish if frozen. Cut fillets into serving size portions. Drain on paper towel. Sprinkle fillets lightly with red pepper and place in an 8x8-inch shallow dish. Drizzle with margarine. Cover and microwave on *high* for 5 minutes, rotating dish once. Fish should flake easily with a fork when done. Drain excess liquid.

Sauce:
2 tablespoons margarine
½ cup almonds, sliced
2 tablespoons lemon juice
1 tablespoon parsley, chopped

½ teaspoon salt
⅛ teaspoon hot pepper sauce
parsley, garnish

Melt margarine in a 2 cup measure; microwave on *high* 30 seconds. Add almonds and microwave on *high* for 2 minutes. Stir in lemon juice, parsley, salt, and hot pepper sauce. Pour sauce over prepared fish. Cover. Just before serving, microwave covered, on *high* 2 minutes to reheat. Garnish with parsley. Serve hot.

POACHED SALMON

Yield: 4 servings

½ cup dry white wine
1 tablespoon lemon juice
1 tablespoon onion, minced
½ teaspoon salt

½ teaspoon white pepper
1½ cups water
4 salmon steaks
sauce

Combine wine, lemon juice, onion, salt, pepper, and water in a 2-quart glass casserole. Microwave on *high* for 5 minutes or until mixture boils. Place salmon steaks in casserole with thick edges toward outside of dish; cover tightly. Microwave on *high* for 2 minutes. Let stand for 5 minutes; drain.

Sauce:
½ cup sour cream
1 tablespoon chives, minced

1 teaspoon lemon juice
½ teaspoon dried dillweed

Combine all ingredients in a small bowl. Microwave on *high* 1 minute just to heat. Serve sauce with salmon.

WILD RICE AND SHRIMP CASSEROLE

Yield: 4 servings

1 (6-ounce) package wild rice
   and long-grain rice mix
2 tablespoons butter
1 cup sour cream
1 cup milk
2 tablespoons all-purpose flour
½ cup onions, thinly sliced
½ cup mushrooms, sliced

¼ cup green peppers, thinly
   sliced
¼ cup butter
1 tablespoon Worcestershire
   sauce
½ teaspoon freshly ground
   pepper
¾ pound cooked small shrimp

Cook rice in microwave or conventionally according to package directions. Meanwhile, melt 2 tablespoons butter in a 1-quart glass bowl. Microwave on *high* for 30 to 40 seconds. Stir in sour cream, milk, and flour, blending thoroughly. Microwave on *high,* stirring frequently until slightly thickened, about 3 to 4 minutes. Set aside. Combine onions, mushrooms, green peppers, and remaining butter in a 2-quart glass baking dish. Cover and microwave on *high* until vegetables are tender, about 4 minutes. Stir in cooked rice, Worcestershire sauce, and pepper. Fold in cream sauce. Cover and microwave on *medium* 15 minutes, turning dish halfway through cooking time. Stir in shrimp and serve hot.

SHRIMP NEWBURG

Yield: 6 servings

1 (10¾-ounce) can cream of
   shrimp soup
2 tablespoons sharp Cheddar
   cheese spread
2 tablespoons margarine
1 tablespoon prepared mustard

1 teaspoon lemon rind
1 (10-ounce) package frozen
   peas
½ pound fresh or frozen shrimp,
   cooked

Combine soup, cheese spread, margarine, mustard, and lemon rind in a
2-quart casserole; stir well. Add peas; cover. Microwave on *high* for 6
minutes, stirring after 3 minutes. Add shrimp. Microwave on *high* for 6
minutes, stirring after 3 minutes. Serve over rice.

COQUILLE ST. JACQUES

Yield: 4 servings

1 pound fresh scallops
⅓ cup fresh mushrooms, sliced
1 tablespoon butter
2 tablespoons chives, snipped
2 tablespoons parsley, snipped
¼ cup dry white wine

1 tablespoon lemon juice
2 teaspoons cornstarch
2 tablespoons milk
4 teaspoons fine dry bread
   crumbs
paprika

Rinse scallops; cut in thirds if large. In a 2-quart casserole, combine
mushrooms and butter. Microwave, uncovered, on *high* for 1½ to 2
minutes, or until tender. Add scallops, chives, parsley, wine, and lemon
juice. Microwave, covered, on *high* for 4 minutes, or until scallops are
tender. Lift scallops and mushrooms from liquid with a slotted spoon;
divide among 4 coquille shells. Stir together cornstarch and milk; add
to liquid in casserole. Microwave, uncovered, on *high* for 3 to 4 minutes
until mixture thickens and bubbles, stirring after each minute. Sprinkle
with a little salt and pepper. Spoon over scallops in shells. Combine
crumbs and paprika; sprinkle over tops. Microwave, uncovered, on *high*
1 to 2 minutes until hot.

Tip:
Do not microwave any food with a sealed skin or covering unless the
skin is well pierced.

FRESH SEAFOOD CASSEROLE

Yield: 4 servings

½ cup celery, minced
¼ cup onion, minced
1 clove garlic, chopped
2 tablespoons butter
¾ pound scallops
¾ pound fresh fish filets
¼ cup fresh bread crumbs

1 tablespoon parsley, chopped
1 tablespoon butter
1 tablespoon all-purpose flour
¼ teaspoon paprika
½ cup milk
2 tablespoons sherry

Combine celery, onion, garlic, and 2 tablespoons butter in a glass bowl. Microwave on *high,* uncovered, 2 minutes, stirring once. Cut scallops and fish into 2-inch pieces. Add them to bread crumbs, parsley, and vegetable mixture; blend thoroughly. In a glass measure place 1 tablespoon butter; microwave on *high* 30 seconds to melt. Stir in flour and paprika; blend thoroughly. Add milk and sherry. Microwave on *high* for 2 minutes, stirring every 30 seconds until sauce boils and thickens. Pour sauce over fish mixture. Blend well. Microwave on *high,* uncovered, for 4 minutes. Stir. Microwave on *high* for 2 more minutes. Decorate with parsley and serve hot.

BROCCOLI AU GRATIN

Yield: 4 servings

2 (10-ounce) packages frozen
    broccoli spears
2 tablespoons butter
2 tablespoons all-purpose flour

¼ teaspoon salt
dash of pepper
1 cup milk
1 cup Cheddar cheese, shredded

Remove wrappers from boxes; place boxes in a flat baking dish and pierce with a fork. Microwave on *high* for 10 minutes or until done, rearranging boxes once. Drain broccoli and set aside. Place butter in a 4-cup glass measure. Microwave on *high* for 30 seconds or until melted. Add flour, salt, and pepper; stir until smooth. Gradually add milk, stirring well. Microwave on *high* for 2 minutes; stir until smooth. Microwave on *high* for 1 to 2 minutes, stirring at 1 minute intervals until thickened and bubbly. Add cheese, stirring until melted. Arrange broccoli on serving platter and top with sauce. Serve immediately.

Tip:
Refrigerate fresh perked coffee. Reheat 1 cup at a time on *high* 1½ to 2 minutes.

BAKED PICNIC BEANS

Yield: 6 servings

8 slices bacon, diced
2/3 cup onion, chopped
2/3 cup green bell pepper,
  chopped
1 clove garlic, chopped
2 (16-ounce) cans pork and
  beans

1/3 cup brown sugar
3 tablespoons dry mustard
1/4 cup Worcestershire sauce
1/2 teaspoon salt
1/2 teaspoon black pepper
1/4 teaspoon red pepper

Place bacon, onion, bell pepper, and garlic in a 7x11-inch baking dish. Cover with waxed paper. Microwave on *high* 5 minutes. Stir in beans, brown sugar, mustard, Worcestershire sauce, and seasonings. Cover with waxed paper. Microwave on *medium-high* for 20 minutes, stirring after 10 minutes. Continue to microwave on *medium-high* for 5 minutes, stirring after 2 minutes. Let stand, covered, 5 minutes before serving.

CAULIFLOWER DAUFUSKIE

Yield: 8 servings

1 small head cauliflower
1/2 cup mayonnaise
1 teaspoon Dijon mustard

3 drops hot pepper sauce
1/4 cup Cheddar cheese,
  shredded

Clean and trim head of cauliflower by taking out some of the stem but keeping the head whole. Place the head of cauliflower on a dish and cover with plastic wrap. Microwave on *high* for 7 minutes or until it is tender to a knife inserted in the stem area. Keep covered until ready to serve. Mix mayonnaise, mustard, and hot pepper sauce together. Cover top of cauliflower with mayonnaise mixture and sprinkle with cheese. Microwave on *high* for 1 1/2 minutes and serve immediately.

Tip:
To peel fresh peaches or tomatoes easily, microwave on *high* 10 to 20 seconds, according to size and quantity. Let stand 10 minutes before peeling.

POTATOES AU GRATIN

Yield: 4 servings

4 medium-sized potatoes
2 yellow onions
4 tablespoons butter

salt and pepper to taste
½ cup light cream
1 cup Cheddar cheese, shredded

Peel potatoes and onions; slice ½ to ¾-inch thick. Place a layer of potatoes and onions in the bottom of a glass 7x11-inch baking dish. Dot with butter. Repeat, ending with potatoes on top. Season with salt and pepper. Pour light cream over potatoes and onions. Sprinkle with cheese. Cover with plastic wrap, but turn up a corner to allow some steam to escape. Microwave on high for 5 minutes. Test for doneness but do not forget potatoes will continue to cook when kept covered. They should be firm to the touch of a fork tine.

PARTY POTATOES

Yield: 6 servings

8 to 10 red potatoes, peeled
   and cut into eighths
2 tablespoons water
1 (8-ounce) package cream
   cheese, softened
1 (8-ounce) carton French
   onion dip

1 teaspoon salt
⅛ teaspoon pepper
½ teaspoon garlic powder
4 tablespoons butter
paprika, garnish
parsley, garnish

Place potatoes in a 2-quart casserole with 2 tablespoons water. Cover tightly with plastic wrap, leaving a corner open to vent. Microwave on high for 9 minutes or until potatoes can be pierced with a fork with little resistance. Set aside, covered, for 8 minutes; drain. Combine cream cheese, onion dip, salt, pepper, and garlic powder in a mixer or food processor. Mix until very smooth. Mash potatoes. Add potatoes gradually to blended ingredients; whip until mixture is light and fluffy. Return to 2-quart glass dish and dot with butter. Microwave, covered with plastic wrap, one corner open, on *medium-high* for 4 to 5 minutes or until heated thoroughly. Sprinkle with paprika before serving. Garnish with parsley.

Tip:
Crisp crackers or potato chips on *high* 45 to 60 seconds.

PARSLEY BUTTERED NEW POTATOES

Yield: 6 servings

2 pounds new potatoes
¼ cup water
¼ cup margarine

2 tablespoons fresh parsley,
  snipped
½ teaspoon lemon juice

Wash potatoes and remove ½-inch peel around center of each potato. Place potatoes and water in a 2-quart casserole, arranging in a circle with smaller potatoes in the center. Cover tightly with plastic wrap or lid. Microwave on *high* 14 minutes. Let sit, covered, 6 minutes. Place margarine, parsley, and lemon juice in a 1-cup measure. Microwave on *high* 1 minute or until hot. Drain potatoes and pour sauce over them.

RICE PILAFF

Yield: 4 servings

1 yellow onion, chopped
1 tablespoon butter

1 cup raw converted rice
2 cups chicken or beef stock

Place chopped onion in a 2-quart glass measure with butter. Microwave on *high* for 2 minutes. Add rice and stock. Cover with plastic wrap and pierce in several places with a pin to vent. Microwave on *high* for 10 to 12 minutes, rotating dish every 3 minutes. Let stand, covered, 5 minutes before serving.

SQUASH MORELLE

Yield: 6 servings

2 pounds yellow squash, sliced
1 cup onions, chopped
1 teaspoon butter
2 eggs, beaten
½ cup sour cream
2 tablespoons butter, softened

1 tablespoon sugar
1½ teaspoons salt
½ cup mozzarella cheese,
  shredded
½ cup almonds, ground

Place squash and onions in a 2-quart casserole dish. Dot with butter and cover tightly with plastic wrap. Microwave on *high* 16 minutes. Shake dish once or twice to rearrange contents. (Shaking eliminates removing the cover.) Drain and mash squash. Mix together eggs, sour cream, butter, sugar, salt, and cheese; stir into squash mixture. Microwave on *high* 4 minutes. Sprinkle with ground almonds and microwave on *high* 4 minutes more. Serve hot.

SUMMER STUFFED TOMATOES

Yield: 6 servings

6 large firm tomatoes
½ teaspoon salt
1 (10-ounce) package frozen
   chopped spinach
2 tablespoons butter, melted
1 large onion, chopped
2 carrots, chopped
⅓ cup green pepper, chopped

2 tablespoons parsley, chopped
¾ cup seasoned dry
   breadcrumbs
⅓ cup milk
1 egg, beaten
1 tablespoon Parmesan cheese,
   grated

Cut a slice ¼-inch thick off top of each tomato. Scoop out insides of each tomato, leaving a shell at least ¼-inch thick. Sprinkle with salt. Place on serving plate. In a 1-quart casserole, microwave spinach 5 to 6 minutes on *high,* covered. Drain and set aside. In the same casserole dish, melt butter in microwave on *high* 30 to 40 seconds. Add onion, carrots, green pepper, and parsley; microwave on *high* 5 to 6 minutes or until tender. Combine with spinach, bread crumbs, milk, and egg; mix well. Spoon vegetable mixture into tomato shells and place in a lightly greased 8-inch baking dish. Sprinkle cheese over tomatoes. Microwave, uncovered, on *high* for 2 minutes or until tomatoes and filling are hot.

APPLE CRISP

Yield: 6 servings

5 cups apples, sliced
¾ cup quick-cooking rolled oats
1 cup all-purpose flour
1 cup brown sugar

½ teaspoon salt
1 teaspoon cinnamon
½ cup butter, cut into 8 pieces

Slice apples with medium slicing disk of food processor and place in a 2-quart glass casserole. In work bowl of food processor, combine oats, flour, brown sugar, salt, cinnamon, and butter pieces; pulse until mixture is crumbly. Sprinkle evenly over apples. Microwave on *high* for 15 minutes. Rotate dish every 2 minutes.

Cathi H. Dillon

BASIC CUSTARD

Yield: 8 servings

½ cup sugar
3 tablespoons all-purpose flour
¼ teaspoon salt

3 cups milk
4 eggs, beaten
1 teaspoon vanilla extract

Combine sugar, flour, and salt in a 2½-quart casserole. Blend thoroughly. Gradually stir in milk. Microwave on *high* 6 to 8 minutes or until thickened. Stir well at 2 minute intervals. Add some of the hot custard to beaten eggs. Gradually stir the egg mixture into the hot custard. Microwave on *medium* 5 to 6 minutes, stirring well at least twice. Add vanilla. Cool to room temperature. Cover and refrigerate. Serve as individual custards or use with recipes calling for cooked pudding.

CHEESECAKE CUPS

Yield: 6 servings

1 (8-ounce) package cream
   cheese
⅓ cup sugar
1 egg

1 tablespoon lemon juice
1 teaspoon vanilla extract
6 vanilla wafers
canned fruit pie filling

Soften cream cheese in a 1-quart mixing bowl; microwave on *medium* 1 minute. Beat in sugar, egg, lemon juice, and vanilla until light and fluffy. Line a micro-muffin pan (or 6 custard cups) with paper liners. Place a vanilla wafer in bottom of each liner and fill each ¾ full with the cream cheese mixture. Microwave on *medium* 2 minutes or until nearly set; rotate pan or dishes once. Top each with 2 tablespoons of pie filling. Chill.

COCONUT PECAN CHOCOLATE CHEESECAKE

Yield: 8 servings

Crust:
2 tablespoons all-purpose flour   ¼ teaspoon cinnamon
2 tablespoons sugar   ¼ cup butter
⅔ cup graham cracker crumbs

In a 9-inch pie plate, combine flour, sugar, and graham cracker crumbs. Sprinkle on cinnamon and top with butter; microwave on *high* 1 minute to melt. Mix and press firmly against bottom and sides. Microwave on *high* 1 to 2 minutes; rotating once during cooking. Set aside.

Filling:
2 (8-ounce) packages cream   ¾ cup sugar
    cheese   1½ teaspoons vanilla extract
3 tablespoons cocoa   2 large eggs

Cut cream cheese into 16 pieces, place in work bowl of food processor. Process until creamy. Add cocoa, sugar, and vanilla; process until smooth. Add eggs one at a time, until filling is very smooth and fluffy. Pour into prepared crust. Microwave 10 to 12 minutes on medium, until filling is almost set. Rotate 2 or 3 times during cooking. Cool.

Coconut Pecan Topping:
½ cup pecans, chopped   ⅓ cup light cream
2 tablespoons butter   ½ teaspoon vanilla extract
2 tablespoons brown sugar   ½ cup coconut, grated
1 egg   whipped cream, garnish

Place pecans in food processor work bowl. Turn machine off/on (pulse) two or three times. Place in small bowl. In work bowl combine butter, brown sugar, egg, and cream; process to blend well. Pour into a 2-cup measure and microwave on *high* about 1 minute just until thickened. Stir once during cooking. Stir in vanilla, coconut, and pecans; cool. Top cooled cheese cake with cooled topping. Chill. Border with whipped cream to serve.

Shirley L. Ballew

MISSISSIPPI MUD CAKE
(Conventional Recipe)

Freezes well   *Yield: 18 servings*

1 cup butter or margarine
4 eggs
2 cups sugar
1½ cups all-purpose flour
¼ teaspoon salt

½ cup cocoa
2 teaspoons vanilla extract
1½ cups pecans, chopped
2 cups miniature marshmallows

Preheat oven to 350°. Melt butter in a 9x13x2-inch pan; cool. Beat eggs and add sugar. Beat well. Sift flour, salt, and cocoa together. Add to egg mixture. Add melted butter, vanilla, and nuts. Pour into pan in which butter was melted. Bake 35 minutes. Place miniature marshmallows over top. Return to oven for 5 minutes or until marshmallows melt. Spread with icing.

Icing:
1 (16-ounce) box powdered
   sugar, sifted
½ cup butter or margarine,
   melted

½ cup evaporated milk
⅓ cup cocoa
dash of salt
1 teaspoon vanilla extract

Combine all ingredients and beat until smooth. Spread over hot cake.

Microwave instructions

Ingredients same as for conventional recipe

Cake:
Microwave butter and cocoa in a 2½-quart glass casserole on *high* 2 minutes. Stir in sugar. Add eggs and beat well. Blend in flour, salt, vanilla, and nuts. Pour batter into a 12x8-inch glass baking dish. Microwave on *high* 10 to 11 minutes. Rotate dish ½ turn after 5 minutes. Leave cake in pan. Spread miniature marshmallows over warm cake. Top with icing.

Icing:
Microwave butter, milk, and cocoa in a 2-quart glass casserole on *high* 2 minutes. Stir in sugar, salt, and vanilla. Spread while warm.

Carol H. Tuttle

CHOCOLATE PECAN BUNDT CAKE

Yield: 12 servings

margarine
1 tablespoon sugar
1/2 cup margarine
2 cups sugar
1 (6-ounce) package semi-sweet
  chocolate morsels

2 eggs, beaten
2 cups all-purpose flour
1 1/2 teaspoons baking powder
1 1/2 cups milk
1 teaspoon vanilla extract
1 cup pecans, chopped

Grease a large ceramic bundt dish with margarine and sprinkle with sugar to coat dish. Cream margarine and sugar in a large mixing bowl. In a 2-cup measure, melt chocolate chips on *high* 1 to 1 1/2 minutes, stirring once. Add chocolate and eggs to creamed mixture. Sift flour and baking powder together. Add alternately with milk to chocolate mixture. Add vanilla and pecans. Mix well. Pour into prepared bundt dish and microwave on *medium* for 9 minutes; rotating dish at 5 minutes. Continue to microwave on *high* for 4 minutes. Use a cake tester or wooden pick to check for doneness. Invert on wire rack after standing 10 minutes. Freeze or refrigerate cake 30 minutes before frosting.

Frosting:
2 (1-ounce) squares semi-sweet
  chocolate
1/2 cup margarine, softened
1 egg, beaten

1 teaspoon lemon juice
1 1/2 cups powdered sugar
1 cup pecans, finely chopped

Melt chocolate in a 1 1/2-quart glass mixing bowl by microwaving on *high* 1 1/2 minutes, stirring at 30 second intervals. Stir until melted. While chocolate is hot, beat in softened margarine and egg. Add lemon juice. Sift in powdered sugar. Beat until well blended. Stir in nuts. Frost cold cake and refrigerate.

Tips:
To toast nuts, place 1 cup nuts in a pie plate with 2 teaspoons butter or oil. Microwave on *high* 2 1/2 to 3 minutes or until lightly browned. Stir every 30 to 45 seconds for even browning.

To shell nuts easily, pour 1 cup water over 2 cups unshelled nuts. Microwave on *high* 4 to 5 minutes.

FANTASTIC FUDGE

Yield: 20 pieces

4 cups sugar
1 (13-ounce) can evaporated
   milk
1 cup butter or margarine
1 (12-ounce) package semi-
   sweet chocolate pieces

1 (7-ounce) jar marshmallow
   creme
1 teaspoon vanilla extract
1 cup walnuts, chopped

Butter a 9-inch square baking dish for thick fudge, or a 12x7½-inch baking dish for thinner fudge; set aside. In a 4-quart bowl combine sugar, milk, and butter. Stirring every 2 minutes, microwave on *high* 18 to 20 minutes or until mixture reaches 234º to 240º, or forms a soft ball when dropped into cold water. *Do not put candy thermometer in microwave oven.* Watch carefully to avoid boiling over. Stir in chocolate and marshmallow creme until blended. Stir in vanilla and nuts. Pour into buttered dish. Cool to room temperature. Cut into squares.

PEANUT BRITTLE

Yield: 1 pound

1 cup sugar
½ cup light corn syrup
1 cup roasted salted peanuts

1 teaspoon butter or margarine
1 teaspoon vanilla extract
¾ teaspoon baking soda

Lightly grease a 15½x10½-inch baking sheet with raised sides; set aside. In a 2-quart bowl combine sugar and syrup. Microwave on *high* 6 to 8 minutes or until syrup turns a light brown color. Stir in peanuts, butter, and vanilla; blend well. Microwave on *high* 1 minute. Place bowl on a hot pad. Syrup will be very hot. Gently stir in baking soda until mixture is light and foamy. Pour evenly onto prepared baking sheet; let cool 30 to 60 minutes. When cool, break into small pieces. Store in an air-tight container.

Note: If raw peanuts are used, add peanuts and ⅛ teaspoon salt to sugar-syrup mixture before cooking. Peanuts will brown in syrup.

Tip:
Sauces prepared in the microwave will not lump, stick or scorch. Use a glass measure 1½ to 2 times larger than the amount being prepared. Stir often for a smooth even texture.

HOT FUDGE SAUCE

May prepare ahead   *Yield: 1 to 1½ cups*

1 (1-ounce) square unsweetened   1 cup granulated sugar
   chocolate   ⅔ cup evaporated milk
2 tablespoons butter   ½ teaspoon vanilla extract
½ teaspoon salt

In a 1½-quart bowl combine chocolate and butter. Microwave on *high*
1½ minutes to melt. Add salt, sugar, and evaporated milk. Microwave
on *high* 4 minutes, stirring every minute. Beat until smooth; add vanilla,
beat to combine. Store covered in refrigerator until ready to use. To
warm, microwave on *high* 30 seconds. Serve warm over ice cream.

Shirley L. Ballew

CHEESE SAUCE

Yield: 1¼ cups

2 tablespoons butter   ½ cup sharp Cheddar cheese,
2 tablespoons all-purpose flour   shredded
½ teaspoon salt   salt and pepper to taste
1 cup milk

Place butter in a 4 cup measure; microwave on *high* 30 seconds to melt.
Stir in flour and salt until smooth. Stir in milk. Microwave on *high* 1
minute; stir. Microwave on *high* 1 minute longer. Stir in cheese. Stirring
twice, microwave on *high* 2 minutes or until creamy. Stir in salt and pepper to taste. Pour over hot vegetables.

HOLLANDAISE SAUCE

Yield: 1 cup

¼ cup butter   2 egg yolks, well beaten
1 tablespoon lemon juice   ½ teaspoon dry mustard
¼ cup light cream   ¼ teaspoon salt

In a 2 cup measure place butter; microwave on *high* 30 seconds to melt.
Stir in lemon juice, cream, and egg yolks. Microwave on *high* 1 to 1½
minutes, stirring every 15 seconds. Stir in dry mustard and salt. Beat until smooth. Serve hot.
Note: Assured success—even for a beginner!

FLAMING SHERRIED MUSHROOM SAUCE

Yield: 1½ cups

8 to 10 medium mushrooms,
  sliced
2 tablespoons green onion,
  chopped
1 teaspoon lemon juice
¼ teaspoon dried leaf tarragon,
  crushed

¼ teaspoon pepper
drippings from roast beef or
  steak
2 tablespoons dry sherry

In a medium bowl or baking dish, stir mushrooms, onions, lemon juice, tarragon, and pepper into meat drippings. Microwave on *high* 2 minutes, stirring once. Pour hot sauce over meat. In a 1 cup measure or heat resistant pitcher with handle, warm sherry in microwave on *high* 30 seconds. Holding pitcher away from you, use a long-handled match to ignite sherry. Pour over meat for a spectacular serving finale.

Note: An elegant sauce to complement an elegant dinner.

BREAD AND BUTTER PICKLES

Yield: 1½ quarts

2 cups water
1 cup sugar
1 cup white vinegar
2 teaspoons pickling spices
1 teaspoon salt

1 teaspoon turmeric
1 teaspoon dry mustard
4 large cucumbers, peeled
  and sliced
1 large onion, sliced

Combine water, sugar, vinegar, spices (place in a piece of cheesecloth and tie), salt, turmeric, and mustard in a 2-quart measure or bowl. Microwave on *high* until mixture boils, about 6 to 7 minutes. Stir in cucumbers and onion. Continue to microwave on *high* until mixture comes to a rolling boil, about 6 to 8 minutes. Transfer to sterile jars. Let cool. Cover and refrigerate until ready to use.

Tip:

Microwave lemons, limes, oranges or grapefruit on *high* 15 seconds to release more juice and flavor. Let stand 3 minutes before squeezing.

GREEN PEPPER JELLY

Yield: 6 (8-ounce) glass jars

¼ cup hot green peppers,
   seeded, finely chopped
¾ cup green bell peppers,
   seeded, finely chopped

6½ cups sugar
1½ cups apple cider vinegar
6 ounces liquid fruit pectin
2 or 3 drops green food coloring

Peppers can be finely chopped in a food processor. Mix peppers and their juices with sugar and vinegar in a 5-quart casserole. Cover and microwave on *high* and bring to a boil, about 10 to 12 minutes, stirring once. Add liquid fruit pectin and 2 or 3 drops of green food coloring. Let stand 5 minutes. Microwave on *high* to a boil; boil 1 minute. Stir well. Pour into hot sterilized jars; seal with lids. Process in a boiling water bath 10 minutes.

Note: This jelly is marvelous as an hors d'oeuvre spread over cream cheese and crisp crackers. It is an excellent condiment for lamb, fowl, beef, pork, and wild game.

Variation: Jelly may be prepared conventionally by bringing peppers, sugar, and vinegar to a hard boil over high heat. Boil 1 minute, stirring constantly. Remove from heat, stir in pectin and food coloring and let stand 5 minutes. Skim off foam; pour liquid quickly into sterilized jars and seal.

Sylvia W. Kercher

SPICY PECANS

Yield: 4 cups

2 cups sugar
2 teaspoons ground cinnamon
1¼ teaspoons salt
1 teaspoon ground nutmeg

½ teaspoon ground cloves
½ cup water
4 cups pecan halves

Combine sugar, cinnamon, salt, nutmeg, cloves, and water in a deep 3-quart casserole, mixing well. Cover with waxed paper. Microwave on *high* for 5 minutes; stir well. Microwave on *high* for 2½ to 4½ minutes or until mixture reaches soft ball stage. (A small amount dropped in cold water forms a soft ball but flattens when removed from water.) Add pecan halves and stir until well coated. Spread pecans on waxed paper and separate with a fork. Cool completely.

CHRISTMAS POPCORN WREATHS OR BALLS

Yield: 12 balls

8 cups popped corn
¾ cup sugar
¾ cup brown sugar
1 teaspoon white vinegar
½ teaspoon light corn syrup
½ cup water
¼ teaspoon salt

¾ cup butter
1 cup little round candy-coated chocolates
1 cup Spanish peanuts
1 cup colored miniature marshmallows

Measure popped corn into a large bowl. In an 8 cup measure, combine sugars, vinegar, corn syrup, water, and salt. Microwave on *high* 12 minutes, stirring every 3 minutes. Cook until a small amount of the mixture dropped into cold water forms a hard ball, or mixture is 260° on a candy thermometer. Add butter and mix well. Pour syrup in a thin stream over popped corn, stirring until all is well coated. Add candy, peanuts, and marshmallows; mix well. Form into 3 or 4-inch rounds. When cool, wrap in plastic wrap and tie with a ribbon.

Note: Children love these!

Katharyn L. Aderholdt

HICKORY
ENTERTAINS

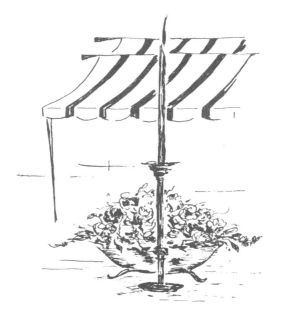

Hickory, North Carolina, is an "entertaining" town. Some of the menus which follow are rather traditional for the area and many came about through MARKET TO MARKET entertaining. Others were adapted for functions surrounding activities that form the cultural hub of our city.

In this section is a smattering of things we love to do, whether that be a picnic or a formal black-tie dinner. We don't always remain regional. Our community is composed of diverse backgrounds and life styles, each of which adds to the unique flavor of Hickory as it entertains.

Service League Antique Fair Luncheon

Antique Fair Vegetable Soup*

Turkey Salad Sandwich* or Salad Plate

Barbecue Pork Sandwich or Salad Plate

Brownstone Front Cake*   French Silk Pie*

Mississippi Mud Cake*

Coffee   Soft Drinks   Tea

Service League Spring Tea

(Honoring Provisional Members)
Lobster Mold*

Open-face Cucumber Sandwiches

Vegetable Sandwiches*

Artichoke Nibble*

Chafing Dish Cheese Dip

Cheese in Chafing Dish with Apples*

Fresh Strawberries
Dipped in White Wine and Powdered Sugar

Crème de Menthe Brownies*   Apricot Pecan Bars*

Strawberry Punch*

(*)Recipes found in index
(**)Suggested wines to complement menu

We are very pleased to offer a menu with recipes included in our cookbook which belong to Anne Byrd. Anne is a friend of the League by virtue of being a teacher to many of us through her vital classes in French cooking. Anne is President of the International Cooking Schools this year. She resides in Charlotte, North Carolina, and has been an instructor for twelve years.

Anne Byrd's Formal Dinner

Stuffed Mushrooms*

Apple Vichyssoise*

Crowned Roast of Pork*

Tomato Gruyére*   Sauté Zucchini*

Cold Lemon Soufflé*

Chateau Laroque 1979**
St. Emilion (red Bordeaux)**
or Cognac

First Nighters After Theater Champagne Dinner

(Hickory Community Threatre)

Romaine Lettuce Soup*

Chicken Crêpés*

Lima Bean Purée*   Carrot Vichy*

Elegant Layered Champagne Salad*

Lemon Bisque*

Frexinet Carta Navada Brut**

(Spanish Champãna)

Golfer's Breakfast

(Given for Visiting Hosiery Executives)

Screwdrivers   Bullshots

Melon and Prosciutto Ham

Bacon and Egg Casserole*

Tomato Pie*

Iced Butterhorns*

Coffee

New Orleans Brunch

(To benefit Catawba County
Council for the Arts)

French 75*

Salted Pecans and Almonds

Shrimp Creole I on Rice*

Louisiana Chef Salad*

Louisiana Popadums*

Bananas Foster*

Robert Mondavi—Chardonay Reserve 1979**

Christmas Brunch

(The Hickory Art Museum Guild)

Sally's Hot Sherried Fruit Crêpes*

Salmon Mousse*

Spinach Supreme Salad*—Country Club French
Dressing*

Lemon Angel Meringues*

Moreau Blanc—Non-Vintage (Frederick Wilsman)**

International Progressive Dinner

(Given for visiting Textile Executives)

Cocktails

Greek Spinach Pie*

Greek-Filled Cheese Bread*

Western Chrysanthemum Bowl*

Green Salad with Vinagarette Dressing*

(Schmitt and Sons)
Halftrocken Riesling 1981**

Braised Filet of Beef Chausser*

Potatoes Alexandre*   Italian Walnut Broccoli*

Russian Black Bread*

Château Beauséjour—St. Estephe 1979**

Pots de Crème*

Cognac   Demi-Tasse

Atlantic Coast Conference Tailgate Party

Cold Cucumber Soup*

Southern Fried Chicken Drumsticks*

Orange Curry Dip*

Picnic Sandwich*

Chilled Relish Tray   Katty's Herb Dip*

Jefferson Davis Tarts*

Beau—Rivage 1981, Blanc DeBland
(White Bordeaux)**
Yukum Gold Lager**

Pasta Party

Antipasto

Tagliatelle Verdi*
(Spinach Fettucine with Pine Nuts)

Ravioli Al Ricotta*
(Cheese-Filled Ravioli)

Insalata Mista*
(Romaine and Boston Salad—Italian Dressing)

Pane All'Olio*
(Italian Olive Oil Bread)

Zabaglione Ice Cream with
Crushed Amaretti Cookies*

Expresso/Cappuccino

Principata Merlot**
THE APRON STRING (A Kitchen Specialty Shop)
Hickory, North Carolina

Luncheon For Four

(À La Microwave)

Wilted Spinach Salad*

Shrimp Thermidor Bake*

Refrigerator Rolls*   Butter Curls

Coffee Ice Cream
with
Hot Fudge Sauce*

Iced Tea   Coffee

Dinner for a Special Occasion

Tequila Sours*, Dry Sherry, Piña Coladas*

Liptauer Cheese*
with Vegetable Garnishes

Coquilles St. Jacques in Scallop Shells*

Hal's Butterfly Lamb*

Potatoes, Carrots, Peas and
Cherry Tomatoes

Curried Brussels Sprouts*   Honeydew-Lime Salad*

Crescent Yeast Rolls*   Butter Curls

Chateau Meyney
St. Estephe 1979 (Rich French Bordeaux)**

Pecan Ice Cream Log with Warm Bourbon Sauce*

Demi-Tasse

Estonian Dinner

(To benefit The Catawba Science Center)

Bouillon

Pirukas*
with Rice and Egg Filling

Kapsarullid*
(Stuffed Cabbage Rolls)

Kartulisalat*   Crab Apples
(Mashed Potatoes)

Türgioad*
(Green Beans)

Kampott*
(Fruit Compote)

Vodka: Stoli-Chnayna**

Wine and Cheese Party

(Honoring Hickory Community Concert
Association Volunteers)

Catawaba County Meatballs*

Peapod Hors D'oeuvres*

Assorted Cheeses:
Danish Cream Havarti   French Brie
Gargonzola   French Port-Salut

Hollowed Round of Pumpernickel filled with
Carrot Mold*

Bread Chunks   Dill Wafers*

Aged Canadian Cheddar

Honey Grapes*   Pears

San Martin—Light Table Wine**

Los Hermanos Gamay, Beaujolais**

Cheeses suggested by KATHRYN'S OF HICKORY

Campaign Pig Pickin'

Roast Pig*

Bill's Coleslaw*   Hush Puppies*

Hot Corn on the Cob

Black Beans in Rum*

Coconut Pumpkin Cake*   Blackberry Jam Cake*

Favorite Pound Cake*

Summertime Iced Tea*

Fischer D'Alsace**   Anstel Light**

Furniture Market Cocktail Buffet

Cocktails

Orange Marmalade Turnovers*

Cheese Olive Balls*

Slice Tenderloin of Beef
or
Teriyaki Flank Steak*

Party Bread of White, Whole Wheat and Rye

Mustard and Mayonnaise Sauce*

Horseradish Sauce*

Barbecue Mushrooms in Chafing Dish*

Ripe Olive Canapés*

Crabmeat Mornay*—Cocktail Party Shells

Deviled Eggs

Oyster Roll*—Toast Points*

Cocktail Quiche with Feta Cheese Filling*

Cheese Mold with Apricot Topping*

Caviar Mousse*

Party Nut Mixture.*

Tired Shoppers Holiday Luncheon

Mushroom-Clam Soup in Mugs*

Vegetable Pockets*   Assorted Fruit on Skewers

Peanut Butter Balls*

One-Pan Brownies*

(Schmitt and Sons) Meringer Goldcupp—
Kabinett 1981**

Picnic On The Grounds

(Hickory Choral Society Pops Concert)
Gazpacho*
Rock Cornish Hens
Cauliflower-Broccoli Delight*
Paté En Croûte*
Assorted Fresh Fruit
Richmond Black Bottoms*
George Duboeuf—Beaujolais Village 1981**

Ice Cream Social

(To benefit The Hickory Landmarks Society)
Vanilla Ice Cream*   Lemon Ice Cream*
Winifred's Butter Pecan Ice Cream*
Butterscotch Sauce*   Mary's Chocolate Sauce*
Rosemary's Pineapple Rum Topping*
Best Ever Pound Cake*   Butter Wafers*

Children's Tea

(To benefit
The Western Piedmont Youth Orchestra)
Miniature Quiche*
Chicken Salad Sandwiches*
Babe Ruth Bars*   Thumbprints*
Cut-Out Sugar Cookies*
Cranberry Punch*

INDEX

( ) Denotes: **(HE) Hickory Entertains**   **(I) International**   **(M) Microwave Recipes**

( ) Denotes: (HE) Hickory Entertains   (I) International   (M) Microwave Recipes

( ) Denotes: (HE) Hickory Entertains   (I) International   (M) Microwave Recipes   **415**

( ) Denotes: (HE) Hickory Entertains   (I) International   (M) Microwave Recipes

( ) Denotes: (HE) Hickory Entertains   (I) International   (M) Microwave Recipes

INDEX

( ) Denotes: (HE) Hickory Entertains   (I) International   (M) Microwave Recipes

( ) Denotes: (HE) Hickory Entertains   (I) International   (M) Microwave Recipes   **419**

( ) Denotes: (HE) Hickory Entertains   (I) International   (M) Microwave Recipes

( ) Denotes: (HE) Hickory Entertains   (I) International   (M) Microwave Recipes   **421**

( ) Denotes: **(HE)** Hickory Entertains   **(I)** International   **(M)** Microwave Recipes   **423**

I
N
D
E
X

424   ( ) Denotes: (HE) Hickory Entertains   (I) International   (M) Microwave Recipes

MARKET TO MARKET
Service League of Hickory, N. C., Inc.
P.O. Box 1563—Hickory, North Carolina 28603

Please send me _____ copies of **MARKET TO MARKET**
   @ $14.50 each   _____
Plus postage and handling @ $1.50 per book   _____
North Carolina residents add 4% sales tax
   @ $ .58 per book   _____
Please gift wrap @ $ .50 per book. Gift card enclosed   _____
Enclosed is my check made payable to **MARKET TO MARKET**
                                  TOTAL _____

Name _____
Address _____
City _____ State _____ Zip _____
All copies will be sent to the same address unless otherwise specified.
Proceeds from the sale of this book support community service projects
sponsored by the Service League of Hickory, N.C., Inc.

MARKET TO MARKET
Service League of Hickory, N. C., Inc.
P.O. Box 1563—Hickory, North Carolina 28603

Please send me _____ copies of **MARKET TO MARKET**
   @ $14.50 each   _____
Plus postage and handling @ $1.50 per book   _____
North Carolina residents add 4% sales tax
   @ $ .58 per book   _____
Please gift wrap @ $ .50 per book. Gift card enclosed   _____
Enclosed is my check made payable to **MARKET TO MARKET**
                                  TOTAL _____

Name _____
Address _____
City _____ State _____ Zip _____
All copies will be sent to the same address unless otherwise specified.
Proceeds from the sale of this book support community service projects
sponsored by the Service League of Hickory, N.C., Inc.

Please list any retail and gift stores in your area who would be interested in stocking MARKET TO MARKET.

Thank you.

Please list any retail and gift stores in your area who would be interested in stocking MARKET TO MARKET.

Thank you.

MARKET TO MARKET
Service League of Hickory, N. C., Inc.
P.O. Box 1563—Hickory, North Carolina 28603

Please send me _____ copies of **MARKET TO MARKET**
   @ $14.50 each   _____
Plus postage and handling @ $1.50 per book   _____
North Carolina residents add 4% sales tax
   @ $ .58 per book   _____
Please gift wrap @ $ .50 per book. Gift card enclosed   _____
Enclosed is my check made payable to **MARKET TO MARKET**
                                 TOTAL _____

Name _____
Address _____
City _____ State _____ Zip _____

All copies will be sent to the same address unless otherwise specified.
*Proceeds from the sale of this book support community service projects
sponsored by the Service League of Hickory, N.C., Inc.*

MARKET TO MARKET
Service League of Hickory, N. C., Inc.
P.O. Box 1563—Hickory, North Carolina 28603

Please send me _____ copies of **MARKET TO MARKET**
   @ $14.50 each   _____
Plus postage and handling @ $1.50 per book   _____
North Carolina residents add 4% sales tax
   @ $ .58 per book   _____
Please gift wrap @ $ .50 per book. Gift card enclosed   _____
Enclosed is my check made payable to **MARKET TO MARKET**
                                 TOTAL _____

Name _____
Address _____
City _____ State _____ Zip _____

All copies will be sent to the same address unless otherwise specified.
*Proceeds from the sale of this book support community service projects
sponsored by the Service League of Hickory, N.C., Inc.*

Reorder Additional Copies

Please list any retail and gift stores in your area who would be interested in stocking MARKET TO MARKET.

Thank you.

Please list any retail and gift stores in your area who would be interested in stocking MARKET TO MARKET.

Thank you.